CURIOUS TEENS & RESPONSIBLE PARENTS

NAVIGATING LIFE'S CHALLENGES TOGETHER

AN OPEN, HONEST, AND MATURE DISCUSSION
BETWEEN A PARENT AND A TEENAGER

STRENGTHEN BONDS: THE PERFECT GIFT FOR
PARENTS AND TEENS TO GROW TOGETHER

PROF. DR. KIRAN MANGALAMPALLI, Ph.D.

INDIA • SINGAPORE • MALAYSIA

ISBN
Paperback 979-8-89556-020-4
Hardcase 979-8-89556-351-9

Dedication

To my Parents, my beloved Wife, my children Krishna, Mahati, and
Sahasra, my students, and my lovely family members,
for their unwavering love, support, and patience,
and for teaching me the true meaning of connection and understanding.

To all the teenagers and parents
who face life's challenges with courage and compassion—
this book is for you.

May your journey together be filled with open conversations,
mutual respect, and lasting bonds.

Contents

Preface

The teenage years are often described as a journey—a complex, exhilarating, and sometimes daunting path filled with growth, exploration, and self-discovery. It's a time when young people begin to assert their independence, grapple with new responsibilities, and carve out their identities. But it's also a period marked by challenges, uncertainties, and pivotal decisions that can shape their lives. As a parent, educator, and counseling Psychologist, I have witnessed firsthand the joys and struggles accompanying this transformative stage.

The relationship between teens and their parents is central to navigating this journey. The seeds of confidence, resilience, and self-worth are sown within this dynamic. Yet, in an era of rapid technological change, shifting societal norms, and increasing pressures, maintaining open and meaningful communication between parents and their teenagers has never been more challenging or crucial.

This book, Curious Teens & Responsible Parents: Navigating Life's Challenges Together (An open, honest, and mature discussion between a Parent and Teenager), is born out of my deep commitment to fostering healthy, supportive, and empowering relationships between teens and their parents. It is designed as a guide—a compass, if you will—to help families navigate the many challenges that arise during the teenage years. Through a series of candid and thoughtful conversations, this book addresses a wide range of topics, from online safety and cyberbullying to body image, career planning, and the complexities of teenage independence.

Each chapter is structured as a dialogue between a parent and a teenager, reflecting the importance of two-way communication. The questions and discussions will be a springboard for deeper conversations within your family. They are designed to help teens express their thoughts, feelings, and aspirations openly while providing parents with insights into their children's minds, fostering understanding, trust, and mutual respect.

This book is not a manual filled with rigid instructions or prescriptive advice. Rather, it is an invitation to engage, listen, and explore together. I believe that the best solutions come from collaboration and recognizing that parents and teens bring valuable perspectives. Through this partnership, we can empower young people to navigate the challenges of adolescence with confidence, clarity, and a strong sense of self.

In writing this book, I have drawn on my years of experience as a scientist, educator, and counseling psychologist and my personal journey as a parent. I have also been inspired by the countless young people and families I have worked with over the years. Their stories, struggles, and triumphs have shaped the content and spirit of this book.

I hope that Curious Teens & Responsible Parents: Navigating Life's Challenges Together (An open discussion between a parent and a teenager) will serve as a trusted companion on your family's journey. Whether you are a parent seeking to understand better and support your teen or a teenager looking for guidance as you navigate the complexities of growing up, this book is here to help you find your way. Together, we can build stronger relationships, foster greater understanding, and create a foundation for lifelong success and happiness.

Thank you for allowing me to be a part of your journey.

Prof. Dr. Kiran Mangalampalli, Ph.D.,

27-August-2024, Chennai

Motivation

The idea to write this book was born out of a deep concern and a heartfelt desire to bridge the growing gap between teenagers and their parents in today's rapidly changing world. As a counseling psychotherapist and educator, I have witnessed firsthand the challenges that both teens and their families face in navigating the complexities of adolescence. While bringing unprecedented access to information and connectivity, the digital age has also introduced new pressures, misunderstandings, and emotional struggles that many young people are ill-equipped to handle.

Today's teenagers are growing up in an environment vastly different from that of previous generations. The constant presence of social media, the relentless pace of technological advancements, and the increasing societal pressures to succeed have created a unique set of challenges that can often lead to feelings of isolation, anxiety, and confusion. These feelings, coupled with the natural process of self-discovery during adolescence, can strain even the strongest family relationships.

As I interacted with countless teens and parents, I noticed a recurring theme: a communication breakdown. Parents, often overwhelmed by the speed at which the world is changing, sometimes struggle to understand the realities their children are facing. Meanwhile, teens, caught between the desire for independence and the need for guidance, often find it difficult to express their emotions and concerns effectively.

This book is my response to these challenges. It is a guide designed to foster understanding, encourage open dialogue, and provide practical advice for both teens and parents as they navigate this critical phase of life together. I aim to equip families with the tools they need to build stronger, more resilient relationships—relationships founded on trust, empathy, and mutual respect.

By addressing these issues head-on and providing a safe space for these important conversations, I believe we can help the current generation of teenagers grow into confident, well-adjusted adults. This book is not just a collection of advice; it is a call to action for parents and teens to reconnect, understand each other better, and support one another through the many challenges and joys that adolescence brings.

In writing this book, I hope it will serve as a beacon of guidance for families everywhere, helping them navigate the often-turbulent waters of adolescence with greater ease, compassion, and understanding. My deepest wish is that this book will inspire meaningful conversations, foster stronger family bonds, and ultimately contribute to the well-being and success of the next generation.

How to Use This Book

Curious Teens & Responsible Parents: Navigating Life's Challenges Together (An open, honest, and mature discussion between a Parent and a Teenager) is designed as a practical guide to foster meaningful conversations between teenagers and their parents. This book is structured to allow you to dive into the topics that matter most to you, whether you're a teenager seeking guidance or a parent looking for ways to support your child during these pivotal years.

Here's how to make the most of this book:

1. **Read Together or Individually:**
   - Each chapter is crafted to be read individually or as a parent-teen duo. If you choose to read separately, consider setting aside time to discuss the questions and topics that resonate with you.

2. **Engage in Open Conversations:**
   - The book has conversation starters, questions, and scenarios designed to encourage open and honest dialogue. Use these prompts to explore different perspectives and understand each other's views on various issues.

3. **Customize Your Journey:**
   - While the chapters are organized thematically, please jump to the sections that address your immediate concerns or interests. You can tailor your reading experience based on your current needs, whether dealing with independence, navigating relationships, or planning.

4. **Reflect and Act:**
   - ➢ After reading each chapter, reflect on the discussion points and how they apply to your life. Consider writing down your thoughts, setting personal goals, or taking specific actions that align with the insights gained from the book.

5. **Revisit and Evolve:**
   - ➢ The teenage years are a time of rapid growth and change. As such, this book is meant to be a resource to return to as you face new challenges and milestones. Revisit chapters as needed, and let your conversations evolve.

6. **Use as a Reference Guide:**
   - ➢ Beyond being a book for active reading, this guide also serves as a reference for specific issues or questions that may arise. Whether it's understanding complex emotions, making important decisions, or simply seeking reassurance, this book offers valuable insights whenever you need them.

7. **Connect with Others:**
   - ➢ This book is also an excellent tool for group discussions, whether in a school setting, community group, or counseling environment. Use it to foster broader conversations among peers or within support networks.

Final Thoughts: This book is not just about offering advice; it's about strengthening the bond between parents and teenagers through shared understanding and mutual respect. Life's challenges are more manageable when faced together, and this book is here to help you navigate those challenges with confidence and care.

The Importance of Open Communication Between Teens and Parents

Open communication between teens and parents is the cornerstone of a strong, healthy, and supportive relationship. As teenagers navigate the complexities of growing up, they encounter new experiences, challenges, and emotions that can sometimes be difficult to understand or express. During this transformative period, having a safe and open line of communication with their parents becomes crucial.

Here's why open communication is so important:

1. **Builds Trust and Strengthens Relationships:**
   - When teens feel they can talk openly with their parents without fear of judgment or punishment, it fosters a sense of trust. This trust is foundational to a strong relationship where both parties feel understood and valued. Regular, honest conversations help solidify this bond, making it easier for teens to approach their parents with concerns, questions, or issues as they arise.

2. **Promotes Emotional Well-being:**
   - Adolescence is a time of emotional upheaval. Teens often experience heightened emotions and stress as they deal with academic pressures, social dynamics, and identity exploration. Open communication provides an outlet for healthily expressing these emotions. Parents who listen actively and empathetically

can offer comfort, guidance, and reassurance, helping their teens manage their emotional well-being more effectively.

3. **Encourages Responsible Decision-Making:**
    - ➤ When parents and teens communicate openly, they can discuss important life choices, such as education, friendships, and personal values. Parents can offer advice based on their own experiences, while teens can voice their thoughts and concerns. This collaborative approach to decision-making helps teens develop critical thinking skills and learn to make responsible, informed choices.

4. **Reduces Misunderstandings and Conflicts:**
    - ➤ Misunderstandings are a common source of conflict between parents and teens. Open communication helps clarify intentions, expectations, and boundaries, reducing the possibility of misinterpretation. When conflicts arise, a foundation of open dialogue makes resolving issues calmly and constructively easier, preserving the relationship's integrity.

5. **Fosters Independence with Guidance:**
    - ➤ As teens seek more independence, they may push boundaries and explore their autonomy. Open communication allows parents to guide their teens through this process, offering advice while respecting their growing need for independence. This balance helps teens develop confidence in navigating the world while knowing they have a supportive safety net at home.

6. **Prepares Teens for Adulthood:**
    - ➤ The skills learned through open communication with parents—such as active listening, empathy, and clear expression—are invaluable for adulthood. These skills enhance personal relationships and are essential in professional and social settings. By fostering open communication, parents help equip their teens with the tools they need to thrive in the future.

Open communication is not just about talking; it's about creating an environment where teens and parents feel heard, respected, and supported. It's about being willing to listen as much as to speak and understanding that every conversation is an opportunity to grow closer. By prioritizing open communication, parents and teens can build a relationship based on mutual trust and respect, making the adolescent journey smoother and more fulfilling.

"Your body is a temple, but only if you treat it as one."
— Astrid Alauda

Chapter 1

Understanding the Body

Parent: Hey dear, can we talk about something important? I know you've been noticing some changes in your body, and I want to ensure you feel comfortable and informed about what's happening.

Teen: Sure, but honestly, it all feels a bit weird. What's going on with my body?

Parent: I get it and trust me, it's normal to feel that way. What you're going through is called puberty—when your body transforms from a child's body into an adult's. It's like a biological rite of passage that every human experiences and sets the stage for your future as an adult. Different cultures have their ways of acknowledging these changes, but at the core, it's a universal experience.

Teen: Why does it have to be so confusing? One day, I'm fine, and the next, everything feels different.

Parent: Puberty can be confusing because it involves so many changes happening all at once, both physically and emotionally. Your body is growing, your hormones are fluctuating, and you're starting to experience feelings and thoughts that are new to you. This can feel like a lot to handle, but it's all part of growing up. Each change has a purpose, even if it's unclear.

Teen: Okay, so what exactly is happening to my body? Why do I need to go through this?

Parent: Great question. Puberty is your body's way of preparing for adulthood and possibly starting a family someday. It's when your reproductive system matures and you develop secondary sexual characteristics. For example, you might notice growth spurts, changes in body shape, and the development of facial hair, breast growth, or a deeper voice. These changes are guided by hormones like estrogen and testosterone like little messengers telling your body how to grow and develop.

Teen: But why do these changes feel so overwhelming? Sometimes I don't even recognize myself.

Parent: It's normal to feel that way. Your body is changing rapidly, and that can be disorienting. Plus, these physical changes are accompanied by emotional and psychological shifts. Hormones can affect your mood, making you feel more sensitive, self-conscious, or irritable than usual. You're also becoming more aware of yourself and how you relate to others, which can lead to a whole range of new feelings. In some cultures, these changes are celebrated, while in others, they might be kept more private—either way, your feelings are valid.

Teen: What if I don't like the way my body is changing? I see everyone else, and it feels like I'm not normal.

Parent: First, there's no such thing as 'normal' regarding bodies. Everyone's body is different, and everyone goes through puberty at their own pace. It's important to remember that your body is unique and valuable just the way it is. Embracing the changes you're experiencing—and understanding that they're part of what makes you, you—is key to building a positive body image. Society might push certain ideals, but beauty and health come in all shapes and sizes. Different cultures worldwide have their own beauty standards, but what matters most is how you feel about yourself.

Teen: That makes sense, but I still have so many questions. For example, what is menstruation, and why does it happen?

Parent: I'm glad you asked. Menstruation, or having your period, is one of the most significant changes that happens for individuals assigned to females at birth. It's part of the menstrual cycle, which prepares the body for the possibility of pregnancy each month. Here's how it works: your uterus builds up a lining of blood and tissue, getting ready to support a fertilized egg. If pregnancy doesn't happen, this lining is shed from the body, and that's what you experience as your period. In some cultures, menstruation is surrounded by specific traditions or taboos, but remember, it's a normal and healthy part of life.

Teen: So, does it hurt? What should I expect?

Parent: Menstruation can be uncomfortable for some people, especially when it comes to cramps or bloating. But it's also something you can manage with the right tools and information. Most periods last between 3 to 7 days, and you'll want to use products like pads, tampons, or menstrual cups to manage the flow. It's also important to know that it's perfectly okay to talk about it openly and ask for help if needed. Understanding your menstrual cycle and what's normal for you is empowering, and it helps reduce any fear or anxiety you might have.

Teen: That's good to know. But what should guys expect during puberty?

Parent: For individuals assigned male at birth, puberty involves different changes. One of the biggest is the production of sperm, which is your body's way of preparing for the possibility of fathering a child in the future. You might also notice your voice getting deeper, facial and body hair growth, and increased muscle mass. These changes are driven by the hormone testosterone, which plays a key role in male development. Around the world, boys may experience these changes in different contexts, but the biological process is the same.

Teen: Sometimes I feel like my emotions are all over the place. Is that normal, too?

Parent: Absolutely. Hormonal changes during puberty can make emotions feel like a rollercoaster. One minute, you might feel on top of the world; the next, you feel down or irritated. This is completely normal. Your brain is still developing, and the hormonal shifts can affect how you process emotions. What's important is finding healthy ways to cope—whether that's talking to someone you trust, journaling, exercising, or just taking a break when you need it. In some cultures, expressing emotions is encouraged; in others, it might be more reserved. Either way, it's important to understand and manage your feelings.

Teen: It seems like there's so much to deal with. How do I know if I'm handling it all okay?

Parent: It's important to remember that there's no right or wrong way to experience puberty. Everyone handles it differently, and it's okay to ask for help when you need it. What matters most is that you care for yourself—physically, emotionally, and mentally. Ensure you eat well, get enough sleep, stay active, and connect with people who support you. And if things ever feel overwhelming, know that it's okay to reach out, whether to me, another trusted adult, or a professional like a counselor. Around the world, people have different ways of seeking support, whether it's through family, community, or professional help.

Teen: What if I don't fit in with everyone else? Sometimes, it feels like I'm the only one going through certain things.

Parent: It's normal to feel like you're the only one going through something, but the truth is, everyone's experience with puberty is different. Some people develop earlier, some later, and everyone's body responds in its way. It's essential to embrace what makes you unique and not compare yourself to others. Fitting in doesn't mean you have to be just like everyone else—instead, it's about finding people who appreciate you for who you are.

Teen: I've noticed some of my friends are already experiencing things I haven't yet. Should I be worried?

Parent: There's no need to worry. Puberty can start at different ages for everyone, and that's perfectly normal. Some people start earlier, and some later, but everyone eventually goes through it. If you are ever concerned about whether what you're experiencing is typical, we can talk to a healthcare provider together. The most important thing is to be patient with yourself and remember that your body knows what it's doing.

Teen: I feel better knowing I'm not alone in this. What should I focus on as I go through these changes?

Parent: Focus on taking care of yourself and embracing the journey. Puberty is a time of growth—physically, emotionally, and mentally. It's a time to explore who you are, build self-confidence, and learn how to navigate the world as a young adult. It's also a time to be kind to yourself, recognizing that change can be challenging but incredibly rewarding. Cultures worldwide view this time differently, but the underlying growth experience is universal.

Teen: What should I do if I feel embarrassed or self-conscious about the changes in my body?

Parent: It's completely normal to feel self-conscious during puberty—after all, your body is going through many changes that can make you feel like you're under the spotlight. The best thing to do is to remind yourself that everyone around you is going through similar changes, even if it doesn't always seem like it. Focus on what makes you feel confident and comfortable in your skin, whether wearing clothes you love, engaging in activities that make you happy, or talking to someone you trust about your feelings.

Teen: How can I manage stress or anxiety during puberty?

Parent: Puberty can bring many new stressors, whether related to school, friendships, or body changes. Managing stress is all about finding healthy outlets that work for you. Some people find exercise helps, whether it's playing a sport, going for a run, or practicing yoga. Others might benefit from creative activities like drawing, writing, or playing music. And sometimes, just talking things out with a friend, family member, or counselor can make a big difference.

Teen: What should I do if I start feeling romantic or sexual feelings during puberty?

Parent: Feeling romantic or sexual feelings during puberty is completely normal. It's part of your body's natural development. What's important is understanding those feelings and making sure you're comfortable with them. It's okay to be curious, but it's also essential to respect your boundaries and those of others. If you have questions or feel unsure about anything, talking to a trusted adult can help you navigate these new experiences in a healthy way.

Teen: How do I know when it's time to talk to a healthcare provider about puberty?

Parent: If you have any concerns about the changes you're experiencing—whether it's about your physical development, your period, your mental health, or anything else—it's a good idea to talk to a healthcare provider. They can provide reassurance, answer your questions, and help you understand what's normal for your body. It's always better to ask questions and get the support you need than to worry alone.

Teen: How can I support my friends going through puberty?

Parent: Supporting your friends during puberty means being there for them, just as you'd want them to be there for you. Listen when they want to talk, offer encouragement, and remind them that feeling uncertain or confused is okay. You can share what you've learned and help them feel less alone in their experiences. Remember, friendship is about lifting each other, especially during times of change.

Teen: Thanks for explaining all this. I think I'm starting to understand it better now.

Parent: I'm always here to help you through it. Remember, puberty is just one part of your journey, leading you toward an exciting future. We'll take it one step at a time together.

Summary: Navigating the Journey of Puberty

In this chapter, we explored puberty, a transformative period during which the body undergoes significant physical and emotional changes. Through an open and supportive conversation, we explored the reasons behind these changes, their impact on a teenager's daily life, and the importance of embracing individuality during this time. We also acknowledged the diverse ways in which puberty is understood and experienced around the world.

Key Takeaways::

1. **Puberty as a Rite of Passage:** Puberty is a natural process that marks the transition from childhood to adulthood, guided by hormones like estrogen and testosterone. It prepares the body for reproductive maturity and brings about changes such as growth spurts, the development of secondary sexual characteristics, and the onset of menstruation.

Cultural perspectives on puberty may vary, but the biological changes are consistent across the globe.

2. **Emotional and Psychological Growth**: Alongside physical changes, puberty is marked by emotional and psychological shifts. Hormonal fluctuations can lead to mood swings, increased self-awareness, and changes in relationships. Understanding and managing these changes is key to building emotional resilience, regardless of cultural context.

3. **Embracing Body Diversity**: Every individual experiences puberty differently. Embracing the diversity of human bodies—recognizing that there's no single 'normal'—is crucial for developing a positive body image. Each body is unique, and that uniqueness should be celebrated. Around the world, different cultures have their beauty standards, but self-acceptance is universally important.

4. **Understanding Menstruation**: For those assigned females at birth, menstruation is a significant aspect of puberty. It's a monthly cycle where the body prepares for the possibility of pregnancy, and understanding it can help dispel myths, reduce anxiety, and promote menstrual health. Cultural attitudes towards menstruation vary, but open communication is key.

5. **Coping with Change**: Puberty can be overwhelming, but it's important to approach it with patience, self-compassion, and openness. Building a strong support system, practicing healthy habits, and seeking guidance when needed can make this transition smoother and more manageable, no matter where you are.

6. **The Bigger Picture**: Ultimately, puberty is about more than just physical changes—it's a journey of self-discovery, personal growth, and preparation for the responsibilities of adulthood. By understanding and embracing this process, teenagers can navigate this period with confidence and resilience, knowing they are part of a global experience.

* * *

"The most important thing in communication is hearing what isn't said."
— *Peter Drucker*

Chapter 2

Relationships and Communication

Parent: Navigating relationships during your teenage years can feel like a rollercoaster. You're at a stage where friendships deepen, romantic feelings might emerge, and you're also figuring out your independence. I want to help you understand how to communicate effectively and build healthy relationships because these skills will shape so much of your life.

Teen: Yeah, sometimes it feels like there's so much pressure to say or do the right thing, and I'm not always sure what that is.

Parent: That's totally understandable. Relationships can be complex, but they're also incredibly rewarding when handled with care. Communication is the key to all healthy relationships—whether with friends, family, or romantic partners. But communication isn't just about talking; it's about listening, understanding, and respecting each other's feelings and boundaries. Different cultures might have their ways of expressing these things, but the core principles of communication remain the same.

Teen: So, how do I get better at communicating with my friends? Sometimes it feels like no one really gets me.

Parent: Let's start by talking about what makes communication effective. It's about getting your point across and connecting with the other person. Here are some strategies that can help:

Teen: What's the best way to communicate with my peers?

Parent: Communicating with your peers effectively starts with understanding that communication is two-way. Here are some ways to improve your communication skills:

- **Active Listening**: This is one of the most important aspects of communication. Active listening means fully concentrating on what the other person is saying without planning your response while they're talking. It's about really hearing their words and trying to understand their perspective. You can show that you're listening by nodding, maintaining eye contact, and not interrupting. In some cultures, active listening is shown through nonverbal cues, but the goal is always to show that you're engaged and respectful.

- **Empathy and Understanding**: Empathy is putting yourself in someone else's shoes. It's about understanding their feelings and where they're coming from. When you respond with empathy, you let the other person know their feelings are valid, even if you disagree. Simple phrases like, 'I can see why you'd feel that way,' can go a long way in building deeper connections. Around the world, empathy is a universal way of fostering closeness and trust.

- **Clear and Respectful Communication**: Be clear and direct about what you're trying to say and be respectful. Use 'I' statements, like 'I feel…' or 'I think…' to express your feelings without sounding accusatory. For example, instead of saying, 'You never listen to me,' you could say, 'I feel unheard when I'm interrupted.' This approach helps to avoid conflict and promotes understanding.

- **Nonverbal Cues**: Your body language, facial expressions, and tone of voice are powerful communication forms. Sometimes, what you don't say is just as important as what you do say. Make sure your nonverbal cues match your words—for example, if you're trying to be supportive, a warm tone of voice and open body posture can reinforce your message. Nonverbal communication may vary across different cultures, but being mindful of these cues helps in any setting.

- **Conflict Resolution Skills**: Conflicts are inevitable in any relationship, but how you handle them makes the difference. When conflicts arise, stay calm, focus on the issue rather than personal attacks, and be willing to compromise. Remember, the goal is to resolve the conflict, not to win the argument.

- **Setting Boundaries**: Boundaries are important because they protect your emotional well-being. They define what you're comfortable with in a relationship and help prevent resentment. Be clear about your boundaries and respect others' boundaries as well.

- **Feedback and Growth**: Finally, be open to giving and receiving feedback. Constructive feedback helps you grow and improve your communication skills. Approach feedback with an open mind and use it as a tool for personal development.

Teen: That makes sense. I guess it's about more than just talking; it's about connecting with people.

Parent: Exactly. The more you practice these skills, the better you'll get at building meaningful, respectful relationships with your peers.

How do I handle conflicts with friends or romantic partners?

Teen: What about when things go wrong? Sometimes, I argue with my friends, or if I had a romantic partner, I'd worry about fighting with them.

Parent: Conflicts are a natural part of any relationship, and they don't have to be negative. In fact, if handled well, conflicts can actually strengthen your relationships. Here's how to navigate them:

- **Stay Calm and Rational**: When a conflict arises, letting your emotions take over is easy. But staying calm is crucial. Take deep breaths, count to ten if needed, and approach the situation clearly. This helps prevent the situation from escalating.

- **Communicate Openly and Honestly**: Honest communication is key to resolving conflicts. Use 'I' statements to express your feelings without blaming others. For example, instead of saying, 'You made me angry,' say,

'I felt angry when this happened.' This approach helps the other person understand your feelings without feeling attacked.

- **Choose the Right Time and Place**: Timing and setting are important when addressing conflicts. Don't bring up a sensitive issue when you are tired, stressed, or in a public place. Find a private, quiet time to discuss the issue so that you both can focus on resolving it without distractions. Some cultures have specific practices or rituals for conflict resolution, which can be valuable in finding the right moment.

- **Focus on the Problem, Not the Person**: Stick to the issue rather than attacking the person. For instance, instead of saying, 'You're so inconsiderate,' you could say, 'I was hurt when you didn't consider my feelings.' This keeps the conversation focused on resolving the issue rather than escalating into a personal attack.

- **Practice Active Listening**: Listening is just as important as speaking during a conflict. Make sure you're really hearing what the other person is saying and acknowledge their feelings. Sometimes, just feeling heard can help diffuse a tense situation.

- **Seek Compromise and Resolution**: The goal in any conflict should be resolution, not winning. Be willing to compromise where you can and find a solution for both of you. Remember, relationships are about give and take.

- **Know When to Take a Break**: If things get too heated, taking a break is okay. Step away, cool down, and return to the discussion when you're both in a better frame of mind. Just ensure you return to the conversation and don't leave the conflict unresolved.

Teen: So, it's about keeping things calm and being willing to work things out together?

Parent: Exactly. Conflicts are opportunities to understand each other better and to grow closer if handled with care and respect.

What are healthy boundaries in relationships?

Teen: What about boundaries? Sometimes, knowing where to draw the line in friendships or with people I care about is hard.

Parent: Boundaries are incredibly important in any relationship because they help you maintain your sense of self while also respecting others. Here's how to establish and maintain healthy boundaries:

- **Understanding Boundaries**: Boundaries are the limits we set to protect our physical, emotional, and mental well-being. They define what we're comfortable with in relationships and help prevent us from feeling overwhelmed or disrespected. These limits can vary depending on cultural norms and personal preferences, but they all serve to maintain balance and respect.

- **Types of Boundaries**: Boundaries can be physical, emotional, or relational. Physical boundaries involve your personal space and how much physical contact you're comfortable with. Emotional boundaries protect your feelings and thoughts, while relational boundaries define the level of intimacy and involvement, you're comfortable with in a relationship.

- **Recognizing Your Needs**: To set healthy boundaries, you need first to understand your own needs and limits. Reflect on what makes you feel safe and respected in a relationship and pay attention to situations where you feel uncomfortable or pressured.

- **Communicating Boundaries**: Once you know your boundaries, it's important to communicate them clearly and assertively. Use 'I' statements to express your boundaries in a direct but respectful way. For example, 'I need some time alone after school to recharge,' or 'I'm not comfortable with that level of physical affection yet.'

- **Respecting Others' Boundaries**: Just as it's important to set your boundaries, it's equally important to respect others'. Everyone has the right to their comfort zones, and respecting those boundaries is key to building trust and respect in any relationship.

- **Setting Limits**: Part of setting boundaries is learning to say No when something doesn't align with your values or makes you uncomfortable. It's okay to decline invitations, requests, or behaviors that don't sit well with you. Your comfort and well-being should always come first.

- **Revisiting and Adjusting Boundaries**: Boundaries aren't set in stone; they can change over time as you and your relationships evolve. It's important to regularly check in with yourself and adjust your boundaries if necessary. If something doesn't feel right, redefining your limits and communicating those changes is okay.

Teen: That helps a lot. It's good to know that it's okay to have boundaries and that it's important to respect them.

Parent: Absolutely. Healthy boundaries are the foundation of any respectful and balanced relationship.

How can I build trust and respect in my relationships?

Teen: How do I ensure my relationships are based on trust and respect? Those things seem really important.

Parent: They are the bedrock of any healthy relationship. Without trust and respect, it's hard for a relationship to thrive. Here's how you can cultivate these qualities:

- **Open and Honest Communication**: Trust is built on honesty. Be open about your thoughts and feelings and encourage the same from those you care about. Avoid keeping secrets or hiding things, as this can erode trust over time. Being transparent helps create a solid foundation of trust.

- **Consistency and Reliability**: Being reliable is key to building trust. If you make a promise, keep it. If you say you'll do something, follow through. Consistency in your words and actions shows that you're dependable, strengthening trust in the relationship.

- **Respect Boundaries and Differences**: Respect is about honoring the boundaries, opinions, and individuality of others. Even if you disagree with someone's viewpoint, respect their right. Respecting differences fosters a culture of mutual respect and understanding in your relationships.

- **Show Empathy and Understanding**: Empathy is crucial for both trust and respect. When you try to understand and share someone else's feelings, you show that you care about their well-being. This deepens your connection and builds trust.

- **Be Authentic and Genuine**: Authenticity is about being true to yourself and honest with others. When you're genuine, people feel they can trust you because you're being real with them. Avoid pretending to be something you're not—authenticity is key to meaningful relationships.

- **Demonstrate Trustworthiness**: Trust is earned through actions. Be trustworthy by keeping your promises, being honest, and acting with integrity. When mistakes happen, take responsibility and make amends. Trustworthiness is about showing through your actions that you're someone who can be relied on.

- **Forgiveness and Repair**: No relationship is perfect, and sometimes trust can be damaged. Forgiveness and willingness to repair the relationship are crucial when this happens. Apologize sincerely when you've hurt someone and be open to forgiving others when they've made mistakes. Repairing trust takes effort, but it's essential to maintaining strong relationships.

Teen: It sounds like building trust and respect happens over time through how you act and treat others.

Parent: Exactly. Trust and respect are earned through consistent, caring actions. They're what make relationships strong and lasting.

How do I navigate peer pressure and make decisions that align with my values?

Teen: Peer pressure can be really tough, especially when everyone else seems to be doing something. How do I make sure I'm making the right decisions?

Parent: Peer pressure is a common challenge, but with the right approach, you can navigate it while staying true to your values. Here's how:

- **Know Your Values**: Knowing what you stand for is the first step. Your values are like your personal compass, guiding your decisions and actions. Consider what's important to you, whether it's honesty, kindness, respect, or something else. Knowing your values makes it easier to make decisions that align with them.

- **Be Confident in Yourself**: Confidence is key to resisting peer pressure. When you're confident in who you are and what you believe, you're less likely to be swayed by others. It's okay to be different, and it's okay to say no if something doesn't feel right to you.

- **Think Independently**: Just because everyone else is doing something doesn't mean it's right for you. Take a step back and think for yourself. Ask yourself, 'Does this align with my values? How will I feel about this decision later?' Thinking independently helps you make choices that reflect who you really are.

- **Set Boundaries**: Part of staying true to yourself is setting boundaries. If something makes you uncomfortable or goes against your values, it's okay to say No. Be clear about your limits and stick to them. This shows others that you respect yourself and your values.

- **Surround Yourself with Supportive Peers**: Having friends who share your values can make it easier to resist peer pressure. Surround yourself with people who respect your choices and encourage you to be yourself. Supportive friends will stand by you, even if your decisions differ from the crowd.

- **Practice Assertiveness**: Assertiveness is about expressing your needs and opinions confidently and respectfully. When faced with peer pressure, practice saying no firmly but politely. You can say something like, 'Thanks, but that's not for me,' or 'I'm not comfortable with that.' Being assertive shows that you're in control of your decisions.

- **Have a Plan**: It can be helpful to consider handling situations where you might face peer pressure. Having a plan gives you confidence and clarity. For example, if you know you'll be in a situation where people might be drinking or doing something risky, decide how you'll respond.

- **Seek Support**: If you're ever unsure about a situation or feeling pressured, don't hesitate to talk to someone you trust—whether that's me, a teacher, or another adult. They can offer guidance and help you make a decision that you'll feel good about.

Teen: So, it's about knowing who I am and what I believe in, and being strong enough to stick with that, even when it's hard?

Parent: Exactly. Peer pressure can be tough, but when you stay true to yourself, you'll make decisions that you can be proud of. And remember, it's always okay to ask for help if needed.

Summary:

This chapter explored the foundational elements of healthy relationships and effective communication. Relationships during adolescence can be complex, but by mastering communication skills, setting boundaries, and building trust, teenagers can form meaningful connections that stand the test of time. We also discussed how different cultural practices can influence communication styles and the importance of understanding these differences.

Takeaway Points:

1. **Effective Communication is Foundational**:
   - Communication is the cornerstone of all healthy relationships. Practice active listening, use "I" statements, and ensure that your thoughts, feelings, and needs are expressed clearly and respectfully.

2. **Empathy and Understanding:**
   - Empathy helps you connect with others on a deeper level. Try to understand things from the other person's perspective and validate their feelings, even if you don't fully agree with them.

3. **Conflict Resolution Skills:**
   - Conflicts are natural in relationships, but how you handle them is crucial. Approach disagreements with calmness, openness, and a focus on finding mutually acceptable solutions rather than assigning blame.

4. **Importance of Boundaries:**
   - Establishing and respecting boundaries is essential for maintaining balance and respect in relationships. Clear boundaries protect your well-being and ensure you and your partner feel safe and respected.

5. **Building Trust and Respect:**
   - Trust is built through consistency, honesty, and reliability. Respect is about valuing each other's opinions, boundaries, and autonomy. Both are fundamental to a healthy relationship.

6. **Navigating Peer Pressure:**
   - Peer pressure can challenge your values and boundaries. Stay true to your beliefs, be confident in your decisions, and don't hesitate to say no. Surround yourself with supportive friends who respect your choices.

7. **Healthy Relationships:**
   - A healthy relationship is based on mutual respect, trust, empathy, and open communication. It involves supporting each other's growth and balancing individuality and togetherness.

8. **Assertiveness and Boundary Setting:**
   - Practice assertiveness by communicating your needs and boundaries clearly and respectfully. Assertiveness helps you stand up for yourself while also respecting others.

9. **Navigating Romantic Relationships**:
   - ➤ In romantic relationships, open communication about expectations, boundaries, and desires is key. Regularly check in with your partner to ensure you are comfortable and satisfied.

10. **Recognizing and Addressing Unhealthy Dynamics**:
    - ➤ Be aware of signs of unhealthy or toxic relationships, such as manipulation, excessive jealousy, or lack of respect. If you encounter these, seek support from trusted adults or professionals.

11. **Continuous Growth and Adaptation**:
    - ➤ Relationships evolve over time, and it is important to be open to growth, change, and adaptation. Continuously work on improving communication, understanding, and trust in your relationships.

* * *

"Education is the most powerful weapon which you can use to change the world."
— Nelson Mandela

Chapter 3

Sexual Health and Education

As a parent, I understand that talking about sex can be uncomfortable, but I also know how important it is to have open and honest conversations about it. I want you to feel safe and informed, not just about the physical aspects of sex, but also about the emotional and social implications. I aim to provide you with the knowledge and support you need to make informed decisions that align with your values and well-being. This isn't just about saying "yes" or "no"—it's about understanding what's right for you and being prepared for the responsibilities that come with your choices.

From a medical standpoint, sexual health is an integral part of your overall well-being. Understanding your body, how it works, and how to protect it is essential as you navigate adolescence and beyond. It's important to be aware of the physical risks associated with sexual activity, such as sexually transmitted infections (STIs) and unplanned pregnancies, and how to prevent them. But sexual health is more than just physical—it's also about making informed choices that are right for you and your future. I aim to ensure you have the correct information to protect your health and make decisions that will keep you safe.

Sexual health also encompasses your emotional and psychological well-being. Adolescence is a time of significant change and self-discovery, and your feelings about sex and relationships are an important part of that journey. It's normal to have questions and even anxieties about these topics. Understanding your readiness, managing emotions, and aligning your decisions with your personal values are all crucial for maintaining a healthy mindset. My focus is on helping you navigate these complex emotions and fostering a sense of confidence and self-respect as you make choices that impact your future.

While there are many positive aspects of sexual relationships, it's also important to be aware of the potential consequences of engaging in sexual activity at an early age. Physically, there's the risk of STIs and unplanned pregnancies, which can have long-term effects on your health and life plans. Emotionally, having sex before you're ready can lead to feelings of regret, confusion, or emotional distress. There's also the impact on your relationships, as sex can change dynamics in ways you might not anticipate.

That said, when approached with the right mindset, education, and maturity, sex can be a healthy and fulfilling part of life. It's about understanding both the pros and cons, being informed, and making choices that are right for you. As we move into the conversation, we'll explore these aspects in more detail, ensuring that you're equipped with the knowledge and support to make decisions that are best for your health, happiness, and future.

Teen: Thanks, Mom, I've been hearing a lot about sex from my friends at school. It seems like everyone has different ideas about it, and honestly, I'm kind of confused. Some of my friends say it's no big deal, while others act like it's serious. I don't really know what to think. Can we talk about it?

Parent: As you're growing up, it's natural to have questions about sexual health and education. These questions are not just about physical changes but also about understanding your emotions, relationships, and the responsibilities that come with sexual activity. I want you to know that it's okay to ask these questions, and I'm here to help you find the answers you need.

Teen: I'm feeling nervous and a bit uncomfortable.

Parent: I completely understand. Talking about sexual health can feel uncomfortable, especially because it's not always discussed openly. But it's such an important part of your overall well-being, and having the right information will help you make informed and confident decisions as you navigate this part of your life.

Teen: I do have a lot of questions, but sometimes, talking about them feels awkward or confusing.

Parent: I'm really glad you brought this up. It's normal to feel confused, especially with all the different messages. Sex is a big topic, and it's important to have a clear, honest understanding of it. First off, what do you think sex is about?

Teen: Well, from what I've heard, it's something people do when they really like each other, but some people at school make it sound like it's just fun to do like it's no big deal. I know it's about more than that, but I'm unsure how to make sense of it all.

Parent: You're right—it's about more than just having fun. Sex is a way people can express their love and intimacy, but it also comes with a lot of responsibility. It's important to understand that sex involves both emotional and physical aspects, and it's not something to rush into without careful thought. Do you feel like you've learned enough about the emotional and physical sides of sex?

Teen: I've heard a little about both, but I'm not sure I understand what it means to be ready. Some of my friends say you know when you're ready, but I don't know if that's true for me.

Teen: How can I tell if I'm truly prepared for the responsibilities and emotions that come with having sex?

Parent: Deciding whether or not to have sex is a deeply personal decision, one that requires careful thought and self-reflection. Here's what to consider when determining if you're ready:

- **Emotional Readiness**: Are you emotionally prepared to handle the intimacy and vulnerability that come with sex? It's important to feel comfortable with your partner and to trust them fully. Ask yourself if you're ready to share this part of yourself and whether you feel secure in your relationship.

- **Physical Readiness**: Understanding the physical aspects of sex is crucial. Are you informed about contraception and how to protect yourself from sexually transmitted infections (STIs) and unplanned pregnancies? Being physically ready also means knowing how to take care of your sexual health.

- **Communication and Consent**: Can you communicate openly with your partner about your boundaries, desires, and concerns? Consent is key—both partners must willingly agree without any pressure or hesitation. Are you comfortable asserting your boundaries and ensuring that you are fully on board?

- **Alignment with Values**: Reflect on your personal values and beliefs. Does engaging in sexual activity align with them? Are you making this decision for yourself, without external pressures? Your decision must align with your morals and the values you hold dear.

- **Maturity and Responsibility**: Sex involves responsibilities—both emotional and physical. Are you prepared to handle any potential consequences, such as changes in your relationship dynamics or the need to manage sexual health proactively? Maturity is about understanding these responsibilities and being ready to face them.

Teen: It sounds like there's a lot to think about. It's not just about whether I want to, but whether I'm really ready in all these different ways.

Parent: Exactly. It's about making sure that when you decide, it's for the right reasons and that you're fully prepared emotionally and physically. And remember, it's okay to take your time. There's no rush, and you should never feel pressured.

Teen: What should I do if I have questions about my sexual health?

Parent: It's completely normal to have questions about your sexual health, and it's important to get accurate, reliable information. Here's how to approach this:

- **No Shame in Asking**: First, understand that there's no shame in having questions about your sexual health. It's vital to your overall well-being;

asking questions is how you learn. Your questions are valid, whether it's about anatomy, STIs, contraception, or anything else.

- **Reach Out to Trusted Sources**: You can always contact me or another trusted adult if you have questions. If you're uncomfortable talking to someone you know, consider speaking with a healthcare provider who can offer professional, confidential advice.

- **Reliable Online Resources**: If you're looking online, make sure to use reputable sources like health organizations or educational websites. Be cautious of misinformation—stick to well-established sites that provide accurate and unbiased information.

- **Confidentiality Matters**: Remember, your conversations with healthcare providers are confidential. They're there to help you, not to judge. You should feel safe discussing any concerns you have with them.

Teen: I guess it's just about finding the right place to ask. I don't want to get the wrong information or feel judged.

Parent: Exactly. The right information and a judgment-free space are key to understanding and taking care of your sexual health.

Teen: How can I practice safe sex and prevent STIs and pregnancy?

Parent: Practicing safe sex is essential to protect yourself and your partner. It's about being responsible and informed. Here's what you should know:

- **Use Contraception**: One of the most effective ways to prevent pregnancy is by using contraception consistently. There are various methods, like condoms, birth control pills, IUDs, and more. Condoms are particularly important because they protect against both pregnancy and STIs.

- **Open Communication**: Talk to your partner about contraception and sexual health before becoming sexually active. Ensure you're both on the same page about using protection and caring for each other's health.

- **Regular STI Testing**: If you're sexually active, regular STI testing is crucial. Many STIs don't show symptoms immediately, so getting tested regularly ensures that you and your partner are healthy and reduces the risk of transmission.

- **Safer Sex Practices**: In addition to using condoms, safer sex practices include avoiding high-risk behaviors and being mindful of your sexual health. This includes using condoms for all types of sex—vaginal, anal, and oral.

- **Stay Informed**: Educate yourself about sexual health and safe sex practices. The more you know, the better equipped you'll be to make informed decisions and protect your health.

Teen: It sounds like a lot to consider, but it's all about being safe and responsible.

Parent: Exactly. Safe sex is about respect—for yourself and your partner—and making sure that both of you are healthy and protected.

Teen: What are the different types of contraception, and how do they work?

Parent: Understanding the different types of contraception helps you make informed decisions about what's best for you. Here's an overview:

- **Barrier Methods**: These include condoms and diaphragms. Condoms are worn on the penis or inside the vagina and prevent sperm from reaching the egg. They also protect against STIs. Diaphragms are placed inside the vagina to cover the cervix, blocking sperm.

- **Hormonal Methods**: These include birth control pills, patches, and injections. They work by regulating hormones to prevent ovulation (the release of an egg) and by thickening cervical mucus to block sperm. These methods are effective for preventing pregnancy but don't protect against STIs.

- **Intrauterine Devices (IUDs)**: IUDs are small devices inserted into the uterus. There are two types: copper IUDs, which release copper to prevent sperm from fertilizing an egg, and hormonal IUDs, which release hormones to prevent ovulation. Both are long-term, reversible options.

- **Permanent Methods**: Permanent options like tubal ligation (for females) and vasectomy (for males) are surgical procedures that permanently prevent pregnancy by blocking or sealing the reproductive tubes.

- **Choosing the Right Method**: The best contraception for you depends on your health, lifestyle, and whether you want to protect against STIs. Discussing your options with a healthcare provider to find what works best for you is a good idea.

Teen: It's good to know there are options. It's just about finding what's right for me.

Parent: Exactly. Being informed helps you make the best decision for your health and your future.

Teen: How do I talk to my partner about sexual health and boundaries?

Parent: Talking about sexual health and boundaries with your partner is crucial for a healthy relationship. Here's how to approach this conversation:

- **Choose the Right Time and Place**: Find a quiet, private space where you both feel comfortable. Avoid discussing sensitive topics in public or when you are stressed or distracted.

- **Be Honest and Open**: Speak from the heart and be honest about your feelings, boundaries, and concerns. Encourage your partner to do the same. Openness builds trust and ensures that both of you feel safe and respected.

- **Use 'I' Statements**: Express your thoughts and feelings using 'I' statements to avoid sounding accusatory. For example, 'I feel more comfortable using protection' instead of 'You never care about protection.' This approach helps to keep the conversation constructive.

- **Respect Each Other's Boundaries**: Respect is key. Understand that your partner's boundaries might differ from yours, and that's okay. Discussing these openly and agreeing on what feels right for both of you is important.

- **Discuss Expectations and Preferences**: Discuss what you expect from the relationship and any sexual activity. This includes discussing contraception, STI prevention, and what each of you is comfortable with.

- **Seek Guidance if Needed**: If you're unsure about how to have this conversation, it's okay to seek advice from a counselor or trusted adult.

They can help you prepare for the discussion and provide tips on effective communication.

Teen: It seems like it's all about being clear and respectful.

Parent: Exactly. When both partners feel heard and respected, it strengthens the relationship and ensures that you are on the same page.

Teen: How do I navigate consent and ensure that all sexual activity is consensual?

Parent: Consent is a fundamental aspect of any sexual relationship. Here's what you need to know:

- **Understand What Consent Is**: Consent means that all parties involved freely agree to participate in sexual activity. It's a clear, enthusiastic 'yes' that can be given verbally or through body language. Importantly, consent must be given without any form of pressure, manipulation, or coercion.

- **Communicate Clearly**: Always ask for consent before engaging in any sexual activity, and make sure your partner feels comfortable expressing their boundaries. Clear, open communication is essential to ensuring that you are on the same page.

- **Listen and Pay Attention**: Closely to your partner's verbal and non-verbal cues. If they seem hesitant, unsure, or uncomfortable, stop immediately and check in with them. Consent should never be assumed.

- **Respect Boundaries**: Always respect your partner's boundaries. If they say no or express discomfort, stop immediately. Consent is about mutual respect and ensuring that both parties feel safe and comfortable.

- **Be Mindful of Power Dynamics**: Be aware of any power imbalances in your relationship, such as differences in age or experience. Make sure that consent is given freely and without influence from these dynamics.

- **Check-In Regularly**: Consent is ongoing—it's not a one-time thing. Continue to check in with your partner throughout any sexual activity to ensure they are still comfortable and enthusiastic.

- **Seek Affirmative Consent**: Affirmative consent means actively seeking and receiving a clear, enthusiastic 'yes' from your partner before proceeding. Avoid assumptions and prioritize explicit verbal consent.

Teen: So it's not just about asking once, but ensuring everything feels right for both people throughout?

Parent: Exactly. Consent is about respect, safety, and ensuring that both of you are fully comfortable with what's happening.

Teen: What are the signs of an unhealthy or abusive relationship, and how can I seek help if I find myself in one?

Parent: It's important to recognize the signs of an unhealthy or abusive relationship early. Here's what to look out for and what to do:

- **Lack of Respect**: In a healthy relationship, both partners respect each other's feelings, boundaries, and autonomy. If your partner consistently disrespects you, belittles you, or disregards your feelings, it's a red flag.

- **Control and Manipulation**: An abusive partner might try to control or manipulate you, whether it's by monitoring your activities, isolating you from friends and family, or making decisions for you. This behaviour is about exerting power and is a serious sign of an unhealthy relationship.

- **Jealousy and Possessiveness**: While some jealousy is normal, excessive jealousy or possessiveness is a warning sign. If your partner is constantly accusing you of cheating, checking your phone without permission, or trying to control who you spend time with, it's a serious issue.

- **Emotional or Verbal Abuse**: Emotional or verbal abuse can be just as damaging as physical abuse. This includes name-calling, insults, threats, or constant criticism. These behaviors can erode your self-esteem over time.

- **Physical Violence**: Any form of physical violence, such as hitting, slapping, or restraining, is abuse. If your partner ever threatens or harms you physically, it's crucial to seek help immediately.

What to Do:

- **Reach Out for Support**: Talk to someone you trust, whether it's a family member, friend, or counselor. They can offer support and guidance and help you explore your options.

- **Educate Yourself**: Learn more about healthy relationships and the warning signs of abuse. Understanding what constitutes abuse can empower you to take action.

- **Create a Safety Plan**: If you're in immediate danger, have a plan to ensure your safety. This might include identifying safe places to go, keeping important documents accessible, and having a code word to signal for help.

- **Seek Professional Help**: Contact a therapist, counselor, or domestic violence hotline for professional support. They can provide resources, referrals, and assistance in developing a safety plan.

- **Know Your Rights**: You have the right to be safe and free from abuse. There are laws and resources to protect you, and you deserve to access them.

Teen: It sounds really scary, but it's good to know that there are ways to get help if I ever find myself in that situation.

Parent: It's important to recognize these signs early and know you're not alone. There are people and resources ready to help you.

Teen: How can I cope with feelings of shame or stigma surrounding sexuality and sexual health?

Parent: It's not uncommon to feel shame or stigma surrounding sexuality, especially with the messages we get from society, media, and sometimes even family. But it's important to know that these feelings don't define you. Here's how to cope:

- **Normalize Your Experience**: Remember that everyone experiences sexual thoughts, feelings, and questions. It's a natural part of being human. Understanding that you're not alone can help reduce feelings of isolation.

- **Educate Yourself**: Knowledge is power. The more you learn about sexuality and sexual health, the less hold shame and stigma will have over you. Seek out reliable, inclusive sources of information that empower you to understand your body and your sexuality.

- **Challenge Negative Beliefs**: Reflect on your internalized negative messages and challenge their validity. Are these beliefs rooted in facts or based on outdated cultural norms and stereotypes? Replace these negative beliefs with positive affirmations.

- **Practice Self-Compassion**: Be kind to yourself. It's okay to feel vulnerable or uncertain as you explore your sexuality. Treat yourself with the same kindness and understanding that you would offer a friend in the same situation.

- **Seek Support**: If you're struggling with feelings of shame, talk to someone you trust. Whether it's a friend, family member, or counselor, sharing your thoughts and feelings can provide relief and perspective.

- **Engage in Positive Activities**: Focus on activities that bring you joy and fulfillment, whether it's spending time with supportive friends, pursuing hobbies, or engaging in self-care. Positive experiences can help boost your mood and self-esteem.

Teen: It's nice to know that there's a way to work through these feelings and that they're not permanent.

Parent: Exactly. You have the power to overcome shame and stigma, and people and resources are here to help you.

Teen: What resources are available for LGBTQ+ [lesbian, gay, bisexual, transgender, queer or questioning, intersex, and asexual] teenagers to access inclusive sexual health information and support?

Parent: LGBTQ+ teenagers need to have access to inclusive and affirming sexual health resources. Here are some options:

- **LGBTQ+ Centers and Organizations**: Many communities have LGBTQ+ centers or organizations that offer resources like sexual health education, counseling, and support groups. These can be valuable places to find information and connect with others.

- **Online Resources**: Many online platforms provide comprehensive sexual health information tailored to LGBTQ+ individuals. Websites like Planned Parenthood, Advocates for Youth, and the Trevor Project offer inclusive and affirming content.

- **Healthcare Providers**: Look for healthcare providers who are knowledgeable and affirming of LGBTQ+ identities. These providers can offer personalized advice, screenings, and treatments, and they'll respect your confidentiality.

- **School-Based Resources**: Some schools provide LGBTQ+-inclusive sexual health education. Check with your school's health department; you might consider advocating for it if it's not offered.

- **Peer Support Groups**: Connecting with peers through support groups or online communities can provide a sense of belonging and understanding. These groups allow you to share experiences and learn from others who have faced similar challenges.

- **Books and Literature**: There are many books and articles written by LGBTQ+ authors that address sexual health topics from an inclusive perspective. These resources can offer valuable insights and relatable experiences.

- **Hotlines and Helplines**: In times of crisis or when you need immediate support, hotlines like the Trevor Project are available to provide confidential assistance specifically for LGBTQ+ youth.

Teen: It's reassuring to know there are places where I can get the information and support I need.

Parent: Absolutely. You deserve access to accurate, affirming information and support; many resources are designed to help.

Teen: How do cultural or religious beliefs influence attitudes towards sex and sexual health, and how can I reconcile them with my values?

Parent: Cultural and religious beliefs often play a significant role in shaping attitudes toward sex and sexual health. Here's how to navigate these influences while staying true to your values:

- **Education and Awareness**: Understand the cultural or religious beliefs that have shaped the attitudes around you. Knowing where these beliefs come from can help you navigate them more effectively.

- **Critical Thinking**: Take a step back and critically evaluate these beliefs. Do they align with your values? It's okay to question and challenge ideas that don't resonate with you or feel right.

- **Open Communication**: Discuss your questions and concerns with trusted family members, mentors, or religious leaders. They may offer perspectives or insights to help you reconcile these beliefs with your values.

- **Personal Values**: Reflect on your own values and how they shape your views on sex and sexual health. It's important to make decisions that feel right for you, even if they differ from the beliefs you were raised with.

- **Seeking Guidance**: If you're struggling, consider seeking support from a counselor or advisor who can help you navigate these complex issues.

- **Respect and Tolerance**: Remember that everyone's beliefs are shaped by their backgrounds. Even if you don't agree, it's important to approach these differences with respect and tolerance.

- **Finding Balance**: Finding a balance between cultural or religious beliefs and your values is a personal journey. Trust yourself to make decisions that feel right for you.

Teen: It's helpful to think about how these beliefs influence me and to know that it's okay to find my path.

Parent: Exactly. It's your journey, and you have the right to navigate it in a way that aligns with who you are.

Teen: What are the potential risks and benefits of engaging in sexual activity, and how can I make decisions that align with my values and priorities?

Parent: Understanding the risks and benefits of sexual activity is crucial for making informed decisions. Here's what to consider:

1. **Potential Risks**:

- **Physical Health**: Sex can involve risks like STIs and unintended pregnancy. Using protection and practicing safe sex can minimize these risks.

- **Emotional Health**: Sex can also have emotional consequences. It's important to be emotionally prepared and ensure that you're in a supportive, consensual relationship.

- **Social Consequences**: Consider how your actions might impact your relationships and reputation. Be mindful of the social implications of sexual activity.

2. **Potential Benefits**:

- **Physical Pleasure**: When experienced safely and consensually, sex can be a source of pleasure and intimacy.

- **Emotional Connection**: Sex can strengthen emotional bonds and deepen your relationship with a partner, provided it's within a healthy, loving context.

- **Exploration and Learning**: Sex can be part of exploring your sexuality, learning about your body, and discovering what feels good for you.

3. **Making Informed Decisions**:

- **Know Your Values**: Reflect on your values and priorities. What feels right to you? Make decisions that align with your beliefs and personal principles. Don't rush into anything because of external pressures—your values should guide your choices.

- **Communication**: Discuss your boundaries, desires, and concerns with your partner. Open, honest communication ensures that you are on the same page and that your relationship is built on mutual respect and understanding.

- **Consent**: Always prioritize consent. Both you and your partner must agree to any sexual activity freely and enthusiastically. Consent should be ongoing, meaning it can be revoked anytime if you feel uncomfortable.

- **Protection**: Use protection to prevent STIs and unintended pregnancies. Condoms are a reliable method that protects against both, but discussing other forms of contraception with a healthcare provider can give you more options.

- **Trust Your Instincts**: Trust your gut if something feels wrong. It's okay to pause, reconsider, or say no at any point. Your comfort and safety are the most important factors.

- **Seek Support**: If you have questions or uncertainties, seek advice from trusted adults, healthcare providers, or counselors. They can provide guidance and help you navigate your decisions with confidence.

Teen: It's clear that there's a lot more to think about than I initially realized, but it makes sense to consider all these aspects.

Parent: Exactly. Being informed and thoughtful about your decisions ensures that you're making choices that truly align with who you are and what you value.

Teen: How do I address misinformation or myths about sex and sexual health that I may encounter from peers or media?

Parent: Misinformation about sex and sexual health is everywhere, especially in today's digital age. Here's how to deal with it:

- **Understand Misinformation**: Misinformation can come from peers, media, or even outdated educational materials. It's important to recognize that not everything you hear or see is accurate.

- **Question and Verify**: When you encounter questionable information, don't accept it at face value. Cross-check with reliable sources like healthcare professionals, sexual health organizations, or trusted educational websites.

- **Educate Yourself**: Proactively educate yourself about sexual health from credible, evidence-based sources. The more informed you are, the easier it will be to spot and correct misinformation.

- **Engage in Critical Thinking**: Develop your critical thinking skills. Ask yourself who is providing the information, what their intentions might be, and whether there's scientific evidence backing their claims.

- **Communicate Effectively**: When addressing misinformation with others, do so with empathy and respect. Instead of being confrontational, share accurate information clearly and non-judgmentally.

- **Promote Open Dialogue**: Encourage open conversations about sexual health with your peers. This helps dispel myths and creates a supportive environment where everyone feels comfortable seeking and sharing accurate information.

- **Seek Support**: If you're unsure how to address certain myths or misinformation, seek advice from trusted adults, educators, or healthcare providers. They can guide you on how to approach these topics effectively.

- **Be an Advocate for Accurate Information**: Actively promote accurate sexual health information in your community. Challenge stigmas, support comprehensive sex education, and be a resource for those who might be misinformed.

Teen: It's good to know that I don't have just to accept everything I hear, and that there are ways to find out what's really true.

Parent: Absolutely. Being informed and critically evaluating the information you encounter empowers you to make better decisions and help others do the same.

Teen: What role does communication play in sexual relationships, and how can I effectively communicate my boundaries, desires, and concerns with my partner?

Parent: Communication is the foundation of any healthy sexual relationship. Here's how to make sure you're effectively communicating your boundaries, desires, and concerns:

- **Understanding the Importance of Communication**: Communication allows both partners to express their needs, desires, and boundaries. It fosters trust, intimacy, and respect, which are essential for a healthy relationship.

- **Setting the Stage for Communication**: Choose a time and place where you both feel comfortable and free from distractions. Approach the conversation with empathy and respect, ready to listen and share.

- **Identifying Your Boundaries and Desires**: Take time to reflect on what you're comfortable with and what you want from the relationship. Being clear with yourself first makes it easier to communicate these feelings to your partner.

- **Expressing Your Needs Clearly**: Use 'I' statements to express your feelings, such as 'I feel more comfortable when…' or 'I would like it if…'. This approach helps avoid placing blame and keeps the conversation positive.

- **Active Listening**: Listen to your partner's responses with empathy and an open mind. Show that you value their perspective by acknowledging their feelings and addressing their concerns.

- **Respecting Each Other's Boundaries**: Respect is a two-way street. Just as you expect your partner to respect your boundaries, you should do the same for them. This mutual respect is key to a healthy relationship.

- **Negotiating and Compromising**: Be prepared to negotiate and find compromises that satisfy both partners' needs. A healthy relationship involves giving and taking, with both people feeling valued and respected.

- **Seeking Support**: If you find it difficult to communicate or if issues arise that you can't resolve on your own, consider seeking help from a counselor or trusted advisor. They can offer guidance and help strengthen your communication skills.

- **Continuous Communication**: Remember, communication in a relationship is ongoing. Regularly check in with each other about your boundaries, desires, and any concerns. This keeps your relationship healthy and responsive to both partners' needs.

Teen: Communication seems to be key to ensuring everyone feels safe and understood.

Parent: Absolutely. Clear, respectful communication is what builds trust, deepens your connection, and ensures that both partners feel valued and heard.

Teen: How can I develop a positive body image and embrace my sexuality in a healthy and empowering way?

Parent: Developing a positive body image and embracing your sexuality is essential for your self-esteem and overall well-being. Here's how you can do that:

- **Understanding Body Image**: Body image is about how you see and feel about your physical appearance. Many factors influence it, including societal standards, media, and personal experiences. It's important to remember that everyone's body is different, and that's okay.

- **Cultivating Self-Acceptance**: Start by accepting and loving your body as it is. Focus on your strengths and qualities beyond your appearance. Practice self-compassion and remind yourself that your appearance doesn't define your worth.

- **Challenging Negative Messages**: Be aware of the negative messages and unrealistic standards often promoted by the media and society. Challenge these messages and replace them with positive affirmations. Surround yourself with supportive influences that celebrate diversity and individuality.

- **Nurturing Your Body**: Take care of your body by engaging in activities that promote your physical and mental well-being. Exercise, eat nutritiously, get enough sleep, and practice self-care. Treat your body with respect and kindness.

- **Exploring Your Sexuality**: Sexuality is a natural part of being human. Educate yourself about your body, sexual health, and what feels right for you. Embrace your sexuality in a way that aligns with your values and beliefs.

- **Understanding Consent and Boundaries**: Know that you have the right to set boundaries and make decisions about your body that feel empowering for you. Respect others' boundaries and communicate openly about your needs and desires.

- **Building Healthy Relationships**: Surround yourself with people who support and uplift you. Avoid those who undermine your self-worth or pressure you into activities you're not comfortable with. Healthy relationships are built on respect, trust, and mutual support.

- **Seeking Support**: If you're struggling with body image or navigating your sexuality, reach out for help. Talking to a trusted adult, counselor, or support group can provide perspective and guidance.

- **Embracing Your Authentic Self**: Celebrate your unique qualities and focus on building self-worth not tied to physical appearance. Embrace who you are and live authentically, pursuing your goals with confidence.

Teen: It's helpful to think about body image more positively and focus on what matters.

Parent: Exactly. Your body is just one part of who you are, and embracing yourself fully is important—body, mind, and spirit.

Teen: What are some strategies for building healthy relationships and fostering mutual respect, trust, and communication with romantic partners?

Parent: Healthy relationships are key to your happiness and well-being. Here are some strategies to build and maintain them:

- **Effective Communication**: Open and honest communication is the foundation of a healthy relationship. Express your thoughts, feelings, and needs clearly, and encourage your partner to do the same. Listen actively and without judgment.

- **Mutual Respect**: Respect is about valuing each other's opinions, boundaries, and autonomy. Treat your partner with kindness and consideration and expect the same in return.

- **Trust and Honesty**: Trust is built through consistent honesty, reliability, and integrity. Be truthful and transparent with your partner and trust them to do the same. Avoid secrets and deception, as these can erode trust.

- **Setting Boundaries**: Establish and respect each other's boundaries. Healthy boundaries are essential for maintaining individuality and ensuring both partners feel safe and respected.

- **Empathy and Understanding**: Practice empathy by putting yourself in your partner's shoes. Understand their feelings and experiences and offer support and validation. Empathy deepens your connection and fosters emotional intimacy.

- **Conflict Resolution**: Conflicts are a natural part of any relationship. Handle them with patience and a focus on finding solutions rather than assigning blame. Stay calm, listen actively, and work together to resolve issues.

- **Quality Time Together**: Spend regular quality time to strengthen your bond. Engage in activities you both enjoy and make time for meaningful conversations. Prioritizing your relationship helps keep the connection strong.

- **Support and Encouragement**: Be your partner's biggest supporter. Celebrate their successes, offer encouragement during tough times, and be there to listen and help when needed. Building each other up strengthens the partnership.

- **Shared Values and Goals**: Discuss and align your values and goals as a couple. Having shared aspirations can bring you closer and give your relationship a sense of purpose and direction.

  - ➤ **Continuous Growth and Adaptation**: Relationships evolve over time. Be open to growth, change, and adaptation. Learn from your experiences and work together to strengthen your relationship.

Teen: It's good to know that there are things I can do to build a strong relationship.

Parent: Absolutely. Healthy relationships require effort but are incredibly rewarding when built on mutual respect, trust, and understanding.

Summary:

Parent: In this chapter, we've explored many aspects of sexual health and education, focusing on the importance of informed decision-making, communication, and mutual respect in relationships. Understanding your body, your sexuality, and the responsibilities that come with sexual activity is crucial as you grow and develop. By addressing these topics openly and honestly, we aim to empower you to make choices that align with your values and ensure your well-being.

Teen: I feel like I have a better understanding now, and it's good to know I can talk to you about these things.

Parent: That's what I'm here for. Remember, these conversations are ongoing, and I'm always here to listen, support, and guide you as you navigate this part of your life.

Takeaway Points:

1. Informed Decision-Making:

- Understand that readiness for sexual activity involves emotional, physical, and mental preparedness. Reflect on your values, communicate openly with your partner, and ensure that all decisions align with your personal beliefs and priorities.

2. Communication is Key:

- Open and honest communication is essential in any relationship, especially regarding sexual health and boundaries. Use clear, respectful language to express your needs and listen actively to your partner's concerns.

3. Consent is Essential:

- Consent must be freely given, enthusiastic, and ongoing. It's important to check in with your partner regularly and ensure that both parties are comfortable and willing to participate in any sexual activity.

4. Practice Safe Sex:

- Protect yourself and your partner by using contraception and getting regular STI screenings. Understand the different types of contraception and choose the method that best fits your needs while also prioritizing your sexual health.

5. Respect Boundaries:

- Establish and respect boundaries in all relationships. Healthy boundaries ensure you and your partner feel safe, respected, and valued.

6. Addressing Misinformation:

- Be critical of the information you encounter, especially from peers and media. Verify facts through reliable sources and engage in open discussions to dispel myths and promote accurate understanding.

7. Positive Body Image and Sexuality:

- Cultivate self-acceptance and challenge negative societal messages about body image. Embrace your sexuality in an empowering way that aligns with your values.

8. Identifying Unhealthy Relationships:

- Recognize the signs of an unhealthy or abusive relationship, such as disrespect, control, and manipulation. Seek support and create a safety plan in such a situation.

9. Support for LGBTQ+ Youth:

- Access inclusive resources tailored to LGBTQ+ individuals, including online platforms, community organizations, and healthcare providers who are knowledgeable and affirming of diverse identities.

10. Cultural and Religious Considerations:

- Understand how cultural and religious beliefs influence attitudes toward sex and sexual health. Reflect on these influences and reconcile them with your own values, seeking guidance if needed.

11. Healthy Relationship Building:

- Focus on mutual respect, trust, and communication in relationships. Support each other's growth, share common goals, and continuously nurture the relationship through empathy, understanding, and quality time.

Additional Discussion: Understanding Sexually Transmitted Infections (STIs)

Teen: Mom, I've heard a lot about STIs at school and in our conversation, but it's still pretty confusing. Can we talk about what they are and why they're important to know about?

Parent: Absolutely, I'm glad you brought this up. STIs, or sexually transmitted infections, are infections that you can get through sexual contact, whether that's vaginal, anal, or oral sex. It's important to understand them because they can have serious health consequences if not treated properly.

Teen: So, are there different types of STIs?

Parent: Yes, there are several types, each caused by different kinds of organisms, like bacteria, viruses, or parasites. Let's go through some of the most common ones.

Teen: Sure. What's the first one?

Parent: One of the most common bacterial STIs is **Chlamydia**. It's caused by the bacteria *Chlamydia trachomatis*. Many people don't have symptoms, but when they do, they might notice painful urination or unusual discharge. If it's not treated, it can cause serious problems, especially for women, like pelvic inflammatory disease (PID), which can lead to infertility.

Teen: That sounds serious. How is it treated?

Parent: It's usually treated with antibiotics like azithromycin or doxycycline. The important thing is to get tested regularly if you're sexually active and to ensure that both partners are treated to prevent reinfection.

Teen: What about Gonorrhea? I've heard that name before.

Parent: Gonorrhea is another bacterial STI, caused by *Neisseria gonorrhoeae*. Like chlamydia, it can be symptomless, but it often causes painful urination and discharge. If left untreated, it can also lead to PID in women and infertility in men. More concerningly, some strains of gonorrhea are becoming resistant to antibiotics, so it's crucial to treat it early with the right antibiotics.

Teen: That's scary. What other STIs should I know about?

Parent: Another important one is **Syphilis**, caused by the bacteria *Treponema pallidum*. Syphilis goes through several stages if untreated. The first stage usually involves a painless sore where the bacteria enter the body. If not treated, it can progress to more serious stages, potentially causing damage to your heart, brain, and other organs.

Teen: Can it be cured?

Parent: Yes, syphilis is treatable with antibiotics, particularly penicillin. But, like with other STIs, early detection is key to preventing serious health issues.

Teen: What about HIV? That's one people talk about a lot.

Parent: HIV, or Human Immunodeficiency Virus, is a virus that attacks the immune system. Early on, it might feel like a flu, but over time, it can weaken your immune system so much that you become vulnerable to other infections. Without treatment, it can develop into AIDS, which is life-threatening. However, with antiretroviral therapy, or ART, people with HIV can live long, healthy lives.

Teen: Is there a cure for HIV?

Parent: Unfortunately, there's no cure yet, but ART can manage the virus effectively, reducing the viral load to undetectable levels, which means it's not transmittable to others and significantly improves the quality of life.

Teen: Are there any other STIs we should talk about?

Parent: There are others, like **Herpes**, caused by the herpes simplex virus, which leads to painful sores around the mouth or genitals, and **HPV**, or Human Papillomavirus, which can cause genital warts and is linked to cervical and other cancers. HPV is particularly common, but there's a vaccine that can prevent the strains most likely to cause cancer.

Teen: So, how do we protect ourselves from these STIs?

Parent: The best way to protect oneself is by using condoms every time one participates in sex with unknown people, as they greatly reduce the risk of transmission for most STIs. Regular testing is also important, especially if one has new or multiple partners. It's all about being informed and taking responsibility for one's sexual health.

Teen: What if someone does get an STI? What should they do?

Parent: If someone thinks they might have an STI, the first step is to get tested as soon as possible. Most STIs are treatable, especially if caught early. It's important to follow the treatment plan exactly as prescribed and inform any sexual partners so they can get tested and treated too. Remember, there's no shame in getting tested or treated—taking care of your health is the priority.

Teen: This is a lot of information, but it's really important. Thanks for explaining it all.

Parent: You're welcome. I'm glad we had this conversation. Remember, if you ever have more questions or need to talk about anything related to your health, I'm here for you.

Takeaway Points:

1. STIs can have serious health consequences if left untreated, so early detection and treatment are crucial.

2. Using protection and getting regular screenings are key to preventing and managing STIs.

3. Open communication about sexual health is important for maintaining overall well-being.

* * *

"The boundaries of your mind are the foundations of your freedom."
— *Anonymous*

Navigating Personal Boundaries: A Guide to Self-Understanding

Understanding and respecting personal boundaries is crucial to developing a healthy sense of self. As you grow and navigate the complexities of adolescence, it's essential to explore and understand your own body, emotions, and desires. This journey of self-discovery involves many aspects of personal identity, including sexuality.

Sexuality is a natural and integral part of who we are, yet it's often surrounded by confusion, misconceptions, and varying cultural messages. One particular aspect of sexuality that is frequently misunderstood and rarely discussed openly is masturbation. Masturbation is a natural part of human sexuality, yet it's a topic that can evoke a range of emotions—from curiosity to embarrassment.

Addressing this topic with teens at an early age is crucial for fostering a healthy and informed perspective on sexuality. Open discussions help dispel myths, reduce feelings of guilt or shame, and provide accurate information that empowers teens to make informed decisions about their bodies. By talking about masturbation and other aspects of sexual health early on, parents can create a supportive environment where teens feel comfortable asking questions and expressing their feelings, leading to a healthier understanding of personal boundaries and self-respect.

This chapter aims to provide a thorough and thoughtful exploration of masturbation. We'll address common questions, concerns, and myths, offering a balanced perspective that respects both the emotional and physical aspects of sexual health. By approaching this subject with honesty and openness, we hope to demystify it and foster healthy attitudes toward sexuality for both teens and parents. This conversation is about understanding the act itself and recognizing and respecting personal boundaries, fostering self-awareness, and developing a positive relationship with your body.

The Conversation Begins:

Teen: Dad, I've been hearing a lot about masturbation lately, and I'm confused. I don't know what to think about it. Can we talk about it?

Parent: I'm glad you asked, and I want you to know that talking about this is okay. Masturbation is something that a lot of people wonder about, but it doesn't always get discussed openly. Let's discuss your questions and try to make sense of everything you've heard.

Teen: Thanks. The first thing I want to know is if it is normal.

Parent: Absolutely. Masturbation is a completely normal part of human sexuality. Most people masturbate at some point in their lives, and it's especially common during adolescence as your body goes through changes and you start to explore your sexuality.

Medical Perspective: What the Science Says

Teen: So, it's not bad for you, right? I've heard some people say it's unhealthy.

Parent: From a medical standpoint, masturbation is not harmful. Many doctors agree that it can be a healthy way to explore your body and relieve sexual tension. Masturbation doesn't cause physical harm or long-term health problems. It's a safe activity that doesn't involve the risks associated with sexual activity with others, like sexually transmitted infections or unintended pregnancy.

Teen: What about some things I've heard like it affecting your growth or causing other health issues?

Parent: There are a lot of myths out there about masturbation, especially when it comes to teens. For example, some people claim that it can stunt your growth, cause blindness, or lead to infertility. These are all unfounded myths with no scientific basis. Masturbation doesn't affect your physical development or health in any negative way. It can have some positive benefits, like helping to reduce stress, improving sleep, and even alleviating menstrual cramps in girls.

Teen: Wow, I didn't know that. But why do these myths exist if they're not true?

Parent: A lot of these myths come from cultural, religious, or societal beliefs that view masturbation as something negative or shameful. For many years, sexual topics, including masturbation, were considered taboo, and this led to misinformation and fear. Unfortunately, these myths have persisted over time, even though we now have a much better understanding of sexual health.

Psychological Perspective: Understanding Emotions and Behaviors

Teen: That makes sense. But what about the way it makes you feel? Sometimes I feel guilty or ashamed afterward. Is that normal?

Parent: It's very normal to have mixed feelings about masturbation, especially because of the way society often talks about it. Psychologically, these feelings of guilt or shame are usually learned—they're not something you're born with. Many people are taught, either directly or indirectly, that masturbation is wrong or dirty, and this can lead to those uncomfortable feelings. But it's important to understand that these feelings don't necessarily reflect reality. Masturbation is a natural behaviour, and feeling curious about your body is normal.

Teen: So, how do I deal with those feelings? I don't want to feel bad about something normal.

Parent: One way to address those feelings is to recognize their origin. Are they based on things you've been told by others? Or are they coming from your understanding and values? It can help to talk about these feelings with someone you trust, whether that's me, another adult, or a counselor. Understanding that masturbation is a normal and healthy part of sexual development can help reduce feelings of guilt or shame. It's also important to develop your perspective on it based on accurate information and self-reflection.

Teen: I guess it's just hard to shake those feelings sometimes, especially when people around you seem to think it's wrong.

Parent: I completely understand, and it's okay to feel conflicted. Remember, it's your body and your experience. Over time, you can work on aligning your feelings with understanding what's normal and healthy. And if those feelings continue to bother you, it might be helpful to talk to a psychologist or counselor who can provide more guidance.

Cultural and Social Perspectives: Navigating External Influences

Teen: You mentioned that some of these feelings come from society or culture. Can we talk more about that? Why do different people have such different views on this?

Parent: Definitely. Views on masturbation can vary widely depending on cultural, religious, and social backgrounds. Some cultures and religions have strict beliefs about sexual behaviour, including masturbation, and may view it as morally wrong or sinful. These beliefs can influence how people feel about masturbation and how they talk about it—or don't talk about it. In other societies, masturbation is seen as a normal and private aspect of sexual health, with less stigma attached to it.

Teen: That's interesting. So, what should I do if I'm getting different messages from different places, like home, school, and friends?

Parent: It can be challenging to navigate different messages, especially when they're conflicting. The key is gathering as much accurate information as possible and then deciding what feels right for you. It's okay to respect the beliefs and values of others, but it's also important to develop your understanding based on facts and your personal values. If you ever feel pressured or confused, don't hesitate to talk to someone you trust. Having open, honest conversations can help you sort through these conflicting messages.

Teen: I guess it's about balancing respecting other people's views and understanding my own.

Parent: Exactly. It's also important to remember that your views might change over time, and that's okay. As you grow and learn more about yourself and the world, your perspective on issues like masturbation might evolve. The most important thing is to stay informed and make choices that are right for you.

Parental Perspective: Addressing Concerns and Building Trust

Teen: Speaking of different views, how do parents generally feel about this? I know some parents don't like the idea of their kids doing this.

Parent: That's true. Some parents might feel uncomfortable with the idea of their child masturbating, often because they were raised with certain beliefs or because they worry about what it might mean for their child's development. Parents need to approach the topic with understanding and without judgment. As a parent, I want to make sure you have accurate information and feel supported rather than shamed or embarrassed.

Teen: What if I don't feel comfortable talking about this with you or another adult? Is that okay?

Parent: It's completely okay to feel that way. Masturbation is a private topic, and it's normal to want to keep it to yourself. If you're not ready to talk about it with me or another adult. But I do want you to know that I'm here if you ever have questions or need to talk. You're not alone, and there are people who can help if you ever feel confused or worried.

Teen: Thanks, that makes me feel better. I guess it's just nice to know that having these feelings and questions is okay.

Parent: It really is. Everyone has different experiences and feelings when it comes to sexuality, and that's perfectly normal. What matters most is that you feel comfortable and informed and that you know you can always reach out for support if you need it.

Exploring Myths and Misconceptions: Dispelling Common Fears

Teen: Can we discuss some of the myths I've heard? Like, what about the idea that masturbation can make you less interested in real relationships?

Parent: That's a common misconception, but it's not true. Masturbation doesn't reduce your ability to form meaningful relationships or diminish your interest in others. In fact, understanding your own body and sexual responses can actually help you have healthier relationships because you'll have a better understanding of what feels good for you. Masturbation and sexual relationships with others are different experiences, and one doesn't replace the other.

Teen: What about the idea that it's addictive or that you can do it too much?

Parent: Masturbation isn't inherently addictive, but like any behaviour, it can become problematic if it starts to interfere with your daily life. If someone is masturbating so much that it's affecting their responsibilities, relationships, or emotional well-being, it might be a sign that they're using it as a way to cope with stress or other issues. In those cases, it's important to talk to someone who can help, like a psychologist or counselor. But for most people, masturbation is a healthy part of their sexual development.

Teen: So, it's okay to do it, as long as it's not taking over your life?

Parent: Exactly. Like with anything, balance is key. Masturbation is a natural and normal activity, but keeping it in perspective and ensuring it doesn't become a way to avoid dealing with other aspects of life is important.

Practical Tips: Navigating Privacy and Boundaries

Teen: What about privacy? I'm worried about someone walking in on me or finding out. How do I handle that?

Parent: Privacy is really important, especially when it comes to something as personal as masturbation. Finding a private space where you feel comfortable and secure is important. If you're worried about someone walking in, you might consider locking your door or finding a time when you know you won't be disturbed. It's also important to be respectful of others' privacy and boundaries. If you share a room or live in a busy household, finding that private time might take a little planning, but it's doable.

Teen: What if I accidentally make someone else uncomfortable? Like if they find out or see something they shouldn't?

Parent: If that happens, handle the situation with care and respect. Apologize if necessary and respect the other person's feelings. It can be awkward, but it's important to be mindful of each other's boundaries. Remember, everyone has different comfort levels when it comes to topics like this, so it's important to be sensitive to that.

Teen: It sounds like it's all about respecting privacy—both mine and other people's.

Parent: That's exactly right. Everyone deserves privacy, especially when it comes to something as personal as their body and sexuality. By being mindful of privacy and boundaries, you can ensure that you and those around you feel comfortable and respected.

Addressing Long-Term Emotional Well-being

Teen: Dad, what about the long-term effects of how I feel about masturbation? Could these feelings affect me as an adult?

Parent: That's a really insightful question. The way you think about and understand your sexuality now can indeed have long-term effects on your emotional well-being. Developing a healthy, informed perspective now can lead to a more positive and fulfilling relationship with your body and others in the future. It's important to address any lingering feelings of guilt or shame so they don't carry over into your adult life. Developing a positive self-image and understanding your needs is key to emotional health in the long run.

Dealing with Peer Influence

Teen: What if my friends have different opinions about this? How do I handle that?

Parent: Peer influence can be strong, especially regarding topics like this. It's important to remember that everyone's experience with sexuality is personal, and what's right for one person might not be right for another. If your friends have different opinions, that's okay. You can listen to their views, but ultimately, your decisions should be based on your understanding and values. If you ever feel pressured or uncomfortable with what your friends say, it's okay to set boundaries or seek advice from a trusted adult.

Fostering a Healthy Dialogue

Parent: Remember, these conversations don't have to end here. Keeping an open dialogue about sexual health is important as you continue to grow and learn. Whether you have new questions or just need to talk through your feelings, I'm here to listen and support you.

Teen: I appreciate that, Dad. It makes me feel more comfortable knowing I can come to you with these things.

Parent: That's exactly what I want—for you to feel supported and understood. Sexual health is an ongoing journey, and being able to talk about it openly is a big part of that.

Conclusion: A Balanced Perspective

In this chapter, we've explored the topic of masturbation from multiple angles—medical, psychological, cultural, and social. The goal has been to provide a well-rounded understanding that helps demystify masturbation and addresses the common questions and concerns that teens and parents might have. Masturbation is a normal part of human sexuality, and it's important to approach it with accurate information, open communication, and respect for personal boundaries. By fostering healthy attitudes toward sexuality, we can support teens in their journey toward understanding their bodies and developing a positive sense of self.

Takeaway Points:

1. **Masturbation is Normal:** Masturbation is a natural and common part of human sexuality, particularly during adolescence. It's a normal way for individuals to explore their bodies and experience sexual pleasure.

2. **Health and Safety:** From a medical perspective, masturbation is safe and does not cause physical harm. It can even offer health benefits such as stress relief, better sleep, and alleviating menstrual cramps.

3. **Myths vs. Facts:** Many myths about masturbation—such as it causing blindness, stunting growth, or leading to infertility—are completely unfounded. These myths often stem from cultural or societal taboos.

4. **Psychological Perspective:** It's normal to experience mixed feelings about masturbation, including guilt or shame. These feelings are often learned from societal attitudes, not inherent to the behaviour.

5. **Cultural and Social Influences:** Views on masturbation can vary widely depending on cultural, religious, and societal backgrounds. Developing a personal understanding based on accurate information and individual values is important.

6. **Respect for Privacy:** Privacy is crucial when it comes to masturbation. It's important to find a private space where you feel comfortable, and to respect the privacy and boundaries of others.

7. **Open Communication:** Discussing masturbation openly with trusted adults can help clarify feelings, dispel myths, and provide support. However, it's also okay to keep this aspect of your sexuality private if that feels more comfortable.

8. **Balancing Independence and Responsibility:** Masturbation is a personal choice, and like any aspect of sexuality, it should be approached with a sense of responsibility and awareness of one's own needs and boundaries.

9. **No Impact on Relationships:** Masturbation does not reduce the ability to form meaningful relationships or diminish interest in others. It's a separate experience from sexual activity with others and can even enhance self-understanding.

10. **Healthy Approach:** It's important to maintain a healthy balance and not let masturbation interfere with daily responsibilities or relationships. If it becomes a coping mechanism for stress or other issues, seeking help from a counselor may be beneficial.

11. **Respecting Boundaries:** Be mindful of others' boundaries and handle any accidental privacy breaches with respect and care. Mutual respect and understanding are key to maintaining healthy relationships.

12. **Ongoing Dialogue:** The conversation about masturbation doesn't have to be a one-time discussion. Ongoing dialogue about sexual health can help foster a deeper understanding and support as teens continue to grow and explore their sexuality.

13. **Empowerment Through Knowledge:** Understanding masturbation as a normal and healthy aspect of sexuality can empower teens to feel confident and informed about their bodies and their choices.

By embracing these insights and fostering open, respectful conversations, teens and parents can build a foundation of trust, understanding, and mutual respect that supports healthy sexual development and personal growth.

* * *

"Open dialogue is the key to guiding young minds through the complex and often confusing landscape of modern influences."
— *Anonymous*

Chapter 5

Understanding Pornography: Consequences and Conversations

In today's digital age, access to information is unprecedented, and this includes exposure to pornography. The topic of pornography can be challenging for both teens and parents to discuss, yet it's a conversation that is increasingly important. As teens grow and begin to explore their sexuality, they may encounter pornography, whether out of curiosity, peer influence, or accidentally. Understanding how to navigate these experiences is crucial for developing a healthy relationship with sexuality.

Pornography presents a complex mix of realities and fantasies that can shape a young person's understanding of sex, relationships, and personal boundaries in ways that may not always be healthy or realistic. Without proper guidance and open conversations, teens may develop distorted views about sexuality, consent, and respect in relationships. Addressing this topic early with teens helps clarify misconceptions, set realistic expectations, and provide a balanced perspective to safeguard their emotional and psychological well-being.

Discussing pornography openly and honestly with teens is essential for several reasons. First, it allows parents to address any misinformation or unrealistic portrayals of sex that teens may encounter. Second, it offers a safe space for teens to express their thoughts and questions, reducing the stigma and secrecy surrounding this topic. Lastly, these conversations help teens to critically assess the content they may come across and understand the potential consequences of engaging with pornography.

In this chapter, we aim to provide a comprehensive discussion on pornography—its portrayal in the media, its potential impact on young minds, and how it can influence perceptions of sexuality and relationships. We will explore the psychological and social consequences of consuming pornography, the importance of consent and mutual respect in real-life relationships, and how to have constructive conversations about this sensitive topic.

By approaching the subject of pornography with openness and clarity, we can help teens navigate this aspect of their sexual development with a more informed and critical mindset. This chapter is not just about understanding pornography itself but also about fostering healthy attitudes toward sex, consent, and relationships and guiding teens in making choices that align with their values and well-being.

Parent: I think it's time we talk about something important but often not discussed enough—pornography. I know it might be awkward, but many teenagers encounter it, and I want us to have an open and honest conversation about it.

Teen: Yeah, I've heard about it from friends and seen some stuff online. But why is it such a big deal? Everyone seems to talk about it like it's normal.

Parent: That's exactly why we need to talk about it. While it's something many people encounter, it's important to understand both the effects it can have and how to approach it in a healthy way. Let's start with the basics— do you know what pornography is?

Teen: I guess it's videos or pictures of people having sex. Some people say it's just entertainment, but others say it's bad. I'm not sure what to think.

Parent: That's a good starting point. Yes, pornography involves explicit sexual content, often presented in videos, images, or even stories. But it's important to recognize that it can affect people differently depending on how and why they engage with it. So, let's break it down together.

Understanding Pornography: What It Is and How It Affects Us

Parent: Pornography is designed to be highly stimulating and can affect the brain in ways similar to other pleasurable activities, like eating your favorite food. But because it's so intense, it can sometimes lead to what experts call 'conditioning'—where the brain constantly expects that stimulation level. This can change how someone experiences real-life sexual relationships.

Teen: Conditioning? Does that mean it's bad for you?

Parent: Not necessarily bad in a black-and-white sense, but it can become problematic, especially if it influences expectations or behaviour. For example, when someone watches porn, they might start to expect that real-life sexual experiences should look or feel like what they see on screen, which isn't always realistic or healthy.

Doctor's Perspective

Parent: From a medical standpoint, watching pornography can have several effects on the brain. Neurologists explain that occasional viewing might not be harmful, but regular exposure can alter brain chemistry. This can lead to desensitization, where normal levels of sexual stimulation don't feel as exciting, and someone might seek more extreme content to feel the same level of excitement.

Teen: So, it's like how people can get addicted to video games or junk food?

Parent: Exactly. It's similar to how the brain responds to other forms of stimulation. Over time, it might lead to issues with sexual function, like difficulty in maintaining arousal or finding satisfaction in real-life relationships.

Psychologist's Perspective

Parent: Now, from a psychological perspective, pornography can shape perceptions and expectations about sex, intimacy, and relationships. If someone's primary exposure to sex is through porn, they might develop unrealistic ideas about what sex should be like, including things like body image, consent, and the emotional aspects of intimacy.

Teen: But if it's not real, why do people get so into it?

Parent: That's a great question. Porn can be appealing because it offers an immediate, low-effort way to experience sexual stimulation. But because it's not real, it often skips over the emotional and relational aspects of sex—things like trust, communication, and mutual respect—which are essential in healthy relationships.

The Influence of Pornography on Relationships

Parent: Let's talk about relationships. Pornography can sometimes give people the wrong idea about what a sexual relationship should be like. For instance, it might make someone think that certain behaviours are normal or expected, even if they're uncomfortable.

Teen: Like what kind of behaviours?

Parent: Things like aggression, a lack of consent, or unrealistic body standards. Pornography often portrays sex in a way that's focused only on physical pleasure and not on the emotional connection between partners. This can lead to misunderstandings and unrealistic expectations in real-life relationships.

Teen: So, it's like when movies show relationships that are all drama and no real communication?

Parent: Exactly! Just like romantic movies can give unrealistic ideas about love, pornography can give unrealistic ideas about sex. In healthy relationships, sex is just one part of a bigger picture that includes trust, communication, and respect.

Doctor's Perspective

Parent: Neurologists also point out that excessive porn use can lead to issues like anxiety or depression, especially if it starts to replace real-life interactions or if someone feels guilty about their use. It's important to remember that while porn might seem like a harmless escape, it can have real effects on mental health.

Teen: But what if someone watches it just because they're curious?

Parent: Curiosity is natural, and it's okay to have questions about sex. The key is to approach those questions in a healthy way. That's why talking openly about these topics, rather than relying on porn as an educator, is so important. Porn is designed to entertain, not to educate.

Psychologist's Perspective

Parent: Relying on porn as a primary source of information about sex can limit a person's understanding of what sex and intimacy can be. For example, it might make someone feel like their body or their sexual preferences don't measure up to what they see on screen, which can lead to issues with self-esteem or body image.

Teen: So, watching porn can make you feel worse about yourself?

Parent: In some cases, yes. If someone constantly compares themselves or their relationships to what they see in porn, it can create unrealistic standards that are hard to meet. This can lead to dissatisfaction with oneself and one's partner.

Cultural and Ethical Considerations

Parent: We also need to consider the cultural and ethical aspects of pornography. Different cultures and societies have different views on porn, and it's important to understand how those views might shape your perspective.

Teen: Like what kind of views?

Parent: For example, some cultures view porn as harmful to society because it can objectify people, particularly women, and reinforce negative stereotypes about sex. Others might see it as a personal choice but still emphasize the need for critical thinking about your consumption.

Parent's Perspective

Parent: From a parental perspective, my main concern is that you understand both the content and the context of what you're watching. Porn often portrays people in ways that aren't realistic, and it's important to approach it critically rather than taking it at face value.

Teen: So, you're not saying I should never watch it, but that I need to be smart about it?

Parent: Exactly. It's not about forbidding you from watching it, but about helping you make informed decisions. If you do encounter porn, ask yourself questions like: Is this how I want to see sex? Does this match my values? How does this make me feel about myself and others?

The Impact of Pornography on Teens

Parent: One thing that concerns many parents and professionals is the impact of porn on teenagers, especially since you're still figuring out what sex and relationships mean to you.

Teen: Why is it different for teens?

Parent: As a teenager, your brain is still developing, and you're still learning about your own sexuality. Doctors explain that because your brain is more plastic or adaptable, you might be more influenced by what you watch. This can shape your attitudes towards sex in ways you might not fully understand until later.

Teen: So, it can change how I think about sex?

Parent: Yes, particularly if it's something you watch regularly. It's important to know how it might influence your thoughts and feelings and remember that real-life relationships are much more complex than what you see on screen.

Psychologist's Perspective

Parent: Porn can affect emotional development. During your teenage years, you're learning how to navigate relationships, and if porn becomes a substitute for real-life experiences, it might hinder your ability to develop healthy, balanced views on intimacy and connection.

Teen: What do you mean by 'substitute for real-life experiences'?

Parent: If someone spends a lot of time watching porn instead of engaging in real-life relationships, they might miss out on learning important skills like communication, empathy, and emotional intimacy. These are the building blocks of healthy relationships, and they can't be fully learned from porn.

Talking About Pornography

Parent: So, what should you do if you find yourself watching porn or feeling curious about it?

Teen: I guess I should try to think critically about it, like you said. But what if I'm not sure how I feel?

Parent: That's completely normal. The most important thing is to keep the conversation open. If you're ever confused or unsure, you can talk to me or another trusted adult about your thoughts or feelings. It's better to talk about it than to keep it to yourself and let it affect you negatively.

Teen: But what if I feel embarrassed?

Parent: I understand that it can be embarrassing, but remember that curiosity about sex is natural. Talking about it openly helps remove some of that embarrassment and makes it easier to understand. We can talk about anything that's on your mind without judgment.

Doctor's Perspective

Parent: Neurologists also advise that if you find yourself watching porn regularly and it starts to feel like it's affecting your life—whether it's your mood, your relationships, or your schoolwork—it's important to talk to someone. Sometimes, speaking with a counselor or therapist who can offer guidance on managing those feelings can be helpful.

Teen: So, it's not just about whether porn is good or bad, but about how it affects me?

Parent: Exactly. It's about understanding its impact on you and making choices that support your overall well-being. Everyone's experience is different, so it's important to be mindful of how it fits into your life.

Healthy Alternatives and Support

Parent: Instead of relying on porn, there are healthier ways to learn about sex and relationships. For example, you can find reliable information from books, educational websites, or through conversations with trusted adults. These sources can give you a more balanced and realistic understanding of sex.

Teen: But those might not be as interesting as what's online.

Parent: I get that, but they're much more likely to give you the full picture. Remember, porn is entertainment—it's designed to be exciting, not necessarily to inform or educate. When you learn about sex from accurate, reliable sources, you're better equipped to make informed decisions about your sexual health.

Psychologist's Perspective

Parent: Psychologists suggest that if you ever feel conflicted about watching porn or if it becomes something you're using to cope with stress or other emotions, it might be helpful to talk to a psychologist. They can help you understand your feelings and find healthier ways to manage them.

Teen: So, if I'm feeling stressed or lonely, watching porn might not be the best way to deal with it?

Parent: That's right. It might temporarily distract you but doesn't address the underlying issue. Finding other ways to manage stress—like talking to someone, exercising, or engaging in a hobby—can be more effective in the long run.

Parental Guidance and Boundaries

Parent: My role as a parent is to guide and support you in making healthy decisions. I'm not here to police everything you do, but to help you navigate these challenges in a safe and supportive way.

Teen: So, what does that mean for how I use the internet?

Parent: While I trust you to make good decisions, I also want to ensure you have the tools to navigate the online world safely. That might involve setting some boundaries, like limiting screen time or using parental controls, but it's all about helping you develop healthy habits.

Teen: I get that. It's just that sometimes it feels like I don't have much privacy.

Parent: I understand that. Privacy is important; you'll have more of it as you age. But until then, it's my job to help guide you, not to invade your privacy but to ensure you're safe and making informed decisions.

Concluding the Conversation

Parent: I hope this conversation has helped you understand pornography a bit better. It's not about making you feel bad for being curious—it's about giving you the information you need to make healthy and positive choices for you.

Teen: Yeah, I get that. I'm glad we discussed it, although it was initially awkward.

Parent: I'm glad too. Remember, you can always come to me with questions or concerns, no matter what they're about. The more we talk openly, the easier it will be to navigate these challenges together.

Teen: Thanks. I'll keep that in mind.

Parent: You're welcome. Remember, you're not alone in figuring this out—we're together.

Takeaway Points:

1. **Pornography is Common but Not Always Beneficial:** While many teens encounter pornography, it's important to understand that it can have significant effects on one's expectations, behaviors, and emotional well-being.

2. **Conditioning and Desensitization:** Regular exposure to pornography can lead to desensitization and unrealistic expectations in sexual relationships, affecting how one perceives real-life intimacy.

3. **Impact on Relationships:** Pornography often portrays sex without the emotional connection, communication, and mutual respect that are essential in healthy relationships. This can lead to distorted views of sex and intimacy.

4. **Psychological and Emotional Effects:** Over-reliance on pornography can lead to issues like anxiety, depression, and low self-esteem, especially if it becomes a substitute for real-life relationships.

5. **Cultural and Ethical Considerations:** Different cultures have varying views on pornography. It's important to critically assess how pornography aligns with personal values and societal norms.

6. **Open Communication is Key:** Talking openly about pornography with trusted adults can help teens navigate their feelings and make informed decisions. Discussing these topics is better than relying solely on what's seen online.

7. **Healthy Alternatives to Porn:** Teens are encouraged to seek out reliable, educational sources for learning about sex and relationships. These sources provide a more balanced and realistic understanding of intimacy.

8. **The Role of Parents:** Parents should provide guidance and support, helping teens develop healthy internet habits while respecting their growing need for privacy.

9. **Managing Curiosity and Stress:** Teens should be mindful of why they're watching porn—whether out of curiosity or as a way to cope with stress—and seek healthier ways to manage their emotions.

10. **Professional Support is Available:** If pornography use becomes problematic, seeking help from a counselor or psychologist can provide strategies for managing its impact and developing healthier coping mechanisms.

11. **Empowerment Through Knowledge:** Understanding the potential consequences of pornography empowers teens to make informed choices that support their overall well-being and healthy sexual development.

* * *

"The foundation of healthy choices is built on trust, understanding, and open communication about values and relationships."
— *Anonymous*

Chapter 6

Premarital Sex and Marriage

The decision to engage in premarital sex is a deeply personal one, influenced by a variety of factors including cultural, religious, and individual beliefs. In today's society, conversations about sex are becoming more open, yet the topic of premarital sex still carries significant weight, particularly when it intersects with the concept of marriage. This chapter aims to explore the complexities surrounding premarital sex and its marriage relationship, offering insights from multiple perspectives to help teens and parents navigate this important aspect of life.

Questions of morality, values, and long-term consequences often surround premarital sex. For teens, understanding the implications of premarital sex is crucial in making informed decisions that align with their values and future goals. Parents, too, play a critical role in guiding their children through these decisions, offering wisdom and support as they navigate the challenges of growing up.

From a psychological perspective, the emotional readiness and impact of premarital sex are significant considerations. Teens may face pressure from peers or partners, and without proper guidance, they may make decisions that they're not fully prepared for emotionally. This chapter will delve into the importance of understanding one's own readiness, the potential emotional consequences, and the importance of building strong, respectful relationships.

From a cultural and societal viewpoint, attitudes toward premarital sex vary widely. Some cultures and families emphasize the importance of waiting until marriage, while others are more accepting of premarital sex within committed relationships. Understanding these different perspectives can help teens navigate the expectations of their family, community, and their own beliefs.

This chapter will also explore the practical aspects of premarital sex, including the potential health risks such as sexually transmitted infections (STIs) and unplanned pregnancies, as well as the importance of contraception and sexual health. By discussing these topics openly, we aim to equip teens with the knowledge they need to make informed, responsible choices.

Marriage is often seen as a significant milestone, and for many, it's intertwined with the idea of sex. Whether viewed as a sacred union or a legal contract, marriage represents a commitment beyond just a physical relationship. This chapter will also touch on how premarital sex might influence future relationships and marriage, including considerations of trust, fidelity, and shared values.

By providing a balanced and thoughtful exploration of premarital sex and marriage, this chapter aims to foster healthy, informed discussions between teens and parents. It's not just about the act of sex itself, but about understanding the broader implications of these choices on one's life, relationships, and future.

Parent: I'm glad you're comfortable discussing these things with me. Premarital sex and marriage are big topics, and it's normal to have questions and concerns about them. Let's dive in.

Teen: Yeah, I've been thinking a lot about what it all means and how it fits into my life. There's so much to consider, and it can be unclear.

Parent: Absolutely. These are complex issues, and it's important to explore them thoughtfully. Let's start by discussing what premarital sex is and why people might choose to engage in it.

Teen: What is premarital sex, and why do people engage in it?

Parent: Premarital sex refers to engaging in sexual activity before marriage. It's a deeply personal decision, influenced by individual values, beliefs, and circumstances. People engage in premarital sex for a variety of reasons, and it's essential to understand that everyone's motivations may differ.

Teen: What are some of those reasons?

Parent: Some people choose to engage in premarital sex because they feel emotionally and physically ready to explore intimacy with their partner. For them, it might be a way to express love, affection, and connection within a committed relationship. Others might see premarital sex as a natural part of the human experience, independent of societal taboos or restrictions.

Teen: And what about those who choose not to?

Parent: On the other hand, some individuals prefer to wait until marriage, guided by religious, cultural, or personal beliefs that prioritize abstinence or chastity. Others may be concerned about the potential risks associated with premarital sex, such as unintended pregnancy, sexually transmitted infections, or emotional consequences. Ultimately, the decision to engage in premarital sex is deeply personal and should be made with careful consideration, respect for oneself and one's partner, and a clear understanding of the potential consequences.

Teen: It sounds like there's a lot to think about before making such a decision.

Parent: Exactly. It's important to have open and honest conversations, seek information, and reflect on your own values and beliefs. That way, you can make informed decisions that align with your aspirations for the future.

Potential risks and consequences of having sex before marriage

Teen: So, what should I know if I'm thinking about this?

Parent: There are several potential risks and consequences to consider when it comes to premarital sex. Here are a few key points:

- **Unplanned Pregnancy**: One of the most significant risks is unintended pregnancy. It's important to consider whether you're emotionally, financially, or socially prepared for parenthood, as it can majorly impact your future goals and aspirations.

- **Sexually Transmitted Infections**: Engaging in sexual activity without protection can increase the risk of contracting STIs, such as HIV, chlamydia, or gonorrhea. These infections can have long-term health consequences and may require medical treatment.

- **Emotional Consequences**: Sex is a deeply intimate experience that can have emotional repercussions. You might experience guilt, shame, regret, or confusion, especially if the relationship ends or the experience doesn't meet your expectations.

- **Relationship Dynamics**: Sex can significantly impact the dynamics of a relationship. While it can deepen feelings of attachment and intimacy, it can also strain the relationship if partners have differing expectations or values regarding sex.

- **Cultural and Religious Considerations**: For some, premarital sex may conflict with cultural or religious beliefs. This can lead to feelings of guilt or shame if there's pressure to conform to societal norms or expectations.

Teen: It's definitely a lot to think about.

Parent: It is, and that's why it's so important to make decisions that are right for you—decisions that respect your values, protect your well-being, and align with your long-term goals.

Teen: How do I know if I'm ready for something like that?

Parent: Making decisions about whether or not to have sex before marriage is a deeply personal process. Here are some steps to help you make informed choices:

- **Understand Your Values and Beliefs**: Reflect on your personal values and beliefs about sex, relationships, and marriage. Consider how your cultural, religious, and family backgrounds influence your perspective.

- **Educate Yourself**: Seek out reliable and accurate information about sexual health, contraception, STIs, consent, and healthy relationships. The more informed you are, the better equipped you'll be to make decisions based on facts, not misconceptions.

- **Consider Your Emotional Readiness**: Ask yourself if you feel emotionally prepared for sex. Consider how you feel about yourself and your partner and the potential positive and negative consequences.

- **Communicate With Your Partner**: If you're in a relationship, have open and honest conversations with your partner about your thoughts, feelings, and expectations regarding sex. Make sure you're both on the same page.

- **Assess the Risks and Consequences**: Consider the potential risks, including unplanned pregnancy, STIs, and emotional impacts. Are you prepared to handle these challenges?

- **Trust Your Instincts**: Listen to your inner voice. If something doesn't feel right, waiting or saying NO is okay.

- **Seek Support and Guidance**: Don't hesitate to talk to trusted adults, like parents, teachers, or healthcare providers. They can offer valuable advice and resources to help you make the right decision for you.

Teen: It sounds like it's about taking the time to really think it through.

Parent: Exactly. There's no rush, and it's important that whatever decision you make is one that you feel confident and comfortable with.

Teen: What about the emotional side of things? How does premarital sex affect that?

Parent: Premarital sex can have various emotional and psychological implications. Here's what to consider:

- **Emotional Intimacy**: Sex often involves a high level of emotional intimacy, which can deepen the bond between partners. But it can also lead to feelings of vulnerability, especially if the relationship isn't well-established.

- **Expectations and Pressure**: Societal or personal expectations about sex can create pressure, leading to anxiety, guilt, or inadequacy if you feel you're not meeting those expectations.

- **Communication and Consent**: Clear communication and consent are crucial. Without them, misunderstandings and emotional distress can occur, which can harm the relationship.

- **Self-Identity and Self-Worth**: Premarital sex can influence how you view yourself and your self-worth. It's important to feel comfortable with your choices and to maintain a positive sense of self.

- **Values and Beliefs**: Conflicts between personal values and actions can lead to inner turmoil. It's important to reconcile your beliefs with your behaviour.

- **Health and Safety**: Concerns about physical health, such as the risk of pregnancy or STIs, can also affect your emotional well-being.

- **Long-Term Implications**: Consider how premarital sex might impact your future relationships, family dynamics, and personal goals. Regret or emotional distress can occur if these decisions conflict with your long-term aspirations.

Teen: It's clear that there's a lot to think about, not just in the moment, but for the future too.

Parent: Exactly. It is important to navigate these emotions with care, open communication, and a clear understanding of what feels right for you.

Teen: If I do decide to have sex, how can I protect myself?

Parent: Protecting yourself is essential. Here's what you should know:

- **Use Contraception**: One of the most effective ways to prevent pregnancy and protect against STIs is by using barrier methods like condoms. Condoms not only help prevent pregnancy but also reduce the risk of STIs.

- **Communicate With Your Partner**: Talk openly with your partner about your sexual history, concerns, and boundaries. Trust and mutual respect are key.

- **Get Regular STI Testing**: If you're sexually active, regular STI testing is crucial. Some STIs don't show symptoms, so testing is the only way to know.

- **Consider Long-Term Contraceptive Options**: Explore other forms of contraception, such as birth control pills, implants, or IUDs, especially if you're in a long-term relationship. Consult a healthcare provider to find what's best for you.

- **Practice Abstinence or Delayed Sexual Activity**: Abstinence or delaying sexual activity until you're in a committed relationship is another effective way to reduce risks. Remember, it's okay to say no if you're not ready.

Teen: It's good to know there are ways to protect myself if I decide to go down that path.

Parent: Absolutely. Being informed and prepared ensures that you're making safe and responsible decisions.

Teen: How do cultural and religious beliefs fit into all of this?

Parent: Cultural, religious, and societal attitudes play a big role in shaping how we view premarital sex. Here's what you should consider:

- **Cultural and Religious Teachings**: In many cultures and religions, premarital sex is often viewed as taboo or morally wrong. Religious teachings might emphasize waiting until marriage to engage in sexual activity, viewing marriage as a sacred union.

- **Societal Norms**: Society's views on premarital sex can vary widely. It may be more accepted in some societies, especially in more liberal cultures. However, even in these societies, there can still be stigma or judgment, particularly for women.

- **Impact on Personal Choices**: These cultural and religious attitudes can significantly impact individual choices. While some people may adhere strictly to traditional values, others might challenge or reject these norms.

- **Respecting Diverse Perspectives**: It's important to approach these discussions with empathy and respect. Everyone's beliefs and choices are shaped by their cultural and religious backgrounds and understanding these perspectives can help you make informed decisions that align with your values.

Teen: So, it's about finding a balance between my beliefs and my influences.

Parent: Exactly. It's your decision, and it's important to make choices that feel right for you, regardless of societal or cultural pressures.

Teen: What exactly is marriage, and why do people choose to get married?

Parent: Marriage is a formal, legally recognized union between two individuals that signifies a commitment to each other. But the reasons people get married can vary widely:

- **Commitment and Partnership**: Marriage often represents a public declaration of love, commitment, and partnership. It symbolizes a lifelong promise to support and care for one another.

- **Cultural and Religious Significance**: For many, marriage carries cultural and religious significance. It's not just a union between two people but often a joining of families or social groups.

- **Practical Benefits**: Marriage can also provide practical benefits, such as legal rights, financial advantages, and social recognition. Married couples may enjoy tax benefits, inheritance rights, and access to healthcare benefits.

- **Emotional and Psychological Fulfilment**: Marriage fulfils the emotional and psychological needs of many people, offering companionship, intimacy, and a sense of belonging. It can also contribute to personal growth and development.

- **Shared Values and Goals**: Marriage often involves aligning shared values and goals, such as family planning, career aspirations, and lifestyle choices. It's about building a life together with mutual respect and support.

Teen: Marriage is a really big decision with many layers to it.

Parent: It is, and it's important to approach it with careful thought and consideration. Marriage is about more than just a ceremony; it's a lifelong commitment that should be based on love, trust, and shared values.

Teen: What legal rights and responsibilities come with marriage?

Parent: Marriage is a legally binding contract that comes with specific rights and responsibilities. Here's what you should know:

- **Right to Make Decisions**: Spouses have the right to make decisions on behalf of each other in emergencies or when one partner is incapacitated. This includes medical and financial decisions.

- **Inheritance Rights**: Upon the death of a spouse, the surviving partner typically has the right to inherit a portion of the deceased spouse's estate, even without a will.

- **Tax Benefits**: Married couples may enjoy certain tax advantages, such as filing joint tax returns and claiming deductions available only to married couples.

- **Healthcare Benefits**: Many employers offer healthcare benefits to spouses, including health insurance coverage and access to medical benefits.

- **Property Rights**: Marriage often establishes joint ownership of property acquired during the marriage. In case of divorce, the property is typically divided equitably.

- **Legal Obligations**: Marriage also entails responsibilities, such as financial support, emotional support, and the duty to communicate and make decisions together.

Teen: It's more than just a relationship—there are legal things to consider, too.

Parent: Exactly. Marriage involves a legal commitment, and it's important to understand the rights and responsibilities that come with it.

Teen: How do I know if I'm ready for marriage?

Parent: Deciding if you're ready for marriage is a significant decision. Here are some factors to consider:

- **Emotional Maturity**: Marriage requires emotional maturity. Are you ready to prioritize your partner's needs, communicate openly, and work through conflicts constructively?

- **Level of Commitment**: Marriage is a lifelong commitment. Consider whether you're ready to prioritize your relationship above all else and make sacrifices when necessary.

- **Shared Values and Goals**: Successful marriages are built on shared values and goals. Discuss important topics like family, finances, and lifestyle preferences with your partner.

- **Financial Stability**: Financial stability is crucial in marriage. Are you and your partner financially independent and capable of supporting yourselves and any potential future family?

- **Communication Skills**: Effective communication is the cornerstone of a healthy marriage. Evaluate your ability to express your thoughts and needs openly and respectfully.

- **Conflict Resolution**: Conflicts are inevitable, but how you handle them matters. Assess your conflict resolution skills and your willingness to compromise.

- **Support System**: A strong support system of family and friends can provide invaluable guidance. Consider whether you have a supportive network to help you through marriage.

- **Personal Growth**: Marriage is a journey of personal growth. Reflect on whether you're ready to continue growing as an individual while supporting your partner's growth.

Teen: It seems like there's a lot to think about before deciding to get married.

Parent: There is, and taking the time to evaluate your readiness is important. Marriage is a lifelong commitment, and being prepared emotionally, financially, and mentally is key to a successful relationship.

Teen: What makes a marriage successful?

Parent: A healthy and successful marriage is built on several key components:

- **Communication**: Effective communication is essential. Express your thoughts, feelings, and needs openly and honestly, and listen actively to your partner.

- **Trust**: Trust is the cornerstone of any successful marriage. Trusting your partner's loyalty, honesty, and integrity is important.

- **Respect**: Respect is fundamental. Value your partner's opinions, honor their boundaries, and treat them with kindness and consideration.

- **Commitment**: Commitment means dedicating yourself to the relationship, even during challenging times. It's about prioritizing your relationship and making sacrifices when necessary.

- **Intimacy**: Intimacy encompasses emotional, physical, and sexual closeness. Sharing your thoughts, feelings, and desires openly deepens your connection.

- **Shared Values and Goals**: Aligning your beliefs, priorities, and aspirations with your partner ensures harmony and unity in the relationship.

- **Flexibility and Compromise**: Flexibility and compromise are crucial for navigating challenges. Be willing to adapt and find solutions that benefit both partners.

- **Quality Time Together**: Spending quality time together strengthens your bond and keeps the relationship vibrant and fulfilling.

Teen: So, it's about building a strong foundation together.

Parent: Exactly. Investing in these components helps cultivate a healthy, fulfilling, and enduring marriage.

Teen: How can I get ready for marriage in the future?

Parent: Preparing yourself emotionally and mentally for marriage is important. Here's how you can start:

- **Self-Awareness**: Reflect on your values, beliefs, and goals. Understand your strengths and areas for growth. Self-awareness helps you identify your needs in a relationship.

- **Emotional Intelligence**: Develop emotional intelligence by recognizing and managing your emotions and empathizing with others. It's essential for building trust and navigating conflicts.

- **Communication Skills**: Work on improving your communication skills. Practice active listening, expressing yourself clearly, and being open to feedback.

- **Conflict Resolution**: Learn healthy ways to resolve conflicts. Practice compromise, problem-solving, and constructive communication.

- **Relationship Readiness**: Assess your readiness for a committed relationship. Consider your level of maturity, stability, and willingness to share your life with someone else.

- **Personal Growth**: Continuously work on personal growth. Pursue hobbies, invest in your well-being, and strive to become the best version of yourself.

- **Understanding of Marriage**: Educate yourself about marriage, its significance, and its commitments. Understanding marriage prepares you for its responsibilities and challenges.

- **Seek Support**: Seek support from trusted friends, family, or mentors. Premarital counseling or workshops can also provide valuable insights.

Teen: It's a lot of work, but it makes sense to be prepared.

Parent: Marriage is a lifelong journey, and preparing yourself now sets the stage for a fulfilling partnership.

Teen: How do cultural and religious beliefs influence marriage?

Parent: Cultural and religious beliefs play significant roles in shaping marriage. Here's how:

- **Foundation of Values**: Cultural and religious beliefs provide values that guide attitudes and behaviors toward marriage, such as commitment, fidelity, and respect for traditional gender roles.

- **Ceremonial Rituals**: Marriage often involves ceremonial rituals that symbolize the union of two individuals and their families. These rituals carry deep cultural and spiritual significance.

- **Family Expectations**: Cultural and religious beliefs may shape family expectations, including partner choice, timing of marriage, and marital roles.

- **Community Support**: Communities provide support networks, offering guidance, counseling, and social connections to help couples navigate marriage.

- **Spiritual Significance**: For many, marriage holds spiritual significance, viewed as a sacred union ordained by a higher power.

- **Adherence to Marital Laws**: Some cultures and religions have specific marital laws governing rights, duties, and divorce procedures.

- **Interfaith and Intercultural Marriages**: In today's diverse world, interfaith and intercultural marriages involve navigating differences in beliefs and practices, fostering understanding and appreciation for diversity.

Teen: It's interesting how marriage can mean different things depending on your background.

Parent: Absolutely. Understanding and respecting these beliefs can enrich your marriage and strengthen your relationship.

Teen: What if I feel pressured by society to get married?

Parent: Navigating societal expectations can be challenging, but your happiness should always come first. Here's how to handle it:

- **Understand Your Own Values**: Reflect on your values and priorities. Consider what you want from life and what kind of partner you envision.

- **Question Societal Norms**: Challenge stereotypes and outdated beliefs about marriage. Everyone's journey is unique, and there's no one-size-fits-all approach.

- **Communicate Openly**: Talk to your family and friends about your thoughts. Open communication helps set boundaries and seek support.

- **Educate Yourself**: Learn about different cultural and religious perspectives on marriage. The more informed you are, the better equipped you'll be to make your own decisions.

- **Set Boundaries**: Establish clear boundaries around marriage expectations. Prioritize your well-being and stick to your principles.

- **Focus on Personal Growth**: Invest in your education, career, and passions. Personal growth builds confidence and resilience.

- **Seek Support**: If societal pressure feels overwhelming, seek guidance from a trusted adult or counselor. They can offer valuable support.

Teen: It's good to know that I don't have to follow society's expectations if they don't fit me.

Parent: Exactly. Marriage is a personal decision, and it's important to trust yourself and make choices that align with your values.

Summary::

Parent: In this chapter, we've explored many aspects of premarital sex and marriage. We've discussed the importance of making informed decisions, understanding the emotional and psychological implications, and navigating societal expectations. Marriage is a significant commitment, and it's essential to approach it with careful consideration and preparation.

Teen: I feel like I have a better understanding now, and it's good to know I can talk to you about these things.

Parent: That's what I'm here for. Remember, these conversations are ongoing, and I'm always here to listen, support, and guide you as you navigate these important aspects of life.

Takeaway Points:

1. **Understanding Premarital Sex**: Premarital sex is a deeply personal decision that requires careful consideration of emotional readiness, potential risks, and societal expectations.

2. **Risks and Consequences**: Engaging in premarital sex can have risks, including unplanned pregnancy, STIs, emotional consequences, and challenges in relationship dynamics.

3. **Informed Decision-Making**: Making informed decisions involves self-reflection, understanding personal values, educating oneself about sexual health, and communicating openly with partners.

4. **Emotional and Psychological Implications**: Premarital sex can impact emotional intimacy, self-identity, and relationship dynamics. Open communication and self-awareness are crucial.

5. **Protection and Safe Sex Practices**: Protecting oneself from STIs and unplanned pregnancy involves using contraception consistently, getting regular STI testing, and practicing safe sex.

6. **Cultural and Religious Influences**: Understanding cultural, religious, and societal attitudes towards premarital sex and marriage helps individuals make decisions that align with their values.

7. **The Institution of Marriage**: Marriage is a significant institution with legal, emotional, and cultural implications. It represents a formal commitment and requires careful consideration.

8. **Legal Rights and Responsibilities**: Marriage comes with legal rights and obligations, including decision-making authority, inheritance rights, tax benefits, and emotional and financial responsibilities.

9. **Readiness for Marriage**: Deciding if one is ready for marriage involves evaluating emotional maturity, commitment levels, shared values, financial stability, and communication skills.

10. **Key Components of a Healthy Marriage**: A successful marriage is built on communication, trust, respect, commitment, intimacy, shared values, and the ability to compromise.

11. **Preparing for Marriage**: Emotional and mental preparation involves self-awareness, emotional intelligence, communication skills, and personal growth. Seeking support can also help.

12. **Cultural and Religious Roles**: Cultural and religious beliefs play significant roles in shaping marriage, influencing values, rituals, expectations, and the spiritual significance of the union.

13. **Navigating Societal Pressures**: Prioritize personal happiness and well-being when navigating societal expectations regarding marriage. Question norms, set boundaries, and seek support to make decisions that align with personal values.

* * *

"Strength doesn't come from avoiding challenges, but from facing them
with resilience, love, and understanding."
— Anonymous

Chapter 7

Navigating Life as a Teenager of Divorced Parents

Divorce is a significant life event that can deeply impact families, especially teenagers, who may find themselves grappling with a whirlwind of emotions and uncertainty. This chapter explores the complexities of divorce and life afterward, addressing the myriad questions and concerns that teenagers often face during this challenging time. By discussing these issues openly and honestly, we hope to offer valuable insights and tools to help teenagers cope with the changes and transitions that come with divorce, fostering resilience and emotional well-being in the process.

Teen: Why are you and Dad getting a divorce? Did I do something wrong?

Parent: I know this is really tough, and you might be wondering why your dad, and I are getting a divorce. From the start, I want you to know this is not your fault. Sometimes, adults face problems in their relationship that they can't fix, no matter how hard they try. We've both tried to make things work, but we've realized that we can no longer be happy together as a married couple. This decision is about our relationship, not anything you've done. We both love you so much, and that will never change. You're the most important person in our lives, and we're here to help you through this, answer your questions, and make sure you feel loved and supported every step of the way.

Teen: What's going to happen to our family now? Will everything change?

Parent: I know you're worried about what this means for our family. While things will change, one thing that won't change is how much we both love you. Even though your Dad and I won't be living together anymore, we are both committed to co-parenting you and making sure you feel safe, loved, and supported. You'll still have a family, just in a new way. You'll have two homes and spend time with both of us. We'll work together to create a schedule that lets you have quality time with each of us. We'll face any challenges that come up together as a family, and we're here to talk whenever you need to.

Teen: Do I have to pick who I live with? Will I still see both of you?

Parent: No, sweetheart, you won't have to choose between us. Your Dad and I want you to have a strong relationship with us. We will work together to ensure you can spend time with both of us regularly. We'll create a custody schedule that works for you and us, so you'll still see both your Dad and me. Your well-being is important to us, and we'll do everything we can to ensure you feel loved and supported, no matter where you are.

Teen: What about money? Will things be different financially?

Parent: It's natural to wonder how this will affect our finances. Divorce can bring about changes, but your Dad and I are both committed to making sure you're taken care of. We'll create a financial plan that puts your needs first. You should know that your basic needs, like food, clothing, and education, will continue to be met. We'll do our best to maintain your stability and security during this transition. If you have any money worries, please ask us. We're here to support you and ensure you have what you need.

Teen: Will I have to change schools or move? What's going to happen to my home?

Parent: I know how important your school and home are to you, and I want to reassure you that our priority is keeping things as stable as possible. While some families might need to move or adjust after a divorce, we'll do our best to minimize disruptions to your life. We'll involve you in decision-making if any changes are necessary and consider what's best for you. We aim to ensure you're comfortable and that this transition is as smooth as possible for you.

Teen: What should I tell my friends and teachers about the divorce? Do I have to tell them everything?

Parent: When it comes to talking about our family situation, it's important that you feel comfortable with what you share. You're not obligated to tell anyone more than you feel ready to share. If you decide to talk to your friends or teachers, you can tell them that our family is going through some changes and that while it's difficult, we're working through it together. It's okay to tell them that you have support and are taking steps to adjust to the changes. Remember, you don't have to go through this alone, and it's perfectly fine to lean on trusted friends and adults for support.

Teen: I'm feeling all kinds of emotions right now—sad, angry, confused. Is that normal?

Parent: Absolutely, it's completely normal to feel all kinds of emotions about the divorce. It's a big change, and feeling sad, angry, confused, or even relieved is natural. Divorce can bring up a lot of different feelings, and it's really important to acknowledge and express them. It's okay to cry, to feel upset, or to need some time to yourself to process everything that's happening. Your feelings are valid, and it's okay to seek support from friends, family members, or a counselor if you're struggling to cope. We're all here for you, no matter what you're feeling.

Teen: Will you and Dad still be friends, or will things be awkward?

Parent: It's natural to wonder how things will change between your Dad and me after the divorce. Our relationship will be different because we won't be together as a couple anymore, but what won't change is our love for you. We will always be your parents, and that will never change. Even though we won't be married, we will continue supporting each other as co-parents and working together to ensure you're happy and well taken care of.

We focus on being the best parents we can be for you and are committed to working together to do that.

Teen: What if I don't feel like visiting the other parent after the divorce? Is that okay?

Parent: Feeling uneasy about visiting the other parent after a divorce is completely understandable. Your feelings are important, and talking to us about your feelings is okay. This is a big change, and adjusting it might take some time. However, it's also really important to spend time with both of us to maintain a strong and healthy relationship with each parent. We hope that, over time, you'll feel more comfortable and secure in your relationship with both of us. We'll work together to find a solution that makes you feel safe and supported, and we're always here to listen to your concerns.

Teen: How can I deal with everything that's happening? It feels overwhelming.

Parent: I know this is a lot to handle, and coping with the changes and emotions can be really challenging. Here are some things that might help you navigate this difficult time:

- **Express Your Feelings**: It's important to acknowledge and express your feelings, whether it's sadness, anger, confusion, or something else. You can talk to a trusted friend, family member, or counselor, write in a journal, or do something creative like art or music to help express your emotions.

- **Seek Support**: Don't hesitate to reach out for support when you need it. Talking to someone you trust can make a big difference. There are also support groups for teens going through similar experiences, which can be really helpful.

- **Take Care of Yourself**: Ensure you care for your physical and mental health. Get enough rest, eat well, and do things that make you happy and relaxed. Exercise can also be a great way to reduce stress and boost your mood.

- **Maintain Routine and Stability**: Try to keep a regular routine for sleeping, eating, and studying. Having consistency in your life can provide stability during times of change.

- **Communicate Openly**: Keep talking to both your Dad and me about how you're feeling. We want to support you, and open communication helps us understand your needs.

- **Focus on the Positive**: Even though this is a challenging time, try to focus on the good things in your life. Look for things to be grateful for and opportunities to grow and learn. Surround yourself with people who lift you up and make you feel good.

- **Seek Professional Help if Needed**: If you're having a really hard time coping, it's okay to ask for help from a therapist or counselor. They can provide the tools and support you need to get through this.

Teen: I'm unsure where to start, but I'll try some of these things.

Parent: That's all I ask. Just take it one step at a time, and remember, we're here for you every step of the way.

Teen: What about holidays and family events? How do I deal with those after the divorce?

Parent: Holidays and family events can be challenging after a divorce because they often bring up memories of how things used to be. Here's how you can handle them:

- **Talk About Plans Early**: We can plan ahead to make sure you know what to expect. Whether we alternate holidays or find ways to celebrate together, we'll work to create new traditions that make you feel comfortable.

- **Be Honest About Your Feelings**: If you're sad or upset about the changes, let us know. It's okay to have mixed emotions, and we'll try to make the experience as positive as possible for you.

- **Focus on What's Important**: Holidays are about spending time with loved ones. Focus on the moments of joy, even if things are different now. We'll do our best to make sure you feel included and loved.

- **Create New Traditions**: We can start new traditions that reflect our current situation. Whether it's a special meal, a new activity, or a different way of celebrating, we'll find ways to make the holidays meaningful for you.

- **Seek Support**: Talk to someone you trust if you're struggling with the changes. Sometimes, just having someone to listen can make a big difference.

Teen: It's hard to imagine different holidays, but new traditions could be nice.

Parent: It may take some time to adjust, but we'll ensure the holidays remain a time of love and togetherness, no matter what.

Teen: How can I stay close to both of you after the divorce?

Parent: Maintaining a strong relationship with both of us is really important. Here's how you can do that:

- **Keep Open Lines of Communication**: Stay in touch with us regularly. Whether it's through phone calls, texts, or visits, keeping open lines of communication helps maintain our bond.

- **Share Your Feelings**: Be honest about how you're feeling. If you're struggling or missing one of us, let us know. We're here to listen and support you.

- **Make Time for Both Parents**: We'll work together to make sure you have quality time with both of us. Whether it's during scheduled visits or special outings, we want to make sure you feel connected to both of us.

- **Respect the Other Parent**: Respecting both parents helps maintain harmony. Even if you're upset with one of us, try to keep communication respectful. We're both here to support you and want to make sure you feel loved and understood.

- **Create New Routines**: Establishing new routines with each parent can help maintain a sense of normalcy. Whether it's a regular weekend activity or a nightly phone call, these routines can help keep our connection strong.

- **Express Your Needs**: Don't hesitate to ask if you need something from either of us—more time together, reassurance, or just someone to talk to. We're here to support you in any way we can.

Teen: I want to stay close to both of you, but it feels weird sometimes.

Parent: It's normal to feel that way, but staying open and honest can keep our relationships strong.

Summary:

Parent: In this chapter, we've explored many aspects of life after divorce, from understanding why it happened to coping with the changes. Divorce is a significant life event, and it's okay to have lots of questions and emotions about it. What's important is that you know you're not alone, and we're here to support you every step of the way.

Teen: I understand things better now, and it helps to know we can talk about it.

Parent: That's what I'm here for. Remember, these conversations are ongoing, and I'm always here to listen, support, and guide you as we navigate this together.

Takeaway Points:

1. **Divorce is Not Your Fault**: The decision to divorce is based on the parents' relationship, and the love for their children remains unchanged.

2. **Family Structure Will Change, But Love Remains**: Divorce changes the family structure, but both parents remain committed to loving and supporting their children.

3. **Co-Parenting and Maintaining Relationships**: Teenagers don't have to choose between parents. Both parents will work together to ensure that the child maintains a strong relationship with both.

4. **Financial Stability Post-Divorce**: Divorce may impact finances, but parents are committed to ensuring that the child's needs are met, providing stability during the transition.

5. **Impact on School and Home Life**: Parents will strive to minimize disruptions to the teenager's life. If changes are necessary, the teenager's preferences will be considered to maintain consistency.

6. **Communication About Divorce**: Teenagers should feel comfortable discussing their family situation with friends or teachers at their own pace.

7. **Normalizing Emotions**: Feeling a range of emotions during a divorce is normal. These feelings are valid and should be acknowledged and expressed in healthy ways.

8. **Evolving Parental Relationships**: While the parents' relationship may change post-divorce, their commitment to co-parenting and supporting their child remains strong.

9. **Visitation and Parental Relationships**: It is important to maintain a relationship with both parents, even if feelings of reluctance or discomfort arise initially.

10. **Coping Strategies**: Effective coping strategies include expressing feelings, seeking support, maintaining self-care routines, and focusing on positive aspects of life.

11. **Handling Family Events and Holidays**: Planning ahead, creating new traditions, and focusing on what's important can help navigate these occasions post-divorce.

12. **Maintaining Strong Relationships with Both Parents**: Open communication, making time for each parent, and expressing needs help maintain strong relationships after divorce.

* * *

"What mental health needs is more sunlight, more candor, and more unashamed conversation."
— Glenn Close

Chapter 8

Mental Health and Well-being

In today's fast-paced world, taking care of your mental health is just as important as your physical health. As a teenager, you might be dealing with school pressures, friendships, social media, and figuring out who you are. All of this can feel overwhelming at times. This chapter is here to help you understand your emotions, cope with stress, and find the right support when you need it. We'll answer some of the most common questions teenagers have about mental health, provide tips for building resilience, and offer guidance on seeking help when it's needed.

How do I cope with stress and anxiety?

Teen: I've been feeling really stressed and anxious lately, and I don't know how to handle it. What can I do?

Parent: I know that stress and anxiety can feel overwhelming, especially when you're juggling so much. Here's how you can manage these feelings:

- **Identify Your Stressors**: It's important to figure out what's causing your stress. Is it school, friendships, or something else? Once you know what's triggering your anxiety, it's easier to address it.

- **Practice Self-Care**: Take care of your body—get enough sleep, eat healthy, exercise, and do things that make you happy. When your body feels good, your mind often does too.

- **Develop Healthy Coping Strategies**: Try deep breathing, meditation, journaling, or listening to your favorite music. Find what works best for calming your mind.

- **Stay Connected**: Talking to friends, family, or other trusted people can really help. You don't have to go through stress alone.

- **Set Realistic Goals**: Break tasks into smaller steps without pressure yourself to be perfect. Celebrate small wins and be kind to yourself if things don't go as planned.

- **Seek Professional Help if Needed**: If stress and anxiety are taking over, it's okay to talk to a counselor or therapist. They can help you find ways to manage these feelings.

Teen: It's hard to admit when I'm stressed, but I'll try these things.

Parent: Remember, learning to cope with stress and anxiety is a process, and it's okay to ask for help. I'm here for you, and together we can figure out what works best.

What should I do if I'm feeling depressed or overwhelmed?

Teen: Sometimes I just feel really down and overwhelmed. What should I do?

Parent: Feeling depressed or overwhelmed can be really tough, and I want to make sure you know what to do:

- **Acknowledge Your Feelings**: It's important to recognize your feelings and understand that feeling this way is okay.

- **Reach Out for Support**: Talk to someone you trust—me, a friend, or a counselor. Sharing your feelings can make a big difference.

- **Take Care of Yourself**: Focus on self-care—get enough sleep, eat well, and do things that usually make you feel good, like hobbies or spending time with loved ones.

- **Practice Stress Management**: Techniques like deep breathing or mindfulness can help calm your mind.

- **Set Realistic Expectations**: Taking things one step at a time is okay. Don't be too hard on yourself.

- **Seek Professional Help**: If these feelings persist, talking to a mental health professional is important. They can help you work through your feelings and find ways to feel better.

Teen: I've been trying to handle it alone, but maybe it's time to talk to someone.

Parent: You don't have to go through this alone. There are people who care about you and want to help you feel better, including me.

How can I build resilience and emotional well-being?

Teen: How can I better handle life's challenges without getting overwhelmed?

Parent: Building resilience and emotional well-being is about learning how to handle life's challenges. Here's how you can do it:

- **Cultivate Self-Awareness**: Know yourself better—your emotions, strengths, and areas where you can grow. Self-reflection can help you understand how to better cope with challenges.

- **Develop Coping Skills**: Practice healthy ways to cope with stress, like deep breathing, mindfulness, or creative outlets like writing or drawing.

- **Build a Support System**: Surround yourself with people who support you—friends, family, teachers, or counselors. Having a strong support network is key to resilience.

- **Focus on Growth Mindset**: Believe that you can grow and learn from challenges. See setbacks as opportunities to learn, not as failures.

- **Practice Self-Care**: Take care of your body and mind—get enough sleep, eat well, exercise, and do things that make you happy.

- **Set Goals and Take Action**: Break down your goals into manageable steps and celebrate your progress along the way.

- **Maintain Perspective**: Keep things in perspective and focus on the positives, even when things are tough.

- **Seek Meaning and Purpose**: Engage in activities that give your life meaning, whether it's helping others, pursuing a passion, or learning something new.

Teen: It sounds about making small changes and building up over time.

Parent: Exactly. Building resilience takes time, but with practice, you can confidently handle life's challenges. I'm here to support you as you build these skills.

What are some healthy coping mechanisms for managing difficult emotions?

Teen: What should I do when I'm feeling really strong emotions and don't know how to handle them?

Parent: Managing difficult emotions is tough, but healthy coping methods exist. Here are some strategies you can try:

- **Mindfulness and Meditation**: Practice mindfulness techniques like deep breathing or guided meditation to help you stay calm and focused.

- **Physical Activity**: Exercise is a great way to boost your mood. Whether it's walking, running, or yoga, find something that makes you feel good.

- **Creative Expression**: Use art, music, or writing to express your emotions. Creativity can be a powerful way to process what you're feeling.

- **Social Support**: Talk to someone you trust about what you're going through. Sometimes just sharing can make a big difference.

- **Self-Care**: Prioritize activities that help you feel good—getting enough sleep, eating well, or spending time on a hobby.

- **Journaling**: Writing down your thoughts and feelings can help you process what you're going through and gain clarity.

- **Mindful Breathing**: Practice deep breathing exercises to help calm your mind and body when feeling overwhelmed.

- **Seek Professional Help**: If you struggle to manage your emotions alone, talking to a therapist or counselor for extra support is okay.

Teen: I've tried some of these before, but maybe I should make them a regular habit.

Parent: That's a great idea. Remember, feeling a range of emotions is okay, and finding healthy ways to cope with them is important. You don't have to go through it alone—I'm here to help.

How do I seek help for mental health issues, and who can I turn to for support?

Teen: What should I do if I think I need help with my mental health? Who can I talk to?

Parent: If you're dealing with mental health issues, it's important to seek help. Here's how you can do that:

- **Talk to a Trusted Adult**: Start by talking to someone you trust, like me, a family member, a teacher, or a school counselor. We're here to support you and help you find your needed resources.

- **School Counselor or Nurse**: Your school's counselor or nurse can provide confidential support and connect you with resources.

- **Mental Health Professionals**: Consider seeing a therapist, psychologist, or psychiatrist. They're trained to help with mental health issues and can provide therapy, medication, or other treatments.

- **Support Groups**: Joining a support group can help you connect with others who are going through similar experiences. It can be really comforting to know you're not alone.

- **Hotlines and Helplines**: There are hotlines you can call if you need immediate support. These services are confidential and available 24/7.

- **Online Resources**: Many online resources offer information and support for mental health issues. Just make sure you're using reputable sources.

- **Family and Friends**: Don't forget to lean on your family and friends for support. We care about you and want to help you through tough times.

- **Emergency Services**: If you ever feel like you're in immediate danger or can't cope, don't hesitate to call emergency services or go to the nearest emergency room.

Teen: I didn't realize there were so many options. It's good to know I'm not alone.

Parent: You're not alone. Remember, seeking help is a sign of strength, not weakness. You deserve to feel supported and understood; many people are here to help you.

What can I do to maintain a positive mental health routine?

Teen: How can I keep my mental health in a good place every day?

Parent: Maintaining a positive mental health routine is all about consistency and self-care. Here are some tips:

- **Create a Daily Routine**: Establish a daily routine that includes time for schoolwork, physical activity, relaxation, and hobbies. Having a structure can help you feel more in control.

- **Practice Gratitude**: Take a few moments each day to reflect on what you're grateful for. This can help shift your focus away from stress and towards positivity.

- **Limit Screen Time**: While enjoying social media and video games is okay, too much screen time can increase anxiety. Try to balance your screen time with other activities.

- **Stay Organized**: Keep track of your assignments, deadlines, and responsibilities. Staying organized can reduce stress and help you manage your time more effectively.

- **Take Breaks**: It's important to take regular breaks throughout the day, especially when you're feeling overwhelmed. Even a few minutes of relaxation can help you recharge.

- **Connect with Others**: Make time to connect with friends and family. Social interaction is essential for your mental well-being, even just a quick chat or a text message.

- **Reflect on Your Day**: Before bed, take a moment to reflect on your day. What went well? What could have gone better? This practice can help you learn from your experiences and set positive intentions for the next day.

Teen: I'll try setting up a routine and see how it goes.

Parent: Creating and maintaining a positive mental health routine takes effort, but it's worth it. I'm here to help you develop a routine that works for you.

How do I recognize when I'm struggling with my mental health?

Teen: Sometimes I'm unsure if I'm feeling just normal stress or something more serious. How can I tell?

Parent: It's important to be aware of the signs that you might be struggling with your mental health. Here's what to look out for:

- **Changes in Mood**: If you notice that you're feeling sad, irritable, or anxious more often than usual, it could be a sign that you're struggling.

- **Withdrawing from Activities**: If you're losing interest in things you used to enjoy, or if you're avoiding social interactions, it might be a sign that something's wrong.

- **Difficulty Concentrating**: If you're having trouble focusing on schoolwork or other tasks, it could be due to mental health issues.

- **Changes in Sleep or Appetite**: Sleeping too much or too little, or changes in your eating habits, can be signs of not feeling well mentally.

- **Feeling Overwhelmed**: If you're constantly feeling overwhelmed or stressed, it might be a sign that you need some extra support.

- **Physical Symptoms**: Sometimes mental health struggles can show up as physical symptoms, like headaches, stomachaches, or fatigue.

Teen: I've noticed some of these things lately. Maybe I need to pay more attention to how I'm feeling.

Parent: If you notice any of these signs, reaching out for help is important. You don't have to deal with this alone—I'm here to support you.

Summary:

Parent: In this chapter, we've talked about many important things related to mental health—how to cope with stress, build resilience, and recognize when you might need help. Taking care of your mental health is just as important as taking care of your physical health, and it's okay to ask for help when you need it.

Teen: I feel like I have a better understanding now, and it's good to know that I can talk to you about this.

Parent: That's what I'm here for. Remember, these conversations are ongoing, and I'm always here to listen, support, and guide you as you navigate your mental health.

Takeaway Points:

1. **Understanding and Managing Stress and Anxiety**:
   - Identify your stressors, practice self-care, develop healthy coping strategies, stay connected, set realistic goals, and seek professional help.

2. **Dealing with Depression or Overwhelm**:
   - Acknowledge your feelings, reach out for support, care for yourself, practice stress management, set realistic expectations, and seek professional help when necessary.

3. **Building Resilience and Emotional Well-being:**
   - ➤ Cultivate self-awareness, develop coping skills, build a strong support system, focus on a growth mindset, practice self-care, set and achieve goals, maintain perspective, and seek meaning and purpose in life.

4. **Healthy Coping Mechanisms:**
   - ➤ Use mindfulness, physical activity, creative expression, social support, self-care, journaling, mindful breathing, and professional help to manage difficult emotions.

5. **Seeking Help for Mental Health Issues:**
   - ➤ Talk to trusted adults, use school resources, see mental health professionals, join support groups, utilize hotlines and online resources, and lean on family and friends for support.

6. **Maintaining a Positive Mental Health Routine:**
   - ➤ Establish a routine, practice gratitude, limit screen time, stay organized, take breaks, connect with others, and reflect on your day.

7. **Recognizing Struggles with Mental Health:**
   - ➤ Pay attention to changes in mood, interest, concentration, sleep, appetite, and physical symptoms.

* * *

"It takes courage to stand alone, even when everyone else is doing something different. Your decisions shape your future, not the crowd's."

Peer Pressure and Decision-Making

Parent: As you navigate your teenage years, you'll encounter various situations where you must make important decisions. Peer pressure can sometimes make these decisions even harder. But remember, you have the strength and wisdom to make choices that reflect your true self. Let's discuss how you can handle these situations with confidence.

How do I handle peer pressure to engage in risky behaviors?

Teen: I sometimes feel pressured to do things I'm not comfortable with, like trying alcohol or skipping school because my friends are doing it. How can I handle that without losing my friends?

Parent: It's tough to go against the crowd, but staying true to yourself is really important. Here's what you can do:

- **Know Your Values**: Consider what's important to you. When you're clear on your values, making decisions that align with who you are is easier.

- **Practice Saying No**: You don't have to go along with something that doesn't feel right. Practice saying no confidently, like, 'No thanks, that's not for me.'

- **Find Supportive Friends**: True friends will respect your choices. If someone pushes you to do something you're uncomfortable with, it might be worth reconsidering that friendship.

- **Create an Exit Plan**: If you find yourself in a situation where you feel pressured, have a plan to leave. It's okay to say, 'I need to go' or 'I have other plans.'

- **Talk to Someone You Trust**: If you're struggling, it's okay to talk to someone like me, a teacher, or a counselor. You don't have to deal with it alone.

Teen: I'll try practicing some of these responses. It's hard, but I don't want to do something I'll regret.

Parent: That's a great start. Remember, it takes courage to stand up for what's right for you, and I'm proud of you for thinking about this.

How can I make decisions that align with my values even when others don't agree?

Teen: Sometimes I know what's right for me, but my friends or others don't agree with my choices. How can I stick to my decisions without feeling guilty?

Parent: It's not always easy to go against the grain, but here's how you can stand firm:

- **Be Clear About Your Values**: Make sure you understand your own values and why they matter to you. This clarity will give you the confidence to make decisions that align with those values.

- **Respectfully Disagree**: It's okay to disagree with others. You can say something like, 'I respect your opinion, but this is what I believe is right for me.'

- **Don't Feel the Need to Justify**: You don't have to explain or justify your decisions to others. Simply stating your choice can be enough.

- **Seek Affirmation**: Talk to people who share your values or who support you. They can help reaffirm that you're making the right choices for yourself.

- **Stay Strong in Your Beliefs**: Remember that it's okay to be different. Sticking to your values shows strength and integrity, and it's something to be proud of.

Teen: It's hard not to feel guilty when others don't agree, but I guess it's important to trust myself.

Parent: Exactly. It's your life, and you're the one who has to live with your decisions. Trusting yourself is key.

What should I do if I'm tempted to give in to peer pressure because I want to fit in?

Teen: I sometimes feel like I should just go along with everyone else so I don't feel left out. What should I do when I'm tempted to give in?

Parent: Wanting to fit in is completely normal, but it's important to consider the consequences. Here's what you can think about:

- **Weigh the Consequences**: Before you act, think about how you'll feel afterward. Will you be proud of your decision, or will you regret it?

- **Ask Yourself Why**: Are you doing this because it's something you want, or just because you want to fit in? Understanding your motivation can help you make a better choice.

- **Find Common Ground**: Look for activities or interests that you and your friends can enjoy together that don't go against your values.

- **Practice Self-Compassion**: It's okay to feel conflicted but remind yourself that you deserve to make right choices.

- **Seek Alternatives**: If you feel left out, find other ways to connect with people who share your values or find new friends who respect your decisions.

Teen: It's hard when everyone else is doing something, but I'll try to remember how I'll feel afterward.

Parent: That's a smart approach. Staying true to yourself will always be more rewarding in the long run.

How can I build confidence in my choices and resist negative influences?

Teen: I want to feel more confident in my choices, but sometimes I doubt myself when others think differently. How can I be surer of myself?

Parent: Building confidence is a process, but here's how you can start:

- **Reflect on Past Successes**: Consider when you made a good decision. What helped you make that choice? Reminding yourself of these moments can boost your confidence.

- **Surround Yourself with Positive Influences**: Spend time with people who support you and encourage you to be your best self. Their positivity can help strengthen your own resolve.

- **Develop a Strong Sense of Self**: Spend time on activities that build your self-esteem, like hobbies, sports, or volunteering. The more you know and like yourself, the less you'll be swayed by others.

- **Learn to Say No Without Guilt**: Practice saying NO in a way that feels good. It's okay to protect your well-being by setting boundaries.

- **Remember Your Long-Term Goals**: Keep your bigger picture in mind. Think about how your choices today will affect your future.

Teen: I need to work on not feeling bad when I say NO, especially when others are disappointed.

Parent: That's understandable. But remember, saying NO is sometimes necessary to take care of yourself, and that's a good thing.

What strategies can I use to say NO and set boundaries in peer situations?

Teen: I find it hard to say NO to my friends, even when I know I should. How can I set boundaries without feeling bad about it?

Parent: It's important to learn how to say NO in a way that respects your needs and friendships. Here's how:

- **Be Honest and Direct**: When you must say NO, do it clearly and calmly. You can say, 'I'm not comfortable with that' or 'That's not something I want to do.'

- **Use the Sandwich Approach**: Start with something positive, say NO, and end with something positive. For example, 'I love hanging out with you, but I'm not into that. Let's do something else instead.'

- **Offer an Alternative**: If you're saying NO to something, suggest another activity that you're comfortable with. This shows you still want to spend time with your friends but on your terms.

- **Practice in Low-Stakes Situations**: Start by saying NO in situations that aren't as emotionally charged. The more you practice, the easier it will become.

- **Respect Your Own Boundaries**: Remind yourself that it's okay to prioritize your own needs and well-being. True friends will understand and respect that.

Teen: I'll try the sandwich approach next time. It might make it easier for me to say NO without feeling bad.

Parent: That's a great idea. Remember, setting boundaries is about taking care of yourself, which you should never feel bad about.

How do I deal with the fear of losing friends if I don't agree with their ideas?

Teen: I'm afraid that they won't like me if I don't do what my friends want. How do I handle that fear?

Parent: It's natural to worry about losing friends, but remember that true friendships are based on respect and understanding. Here's how to manage that fear:

- **Evaluate Your Friendships**: Ask yourself if these friends truly support you. Friends who pressure you to do things that make you uncomfortable might not be the best influences in your life.

- **Communicate Openly**: If you're worried about how your friends will react, talk to them about it. You can say, 'I really value our friendship, but I need to do what feels right for me.'

- **Stay True to Yourself**: It's better to have a few close friends who respect you than many friends who don't. Being authentic will attract people who appreciate you for who you are.

- **Seek New Friendships**: If you lose friends because you stood up for yourself, it might be time to find new ones who share your values and respect your choices.

- **Remember Your Worth**: You deserve friends who like you for who you are, not for what you do for them. Don't compromise your values for the sake of fitting in.

Teen: It's hard to think about losing friends, but you're right. I need to focus on who really respects me.

Parent: Exactly. It's tough, but the friends who truly care about you will stay, and those are the ones worth keeping.

How do I handle peer pressure in online or social media settings?

Teen: Sometimes I feel pressured to post things or act a certain way online because everyone else does it. How can I handle this kind of peer pressure?

Parent: Online peer pressure can be tricky, but you can navigate it with these strategies:

- **Think Before You Post**: Before sharing anything online, ask yourself if it aligns with your values and if you're comfortable with everyone seeing it. If the answer is no, it's okay not to post.

- **Curate Your Online Circle**: Surround yourself with positive influences on social media. Follow accounts that inspire you and unfollow or mute those that make you feel pressured or anxious.

- **Set Boundaries**: Decide how much time you want to spend on social media and what you're comfortable sharing. Stick to these boundaries, even if others are doing something different.

- **Don't Compare**: Remember that people often post only their highlights, not their whole lives. Don't compare yourself to what you see online, and focus on your own journey.

- **Seek Real Connections**: Prioritize real-life connections over online validation. Spend time with friends who make you feel good about yourself, both online and offline.

Teen: It's hard not to compare myself to others online, but I'll try to remember that it's just their highlights.

Parent: That's a good perspective. What you see online is only part of the story, so focus on what makes you happy and fulfilled.

How do I navigate peer pressure when it comes to academic decisions?

Teen: Sometimes I feel pressured to take certain classes or join certain clubs because that's what everyone else does, even if it's not what I want. How do I handle that?

Parent: Academic decisions are important, and making choices that align with your interests and goals is essential. Here's how to navigate that pressure:

- **Identify Your Interests**: Focus on what you enjoy and are passionate about. Choose classes and activities that excite you, not just what's popular.

- **Set Your Own Goals**: Think about your future and your goals. Make decisions that will help you reach your goals, even if they differ from your friends' goals.

- **Seek Advice**: Talk to a counselor, teacher, or mentor about your options. They can provide guidance based on your strengths and interests, helping you make informed choices.

- **Be Confident in Your Path**: It's okay to take a different path from your friends. What matters is that you're pursuing what's right for you.

- **Stay True to Yourself**: Remember that your academic journey is yours alone. Don't let others dictate your choices—do what feels right for you.

Teen: It's hard not to follow the crowd, but I want to do what's best for me.

Parent: That's the right approach. Your future is yours to shape, so make choices to help you get where you want to go.

Takeaway Points:

1. **Handling Peer Pressure**:
   - Know your values, practice saying NO, and surround yourself with supportive friends.
   - Create an exit plan for situations where you feel pressured and talk to someone you trust if needed.

2. **Making Decisions**:
   - Understand your values, respect others' opinions, and don't feel the need to justify your decisions.
   - Seek affirmation from supportive people and stay strong in your beliefs.

3. **Building Confidence**:
   - Reflect on past successes, surround yourself with positivity, and develop a strong sense of self.
   - Learn to say NO without guilt and keep your long-term goals in mind.

4. **Setting Boundaries**:
   - Be honest and direct, use the sandwich approach, and offer alternatives.
   - Practice in low-stakes situations and remember that it's okay to prioritize your well-being.

5. **Navigating Friendships**:
   - Evaluate friendships, communicate openly, and stay true to yourself.
   - Seek new friendships if needed, and remember your worth.

6. **Handling Online Peer Pressure:**
   - ▷ Think before you post, curate your online circle, and set boundaries.
   - ▷ Don't compare yourself to others online, and seek real-life connections.

7. **Academic Decisions:**
   - ▷ Identify your interests, set your own goals, and seek advice from mentors.
   - ▷ Be confident in your academic path and stay true to what feels right.

8. **Resisting Negative Influences:**
   - ▷ Stay strong in the face of negative influences by remembering your worth, setting clear boundaries, and seeking support when needed.

9. **Empowerment through Self-Knowledge:**
   - ▷ Knowing yourself—your values, strengths, and goals—empowers you to make decisions that lead to a fulfilling and authentic life.

10. **Seeking Support:**
   - ▷ It's okay to ask for help when navigating difficult situations. Trusted adults, friends, and mentors can offer valuable guidance and support.

These points remind you that you can make choices that reflect your true self and navigate the challenges of peer pressure with confidence and integrity.

* * *

"With great power comes great responsibility."
— *Stan Lee*

Chapter 10

Online Safety and Cyberbullying

Parent: Hey, I've meant to talk to you about something important—online safety. With so much of our lives happening online, I want to ensure you're prepared to navigate it safely.

Teen: I've heard about online dangers, but it all seems overwhelming sometimes. What should I be doing to protect myself?

Teen: How can I protect my privacy and safety online?

Parent: Protecting your privacy online starts with being aware of what you share and who you share it with. Here are a few tips:

- **Use Strong Passwords**: Make sure your passwords are complex, with a mix of letters, numbers, and symbols. Avoid using easily guessable information like your birthdate.

- **Think Before You Share**: Be mindful of the personal details you post online. Others can use information like your location, school, or routine in ways you might not expect.

- **Enable Privacy Settings**: Most social media platforms allow you to control who sees your posts. Adjust your settings to ensure only people you trust can see your personal information.

- **Be Cautious with Strangers**: Don't accept friend requests or follow requests from people you don't know. Even if they seem friendly, it's better to be safe.

- **Update Software Regularly**: Keep your devices and apps updated to protect against the latest security threats.

Teen: That makes sense. I'll start being more careful with what I share.

Parent: That's a great idea. Your privacy is your responsibility, and the best way to protect it is to be cautious.

Teen: What should I do if I'm being cyberbullied or harassed online?

Parent: If you ever find yourself being targeted online, there are steps you can take to protect yourself and get help:

- **Don't Respond**: Engaging with the bully can sometimes make things worse. Instead, take screenshots of the messages or posts as evidence.

- **Block and Report**: Use the platform's tools to block the person and report the behaviour. Most platforms take harassment seriously and have policies to deal with it.

- **Talk to Someone You Trust**: Don't keep it to yourself. Reach out to me, a teacher, or another trusted adult. We can help you figure out the best course of action.

- **Practice Self-Care**: Cyberbullying can be really tough emotionally. Make sure you take care of yourself, whether taking a break from social media or doing something you enjoy to de-stress.

Teen: I didn't know I could block people like that. It's good to know I have options if I need them.

Parent: Absolutely. You control your online experience, and no one should make you feel unsafe or uncomfortable.

Teen: How do I navigate social media in a healthy way?

Parent: Social media can be fun, but it's important to use it wisely:

- **Set Limits**: It's easy to lose track of time online. Setting limits on how long you spend on social media daily can help you stay balanced.

- **Curate Your Feed**: Follow accounts that make you feel good about yourself and unfollow those that don't. It's your feed—make it a positive space.

- **Avoid Comparison**: Remember that people often only post the highlights of their lives. Don't compare your everyday life to someone else's curated posts.

- **Be Mindful of What You Post**: Consider how your posts might affect others and yourself in the long run. Once something is online, it's hard to take back.

- **Take Breaks**: If you're feeling overwhelmed or anxious, taking a break from social media is okay. Your mental health is more important.

Teen: I've definitely fallen into the comparison trap before. I'll try to be more mindful about how much time I spend online and who I follow.

Parent: That's a great approach. Social media should enhance your life, not something that brings you down.

Teen: What are the risks of online interactions, and how can I stay safe?

Parent: Online interactions can sometimes lead to risky situations. Here's how you can stay safe:

- **Be Skeptical of New Contacts**: If someone you don't know well suddenly reaches out, be cautious. They might not be who they say they are.

- **Avoid Sharing Personal Information**: Even in casual conversations, be careful about sharing details like your address, phone number, or school name.

- **Trust Your Gut**: Trust your instincts if something feels off or makes you uncomfortable. It's better to be safe and step away from the conversation.

- **Be Aware of Scams**: Many scams are out there, from phishing emails to fake online contests. Always verify the source before clicking on links or providing any information.

- **Stay Informed**: Keep up with the latest online safety tips and trends. The more you know, the better equipped you'll be to recognize and avoid potential dangers.

Teen: I'll keep an eye out for anything suspicious. Better safe than sorry, right?

Parent: Exactly. Being cautious online is just as important as being cautious in the real world.

Teen: How do I recognize and respond to online grooming and predatory behaviour?

Parent: It's important to recognize the signs of online grooming and know how to respond:

- **Watch for Red Flags**: If someone is overly interested in your personal life, tries to isolate you from friends or family, or makes you uncomfortable with inappropriate comments, those are red flags.

- **Limit Sharing Personal Details**: Avoid sharing too much too soon, especially with people you've just met online.

- **Don't Meet Up Alone**: Never agree to meet someone in person that you've only known online without discussing it with a trusted adult first.

- **Report Suspicious Behavior**: If someone makes you uncomfortable or seems suspicious, report them to the platform and talk to an adult immediately.

- **Educate Yourself**: Learn about predators' online tactics so you can recognize and avoid them. Knowledge is power.

Teen: I didn't realize how sneaky some people could be online. I'll be more careful and talk to you if anything feels off.

Parent: That's the right thing to do. Always trust your instincts, and never hesitate to ask for help.

Teen: What steps should I take if my personal information is compromised online?

Parent: If your personal information is ever compromised online, here's what you should do:

- **Change Passwords Immediately**: Update your passwords on all affected accounts, especially those related to banking or social media.

- **Enable Two-Factor Authentication**: This adds an extra layer of security by requiring a second form of verification when logging in.

- **Monitor Your Accounts**: Monitor your bank statements, emails, and social media accounts for any suspicious activity. Report anything unusual to the appropriate service providers.

- **Alert Friends and Contacts**: If your account has been hacked, let your friends and contacts know so they don't fall for any scams or phishing attempts from your compromised account.

- **Report the Incident**: Report the breach to the platform or service where it occurred. They might have specific steps you need to follow to secure your account.

Teen: That sounds scary, but it's good to know I can take steps to minimize the damage.

Parent: It can be stressful, but acting quickly can help protect your information and prevent further problems.

Teen: How can I support a friend who is being cyberbullied?

Parent: Supporting a friend who is being cyberbullied is important. Here's how you can help:

- **Listen and Be There**: Sometimes, just being there to listen can make a big difference. Let your friend know they're not alone.

- **Encourage Them to Talk to an Adult**: Suggest that they talk to a trusted adult, like a parent, teacher, or counselor, who can help them take the right steps to stop the bullying.

- **Don't Join In**: Even if it's meant as a joke, don't participate in or encourage any bullying behaviour. Stand up for your friend if you feel safe doing so.

- **Report the Bullying**: If your friend is reluctant to report the bullying themselves, you can help by reporting it on their behalf. Many platforms allow you to report harassment anonymously.

- **Help Them Disconnect**: Encourage your friends to take breaks from social media and focus on activities that make them feel good.

Teen: I'll definitely look out for my friends and make sure they know they can talk to me.

Parent: That's great. Being a good friend means being there when it really counts.

Teen: What are the legal consequences of cyberbullying?

Parent: Cyberbullying can have serious legal consequences. Here's what you should know:

- **School Policies**: Many schools have strict policies against cyberbullying. Students found guilty can face suspension, expulsion, or other disciplinary actions.

- **Criminal Charges**: In severe cases, cyberbullying can lead to criminal charges. This could include charges like harassment, stalking, or even hate crimes, depending on the nature of the bullying.

- **Civil Lawsuits**: Victims of cyberbullying can sometimes file civil lawsuits against the bully or their guardians for damages, especially if the bullying has caused significant harm.

- **Permanent Record**: Legal actions taken against cyberbullying can stay on a person's record, potentially affecting future opportunities like college admissions or employment.

Teen: I didn't realize cyberbullying could have such serious consequences. It's not something to take lightly.

Parent: Exactly. Cyberbullying can have lasting effects on everyone involved, which is why it's so important to be kind and responsible online.

Teen: How can I safely manage multiple social media accounts?

Parent: Managing multiple social media accounts can be tricky. Here's how to do it safely:

- **Use Different Passwords**: Don't use the same password for all your accounts. If one account gets hacked, having different passwords will help protect the others.

- **Keep Track of Your Accounts**: It's easy to lose track of old accounts. Regularly review and delete accounts you no longer use to reduce your online footprint.

- **Separate Personal and Public Accounts**: If you have accounts for different purposes (like one for close friends and one for public use), keep them separate and manage privacy settings accordingly.

- **Be Cautious with Third-Party Apps**: Some apps and websites request access to your social media accounts. Be selective about which apps you grant access to, as they can sometimes misuse your data.

- **Monitor Activity**: Regularly check your accounts for any unusual activity, such as login attempts from unknown devices or locations. Most platforms will alert you if something suspicious occurs.

Teen: I'll make sure to review my accounts and keep everything organized and secure.

Parent: That's a smart move. The more organized you are, the safer you'll be online.

Teen: What should I do if I accidentally share something I regret online?

Parent: It happens to the best of us—here's what you can do if you share something you regret:

- **Delete the Post**: Delete the post or content as soon as you realize the mistake. The quicker you act, the less likely it is to spread.

- **Apologize If Necessary**: If your post has hurt someone or caused misunderstanding, consider reaching out to apologize. A sincere apology can go a long way.

- **Use Social Media's 'Undo' Features**: Some platforms allow you to retract messages or posts shortly after posting. Familiarize yourself with these features if you need them.

- **Address the Issue Publicly or Privately**: Depending on the situation, you might need to make a public statement to clarify or correct your post or address it privately with those involved.

- **Learn from the Experience**: Reflect on what led to the mistake and consider how to avoid it in the future. It might be a good time to reassess your online habits.

Teen: It's good to know I have options if I ever make a mistake online. I'll be more careful, but having a plan is nice.

Parent: Exactly. Mistakes happen, but how you respond to them is what really counts.

Key Takeaways:

1. **Privacy First:**
   - Protect your personal information by using strong passwords, adjusting privacy settings, and being cautious about what you share online.

2. **Respond to Cyberbullying:**
   - If you experience cyberbullying, don't engage with the bully. Instead, block, report, and seek support from trusted adults.

3. **Healthy Social Media Use:**
   - Curate your social media feed, avoid comparisons, and set time limits to maintain a healthy relationship with online platforms.

4. **Recognize Risks**:
   - ➢ Stay alert to online scams, suspicious contacts, and inappropriate behaviour, and trust your instincts to avoid risky situations.

5. **Respond to Predatory Behavior**:
   - ➢ Learn to recognize the signs of grooming and predatory behaviour online, and take immediate action by reporting and seeking help.

6. **Act Quickly if Compromised**:
   - ➢ If your personal information is compromised online, immediately secure your accounts and prevent further damage.

7. **Support Friends**:
   - ➢ If a friend is being cyberbullied, offer support, encourage them to seek help, and report the bullying if necessary.

8. **Understand Legal Implications**:
   - ➢ Be aware of the serious legal consequences that can arise from cyberbullying, including criminal charges and civil lawsuits.

9. **Manage Accounts Wisely**:
   - ➢ Safely manage multiple social media accounts by using different passwords, regularly monitoring activity, and being cautious with third-party apps.

10. **Handle Mistakes Gracefully**:
    - ➢ If you share something you regret online, delete it promptly, apologize if needed, and learn from the experience to avoid future mishaps.

This chapter empowers you with the tools and knowledge to navigate the online world safely and confidently. Remember, the internet is a powerful tool, but staying informed and cautious is key to making the most of it while protecting yourself. This chapter also provides practical advice to handle common online challenges and emphasizes the importance of staying informed, being cautious, and acting responsibly online.

* * *

"It is time that we all see gender as a spectrum instead of two sets of opposing ideals."
— Emma Watson

Chapter 11

Gender and Sexuality

Parent: You know, understanding gender and sexuality can be a complex journey, and it's okay to have questions. Let's talk through some of them together.

Teen: Yeah, I've been thinking about these topics a lot. Sometimes it feels like there's so much to understand, and I'm unsure where to start.

Parent: That's completely normal. It's a journey, not just for you but for everyone. Why don't we start with some questions you might have?

How do I explore and understand my sexual orientation and gender identity?

Teen: I've been thinking about this a lot. It feels overwhelming sometimes, not knowing exactly who I am or what label fits me.

Parent: I can understand that. Exploring your sexual orientation and gender identity is a deeply personal journey, and it's okay to feel uncertain or confused. The important thing is to approach this process with an open mind, without pressuring yourself to fit into any particular label right away.

Teen: But how do I even start? I feel like I don't know where to begin.

Parent: Reflect on your feelings and experiences is a good place to start. What kinds of attractions or emotions have you noticed in yourself? Journaling might help you sort through your thoughts. And remember, there's no rush. It's okay to take your time to explore.

Teen: I've heard about different sexual orientations and gender identities, but sometimes it's hard to relate to any of them.

Parent: That's perfectly normal. Sexual orientation and gender identity exist on a spectrum, and not everyone fits neatly into a single category. It's okay if you don't feel like you fit into one specific box. You might find that your understanding of yourself evolves over time, and that's part of the journey.

Teen: What if I don't ever figure it out?

Parent: It's okay if you don't have all the answers right now. Your identity is something that you define for yourself, and it's okay if that definition changes over time. What's important is that you feel comfortable with who you are and have support as you explore.

What does it mean to have a healthy understanding of gender and sexuality?

Teen: What does it mean to have a healthy understanding of gender and sexuality?

Parent: Having a healthy understanding of gender and sexuality means recognizing and respecting the diversity of identities and experiences, both in yourself and in others. It's about embracing yourself and allowing others to do the same.

Teen: That sounds great, but how do I do that?

Parent: Start by educating yourself. Read about different gender identities and sexual orientations. Listen to the experiences of people from different backgrounds. The more you understand, the more you can appreciate the diversity of human experiences.

Teen: So, it's about learning and being open-minded?

Parent: Exactly. And it's also about challenging stereotypes and misconceptions that you might encounter. It's important to recognize that there's no one right way to be. Everyone's experience is valid, and everyone deserves to be treated with respect.

Teen: I guess that also means speaking up when I hear something wrong?

Parent: Yes, being an ally is a big part of having a healthy understanding. Stand up against discrimination and support those who might be marginalized. It's about creating a community where everyone feels safe and valued.

How can I support friends or peers exploring their gender and sexuality?

Parent: Supporting your friends or peers starts with listening. Make sure they know you're there for them without judgment.

Teen: But what if I say the wrong thing?

Parent: It's okay to make mistakes as long as you're coming from a place of care. If you're not sure about something, ask them respectfully. They'll appreciate your willingness to understand.

Teen: I've heard it's important to use the right pronouns. How do I make sure I'm doing that?

Parent: Absolutely. Using the correct pronouns is a simple but powerful way to show respect. If you're unsure, it's okay to ask someone what their preferred pronouns are. And if you make a mistake, just apologize and correct yourself.

Teen: What else can I do?

Parent: Educate yourself about the issues they might be facing, stand up for them if they're being treated unfairly, and be there to support them in any way you can. It's also important to respect their privacy and not share their personal information without their permission.

What are common misconceptions about gender and sexual orientation?

Parent: There are quite a few, unfortunately. For instance, some people think that gender and sexual orientation are binary—like you're either male or female, or you're straight or gay. But the truth is that both gender and sexual orientation exist on a spectrum.

Teen: So, it's not just one or the other?

Parent: Exactly. Another misconception is that gender and sexual orientation are choices. But they're inherent parts of who you are. People can't choose their gender identity or who they're attracted to any more than they can choose their height or eye color.

Teen: I've heard some people say that being LGBTQ+ is just a phase. Is that true?

Parent: No, it's not. LGBTQ+ (Lesbian, Gay, Bisexual, Transgender, Queer or Questioning. "+" represents other sexual orientations, gender identities, and expressions that are not specifically covered by the initial letters, such as Intersex, Asexual, and Pansexual, among others) identities are valid and enduring. For many people, their gender identity or sexual orientation is something they've understood about themselves for a long time, even if it takes time to express it fully.

Teen: What about the idea that LGBTQ+ people fit certain stereotypes?

Parent: That's another misconception. LGBTQ+ individuals are just as diverse and unique as anyone else. There's no one way to be LGBTQ+, and stereotypes can be harmful because they ignore that diversity.

How can I promote inclusivity and acceptance of diverse identities in my community?

Teen: I want to help make my school and community more inclusive. How can I do that?

Parent: Promoting inclusivity starts with educating yourself and being respectful. Make an effort to learn about different identities and experiences.

Teen: What else can I do besides learning?

Parent: You can challenge stereotypes when you hear them and speak up against discrimination. Being an ally means standing up for others, even when it is difficult.

Teen: I've noticed that some places don't feel very inclusive. What can I do about that?

Parent: You can work to create safe spaces where everyone feels welcome. This might mean advocating for gender-neutral restrooms, supporting LGBTQ+ groups, or starting a diversity initiative at school.

Teen: It sounds like a lot, but I want to make a difference.

Parent: And you can. Every small action counts. Leading with kindness and respect can help create a more inclusive and accepting environment for everyone.

How do I talk to adults about my gender and sexuality?

Teen: What if I want to talk to other adults about my gender and sexuality? How should I approach it?

Parent: It's important to approach these conversations with honesty and openness and to choose a time when you feel safe and ready. You might start by gradually sharing your thoughts or feelings and gauging their reaction. It's okay if the conversation takes time—what matters is that you feel heard and respected.

Teen: What if they don't understand?

Parent: Not everyone will understand right away, and that's okay. Some people might need time to process what you're telling them. Be patient, and if necessary, provide them with resources to help them learn more. If someone is unwilling to accept you, remember that others will support and celebrate who you are.

How can I find communities that support my gender and sexual identity?

Teen: Where can I find people who will support me and understand what I'm going through?

Parent: There are many communities, both online and offline, that offer support for people exploring their gender and sexual identity. Look for local LGBTQ+ centers, support groups, or online forums where you can connect with others who share similar experiences. Finding a community can provide a sense of belonging and help you feel less alone.

Teen: Is it safe to join these communities online?

Parent: While many online communities are supportive, it's important to be cautious. Make sure the groups you join are reputable and respectful of privacy. Never share personal information with someone you don't trust and be aware of the risks of online interactions. Your safety is always the top priority.

Parent: I'm so glad we're talking about these things. It's important to remember that your journey is your own, and it's okay to take your time figuring things out.

Teen: Thanks for being so open about this. It makes me feel like I'm not alone in figuring everything out.

Parent: You're not alone. We're in this together, and I'm here to support you every step of the way.

Key Takeaways:

1. **Exploring Identity:**
   - Understanding your gender and sexual identity is a personal journey. Take your time, and don't feel pressured to fit into a specific label.

2. **Healthy Understanding:**
   - A healthy understanding of gender and sexuality involves respecting the diversity of identities and challenging stereotypes.

3. **Supporting Others:**
   - Be a supportive friend by listening, using correct pronouns, and standing up against discrimination.

4. **Challenging Misconceptions:**
   - Gender and sexual orientation are not binary, and they are not choices. Challenge harmful stereotypes and promote understanding.

5. **Promoting Inclusivity:**
    - ▷ Advocate for inclusivity in your community by creating safe spaces, challenging discrimination, and educating yourself and others.

6. **Talking to Adults:**
    - ▷ Approach conversations about your gender and sexuality with honesty, and be patient if others need time to understand.

7. **Finding Supportive Communities:**
    - ▷ Seek out supportive online and offline communities, but always prioritize your safety and privacy.

8. **Personal Journey:**
    - ▷ Your journey is unique, and taking your time is okay. Seek support from those who respect and celebrate your identity.

This chapter provides a compassionate and thoughtful approach to understanding gender and sexuality. It encourages open dialogue, self-exploration, and the promotion of inclusivity and respect for all identities.

* * *

"To be beautiful means to be yourself. You don't need to be accepted by others. You need to accept yourself."
— *Thich Nhat Hanh*

Chapter 12

Body Image and Self-Esteem

Parent: Hey dear, can we talk for a bit? As you're growing up, you might feel a lot of pressure about your appearance, which can sometimes mess with how you feel about yourself. I've noticed how much society—social media, TV, magazines—pushes this idea of what we should look like. But here's the thing: your worth isn't tied to your appearance. How you feel about your body and you is so important, and I want us to explore that together. Are you up for it?

Teen: Yeah, I guess it's been on my mind. Everyone seems to care so much about their appearance, and sometimes it feels like I can't measure up.

Parent: I get that. It's tough out there with all these unrealistic standards. But let's dig into this together and see if we can find ways to help you feel more confident and comfortable in your own skin.

How can I develop a positive body image and self-esteem?

Teen: It's hard not to compare myself to others, especially online. How can I start feeling better about myself?

Parent: It starts with self-compassion. Imagine talking to yourself the way you'd talk to your best friend. You wouldn't be harsh or critical. So, why do that to yourself? Be kind to yourself, especially when you're feeling insecure. Remember that everyone has unique qualities, and your value doesn't depend on your appearance.

Teen: I guess it's easier said than done. What else can I do?

Parent: Surround yourself with positivity. Hang out with people who lift you up, not those who bring you down. Focus on what makes you feel good—exercising, eating well, or getting enough rest. And when those negative thoughts pop up, challenge them. Ask yourself if they're really true or if they're just coming from a place of insecurity. Replace them with positive affirmations.

Teen: I've heard about that—positive affirmations. Do they really work?

Parent: Absolutely. It might initially feel awkward, but it helps shift your mindset. Also, practice gratitude. Think about what you like about your body and what it allows you to do, and appreciate those things. It's about focusing on health and well-being, not just appearance.

Teen: And what about all those perfect bodies on social media? It's hard to ignore them.

Parent: That's a great point. Be mindful of what you're consuming on social media. Remember, a lot of what you see is edited or filtered. It's not real life. Surround yourself with diverse and realistic representations of beauty, and don't be afraid to unfollow accounts that make you feel bad about yourself.

What should I do if I'm struggling with body image issues or eating disorders?

Teen: What if it's more than just feeling down sometimes? What if I'm really struggling with my body image or even eating habits?

Parent: If you're feeling like that, reaching out is important. You don't have to go through it alone. Talk to someone you trust—me, another family member, or a close friend. Sharing how you feel can really help lighten the load.

Teen: But what if talking to you isn't enough?

Parent: Then we should look into getting some professional help. Therapists or counselors who specialize in body image issues or eating disorders can provide the guidance and support you need. Recovery is a process, and it's okay to seek help.

Teen: What else can I do to start feeling better?

Parent: Educate yourself about body image and eating disorders. Understanding what you're going through can be empowering. Also, practice self-care—this means taking care of your body with proper nutrition, exercise, and rest, but also taking care of your mind. And remember, progress might be slow, but every small step counts.

Teen: I'll try. I just want to feel better.

Parent: And you will, with time and support. Remember, recovery is a journey; you're not expected to do it alone.

How do I appreciate and celebrate my body for its uniqueness?

Teen: How do I start liking my body for what it is, not what it isn't?

Parent: Start by practicing gratitude. Every day, take a moment to appreciate what your body can do—whether it's something simple like walking or something joyful like dancing. Celebrate your body's abilities instead of focusing solely on its appearance.

Teen: But it's tough when everyone around me seems to care about looks.

Parent: It is, but you can shift your focus. Think about what makes your body unique and special. Maybe it's your strength, your resilience, or how you can express yourself through movement. Challenge those unrealistic beauty standards by embracing what makes you, you.

Teen: And if I don't feel that way right now?

Parent: That's okay. It's a journey, not a destination. Surround yourself with people and messages celebrating diversity in body shapes and sizes. And remember, self-love isn't about thinking you're perfect—it's about accepting and caring for yourself as you are.

What are some strategies for building self-confidence and self-acceptance?

Teen: I want to feel more confident but don't know where to start.

Parent: Building confidence starts with understanding yourself. Get to know your strengths and values. Knowing who you are and what you stand for makes it easier to feel self-confident.

Teen: But what if I focus too much on my weaknesses?

Parent: We all have areas where we can grow, but it's important to balance that with recognizing your strengths. Set small, realistic goals and celebrate each achievement, no matter how minor it might seem. Each step forward is a win.

Teen: And what about when I'm really hard on myself?

Parent: That's when you need to challenge those negative thoughts. When you are self-critical, pause and ask if you'd say those things to a friend. Practice self-compassion and replace negative self-talk with positive affirmations.

Teen: It sounds like a lot of work.

Parent: It can be, but it's worth it. Confidence and self-acceptance aren't built overnight—they're cultivated through consistent effort. Surround yourself with positivity, whether that's people, activities, or thoughts, and you'll see a difference over time.

How do I challenge societal beauty standards and embrace body shape and size diversity?

Teen: It feels like there's this one standard of beauty everywhere I look. How do I not get caught up in it?

Parent: Start by educating yourself about the harm these narrow beauty standards can cause. Once you understand that they're unrealistic and often unattainable, pushing back against them is easier. Challenge stereotypes whenever you encounter them.

Teen: How do I do that?

Parent: Speak up when you hear or see something perpetuating these standards. Advocate for diversity in the media you consume and support body-positive movements. It's about celebrating all body types, not just the ones society deems ideal.

Teen: But what if I still feel pressured?

Parent: That's normal. We're all influenced by the world around us, but you can create a more positive environment by being mindful of the media you consume and the language you use. And remember, you can lead by example. Embrace your own body and show others that true beauty comes in all shapes and sizes.

Teen: It sounds empowering but also challenging.

Parent: It is both. But by promoting body diversity and rejecting harmful standards, you're not just helping yourself—you're contributing to a more inclusive world where everyone can feel valued for who they are, not just how they look.

How can I deal with body shaming and negative comments about my appearance?

Teen: What should I do if someone makes fun of my appearance or says something mean about my body?

Parent: That's a tough situation, and I'm sorry you've had to deal with it. Remember, body shaming says more about the person doing it than it does about you. You can choose to ignore it, or calmly let the person know that their comment is hurtful and not okay. Surround yourself with people who respect and support you and try not to let negative comments define how you see yourself.

Teen: It's hard not to take it personally, though.

Parent: I know, but it's important to remember your worth isn't tied to anyone else's opinion. Keep focusing on your strengths and the things you love about yourself.

How do I stay positive about my body on days when I'm feeling down?

Teen: What if I just wake up feeling bad about myself one day? How do I get out of that funk?

Parent: We all have those days. When you're feeling down, try doing something that lifts your spirits—whether it's listening to music, going for a walk, or talking to someone who makes you feel good. Sometimes a little self-care can make a big difference. Also, remind yourself that it's okay to have bad days. They don't define you, and tomorrow is a new day.

Teen: So, it's okay to feel bad sometimes, as long as I don't stay there?

Parent: Exactly. Feelings are temporary, and being kind to yourself on those tough days is important. You're always enough, no matter how you're feeling.

How can I help friends who struggle with body image issues?

Teen: What if I have a friend who's really struggling with how they see themselves? How can I help?

Parent: That's a great question. Start by being a good listener—sometimes, just knowing someone cares can make a big difference. Encourage your friend to focus on their strengths and remind them of their special qualities. If they're really struggling, suggest they talk to a trusted adult or professional. And of course, continue being supportive and patient.

Teen: So just being there for them can help?

Parent: Absolutely. Your support can mean a lot, and sometimes knowing they have someone to lean on can make all the difference.

Takeaway Points:

Parent: I hope this conversation helped you see that body image and self-esteem are about so much more than looks. It's about how you feel inside, how you treat yourself, and how you view the world around you.

Teen: Yeah, I've learned a lot. I guess the key is to be kind to myself and others, and not let society tell me how I should look or feel.

Parent: Exactly. Remember, your body is just one part of who you are—it doesn't define your worth. Keep focusing on what makes you unique, and don't be afraid to challenge those unrealistic standards. You're amazing just as you are.

Teen: Thanks, I feel a lot better about this now. I'll keep working on seeing myself in a more positive light.

Parent: That's the spirit! And remember, I'm always here if you want to talk more about this or anything else. We're in this together.

This chapter emphasizes the importance of developing a positive body image and self-esteem by focusing on self-compassion, challenging societal beauty standards, and supporting others. It encourages Teens to embrace their uniqueness, build confidence, and promote inclusivity in their communities.

* * *

"The best way to find yourself is to lose yourself in the service of others."
— *Mahatma Gandhi*

Chapter 13

Responsible Behavior and Citizenship

Parent: Hey, my love! I've been thinking—it's really important to talk about what it means to be a responsible citizen. I know it sounds like a big topic, but it's really about how we live our lives every day and how we can make the world a better place. Are you up for chatting about it?

Teen: Sure, I've been thinking about this too, especially with everything happening worldwide. Sometimes it feels like there's so much to do, and I'm unsure where to start.

Parent: That's exactly why this conversation is so important. Being a responsible citizen is about knowing your rights and responsibilities and finding ways to positively impact, whether big or small.

What are my rights and responsibilities as a citizen?

Teen: So, what are my rights and responsibilities as a citizen?

Parent: Great question. As a citizen, you have certain rights that protect your freedom and well-being, but with those rights come responsibilities that help maintain the community and society. Let's break them down:

Rights:

- **Right to Vote**: You can influence how your community and country are run by voting in elections.

- **Freedom of Speech**: You can freely express your thoughts and ideas, as long as it doesn't harm others.

- **Right to Assembly**: You can gather with others peacefully to discuss, celebrate, or advocate for change.

- **Right to a Fair Trial**: If you're accused of a crime, you're entitled to a just legal process.

- **Right to Privacy**: Your personal life is protected from unwarranted intrusion.

- **Right to Education**: You deserve access to quality education to help you grow and succeed.

Responsibilities:

- **Voting**: It's your responsibility to use your vote to help shape the future.
- **Obeying the Law**: Following the rules keeps society safe and orderly.
- **Paying Taxes**: Your contributions help fund public services like schools, roads, and healthcare.
- **Civic Engagement**: Stay informed and participate in community activities to help improve society.
- **Serving on Juries**: When called upon, you help ensure that justice is served.
- **Respecting Others**: Treat everyone with dignity, regardless of their background or beliefs.

How can I contribute positively to my community and society?

Teen: How can I actually make a difference in my community?

Parent: You can contribute in so many ways, and they don't all have to be big gestures. Even small actions can create a positive ripple effect. Here are some ideas:

- **Volunteer**: Whether it's helping at a local shelter, cleaning up parks, or tutoring kids, your time and effort can make a huge difference.

- **Support Local Businesses**: Shopping locally helps strengthen your community's economy and supports your neighbours.

- **Advocate for Social Justice**: Stand up for what's right by supporting causes that fight for equality and justice, whether through peaceful protests, spreading awareness, or supporting marginalized groups.

- **Mentorship**: Share your knowledge and experiences to guide others, whether it's younger kids or peers.

- **Environmental Stewardship**: Protect the planet by reducing waste, recycling, and supporting sustainable practices.

- **Civic Engagement**: Get involved in local politics or community boards to help shape decisions that affect your life and community.

- **Acts of Kindness**: Even simple gestures like helping a neighbour or being kind to someone in need can create a positive environment.

What are the laws and regulations regarding consent and sexual behaviour?

Teen: There's a lot of talk about consent nowadays. What should I know about it legally?

Parent: Consent is incredibly important, both ethically and legally. Here's what you need to know:

- **Age of Consent**: The law sets a minimum age for giving legal consent to protect minors. It varies by location but is designed to ensure that people are mature enough to make informed decisions.

- **Capacity to Consent**: A person must be mentally capable of understanding and agreeing to the activity.

- **Continuous Consent**: Consent must be given freely and can be withdrawn at any time. It's not something you give once and forget about.

- **Incapacitation**: If someone is intoxicated, unconscious, or otherwise incapacitated, they cannot give consent. Engaging in sexual activity under these circumstances is illegal and considered assault.

- **Legal Consequences**: Violating consent laws can lead to serious legal consequences, including imprisonment and a permanent criminal record.

How do I recognize and report instances of discrimination and injustice?

Teen: What if I see someone being treated unfairly? How do I handle that?

Parent: First, it's important to recognize discrimination or injustice when you see it. This could be based on race, gender, sexual orientation, disability, or other factors. Here's what you can do:

- **Educate Yourself**: Understand the different forms of discrimination and their impact on people.

- **Be Observant**: Pay attention to behaviors or situations that seem unfair or discriminatory.

- **Speak Up**: If you feel safe, challenge the behaviour by standing up for the mistreated person. Use your voice to support those who may be marginalized.

- **Support Victims**: Offer help and listen to those affected. Sometimes, just knowing someone cares can make a big difference.

- **Report It**: If the situation is serious, report it to the relevant authorities, whether it's a teacher, employer, or law enforcement.

- **Document Evidence**: Record what you saw, including dates, times, and details. This can be crucial if the issue escalates.

How can I advocate for social change and support causes that are important to me?

Teen: What if I want to get involved in bigger causes? How can I do that?

Parent: Advocating for social change is a powerful way to make a positive impact. Here's how you can start:

- **Identify Your Passion**: What issues matter most to you? Whether it's climate change, racial equality, or another cause, find what drives you.

- **Educate Yourself**: Learn as much as you can about the issue. The more you know, the more effective you'll be.

- **Join a Cause**: Look for groups or organizations already working on the issue. They often have resources and platforms where you can make a difference.

- **Raise Awareness**: Use social media, organize events, or talk to people. Spreading awareness is often the first step toward change.

- **Engage with Policymakers**: Write letters, attend meetings, and speak directly to those in power to advocate for change.

- **Collaborate**: Work with others who share your passion. Together, you can amplify your voice and increase your impact.

- **Practice Self-Care**: Activism can be challenging. Make sure to take care of your own well-being so you can keep going for the long haul.

How can I balance my personal goals with my responsibilities as a citizen?

Teen: Sometimes it feels like my personal goals and ambitions might conflict with my responsibilities as a citizen. How can I balance these?

Parent: Balancing personal goals with citizenship responsibilities is definitely a challenge, but it's possible with some planning and mindfulness. Here are some tips:

- **Prioritize**: Identify what's most important to you in both your personal and civic life. Prioritizing can help you allocate time and resources effectively.

- **Set Goals**: Create specific, achievable goals for both areas. For example, if you want to advance in your career while also volunteering, set clear objectives for each.

- **Integrate Efforts**: Find ways to combine your personal ambitions with civic responsibilities. If you're passionate about the environment, pursuing a career in environmental science can align with your commitment to sustainability.

- **Manage Time**: Use time management strategies to balance your commitments. Create a schedule that includes time for personal development and civic engagement.

- **Seek Support**: Connect with mentors or advisors who can help you navigate your responsibilities and goals, providing guidance and encouragement.

What role does empathy play in responsible behaviour and citizenship?

Teen: How important is empathy in being a good citizen and behaving responsibly?

Parent: Empathy is crucial for responsible behaviour and citizenship because it helps you understand and connect with others' experiences and perspectives. Here's why empathy matters:

- **Promotes Understanding**: Empathy allows you to see things from others' viewpoints, which can lead to more respectful and considerate interactions.

- **Fosters Compassion**: When you empathize with others, you're more likely to support and help them, contributing to a caring community.

- **Encourages Fairness**: Empathy helps you recognize and address injustices, leading to more equitable and just actions and decisions.

- **Strengthens Relationships**: By understanding and responding to others' needs, you build stronger, more supportive relationships, which are essential for a thriving society.

How can I effectively communicate with others who have different opinions?

Teen: What's the best way to have conversations with people who don't share my views?

Parent: Engaging in respectful dialogue with people who have different opinions is essential for constructive discussions and building mutual understanding. Here are some strategies:

- **Listen Actively**: Pay attention to what the other person is saying without interrupting. Show that you value their perspective.

- **Stay Open-Minded**: Approach the conversation with an open mind, and be willing to consider their viewpoint even if you disagree.

- **Express Yourself Clearly**: Share your thoughts and feelings honestly, but do so in a respectful and non-confrontational manner.

- **Find Common Ground**: Look for shared values or interests to build a foundation for your conversation.

- **Avoid Personal Attacks**: Focus on discussing ideas rather than criticizing the person. This helps keep the conversation productive.

- **Agree to Disagree**: Sometimes, you may not reach a consensus. It's okay to respectfully agree to disagree and move on.

What are some ways to educate myself about current social and political issues?

Teen: How can I stay informed about what's happening in the world?

Parent: Staying informed about social and political issues is key to being an engaged and responsible citizen. Here are some methods to help you stay educated:

- **Read Reliable News Sources**: Follow reputable news outlets that provide balanced and accurate reporting.

- **Follow Expert Opinions**: Look for analyses and insights from experts in the field to understand complex issues better.

- **Engage with Educational Content**: Watch documentaries, listen to podcasts, and read books that explore current issues in depth.

- **Participate in Discussions**: Join community forums, attend lectures, and engage in conversations to hear diverse perspectives.

- **Use Social Media Wisely**: Follow credible organizations and thought leaders to stay updated, but be cautious of misinformation.

How can I support and advocate for marginalized communities?

Teen: What are some effective ways to support marginalized groups?

Parent: Supporting and advocating for marginalized communities involves both understanding their experiences and taking action to promote equity. Here's how you can contribute:

- **Educate Yourself**: Learn about the challenges faced by marginalized groups and the history of their struggles.

- **Listen to Their Voices**: Amplify and support the voices of those from marginalized communities. Listen to their experiences and respect their perspectives.

- **Advocate for Policy Change**: Support policies and initiatives that aim to reduce inequality and provide resources to these communities.

- **Donate and Volunteer**: Contribute to organizations and causes that support marginalized groups through donations or volunteer work.
- **Challenge Discrimination**: Speak out against prejudice and discrimination when you encounter it, and support inclusive practices in your community.

Takeaway Points:

Parent: I hope this conversation helped you see that being a responsible citizen is about more than just following rules. It's about making a positive impact on the world around you.

Teen: Yeah, I've learned a lot. It seems like there's always something I can do, no matter how small, to make a difference.

Parent: Exactly. Citizenship is not just a status—it's an ongoing process of contributing to the greater good. By embracing these principles, you can help build a better, more inclusive world for everyone.

Teen: Thanks, I feel more confident about how I can make a difference. I'll definitely keep these ideas in mind.

Parent: That's the spirit! And remember, I'm always here if you want to talk more about this or anything else. We're in this together.

* * *

"The future depends on what you do today."
— *Mahatma Gandhi*

Chapter 14

Life Skills and Future Planning

Parent: Hey dear!, I've noticed you've been thinking a lot about your future and how to manage everything that's going on. It's a lot to juggle, and I want to help you figure out how to navigate it all. Want to talk about some strategies?

Teen: Yeah, that sounds good. Sometimes, I feel overwhelmed with school, thinking about college, and everything else. I'm not sure where to start when it comes to planning for the future.

Parent: That's completely normal. Let's break it down into manageable steps and talk about some skills that can help you not just now, but throughout your life.

How do I manage my time effectively and set goals for the future?

Teen: I have so many things on my plate. What's the best way to organize everything?

Parent: Time management is key to balancing everything. Start by prioritizing your tasks. Make a list of what you must do, then figure out what's most important and what can wait. From there, create a schedule that includes work, school, and relaxation time. Planners or apps can help you keep track of everything.

Teen: What about setting goals? I have so many things I want to achieve, but it's hard to stay focused.

Parent: For goal setting, use the SMART criteria: Specific, Measurable, Achievable, Relevant, and Time-bound. Break larger goals into smaller, actionable steps and set deadlines for each. For instance, if your goal is to get better grades, break it down into setting study schedules for each subject and sticking to them.

Teen: What if I get overwhelmed by everything I have to do?

Parent: That's a common feeling. Break tasks into smaller steps to make them feel more manageable. Avoid multitasking—focus on one task at a time, and don't forget to take breaks to recharge. Remember, it's okay to ask for help if you need it.

What skills do I need to navigate adulthood and pursue my dreams?

Teen: Besides managing time, what other skills are important as I become an adult?

Parent: Several key skills will help you navigate adulthood:

- **Communication Skills**: Being able to express yourself clearly and listen effectively is crucial for building relationships and resolving conflicts.

- **Critical Thinking**: This skill involves analyzing information and making informed decisions, essential for problem-solving and adapting to new challenges.

- **Problem-solving**: Learn to identify issues and find creative solutions.

- **Resilience**: Life will have its setbacks, and it is essential to bounce back and learn from failures.

- **Adaptability**: The world changes, and flexibility helps you handle new situations and opportunities.

- **Financial Literacy**: Understanding budgeting, saving, and investing will help you manage your finances wisely.

- **Emotional Intelligence**: Recognize and manage your emotions and understand others' feelings to build strong relationships.

- **Networking**: Build and maintain relationships that can provide support and opportunities.

Teen: How can I improve these skills?

Parent: Practice them regularly in your daily life. For example, communicate openly with friends and family, tackle problems head-on, and stay curious and engaged in learning. Building a strong support network and seeking out mentors can also provide guidance and feedback.

How can I prepare for challenges and setbacks in life?

Teen: Life isn't always smooth sailing. How do I prepare for tough times?

Parent: Preparing for challenges involves developing a mindset and strategies to handle difficulties:

- **Cultivate a Growth Mindset**: View setbacks as opportunities to learn and grow rather than as failures.

- **Develop Self-Awareness**: Know your strengths and weaknesses to handle challenges better.

- **Build a Support Network**: Surround yourself with supportive people who can offer advice and encouragement.

- **Practice Mindfulness**: Techniques like meditation can help you stay calm and focused during tough times.

- **Develop Problem-Solving Skills**: Break problems into steps and explore different solutions.

- **Set Realistic Expectations**: Avoid setting yourself up for disappointment by being realistic about your goals and progress.

- **Practice Self-Care**: To build resilience, take care of your physical and emotional well-being.

- **Learn from Setbacks**: Reflect on what went wrong and how you can improve in the future.

- **Seek Professional Help**: Talking to a counselor or therapist can provide additional support if you're struggling.

Teen: Can you give me an example of how this might work in real life?

Parent: Sure! If you're facing a tough academic challenge, you might break the problem into smaller tasks, seek advice from a teacher or tutor, and practice stress management techniques. Reflect on what strategies worked or didn't work and adjust your approach as needed.

What are some strategies for building resilience and adaptability?

Teen: How can I become more resilient and adaptable?

Parent: Building resilience and adaptability is all about developing a strong mindset and flexible approach:

- **Cultivate a Growth Mindset**: Embrace challenges as chances to learn and improve.

- **Develop Self-Awareness**: Recognize your emotional responses and triggers to handle stress better.

- **Build a Support Network**: Having people to lean on can help you navigate tough times.

- **Practice Mindfulness**: Techniques like deep breathing can help manage stress and maintain focus.

- **Develop Problem-Solving Skills**: Break down problems into manageable parts and consider different solutions.

- **Foster Flexibility**: Be open to changing plans and adapting to new situations.

- **Set Realistic Expectations**: Set achievable goals and celebrate your progress.

- **Practice Self-Care**: Maintain your physical and emotional health through healthy habits.

- **Learn from Setbacks**: Use failures as learning opportunities rather than as reasons to give up.

- **Maintain Perspective**: Remember that setbacks are temporary and part of the journey.

Teen: How do I stay motivated when things get tough?

Parent: Focus on your goals and the reasons behind them. Celebrate small victories along the way and remind yourself of your progress. It's also helpful to stay connected with your support network for encouragement.

How do I create a vision for my future and take steps toward achieving it?

Teen: I have big dreams but don't know where to start. How do I create a vision for my future?

Parent: Creating a vision for your future involves defining your aspirations and taking actionable steps:

- **Reflect on Your Values and Interests**: Identify what matters to you and what you're passionate about.

- **Define Long-Term Goals**: Set specific goals for different areas of your life, such as career and personal development.

- **Visualize Your Ideal Future**: Imagine your life when you've achieved your goals.

- **Set SMART Goals**: Break down your vision into specific, measurable, achievable, relevant, and time-bound goals.

- **Create a Vision Board**: Use images and quotes to visualize your future and keep your goals in sight.

- **Develop a Plan**: Outline the steps you need to take and the resources you'll need.

- **Take Consistent Action**: Act on your plan and stay focused on your goals.

- **Stay Flexible**: Be open to adjusting your goals as circumstances change.

- **Seek Support and Accountability**: Surround yourself with people who support your vision.

- **Celebrate Milestones**: Acknowledge your achievements to stay motivated.

Teen: How do I keep my vision and goals realistic?

Parent: Regularly review and adjust your goals based on your progress and any new information. Make sure your goals are challenging but achievable and be prepared to adapt as needed.

How can I effectively manage stress and avoid burnout while juggling multiple responsibilities?

Teen: With school, extracurriculars, and social life, I sometimes feel overwhelmed. How can I manage stress better?

Parent: Managing stress and avoiding burnout is crucial for maintaining well-being. Here's how you can do it:

- **Prioritize Self-Care**: Ensure you get enough sleep, eat well, and exercise regularly. These basics are essential for handling stress.

- **Practice Time Management**: Use scheduling tools to balance your responsibilities and avoid overcommitting yourself.

- **Set Boundaries**: Learn to say no when necessary and set clear boundaries between work and relaxation time.

- **Break Tasks into Smaller Chunks**: Divide large tasks into smaller, more manageable steps to reduce feelings of being overwhelmed.

- **Incorporate Relaxation Techniques**: Engage in activities that help you relax, such as deep breathing, meditation, or hobbies you enjoy.

- **Seek Support**: Talk to friends, family, or a counselor if you're feeling overwhelmed. Sharing your feelings can provide relief and practical solutions.

Teen: What should I do if I feel like I'm on the verge of burnout?

Parent: If you're feeling close to burnout, take immediate steps to reduce your stress:

- **Take a Break**: Allow yourself some time to rest and recharge. Even a short break can make a difference.

- **Reevaluate Your Commitments**: Assess your current responsibilities and see if you can adjust or delegate tasks.

- **Practice Mindfulness**: Engage in mindfulness exercises to calm your mind and reduce stress.

- **Reach Out for Help**: Don't hesitate to ask for support from family, friends, or a mental health professional.

How do I balance personal aspirations with societal expectations and family responsibilities?

Teen: Sometimes, it feels like my personal goals are at odds with what's expected of me by society or my family. How can I balance these?

Parent: Balancing personal aspirations with societal expectations and family responsibilities involves thoughtful navigation:

- **Communicate Openly**: Share your goals and aspirations with your family and discuss how they can support you. Clear communication helps align expectations.

- **Set Boundaries**: Define your personal priorities and ensure that you're making time for what matters most to you while also fulfilling necessary responsibilities.

- **Seek Compromise**: Find middle ground between personal goals and family expectations. For example, if you have a strong academic focus but also need to help at home, discuss ways to balance both.

- **Stay True to Yourself**: While it's important to consider others' expectations, make sure you're pursuing goals that are genuinely meaningful to you.

Teen: How can I manage societal pressures while still pursuing my dreams?

Parent: Societal pressures can be challenging, but remember:

- **Focus on Your Values**: Keep your core values and interests at the forefront of your decision-making.

- **Build Confidence**: Strengthen your confidence in your choices by setting small goals and celebrating your progress.

- **Surround Yourself with Support**: Build a network of people who encourage and support your aspirations.

- **Educate Yourself**: Understand the reasons behind societal expectations and assess if they align with your personal values and goals.

How can I develop a growth mindset and use it to overcome challenges?

Teen: What exactly is a growth mindset, and how can it help me when I face difficulties?

Parent: A growth mindset is the belief that abilities and intelligence can be developed through effort and learning. Here's how it can help:

- **Embrace Challenges**: View challenges as opportunities to grow rather than obstacles.

- **Learn from Criticism**: Accept constructive feedback and use it to improve your skills and knowledge.

- **Celebrate Effort**: Focus on your effort and progress rather than just the outcome.

- **Persevere**: Keep trying even when you encounter setbacks. A growth mindset encourages persistence and resilience.

Teen: Can you give an example of how adopting a growth mindset can make a difference?

Parent: Certainly! If you're struggling with a difficult subject in school, approach it as a chance to learn more instead of seeing it as a failure. By seeking help, practicing regularly, and reflecting on what strategies work best for you, you'll improve over time and develop a stronger understanding of the subject.

What role does continuous learning play in personal and professional growth, and how can I cultivate it?

Teen: I want to keep growing and learning throughout my life. How can I make continuous learning a part of my routine?

Parent: Continuous learning is vital for personal and professional development. Here's how to cultivate it:

- **Stay Curious**: Foster a curious mindset by exploring new topics, hobbies, and interests.

- **Seek Out Opportunities**: Take advantage of workshops, online courses, and educational resources.

- **Read Regularly**: Read books, articles, and journals related to your interests and career goals.

- **Set Learning Goals**: Identify areas you want to improve and set specific learning goals.

- **Reflect on Learning**: Regularly review what you've learned and how it applies to your goals and life.

Teen: How can I find time to learn amidst a busy schedule?

Parent: You can integrate learning into your daily routine by:

- **Scheduling Learning Time**: Set aside dedicated time for learning each week, even if it's just 15-30 minutes a day.

- **Utilizing Downtime**: Use spare moments, such as during commutes or breaks, to engage in learning activities like educational podcasts.

- **Combining Interests**: Incorporate learning into activities you already enjoy. For instance, if you like cooking, read about nutrition or cuisines.

How can I create a balanced approach to setting and achieving long-term goals?

Teen: I have big dreams but worry about staying motivated over the long haul. How can I keep a balanced approach?

Parent: Creating a balanced approach involves setting realistic milestones and maintaining motivation:

- **Break Down Goals**: Divide your long-term goals into smaller, manageable milestones to make progress more achievable and trackable.

- **Set Short-Term Objectives**: Establish short-term goals leading to your long-term vision. This helps maintain motivation and provides regular achievements to celebrate.

- **Maintain Flexibility**: Be prepared to adjust your goals and plans as circumstances change. Flexibility ensures that you stay aligned with your evolving interests and situations.

- **Regularly Review Progress**: Assess your progress periodically to stay on track and make necessary adjustments.

- **Stay Motivated**: Remind yourself of the reasons behind your goals and their benefits. Visualize your success and seek support from mentors or peers.

Teen: What if I encounter unexpected obstacles while working towards my goals?

Parent: Obstacles are part of the journey. Address them by:

- **Assessing the Situation**: Identify the nature of the obstacle and consider alternative strategies to overcome it.

- **Seeking Advice**: Consult with mentors, peers, or experts who can offer guidance and solutions.

- **Adjusting Your Plan**: Modify your approach if needed, while keeping your ultimate goal in mind.

Takeaway Points:

Parent: Navigating life and future planning requires a combination of essential skills, strategic thinking, and ongoing personal development. Effective time management, goal setting, stress management, and resilience are crucial for balancing responsibilities and achieving your aspirations. Cultivating a growth mindset, embracing continuous learning, and maintaining flexibility in your goals are key to long-term success. By actively engaging with these strategies, you can build a fulfilling and balanced life that aligns with your values and dreams.

Teen: Thanks, this really helps. I feel like I have a clearer idea of what I need to do and how to approach things.

Parent: I'm glad to hear that. Remember, I'm always here to support you on this journey. We'll figure it out together.

* * *

"The single biggest problem in communication is the illusion that it has taken place."
— George Bernard Shaw

Chapter 15

Family Dynamics and Communication

Parent: You know, I've been thinking a lot about how we interact as a family. Sometimes it feels like we're not really connecting, or we misunderstand each other. What do you think we could do to improve our communication and make our home life more positive?

Teen: Yeah, I've noticed that too. It seems like we're often busy or distracted, and when we talk, it doesn't always feel like we're really listening. What can we do to make our conversations more meaningful?

Parent: I think one key strategy is practicing active listening. That means when someone is speaking, we focus entirely on what they're saying without interrupting or thinking about what we're going to say next. It also helps to reflect back on what you've heard to make sure you understood correctly. Another idea could be setting up regular family meetings where everyone has a chance to talk and share. What do you think about setting aside some time each week for these kinds of conversations?

Teen: I like the idea of family meetings. It would give us a chance to talk things out before they become bigger issues. But what about when we have disagreements? How can we handle those without things getting heated?

Parent: Great point. Handling disagreements effectively is really important. It's helpful to use 'I' statements, like saying, "I feel upset when…" instead of blaming someone else. This way, we focus on our feelings and avoid putting others on the defensive. It's also important to stay calm and try to work together to find a solution rather than assigning blame. Do you think it would help if we brainstormed solutions together when conflicts come up?

Teen: Yeah, that sounds like a good way to approach it. But sometimes, it's hard to know what's okay in terms of personal space and boundaries. How do we figure that out as a family?

Parent: Boundaries are crucial for maintaining respect and personal space in any relationship. First, it's important to reflect on what you personally need in terms of privacy and communication. Then, we should discuss these needs openly as a family so that we can set mutual guidelines. It's also important to be flexible and willing to adjust these boundaries as needed. Do you have any ideas on how we could better respect each other's space?

Teen: Maybe we could have a family discussion where everyone talks about what they need in terms of space and communication. We could agree on some ground rules that work for everyone. And what about showing appreciation? Sometimes it feels like we don't really acknowledge each other's efforts.

Parent: You're right—showing appreciation is really important for a positive family dynamic. Simple things like saying thank you, complimenting, and celebrating each other's achievements can make a big difference. How do you think we could incorporate more appreciation into our daily lives?

Teen: We could make it a habit to complement each other more often and actively support each other's interests and achievements. Maybe we could also set up a special time to recognize and celebrate milestones, like a family dinner where we share our successes.

Parent: That's a fantastic idea! Creating a tradition of celebrating successes and milestones can really strengthen our family bonds and make everyone feel valued. How do you feel about creating a family calendar where we mark important dates and achievements?

Teen: I like that idea. It would remind us to celebrate and appreciate each other more. What about supporting each other during tough times? How can we improve in that area?

Parent: Support during challenging times is essential. Being there for each other, actively listening, and offering practical help can make a big difference. We should also create an environment where everyone feels comfortable sharing their struggles. Do you have any ideas on how we can be more supportive of each other?

Teen: We could establish regular check-ins to see how everyone is doing and offer help when needed. Maybe we could also have a family ritual to discuss our day and any challenges, like during dinner or before bed.

Parent: That's a great approach. Regular check-ins and having a routine for discussing our day can help us stay connected and provide the support we need. How about understanding each other's roles and contributions to the family? Sometimes, it feels like we don't fully appreciate what everyone brings to the table.

Teen: I agree. Understanding and appreciating each other's roles can help us work better together. Maybe we could have a family meeting to discuss each person's contributions and how we can support each other in our roles.

Parent: That's an excellent idea. Recognizing and valuing each family member's unique contributions helps build a stronger sense of unity and cooperation. Let's also make it a point to discuss and adjust our roles and responsibilities as needed. What else should we focus on to improve our family dynamics?

Teen: We should also work on handling stress and changes together. Sometimes, transitions or unexpected events cause us to struggle, which affects our interactions.

Parent: Handling stress and changes together is crucial for maintaining harmony. We can work on being more adaptable and supportive during transitions. It's important to communicate openly about our feelings and find ways to support each other through changes. How about creating a family plan for dealing with major changes or stressful situations?

Teen: That sounds like a good idea. A plan could help us feel more prepared and connected during tough times. What about when we need to address deeper issues or conflicts? Should we consider seeking outside help?

Parent: Seeking outside help can be very beneficial if we struggle with deeper issues or persistent conflicts. Family therapy or counseling can provide guidance and support in improving our dynamics and communication. It's important to be open to seeking help when needed. Do you think having a family counselor might be something we should consider?

Teen: It could be helpful if we ever feel stuck or overwhelmed. A neutral third party could give us new perspectives and strategies for improving our family dynamics.

Parent: I agree. A counselor can offer valuable insights and tools for improving communication and resolving conflicts. Let's consider that option if we ever feel it's needed. Finally, how can we ensure that we continuously work on these aspects and keep our family dynamic positive?

Teen: I think it's important to keep having these conversations and be open to making adjustments as needed. Regular check-ins on how we're doing with our communication, boundaries, and support can help us stay on track.

Parent: Absolutely. Regular discussions and being open to making changes will help us maintain a positive family dynamic. Let's commit to working together on these aspects and supporting each other in building a stronger, more connected family.

Teen: I'm on board with that. These changes will help us improve our relationships and strengthen our family.

Parent: One more thing to consider is how we handle technology in our family. It can be a great tool, but it can also create distractions that make it harder to connect. How could we balance using technology while still making time for each other?

Teen: That's a good point. Sometimes it feels like we're all in the same room but not together because we're on our phones or watching TV. Maybe we could set some rules around tech use, like no phones during dinner or having a tech-free hour daily.

Parent: I love that idea. Setting aside specific times to unplug and focus on each other can help us reconnect and strengthen our bonds. It's important to remember that while technology can be a part of our lives, it shouldn't replace our face-to-face interactions. How about we try out a tech-free hour after dinner and see how it goes?

Teen: That sounds like a good start. I think it would help us spend more quality time together. What about planning more family activities? Sometimes it feels like we don't do much together outside of our routines.

Parent: Planning regular family activities is a great way to build stronger connections and create lasting memories. We could start by making a list of things we all enjoy, like hiking, playing board games, or cooking together, and then schedule time for these activities regularly. How do you feel about creating a family tradition, like a monthly outing or a weekly game night?

Teen: I think that would be fun. It would give us something to look forward to and help us bond more as a family. Plus, it's a good way to relax and enjoy each other's company.

Parent: I agree. Creating regular opportunities to have fun together is important for maintaining a positive and supportive family environment. Let's start planning our first family outing or game night this week.

Teen: Sounds good to me. All these changes will help us communicate better and make our home life more positive.

Parent: I'm glad we're on the same page. Working together on these goals will help create a stronger family. Remember, it's all about being open, supportive, and willing to adjust as needed. We're all in this together, and we can improve our family dynamics with little effort.

Teen: I look forward to seeing how these changes will help us. Thanks for having this conversation with me.

Parent: Thank you for being open and willing to work together. I'm proud of the way we're approaching this as a team. Let's keep the lines of communication open and continue supporting each other as we move forward.

Takeaway Points:

1. **Active Listening:** Commit to truly understanding each other's perspectives without interruptions. Try to listen fully and reflect on what's being said before responding.

2. **Effective Conflict Resolution:** Use 'I' statements, stay calm, and collaborate on finding solutions. Focus on feelings rather than assigning blame and work together to resolve disagreements constructively.

3. **Setting Boundaries:** Identify and communicate personal needs clearly and respect each other's boundaries. Regularly revisit these boundaries to ensure they continue to work for everyone.

4. **Showing Appreciation:** Regularly acknowledge and celebrate each other's efforts and achievements. Create rituals or traditions for recognizing milestones and showing gratitude within the family.

5. **Providing Support:** Offer emotional and practical help, and create a safe space for sharing struggles. Establish regular check-ins and encourage open discussions about challenges and how to support each other.

6. **Understanding Roles:** Recognize and value each family member's contributions and perspectives. Have open conversations about roles and responsibilities and be willing to adjust them as needed.

7. **Handling Stress and Changes:** Be adaptable, support each other during transitions, and create a plan for managing stress. Develop strategies for coping with unexpected events and changes together as a family.

8. **Seeking Outside Help:** Consider family therapy or counseling to address deeper issues or persistent conflicts. Be open to professional guidance when necessary to improve family dynamics.

9. **Technology Balance:** Set guidelines for technology use to ensure it doesn't interfere with family connections. Create tech-free times to focus on each other and engage in meaningful conversations.

10. **Family Activities:** Plan regular family activities to strengthen bonds and create shared experiences. Establish traditions that bring everyone together and promote a sense of unity and enjoyment.

11. **Continuous Improvement:** Regularly check in on family dynamics and be open to making necessary adjustments to maintain a positive environment. Keep the focus on growth and improvement, recognizing that family dynamics evolve over time.

By focusing on these areas, families can enhance their communication, strengthen relationships, and create a supportive, understanding environment where every member feels valued and connected. These efforts will help ensure that the family remains a source of comfort, support, and happiness for everyone involved.

* * *

"The future belongs to those who believe in the beauty of their dreams."
— *Eleanor Roosevelt*

Chapter 16

Academic and Career Planning

Parent: I've noticed you've been thinking about your future lately. Have you started setting any academic or career goals for yourself?

Teen: I've been thinking about it, but I'm not sure where to start. How do I figure out what I want to do?

Parent: It can be overwhelming initially, but the key is to start by understanding your interests, strengths, and values. What subjects or activities do you enjoy the most?

Teen: I enjoy science and technology, but I'm unsure how to turn that into a career.

Parent: That's a great starting point. From there, you can research careers in those fields, maybe even look into internships or job shadowing opportunities to see what interests you most. Have you thought about setting some SMART goals?

Teen: What are SMART goals?

Parent: SMART goals are Specific, Measurable, Achievable, Relevant, and Time-bound. They help you create a clear plan. For example, if you're interested in engineering, you might set a goal to research three different engineering fields and talk to someone in each field by the end of the month.

Teen: That sounds helpful. What if I'm interested in more than one thing?

Parent: It's okay to explore multiple interests. You can set goals in each area and see where your passion leads you. Just remember to be flexible and adjust your goals as you gain more experience and insight.

What resources are available to help me explore different career paths?

Teen: What resources are out there to help me explore different career paths?

Parent: There are so many resources available! Career counseling services at school, online career assessments, and the Occupational Outlook Handbook or National Career Service are all great places to start. Have you ever used any career assessment tools?

Teen: I've heard about them but haven't tried any. How do they work?

Parent: They typically ask you questions about your interests and strengths and then suggest careers that might be a good fit. It's a great way to explore options you might not have considered. Networking with professionals and job shadowing can also give you real-world insights. What fields would you like to learn more about?

Teen: I'm curious about healthcare and maybe something in environmental science.

Parent: Those are both important and growing fields. You could look into internships or volunteer opportunities to get some hands-on experience. That way, you can see if you'd like to pursue it further.

What skills do I need to succeed in school and later in a job?

Teen: What skills do I need to succeed in school and later in a job?

Parent: Several key skills are important, both academically and professionally. Time management, communication, and critical thinking are some of the basics. How do you feel about your time management right now?

Teen: I'm okay at it, but I get distracted easily.

Parent: That's normal. One way to improve is by setting specific times for studying and breaks. Also, practicing communication skills by participating in class discussions or joining a debate club can really help. How do you feel about problem-solving and working in teams?

Teen: I like solving problems, but teamwork can be challenging sometimes.

Parent: Teamwork is a skill that improves with practice. Group projects at school or team sports can be good practice. It's also important to stay adaptable and flexible, especially since things can change quickly in both school and work environments.

Teen: What about technology skills? Do I need to focus on those?

Parent: Absolutely. Technology is everywhere now, and being comfortable with computers, software, and other digital tools is essential. You might consider taking a coding or digital literacy course to stay ahead.

How do I balance schoolwork with extracurricular activities and hobbies?

Teen: How do I balance my schoolwork with extracurricular activities and hobbies?

Parent: It's all about prioritization and time management. Start by listing out your academic responsibilities and extracurricular activities. How do you usually spend your time after school?

Teen: I usually do my homework first, but sometimes I get caught up in activities and do it late.

Parent: That's a common challenge. Creating a weekly schedule that includes time for both homework and activities can help. It's also important to make time for self-care and relaxation. How do you unwind?

Teen: I like reading or playing video games.

Parent: Those are great ways to relax, but make sure you get enough sleep and eat well. Balancing these will help you stay healthy and perform your best.

Teen: What if I'm feeling overwhelmed?

Parent: If you're feeling overwhelmed, it's important to talk to someone, whether it's a teacher, counselor, or even me. Sometimes you might need to cut back on activities or adjust your schedule. Remember, saying 'NO' to things that don't align with your goals is okay.

How do I prepare for college or vocational training?

Teen: What should I do to prepare for college or vocational training?

Parent: The first step is to assess your interests and strengths to determine what kind of education or training aligns with your career goals. Have you considered whether you want to go to college or pursue vocational training?

Teen: I'm leaning towards college, but I'm not 100% sure.

Parent: That's okay. You can start by researching different colleges or vocational programs, visiting campuses, and talking to current students. Have you started thinking about standardized tests like JEE for engineering, NEET for medical courses, CLAT for law programs, CUET for central university admissions, CAT for management studies, and GATE for postgraduate engineering. Other options include NID DAT for design, NATA for architecture, GMAT/GRE for global or local postgraduate programs, and even SAT , which is gaining acceptance among Indian universities. These exams guide students toward specialized academic and career paths.

Teen: I know I need to take them, but I'm unsure when to start preparing.

Parent: It's good to start preparing early. You can take practice tests to see where you stand and focus on areas that need improvement. Also, don't forget to explore financial aid options like scholarships and grants. How do you feel about applying for financial aid?

Teen: I'm a bit nervous about it. It doesn't seem very easy.

Parent: It can be, but there are resources to help. You can start exploring the NSP (National Scholarship Portal), which is a comprehensive platform for various scholarships from central and state governments. Many universities offer Merit-based Scholarships or need-based aid, and workshops are often held to guide students on applying for scholarships. Additionally, Vidya Lakshmi Portal helps students apply for education loans. Building a strong resume is equally important, and resources like internships, volunteer work, and platforms like NCS (National Career Service) offer support to develop career skills. What about building a strong resume—have you thought about that?

Teen: Not really. What should I include?

Parent: Your resume should highlight your academic achievements, extracurricular activities, volunteer work, and work experience. It is important to present a well-rounded profile that reflects your interests and skills.

Teen: What if I don't know exactly what I want to study?

Parent: That's completely normal. Many students start college undecided or change their major along the way. You can take general education courses to explore different fields before deciding. What's important is to stay curious and open-minded.

How do I stay flexible and adjust my goals as I learn more about myself?

Teen: What if I set a goal and then realize it's not what I want anymore?

Parent: That's a natural part of the process. It's important to stay flexible and be willing to adjust your goals as you gain new experiences and insights. If you find that a goal no longer aligns with your interests, don't be afraid to change direction.

Teen: But how do I know when to adjust a goal?

Parent: Reviewing your goals and assessing your progress regularly is a good idea. Ask yourself if you're still passionate about the goal and if it still aligns with your long-term vision. If not, consider tweaking it or exploring other options. Talking to mentors or advisors who can offer guidance is also helpful.

How do I balance personal aspirations with family and societal expectations?

Teen: Sometimes, it feels like my personal goals are at odds with what society or my family expects of me. How can I balance these?

Parent: Balancing personal aspirations with family and societal expectations can be challenging, but staying true to yourself is important. Open communication is key—talk to your family about your goals and see how you can find common ground.

Teen: What if they don't understand my goals?

Parent: It's okay if they don't fully understand right away. Be patient and explain why these goals are important to you. At the same time, listen to their concerns and try to address them. It's possible to find a compromise that respects both your aspirations and their expectations.

How can I effectively manage stress and avoid burnout while working towards my goals?

Teen: With school, extracurriculars, and planning for the future, I sometimes feel overwhelmed. How can I manage stress better?

Parent: Managing stress and avoiding burnout is crucial. Start by setting realistic goals and prioritizing your tasks. Make sure to take regular breaks and practice self-care, like getting enough sleep, eating well, and engaging in activities you enjoy.

Teen: What if I still feel overwhelmed?

Parent: If you're feeling overwhelmed, it's important to reach out for support. Talk to a teacher, counselor, or even me. Sometimes, you need to adjust your schedule or cut back on activities. Remember, it's okay to ask for help when you need it.

Takeaway Points:

1. **Start Early**: Begin setting academic and career goals early to give yourself time to explore your interests and develop a clear plan.

2. **Use Available Resources**: Explore various career paths by taking advantage of career counseling, online assessments, internships, and networking opportunities.

3. **Develop Key Skills**: Focus on building essential skills like time management, communication, critical thinking, and adaptability to succeed in both academics and the workplace.

4. **Balance Responsibilities**: Learn to manage your time effectively to balance academic responsibilities, extracurricular activities, and personal interests.

5. **Prepare for the Future**: Research college or vocational training options, prepare for standardized tests, and build a strong resume to ensure you're ready for the next step after high school.

6. **Stay Flexible**: As you learn more about yourself and your interests, be open to adjusting your goals and exploring new opportunities.

7. **Seek Support**: When you need it, don't hesitate to ask for guidance and support from family, teachers, mentors, or counselors.

By following these steps and staying proactive, you can create a solid foundation for your academic and career journey, positioning yourself for success and fulfilment in the future.

* * *

"It's not how much money you make, but how much money you keep, how hard it works for you, and how many generations you keep it for."
— *Robert Kiyosaki*

Chapter 17

Financial Literacy and Responsibility

Parent: You know, money isn't just about spending it; it's about understanding it, managing it, and making it work for you. Learning how to handle your finances now can set you up for a secure and stress-free future. I wish I had learned more about financial literacy when I was your age—it would have saved me a lot of headaches!

Teen: I understand that managing money is important, but it seems difficult. Where do I even start? How do I make sure I'm not just blowing through my money and saving for the future?

Parent: Great question! Financial literacy is about building good habits and understanding how money works. Let's discuss some key concepts to help you manage money wisely, avoid debt, and start investing in your future.

How do I manage money responsibly and budget for expenses?

Parent: The first step to financial freedom is learning how to budget your money. It might sound boring, but trust me, it's the foundation of financial success.

Teen: Okay, what's the first thing I must do?

Parent: You need to start by tracking your income and expenses. Think of it like a game—you're in control, and the goal is to ensure your income always outpaces your expenses. Here's how you can do it:

- **Track Your Income and Expenses**: Start by recording all sources of income, whether it's from a part-time job, allowances, or side gigs. Next, track your expenses by dividing them into fixed expenses like rent or bills and variable expenses like food, clothes, and entertainment. This will help you see where your money is going.

- **Create a Budget**: Once you know where your money goes, create a budget. Allocate a portion of your income towards essentials—like housing, utilities, and groceries—and set aside some money for savings and fun. The key is to live within your means and avoid overspending.

- **Prioritize Saving**: Saving should always be a priority. Aim to put away some of your income for emergencies and future goals. This might mean saving for a new laptop, a trip, or even college. A good rule of thumb is the 50/30/20 rule—50% of your income goes to needs, 30% to wants, and 20% to savings.

Teen: That sounds simple enough, but what if something unexpected comes up? What if my phone breaks, and I need a new one?

Parent: That's where an emergency fund comes in. It's a stash of money you set aside specifically for unexpected expenses. This way, you won't have to dip into your savings or go into debt to cover it.

What are the basics of saving, investing, and financial planning?

Teen: So, I get saving, but I've heard people talk about investing. Isn't that risky? How do I know what's safe?

Parent: Investing can seem intimidating, but it's one of the most powerful ways to grow your wealth over time. Here's a breakdown of saving, investing, and financial planning:

- **Saving**: This is the money you set aside for short-term needs or emergencies. Your emergency fund, for example, should have enough to cover three to six months of living expenses. This money should be kept in a separate savings account so it's easily accessible when needed.

- **Investing**: Investing involves putting your money into assets—like stocks, bonds, or real estate—that have the potential to grow over time. The key is starting early, even with small amounts, and diversifying your investments. This means spreading your money across different types of investments to reduce risk. Remember, investing is about the long game—your money grows as the value of your investments increases over time.

- **Financial Planning**: This is your roadmap to financial success. It involves setting financial goals—like buying a car, saving for college, or even retirement—and creating a plan to reach them. A good financial plan considers your income, expenses, savings, investments, and any debt you might have. It's something you should review and adjust as your life changes.

Teen: It sounds like I should start saving and maybe dip my toes into investing once I have enough saved up. But how do I avoid making mistakes, like spending too much or getting into debt?

How can I avoid common pitfalls, such as overspending or accruing debt?

Parent: Avoiding financial pitfalls is all about being mindful of your habits and staying disciplined. Here are some tips to keep you on track:

- **Budgeting**: Stick to the budget you've created. It's easy to overspend if you don't have a plan. Use apps or tools to help you track your spending and ensure you're not going over your budget.

- **Saving First**: Always pay yourself first. This means setting aside money for savings before spending on other things. It's easier to avoid debt when you've built a savings cushion.

- **Debt Management**: Be very cautious about taking on debt. If you use credit cards, make sure to pay off the balance in full every month. High-interest debt can spiral out of control quickly if you're not careful.

- **Smart Spending**: Think twice before making big purchases. Ask yourself if it's something you really need or just something you want. If it's a want, consider waiting a few days before buying to see if you still feel the same way.

Teen: I've heard about people getting into trouble with credit cards. Should I avoid them altogether?

Parent: Not necessarily. Credit cards can be a useful tool if used responsibly. They help build your credit score, which you'll need if you ever want to take out a loan for something like a car or a house. The key is to use them wisely—only charge what you can pay off in full each month, and never miss a payment.

What resources are available to help me learn about financial literacy and independence?

Teen: This is all really helpful, but where can I learn more? I want to make sure I'm fully prepared to handle my money.

Parent: There are so many great resources out there. Here are a few you can check out:

- **Online Courses and Workshops**: Websites like Coursera, Udemy, and Khan Academy offer free or affordable courses on personal finance. These can help you dive deeper into budgeting, saving, and investing.

- **Personal Finance Books**: There are tons of books that make personal finance easy to understand. Some popular ones include *Rich Dad Poor Dad* by Robert Kiyosaki, *The Total Money Makeover* by Dave Ramsey, and *The Millionaire Next Door* by Thomas J. Stanley and William D. Danko.

- **Financial Literacy Websites and Blogs**: Investopedia, The Balance, and NerdWallet offer many articles and tools to help you manage your money.

- **Podcasts and Videos**: Sometimes, learning by listening or watching is easier. You can find financial podcasts on Spotify or Apple Podcasts that discuss everything from saving tips to investing strategies.

- **Government and Nonprofit Organizations**: The National Centre for Financial Education (NCFE) provides resources to enhance financial education, and the Reserve Bank of India (RBI) has initiatives like the RBI Financial Education website, offering guides on managing finances. Additionally, the Securities and Exchange Board of India (SEBI) promotes financial literacy through programs and workshops. Nonprofits like Sankalp Foundation and Moneylife Foundation also focus on providing financial education and resources to the public.

Teen: These resources sound great! I'll check them out. But how do I put all this knowledge into practice?

How do I make informed decisions about spending, saving, and investing for my future?

Parent: It all starts with education and setting clear goals. Here's how you can make informed financial decisions:

- **Educate Yourself**: Knowledge is power. Continue learning about personal finance topics like budgeting, saving, and investing. The more you know, the better decisions you can make.

- **Set Financial Goals**: Whether it's saving for a car, college, or even a rainy day, having specific goals gives you direction. Write down your goals and create a plan to achieve them.

- **Create a Budget**: Stick to your budget and adjust as needed. Track your spending to stay within your limits and save for your goals.

- **Build an Emergency Fund**: Before investing, ensure you have an emergency fund in place. This will give you peace of mind and prevent you from going into debt if something unexpected happens.

- **Pay Off High-Interest Debt**: If you have any debt, especially high-interest debt like credit cards, focus on paying it off as quickly as possible. This will free up more money for saving and investing.

- **Save for the Future**: Start contributing to retirement accounts, like National Pension Scheme (NPS) in India, regulated by the Pension Fund Regulatory and Development Authority which is under the jurisdiction of the Ministry of Finance of the Government of India, as early as possible. The sooner you start, the more time your money has to grow.

- **Diversify Your Investments**: Don't put all your eggs in one basket. Spread your investments across different types of assets to reduce risk and increase your chances of earning a good return.

- **Stay Informed**: Keep up with economic trends, market developments, and new investment opportunities. This will help you make informed decisions and adjust your financial plan as needed.

- **Review and Adjust**: Regularly review your financial plan, budget, and investment portfolio. Life changes, and so should your financial strategy.

Takeaway Points:

- **Financial Literacy**: Understanding how money works is crucial for managing it responsibly and achieving financial independence.

- **Budgeting**: Start by tracking your income and expenses, then create a budget that prioritizes saving.

- **Investing**: To grow your wealth over time, begin investing early, diversify your portfolio, and stay informed.

- **Avoiding Debt**: Be cautious with credit and avoid high-interest debt by sticking to a budget and paying off balances in full.

- **Learning Resources**: To improve your financial knowledge, utilize online courses, books, podcasts, and financial literacy websites.

- **Goal Setting**: Set specific, measurable financial goals and create a plan to achieve them.

- **Emergency Fund**: Build an emergency fund to cover unexpected expenses and protect your financial stability.

Teen: Wow, I didn't realize there was so much to learn about money! But I feel more confident now that I know where to start.

Parent: And that's the key—starting now. The sooner you manage your money wisely, the more secure your future will be. Remember, it's not about how much you earn, but how well you manage what you have. Financial freedom is within your reach, and I'm here to support you every step of the way.

* * *

"It is health that is real wealth and not pieces of gold and silver."
— Mahatma Gandhi

Chapter 18

Health and Wellness

Maintaining health and wellness isn't just about avoiding illness—it's about living your best life, feeling good in your body, and having the energy and mindset to pursue your dreams. As a teenager, you're laying the foundation for your future health, and the habits you build now can influence how you feel for the rest of your life. But health isn't just about what you eat or how often you exercise—it's also about how you take care of your mind and emotions. In this chapter, let's dive into what it really means to prioritize your physical and mental health, and how you can build a lifestyle that supports your well-being every day.

Parent: I know a lot is happening in your life right now—school, friends, maybe even a part-time job or extracurricular activities. With so much happening, letting your health take a backseat can be easy. But your physical and mental well-being are the foundation of everything you do. How do you think you could start prioritizing your health more?

Teen: It feels like there's never enough time! But I could start by trying to eat better and get more sleep. Is that enough?

Parent: That's a great start! Prioritizing your physical and mental health is key to feeling your best and handling everything life throws. Let's break down how you can prioritize your health in your daily life.

How do I prioritize my physical and mental health in my daily life?

Teen: I want to be healthier, but with school and everything, it's hard to know where to start. What should I focus on first?

Parent: Start with the basics—exercise, nutrition, and sleep. These three pillars are essential for physical and mental health. Try to include at least 30 minutes of physical activity into your day, even if it's just a brisk walk. Exercise doesn't just keep your body fit; it also helps clear your mind, reduce stress, and improve your mood.

Aim for balanced meals with plenty of fruits, vegetables, whole grains, and lean proteins for nutrition. Think of food as fuel for your body and mind. And don't forget to drink plenty of water—it's easy to overlook, but staying hydrated is crucial.

Sleep is another big one. Aim for 7-9 hours each night. Good sleep improves your focus, mood, and energy levels. And remember, your mental health is just as important as your physical health. Make time for activities that help you relax and recharge—whether that's reading, listening to music, or practicing mindfulness.

Teen: That makes sense. But what about when I'm really stressed or feeling down? How can I manage those feelings better?

Parent: Managing stress and maintaining your mental health is about developing healthy coping mechanisms. When you feel stressed, try relaxation techniques like deep breathing or meditation. Even just taking a few moments to breathe deeply can help you feel calmer and more centered. It's also important to talk about what's on your mind—whether with me, another family member, or a friend. Sometimes, just sharing what you're going through can make a huge difference.

What are the benefits of regular exercise, healthy eating, and sufficient sleep?

Teen: I've heard that exercise and eating right are important, but what do they do for me?

Parent: The benefits of regular exercise, healthy eating, and sufficient sleep are huge! Exercise helps your heart stay strong, improves your lung capacity, and even reduces your risk of chronic diseases like diabetes. It also boosts your mood by releasing endorphins, your body's natural feel-good chemicals.

A healthy, balanced diet gives your body the nutrients it needs to function at its best. This means you'll have more energy, a stronger immune system, and a better ability to concentrate and learn.

And sleep—never underestimate the power of a good night's sleep! During sleep, your body repairs, your brain processes information, and your mood stabilizes. Without enough sleep, it's harder to focus, you might feel irritable, and your immune system can weaken. These three—exercise, nutrition, and sleep—work together to keep you feeling your best.

Teen: That sounds like a lot, but I see how it all connects. What about specific eating habits? Are there certain things I should be eating more or less of?

Parent: Yes, some guidelines can help you make healthier food choices. Here's what to focus on:

- **Eat More Whole Foods:** Focus on whole grains, fruits, vegetables, lean proteins, and healthy fats. These foods are packed with nutrients that your body needs to function optimally.

- **Limit Processed Foods:** Avoid or limit foods high in sugar, salt, and unhealthy fats. Processed foods often have empty calories, providing energy but little nutritional value.

- **Stay Hydrated:** Water is essential for almost every function in your body. Aim to drink at least 8 glasses daily, and more if you're active.

- **Balance Your Plate:** Mix half your plate with vegetables and fruits, a quarter with lean protein, and a quarter with whole grains. This balance ensures you're getting a variety of nutrients.

Teen: That's really helpful. I think I can start by making some small changes, like swapping out soda for water and adding more veggies to my meals.

How can I develop healthy habits for managing stress and maintaining well-being?

Teen: Sometimes I feel like I'm just juggling too much, and I end up really stressed. How can I handle it better?

Parent: Stress is a part of life, but managing it makes all the difference. Developing healthy habits can help you navigate stressful times without feeling overwhelmed. Here are a few strategies:

- **Practice relaxation techniques:** Deep breathing, meditation, and yoga are great ways to calm your mind and body. Even just a few minutes a day can make a big difference.

- **Prioritize self-care:** Make time for activities that make you happy and relaxed, whether that's playing a sport, spending time in nature, or just reading a good book.

- **Set boundaries:** It's okay to say no sometimes. Protect your time and energy by setting boundaries with school, work, and even friends if necessary.

- **Stay connected:** Surround yourself with supportive people. Friends and family can offer a listening ear, advice, or a fun distraction when needed.

- **Mindfulness:** Stay present and not get too caught up in what-ifs. Mindfulness practices can help you stay grounded, especially during tough times.

- **Seek support when needed:** Never hesitate to reach out to a trusted adult or a mental health professional if things feel too heavy to handle on your own.

Teen: That's really helpful. I could start by trying some of those relaxation techniques and maybe setting better boundaries with my time.

What role do self-care practices, such as mindfulness and relaxation techniques, play in health?

Teen: You've mentioned mindfulness and relaxation before. Do they really make that big of a difference?

Parent: Absolutely! Mindfulness and relaxation techniques are powerful tools for maintaining both physical and mental health. They help reduce stress, which is important because stress can affect your body and mind. For example, mindfulness can lower blood pressure, improve sleep, and even boost your immune system.

Mentally, these practices help you become more aware of your thoughts and feelings, which can prevent you from getting stuck in negative thinking patterns. They also enhance your emotional resilience, making it easier to bounce back from challenges. And since they encourage relaxation, they help reduce anxiety and improve your overall sense of well-being.

Teen: I guess I didn't realize how much impact these small practices could have. How do I get started with mindfulness?

Parent: Getting started with mindfulness can be as simple as taking a few minutes each day to focus on your breathing. You can sit quietly, close your eyes, and just pay attention to your breath as it goes in and out. If your mind starts to wander, gently bring it back to your breath. Many apps and online resources offer guided mindfulness practices, which can be really helpful when you're just starting out.

Teen: I'll give it a try. It sounds like it could really help me stay calm and focused, especially when things get hectic.

How do I access healthcare resources and advocate for my own health needs?

Teen: I'm not sure I understand how to handle things like doctor's appointments or even know when to go. How do I figure all that out?

Parent: It's important to start taking an active role in your healthcare. First, ensure you have a primary care provider—a doctor you see for regular check-ups. They can help you stay on top of your health and address any concerns you might have. If you ever feel unwell or have questions about your health, don't hesitate to contact them.

When you go to appointments, it's important to communicate openly with your healthcare provider. Be honest about your feelings, ask questions, and don't fear expressing any concerns. It's also okay to seek a second opinion if something feels wrong.

Finally, knowing your rights as a patient is crucial. You have the right to understand your treatment options, ask questions, and be involved in decisions about your care. If you ever feel uncertain or uncomfortable, speak up! Your health is too important to leave in anyone else's hands.

Teen: I didn't realize there was so much I could do to manage my health. I'll try to be more proactive about it from now on.

How can I build a balanced lifestyle supporting my academic and personal goals?

Teen: Sometimes it feels like balancing school, friends, and everything else is impossible. How do I make sure I'm not burning out?

Parent: Balancing different aspects of your life is challenging, but it's possible with some planning and self-awareness. Here's how you can create a balanced lifestyle:

- **Time management:** Create a schedule that includes time for schoolwork, hobbies, physical activity, and rest. Prioritize your tasks and make sure to include breaks.

- **Set realistic goals:** Set academic and personal goals that are challenging but achievable. Don't try to do too much at once—focus on what's most important to you.

- **Stay flexible:** Life doesn't always go according to plan, so be willing to adjust your schedule and goals as needed.

- **Make time for self-care:** Include activities that help you relax and recharge in your routine. This could be anything from reading a book to spending time with friends.

- **Seek support:** Don't be afraid to ask for help if you feel overwhelmed. Teachers, friends, and family are there to support you.

Teen: I like the idea of setting realistic goals and staying flexible. I'll start by creating a schedule that includes time for everything I need to do, including some downtime.

How do I stay motivated to maintain a healthy lifestyle when busy?

Teen: It's easy to start off strong with healthy habits, but I often lose motivation when things get busy. How can I stay consistent?

Parent: Staying motivated is a common challenge, especially when hectic. Here are some strategies to help you maintain a healthy lifestyle even when you're busy:

- **Set small, achievable goals:** Break down your larger health goals into smaller, manageable steps. This makes it easier to stay on track and feel accomplished.

- **Find what you enjoy:** Whether it's a type of exercise, a hobby, or a healthy food you love, focus on activities that you enjoy. This makes it more likely that you'll stick with them.

- **Create a routine:** Consistency is key. Make healthy habits a part of your daily routine so they become second nature.

- **Track your progress:** Keep a journal or use an app to track your progress. Seeing how far you've come can be a great motivator.

- **Reward yourself:** Celebrate your successes, no matter how small. Treat yourself when you reach a milestone—just ensure the reward supports your healthy lifestyle.

- **Stay connected:** Share your goals with friends or family members who can support and encourage you. Sometimes, having someone to check in with can keep you accountable.

Teen: I think tracking my progress and setting small goals could really help. I'll try to focus on the things I enjoy and make them a regular part of my day.

How can I recognize and address signs of burnout before they become overwhelming?

Teen: I've heard people talk about burnout, but I'm not sure I'd recognize it. How do I know if I'm getting burned out?

Parent: Burnout can sneak up on you, especially when you're juggling a lot of responsibilities. Recognizing the signs early is important to take action before it becomes overwhelming. Here's what to watch for:

- **Physical symptoms:** Frequent headaches, stomach aches, or feeling tired all the time can be signs of burnout.

- **Emotional symptoms:** If you're feeling constantly stressed, irritable, or overwhelmed, it could be a sign that you're heading toward burnout.

- **Behavioral changes:** If you notice that you're withdrawing from activities you used to enjoy, procrastinating more, or having trouble focusing, these could be warning signs.

- **Lack of motivation:** Feeling unmotivated or disconnected from your goals is another sign that you might be experiencing burnout.

If you recognize these signs, taking a step back and reassess your situation is important. Here's what you can do:

- **Take a break:** Give yourself permission to rest and recharge. This might mean taking a day off, reducing your workload, or simply spending some time doing something you enjoy.

- **Prioritize self-care:** Make sure you're taking care of your basic needs—eating well, sleeping enough, and staying active.

- **Seek support:** Talk to someone you trust about what you're going through. Sometimes just having someone listen can make a big difference.

- **Reevaluate your goals:** It might be time to adjust your goals or expectations if you're feeling overwhelmed. It's okay to scale back if it means protecting your health.

Teen: I'll definitely watch out for those signs. Taking breaks and talking to someone when I'm feeling stressed will help me stay balanced.

Takeaway Points:

1. **Physical and Mental Health:** Both are equally important. To support your overall well-being, incorporate exercise, good nutrition, and quality sleep into your daily routine.

2. **Stress Management:** Develop healthy coping mechanisms, such as relaxation techniques, setting boundaries, and maintaining supportive relationships.

3. **Self-Care:** Regular self-care practices, such as mindfulness and relaxation, can significantly reduce stress and improve physical and mental health.

4. **Healthcare Advocacy:** Be proactive about your health by staying informed, communicating openly with healthcare providers, and knowing your rights as a patient.

5. **Balanced Lifestyle:** Create a balanced lifestyle by managing your time effectively, setting realistic goals, and making time for self-care and relaxation.

6. **Consistency and Motivation:** Stay motivated by setting small goals, tracking your progress, and focusing on activities you enjoy. Celebrate your successes and stay connected with supportive people.

7. **Burnout Prevention:** Recognize the signs of burnout and take action early by resting, prioritizing self-care, and seeking support when needed.

Parent: Taking charge of your health and wellness is an ongoing process, but it's one of the most important things you can do for yourself. With the right habits and mindset, you'll be better equipped to face challenges, enjoy your life, and reach your full potential.

Teen: Thanks. I now have a much clearer idea of how to take care of myself. I'll start making some of these changes right away.

Parent: That's great to hear. Remember, I'm here to support you every step of the way. We're in this together!

* * *

> *"Friendship is born at that moment when one person says to another, 'What! You too? I thought I was the only one.'"*
> — *C.S. Lewis*

Chapter 19

Peer Relationships and Social Skills

Navigating peer relationships as a Teen can be both rewarding and challenging. These relationships often play a significant role in your social development and self-identity. Whether it's learning to connect with others, managing conflicts, or resisting peer pressure, developing strong social skills is crucial for building healthy, supportive friendships. This chapter will guide you through the complexities of peer relationships, offering strategies for effective communication, empathy, and resilience.

Parent: Hey, how's everything going with your friends these days?

Teen: It's… complicated, I guess. Sometimes it feels like there's a lot of pressure to fit in, and I'm not always sure how to deal with it.

Parent: I get it. Peer relationships can be tricky, especially when figuring out who you are and where you belong. But they're also some of the most important relationships you'll have, and they can teach you a lot about yourself and others.

Teen: Yeah, I want to be a good friend and make the right choices, but it's hard sometimes. How do I know what's right for me?

Parent: That's a great question. It's all about understanding your values, communicating effectively, and recognizing the qualities of healthy relationships. You must also know how to handle peer pressure and what to do when a friendship isn't good for you. Let's talk about all that—how to build strong, supportive friendships, stand up for yourself, and grow as a person through your relationships with others.

Teen: That sounds like a lot to take in. Where do we start?

Parent: Let's start by discussing peer pressure. Then, we'll move on to what makes a friendship healthy, how to resolve conflicts, and how to spot a toxic relationship. Along the way, we'll discuss how to build empathy, set boundaries, and develop the social skills you need to navigate all kinds of relationships. Ready?

Teen: I'm ready. Let's do this.

How do I navigate peer pressure and make choices that align with my values?

Teen: Peer pressure is everywhere. How can I stay true to myself when everyone else does something different?

Parent: Navigating peer pressure is tough but also an opportunity to strengthen your sense of self. First, take time to understand your values—what really matters to you. Once you know your values, making decisions that reflect who you are is easier, even when others might try to sway you.

Teen: But what if I feel left out or judged?

Parent: It's normal to feel that way, but remember, those who truly care about you will respect your choices. Surround yourself with friends who support your values, and practice saying 'no' respectfully but firmly. It helps to plan ahead for situations where you might face pressure so you're prepared to stick to your choices.

Teen: What if I mess up and give in to peer pressure?

Parent: Everyone makes mistakes. It is important to learn from them and make better choices next time. Reflect on what happened, why you felt pressured, and how you can handle it differently in the future. And remember, you can always talk to someone you trust for support.

What are the qualities of healthy friendships, and how do I cultivate them?

Teen: How do I know if my friendships are healthy?

Parent: Healthy friendships are built on trust, respect, and support. Ask yourself if you feel valued, heard, and respected by your friends. Do they encourage you to be your best self or pressure you to do things that don't align with your values?

Teen: What if I realize a friendship isn't healthy?

Parent: It's important to address any issues by communicating openly with your friends. Let them know how you feel and what you need from the friendship. It might be time to reconsider the relationship if things don't improve. Surround yourself with friends who lift you up and respect your boundaries.

Teen: How can I be a better friend?

Parent: Be trustworthy, honest, and supportive. Show empathy, listen actively, and respect your friends' feelings and boundaries. Friendship is a two-way street—make sure it's balanced, with both of you giving and receiving care and respect.

How do I build empathy and compassion for others in my social interactions?

Teen: I want to understand others more, but it's not always easy to relate.

Parent: Empathy is about putting yourself in someone else's shoes. Start by listening when others talk—pay attention to their words and emotions. Try to understand their perspective, even if it differs from yours.

Teen: But what if I don't agree with them?

Parent: You don't have to agree to show empathy. You can validate their feelings and express compassion without compromising your views. It's about acknowledging their experience and being kind, even if you see things differently.

Teen: How can I practice this more in everyday life?

Parent: Engage in small acts of kindness, ask questions to learn more about others, and reflect on how your own experiences shape your reactions.

Volunteering or helping others in need can also deepen your sense of empathy and compassion.

What strategies can I use to resolve conflicts and communicate effectively with peers?

Teen: Conflicts with friends are the worst. How can I handle them better?

Parent: Conflicts are a normal part of any relationship, but how you handle them matters. Start by practicing active listening—really hear what the other person is saying without interrupting. Then, express your feelings clearly using 'I' statements, like 'I feel hurt when…' instead of blaming.

Teen: What if the conflict doesn't get resolved?

Parent: If the conflict persists, it might help to take a break and revisit the conversation later when emotions have cooled. Sometimes, seeking a neutral third party, like a counselor, can also help. Remember, the goal is to understand each other and find a solution, not to 'win' the argument.

Teen: Is it okay to agree to disagree?

Parent: Absolutely. Not every conflict will have a perfect resolution. Sometimes, agreeing to disagree while respecting each other's perspectives is the best outcome.

How do I recognize and address toxic or unhealthy relationships in my life?

Teen: How can I tell if a relationship is toxic?

Parent: Toxic relationships often involve manipulation, disrespect, control, or constant negativity. If you feel drained, anxious, or unhappy more often than not, it's a sign that something isn't right. Trust your instincts—if something feels off, it probably is.

Teen: What should I do if I'm in a toxic relationship?

Parent: Start by setting clear boundaries and communicating your concerns to the other person. If the behaviour doesn't change, it may be necessary to distance yourself or end the relationship altogether. Your well-being comes first, and protecting yourself from harm is important.

Teen: But what if I'm scared to leave the relationship?

Parent: Leaving a toxic relationship can be difficult, especially if you fear the consequences. Seek support from trusted friends, family members, or a counselor. They can help you develop a plan and provide the emotional backing you need. Remember, you deserve to be in relationships that uplift and support you.

How can I balance being authentic with fitting in socially?

Teen: I want to be myself, but sometimes I feel like I have to change to fit in. How do I find a balance?

Parent: It's natural to want to fit in, but staying true to yourself is important. Start by identifying what aspects of yourself are non-negotiable—your core values, beliefs, and passions. You should never compromise these things, even if it means standing out or being different.

Teen: What if I feel pressured to hide those parts of myself?

Parent: It can be tough but remember that the right friends will appreciate you for who you are, not who you pretend to be. You don't have to change yourself to fit in; instead, find a group where you can be authentic. It's better to have a few close friends who accept you than a large group where you must hide who you are.

How do I deal with jealousy and envy in friendships?

Teen: Sometimes I feel jealous of my friends, like when they succeed at something. How do I deal with those feelings?

Parent: Jealousy and envy are normal emotions, but it's important to manage them in a healthy way. Start by acknowledging your feelings without judgment—everyone feels this way sometimes. Then, try to shift your focus from comparing yourself to others to celebrating their successes and recognizing your own strengths.

Teen: But what if I still feel bad about myself?

Parent: It's okay to feel that way. Use these moments to reflect on what you really want and how you can work toward your goals. Instead of letting jealousy create distance, use it as motivation to improve and grow. And remember, your friends' success doesn't detract from your potential.

How can I build and maintain trust in my friendships?

Teen: Trust is important, but how do I build it with friends?

Parent: Trust is built over time through consistent, reliable actions. Be honest, keep your promises, and respect your friends' privacy. If you make a mistake, own up to it and apologize. It's also important to show that you can be trusted with their feelings—be a good listener and avoid gossip.

Teen: What if someone breaks my trust?

Parent: If someone breaks your trust, talk to them about how it made you feel. Depending on their response, you can decide whether to rebuild the trust or set new boundaries. Rebuilding trust takes time and effort from both sides, so be patient with the process.

How do I deal with peer pressure related to social media?

Teen: Social media can be overwhelming. How do I handle the pressure to post and keep up with everything?

Parent: Social media can create a lot of pressure to present a certain image or keep up with trends. Start by setting boundaries for yourself—decide how much time you want to spend online and what kind of content you want to engage with. Remember, you don't have to share everything about your life online.

Teen: But what if I feel like I'm missing out?

Parent: It's easy to feel like you're missing out, but remember that social media often shows a curated version of reality. Focus on living in the moment and engaging with the real world. You can stay connected with friends without feeling pressured to document every detail. It's okay to take breaks and prioritize your mental health over social media.

How can I handle disagreements with friends without damaging the relationship?

Teen: What if I disagree with a friend? How do I keep it from hurting our relationship?

Parent: Disagreements are a natural part of any relationship, but how you handle them makes all the difference. Approach the situation with empathy—try to understand your friend's perspective and express your own feelings calmly and respectfully. Avoid personal attacks and focus on the issue at hand.

Teen: What if we still don't agree?

Parent: It's okay to have different opinions. The key is to respect each other's viewpoints and find a compromise if possible. If the disagreement concerns something important, you might need to agree to disagree and move forward. The goal is to maintain the friendship while acknowledging that it's okay not to see eye to eye on everything.

How do I set boundaries with friends without hurting their feelings?

Teen: Sometimes I feel like I need space, but I don't want to hurt my friends' feelings. How do I set boundaries?

Parent: Setting boundaries is an important part of maintaining healthy relationships, and it's possible to do so without causing hurt. Be honest and clear about your needs—explain that it's not about them but about what you need to feel comfortable and happy.

Teen: What if they don't take it well?

Parent: If a friend doesn't respect your boundaries, that indicates an unhealthy dynamic. It's important to stand firm and prioritize your well-being. A true friend will understand and respect your need for space or time alone. You can also reassure them that the boundary doesn't change how much you value the friendship.

How can I handle feelings of loneliness or isolation in social settings?

Teen: Even when I'm around people, I sometimes feel lonely. What can I do about that?

Parent: Feeling lonely in a crowd is more common than you might think. It often happens when we feel disconnected from others or not fully engage with the people around us. Try to focus on quality over quantity in your social interactions—build deeper connections with a few people rather than spreading yourself too thin.

Teen: But what if I don't have anyone to connect with?

Parent: If you're feeling isolated, consider joining clubs, groups, or activities where you can meet people with similar interests. Building new friendships takes time, so be patient with yourself. In the meantime, reach out to someone you trust to talk about your feelings—it can help to share what you're going through and feel less alone.

How do I deal with the fear of missing out (FOMO) when I'm not included in social activities?

Teen: I hate feeling left out when my friends do something without me. How do I deal with FOMO?

Parent: FOMO is common, especially with social media, which makes it easy to see what others are doing. Remember, you don't have to be a part of everything to have meaningful relationships. Focus on the activities and friendships that bring you joy and fulfilment rather than trying to be everywhere at once.

Teen: But it still feels bad to be left out.

Parent: It's natural to feel that way, but try to shift your focus to what you're doing and enjoying rather than what you're missing. Engage in activities that make you happy, and remind yourself that it's okay to miss out sometimes. Everyone experiences FOMO at some point, but it doesn't define your worth or your friendships.

How can I develop better communication skills with my peers?

Teen: I sometimes struggle to express myself or understand others. How can I improve my communication skills?

Parent: Effective communication starts with active listening—paying attention to what the other person is saying without planning your response while talking. When it's your turn to speak, be clear and concise, and use 'I' statements to express your feelings and needs.

Teen: What if I'm nervous about speaking up?

Parent: It's normal to feel nervous, especially in new or challenging situations. Practice in low-stakes environments, like with close friends or family, to build your confidence. Also, non-verbal communication is just as important—maintain eye contact, use open body language, and be mindful of your tone. Over time, these skills will become more natural, and you'll feel more comfortable communicating with others.

How do I deal with rejection or feeling left out by friends?

Teen: What should I do if I feel rejected or left out by my friends?

Parent: Rejection is painful, but everyone experiences it at some point. Start by acknowledging your feelings—feeling hurt or disappointed is okay. Then, try to understand the situation from a broader perspective. Sometimes, people don't realize they're excluding others or might be going through their own issues.

Teen: Should I talk to them about it?

Parent: If it's really bothering you, it's worth conversing. Approach the topic calmly, without accusations, and express how you feel. For example, you could say, 'I felt left out when...' This opens the door for them to explain and for you to work through it together. However, if this happens frequently, it might be a sign that the friendship isn't as healthy as it should be, and it may be time to reassess the relationship.

How can I build resilience in the face of social challenges?

Teen: Dealing with social challenges can be exhausting. How can I build resilience?

Parent: Building resilience is about learning to bounce back from difficulties. One way to develop it is by viewing challenges as opportunities to learn and grow. When you face a social setback, take a moment to reflect on what happened and what you can learn from it.

Teen: But what if I keep making the same mistakes?

Parent: It's okay to make mistakes—that's part of learning. The important thing is to be kind to yourself and recognize that growth takes time. Surround yourself with supportive people, practice self-care, and don't be afraid to seek help when needed. Over time, you'll find that you can handle challenges more effectively and confidently.

How do I support a friend who is going through a tough time?

Teen: I want to help a friend who's having a hard time, but I'm unsure what to do.

Parent: Supporting a friend during tough times means being respectful and compassionate. Start by letting them know you care and are available to listen if they want to talk. Sometimes, just being a good listener is the most valuable thing you can do.

Teen: What if they don't want to talk about it?

Parent: Respect their boundaries and give them space if they're not ready to open up. You can still offer support by checking in on them, spending time together, or doing something kind for them. If their situation seems serious and you're worried about their well-being, it's okay to encourage them to seek help from a trusted adult or a professional.

Takeaway Points:

1. **Know Your Values:** Understanding your own values helps you navigate peer pressure and make choices that align with who you are.

2. **Healthy Friendships:** Look for trust, respect, and support in friendships. Be the kind of friend you want to have.

3. **Empathy and Compassion:** Practice putting yourself in others' shoes, listening actively, and showing kindness in your interactions.

4. **Conflict Resolution:** Handle conflicts with patience, active listening, and clear communication. Aim to understand rather than to win.

5. **Recognizing Toxic Relationships:** Trust your instincts and prioritize your well-being. Don't hesitate to set boundaries or walk away from unhealthy relationships.

6. **Seek Support:** Whether navigating peer pressure, conflict, or toxic relationships, don't be afraid to reach out to trusted individuals for guidance and support.

7. **Balanced Social Life:** Focus on quality over quantity in your social interactions, and don't let FOMO dictate your choices.

8. **Communication Skills:** Practice active listening, clear expression, and non-verbal communication to build stronger connections with others.

9. **Resilience:** Embrace challenges as opportunities to grow, and remember that mistakes are part of the learning process.

10. **Supporting Others:** Be a compassionate listener and respect boundaries when helping friends through difficult times.

Parent: Remember, your relationships play a big role in shaping who you are and who you will become. Developing strong social skills and surrounding yourself with positive, supportive friends set the foundation for healthy, fulfilling relationships.

Teen: Thanks. This really helps. I now have a better understanding of what I need to do.

Parent: I'm glad to hear that. Remember, it's all a learning process. Take it one step at a time, and don't be too hard on yourself. You're doing great.

* * *

"We cannot become what we want by remaining what we are."
— Max DePree

Chapter 20

Personal Development and Growth

Parent: Hey Dear! You know how we often talk about growing and becoming the best versions of ourselves?

Teen: Yeah, like improving and reaching our goals, right?

Parent: Exactly! Personal development is all about that journey of self-discovery and growth. It's about constantly improving who we are and what we can do. It helps us understand ourselves better, set meaningful goals, and overcome obstacles. It's also about building resilience, learning from our experiences, and becoming more adaptable. Let's dive into how to start this journey and make the most of it!

Teen: Sounds interesting, but where do we even start?

Parent: Let's start by exploring what personal development means and why it's important. Then, we'll talk about setting goals, building resilience, staying motivated, and balancing personal growth with other responsibilities. Ready to get started?

Teen: Definitely! I'm curious to learn more.

What does personal development mean, and why is it so important?

Teen: So, what exactly does personal development mean, and why is it so important?

Parent: Personal development is essentially the process of growing as a person. It means understanding your strengths and weaknesses, setting goals, and becoming your best version. It's important because it helps you tackle life's challenges more effectively, confidently pursue your dreams, and create a fulfilling life. Personal development isn't just about achieving success; it's about finding purpose, improving relationships, and enhancing overall well-being.

Teen: Is it only about career goals, or does it include other aspects of life?

Parent: Great question! Personal development covers all aspects of your life—career, relationships, health, hobbies, and mental and emotional well-being. It's about becoming a well-rounded individual who can adapt to change, overcome obstacles, and grow in all areas of life.

Teen: So, it's like working on being the best version of myself in every way?

Parent: Exactly. It's about striving to improve every day, even if it's just a little bit. It's about setting the foundation for a life that's not only successful but also meaningful and fulfilling. And the best part? It's a journey that lasts a lifetime, so there's always room for growth and learning.

How can I set meaningful goals and create a vision for my future self?

Teen: How can I set meaningful goals and create a vision for my future self?

Parent: Start by reflecting on what truly matters to you. What are your passions, values, and aspirations? Setting meaningful goals begins with understanding what you want to achieve and why. Think about where you want to be academically, professionally, and personally in the next few years. Create a vision for your future self that excites and motivates you.

Teen: How do I make sure these goals are realistic?

Parent: Break your goals down into smaller, manageable steps. This makes them less overwhelming and easier to tackle. Setting SMART goals—specific, Measurable, Achievable, Relevant, and Time-bound—is also important. This framework helps ensure your goals are clear and attainable.

Teen: Can you give me an example of a SMART goal?

Parent: Sure! You're passionate about writing and want to become a published author. A SMART goal might be: 'I will write a 1,500-word short story every month for the next six months, revise it, and submit at least two stories to literary magazines by the end of the year.' This goal is specific, measurable, achievable, relevant to your passion, and time bound.

Teen: What if I have several goals in different areas of my life?

Parent: That's perfectly fine! It's good to have various goals that address different aspects of your life. Just prioritize them based on what's most important to you. You can focus on a few goals at a time to avoid feeling overwhelmed.

Teen: What should I do if I start feeling overwhelmed?

Parent: If you start feeling overwhelmed, it's okay to reassess and adjust your goals. Life can be unpredictable, so being flexible is key. Take a step back, evaluate your progress, and decide if you need to break your goals down further or shift your focus for a while. Remember, it's about progress, not perfection.

What strategies can help me overcome obstacles and focus on self-improvement?

Teen: What strategies can help me overcome obstacles and focus on self-improvement?

Parent: Obstacles are a natural part of any journey, but they are also opportunities to learn and grow. One strategy is to break down challenges into smaller, more manageable tasks. This makes them less intimidating and easier to tackle. For example, if you're struggling with a big project at school, break it down into smaller tasks like research, outlining, and drafting.

Teen: What if I keep facing the same obstacles over and over?

Parent: That's when self-compassion becomes really important. It's easy to get frustrated when you hit the same roadblocks, but instead of being hard on yourself, try to approach the situation with curiosity. Ask yourself, 'What can I learn from this? How can I approach this differently?' Sometimes, seeking advice from someone who has faced similar challenges can provide new insights.

Teen: How do I stay focused on self-improvement, especially when things get tough?

Parent: Staying focused on self-improvement requires persistence and patience. Make personal development a part of your daily routine—whether it's reading, practicing a new skill, or reflecting on your progress. Celebrate small victories along the way to keep yourself motivated. And when things get tough, remind yourself why you started. Keep your long-term vision in mind, and remember that every step brings you closer to your goals, no matter how small.

How can I cultivate resilience and adaptability when things get tough?

Teen: How can I cultivate resilience and adaptability when things get tough?

Parent: Resilience and adaptability are essential skills for navigating life's challenges. To build resilience, start by viewing setbacks as opportunities for growth rather than failures. When faced with adversity, ask yourself, 'What can I learn from this experience? How can I grow stronger because of it?'

Teen: What if I'm struggling to stay positive during tough times?

Parent: Feeling down during difficult times is natural, but cultivating a positive mindset can make a big difference. Practice gratitude by focusing on what you're thankful for, even in tough situations. Surround yourself with supportive people who lift you up. And remember, it's okay to seek help when you need it—whether it's talking to a friend, family member, or counselor.

Teen: How does adaptability fit into all of this?

Parent: Adaptability is about being open to change and willing to adjust your plans when necessary. Life rarely goes as planned, so being flexible allows you to navigate unexpected challenges easily. Embrace change as a chance to learn and grow, and be willing to try new approaches when faced with obstacles. The more you practice resilience and adaptability, the stronger and more confident you'll become in handling whatever life throws your way.

What role do self-reflection and self-awareness play in personal growth?

Teen: What role do self-reflection and self-awareness play in personal growth?

Parent: Self-reflection and self-awareness are at the core of personal growth. By regularly reflecting on your thoughts, feelings, and actions, you gain valuable insights into who you are and how you interact with the world. This awareness helps you understand your strengths, identify areas for improvement, and make intentional choices that align with your values and goals.

Teen: How do I practice self-reflection without being too critical of myself?

Parent: It's important to approach self-reflection with kindness and curiosity rather than judgment. Focus on what you can learn from your experiences rather than dwelling on what went wrong. Ask yourself questions like, 'What did I learn from this situation?' or 'How can I grow from this experience?' Journaling can be a helpful tool for processing your thoughts and tracking your growth over time.

Teen: What if I discover things I don't like about myself?

Parent: That's part of the process. The goal of self-reflection isn't to be perfect, but to be aware of who you are and to work on areas where you want to grow. Remember, personal development is a journey, and it's okay to have aspects of yourself that you're still working on. The important thing is to approach these areas with a growth mindset and a willingness to improve.

How do I stay motivated while working towards my goals?

Teen: How do I stay motivated while working towards my goals?

Parent: Staying motivated can be challenging, especially when the initial excitement fades. One way to maintain motivation is by setting short-term goals that lead to your larger, long-term objectives. This gives you regular milestones to celebrate, which helps keep you motivated.

Teen: What if I start losing interest in my goals?

Parent: If you start losing interest, revisit your goals and the reasons why you set them in the first place. Ask yourself if the goals still align with your values and aspirations. Sometimes, adjusting your goals or setting new ones is okay if your interests or circumstances have changed. Also, try to mix things up to keep your journey exciting—experiment with new approaches or reward yourself for hitting key milestones.

Teen: How do I deal with setbacks that make me want to give up?

Parent: Setbacks are a natural part of the journey, but they don't define your ability to succeed. When you encounter a setback, take a moment to process your feelings, then shift your focus to problem-solving. Ask yourself, 'What can I do differently next time? How can I turn this challenge into an opportunity to learn?' Surrounding yourself with a support system of friends, family, or mentors can also help you stay motivated during tough times.

How do I balance personal development with other responsibilities?

Teen: How do I balance personal development with other responsibilities?

Parent: Balancing personal development with other responsibilities requires good time management and prioritization. Start by identifying your top priorities—both in terms of personal growth and daily responsibilities. Then, create a schedule that includes dedicated time for personal development activities, whether it's reading, practicing a skill, or reflecting on your progress.

Teen: What if I feel like I don't have enough time for everything?

Parent: It's all about finding a balance that works for you. Sometimes, you might need to adjust your schedule or scale back on certain activities to make room for what's most important. It's also important to be realistic about what you can achieve in a given timeframe. Personal development is a lifelong journey, so taking it one step at a time is okay.

Teen: How do I avoid burnout while trying to improve myself?

Parent: To avoid burnout, prioritize self-care and allow yourself time to rest and recharge. It's easy to get caught up in the drive for self-improvement, but rest is a crucial part of the process. Schedule regular breaks, practice mindfulness, and make time for activities that bring you joy and relaxation. Balance is key to sustaining long-term growth without sacrificing your well-being.

How can I build self-discipline to stick to my personal development goals?

Teen: How can I build self-discipline to achieve my personal development goals?

Parent: Building self-discipline starts with creating a routine that supports your goals. Set specific times each day or week for activities related to your personal development. Consistency is key—over time, these activities will become habits that are easier to stick to.

Teen: What if I struggle to stay disciplined?

Parent: It's normal to struggle with self-discipline at times. One strategy is to break your goals down into very small steps that are easy to achieve. This way, you build momentum with small successes. Another approach is to remove distractions that make it harder to stay focused. For example, if you're trying to study, turn off your phone or use apps that block social media during your study time.

Teen: How do I get back on track if I slip up?

Parent: Don't be too hard on yourself if you slip up. It's all part of the learning process. Reflect on what caused the slip-up and think about how you can prevent it in the future. Then, refocus on your goals and get back on track. Self-discipline is like a muscle—the more you practice it, the stronger it becomes.

How do I handle criticism and feedback as part of my growth process?

Teen: How do I handle criticism and feedback as part of my growth process?

Parent: Handling criticism and feedback can be challenging, but it's essential to personal growth. The first step is to approach feedback with an open mind. Instead of seeing it as a personal attack, view it as an opportunity to learn and improve.

Teen: But what if the criticism feels unfair or harsh?

Parent: Not all criticism is constructive, so it's important to evaluate the feedback you receive. Ask yourself if there's any truth to the criticism and if you can learn anything from it. If the feedback is harsh or unfair, try not to take it personally. Instead, focus on the constructive elements and let go of any negativity. If you're unsure about the feedback, seeking a second opinion from someone you trust can be helpful.

Teen: How do I use feedback to improve?

Parent: Use feedback as a guide for your next steps. Identify specific areas for improvement and set goals to address them. For example, if you receive feedback that your writing could be clearer, you might set a goal to practice writing more frequently or to study examples of effective writing. Remember, feedback is a tool for growth, and embracing it can help you achieve your personal development goals more effectively.

How do I maintain a positive mindset and stay resilient in the face of challenges?

Teen: How do I maintain a positive mindset and stay resilient in facing challenges?

Parent: Maintaining a positive mindset is crucial for resilience. Start by practicing gratitude—regularly reflect on the things you're thankful for, no matter how small. This helps shift your focus from what's going wrong to what's going right.

Teen: What if I'm struggling to stay positive during tough times?

Parent: It's okay to have moments of doubt or frustration but try to keep them in perspective. Remind yourself that challenges are temporary and that you have the strength to overcome them. Surround yourself with positive influences—people who encourage and support you, and activities that bring you joy.

Teen: How can I bounce back when things don't go as planned?

Parent: Resilience is about bouncing back and learning from setbacks. When things don't go as planned, reflect on what happened and what you can learn from the experience. Then, adjust your approach and keep moving forward. Remember, every challenge is an opportunity to grow stronger and more resilient.

Takeaway Points:

1. **Embrace the Journey:** Personal development is a continuous process of growth and self-discovery. It's important to stay open to learning and evolving.

2. **Set Meaningful Goals:** Reflect on your values and aspirations to set clear, achievable goals that align with your vision for the future.

3. **Overcome Obstacles:** Approach challenges with resilience and problem-solving skills. Seek support when needed and celebrate your progress.

4. **Cultivate Resilience:** Develop a positive mindset, practice mindfulness, and build a support network to help you adapt to changes and setbacks.

5. **Utilize Self-Reflection:** Self-reflection and self-awareness are tools for personal growth. They help you understand yourself better and make intentional choices.

6. **Stay Motivated:** Keep your goals in mind, celebrate milestones, and surround yourself with supportive people to maintain motivation.

7. **Balance Responsibilities:** Manage your time effectively to balance personal development with other responsibilities, ensuring you make room for both growth and daily tasks.

8. **Build Self-Discipline:** Create routines and habits that support your personal development goals. Practice consistency and remove distractions to stay on track.

9. **Handle Feedback Constructively:** Approach criticism and feedback with an open mind, using it as a tool for growth. Focus on the constructive elements and set goals for improvement.

10. **Maintain a Positive Mindset:** Practice gratitude, surround yourself with positive influences, and view challenges as opportunities for growth.

Parent: Remember, personal development is a lifelong journey. It's about continually striving to be the best version of yourself, learning from your experiences, and staying true to your values and goals.

Teen: Thanks for the advice. I feel more confident about working on my personal growth now.

Parent: I'm glad to hear that. Keep moving forward, and remember, I'm always here to support you along the way.

* * *

"The mind is everything. What you think, you become."
— *Buddha*

Chapter 21

Media Literacy and Critical Thinking

Parent: Hey dear! Let's chat about something super important—how we interact with the media and information we encounter daily. With all the media and advertising around us, it's easy to get swayed by what we see and hear. However, learning how to navigate these influences and think critically about what we consume can make a huge difference in how we perceive the world and make decisions.

Teen: That sounds pretty relevant. I feel like I'm bombarded with so much information online and on TV. Sometimes, it's hard to tell what's true and what's not.

Parent: Absolutely, it can be overwhelming. That's why developing media literacy and critical thinking skills is so crucial. It's not just about spotting fake news, but also about understanding how media shapes our perceptions and behaviors. Let's dive into some key questions to help you become more discerning and informed.

How do I navigate the influence of media and advertising on my perceptions and behaviors?

Teen: Media and advertising are everywhere. How can I ensure they're not affecting my thoughts or behaviour?

Parent: Navigating media and advertising is like being a detective. Start by asking yourself: Who is behind this message? What might they be trying to achieve? Often, media and ads have an agenda, whether it's selling a product, promoting a certain lifestyle, or shaping opinions.

Teen: So, I should be skeptical about everything I see?

Parent: Be not skeptical but thoughtful. Consider the source of the message and look for multiple viewpoints. Ask yourself if the information is backed by evidence and reflect on how it makes you feel. Advertising, for example, is designed to trigger emotions—like making you feel that you need something to be happy or successful. Being aware of these tactics helps you make more informed choices.

Teen: What if I feel the media influences me too much?

Parent: It's important to take breaks from media and spend time doing non-media-related activities. This helps you gain perspective. Also, surround yourself with diverse sources of information to ensure you see the world from multiple angles, not just through the lens of one media outlet or platform.

What are the dangers of misinformation and fake news, and how do I discern credible sources?

Teen: I keep hearing about misinformation and fake news. Why is it so dangerous, and how can I tell if a source is credible?

Parent: Misinformation and fake news can spread quickly and have real-world consequences, like influencing public opinion, inciting fear, or even affecting elections. To discern credible sources, look for reputable organizations known for accurate and balanced reporting. Cross-reference information with multiple reliable outlets and use fact-checking websites to verify the truth.

Teen: What should I look for in a reliable source?

Parent: A reliable source typically has a clear and transparent editorial policy, cites experts and credible research, and avoids sensationalist language. Check the organization's background—does it have a trustworthy reporting history? Does evidence back their claims? If something sounds too sensational or emotionally charged, it's worth investigating further before believing or sharing it.

Teen: How can I practice verifying information on my own?

Parent: You can start by comparing news stories from different outlets. Look for consistency in facts and figures. Pay attention to the report's tone—credible news presents facts without excessive bias or emotional manipulation. Fact-checking tools like Snopes, FactCheck.org, or the International Fact-Checking Network can also help.

How can I develop critical thinking skills to evaluate information and make informed decisions?

Teen: Critical thinking sounds important, but how do I develop those skills?

Parent: Critical thinking is about questioning and analyzing information rather than accepting it at face value. Practice by asking probing questions like: What evidence supports this claim? Are there any biases at play? Who benefits from this information being spread? Engage in discussions and debates to challenge your views and consider alternative perspectives.

Teen: What's a good way to start practicing this?

Parent: Start by analyzing news articles or social media posts critically. Look at how arguments are constructed—are they based on facts, or are they relying on emotional appeal? Identify any logical fallacies, such as generalizations or false cause-and-effect relationships. Engaging in discussions with friends or online forums where different viewpoints are debated can also help sharpen your critical thinking skills.

Teen: How can I tell if my own thinking is biased?

Parent: We all have biases, but recognizing them is the first step. Reflect on your assumptions and consider how they might affect your interpretation of information. Challenge yourself to see things from different perspectives and seek out sources that contradict your initial beliefs to gain a more balanced view.

What are the ethical considerations of media consumption and online interactions?

Teen: I know it's important to be careful online, but what does it mean to be ethical in consuming media and interacting online?

Parent: Ethics in media and online interactions involve respecting others and being truthful. This means avoiding spreading false information, not engaging in or encouraging harmful behaviors like cyberbullying, and being mindful of the impact of your online actions. It's about being a responsible digital citizen.

Teen: How can I make sure I'm behaving ethically online?

Parent: Think before you post or share content. Ask yourself if it's respectful and truthful and if it could harm others. If you wouldn't say something face-to-face, it's probably best not to say it online. Also, respect others' privacy—don't share personal information or photos without consent. Being ethical online also means being mindful of how your interactions affect others and striving to create a positive digital environment.

Teen: What should I do if I see unethical behaviour online?

Parent: If you see unethical behaviour like cyberbullying or spreading misinformation, consider reporting it to the platform administrators. If it's safe, you can also contact the person involved and encourage them to reconsider their actions. Sometimes, just speaking out against harmful behaviour can make a big difference.

How do I promote digital citizenship and responsible use of technology?

Teen: What does being a good digital citizen mean, and how can I promote responsible use of technology?

Parent: Digital citizenship involves using technology responsibly, respectfully, and safely. This includes protecting your own privacy and security, respecting the rights of others online, and advocating for ethical use of digital platforms. It also means being aware of the digital footprint you leave behind and understanding how your online actions can have long-term consequences.

Teen: What practical steps can I take to promote digital citizenship?

Parent: Lead by example—use technology responsibly, engage positively in online communities, and help others learn about digital safety. Support initiatives that promote online ethics, such as campaigns against cyberbullying, and advocate for policies that enhance digital rights and security. You can also educate your peers about the importance of digital literacy and responsible tech use.

Teen: How can I protect my digital footprint?

Parent: Be mindful of the information you share online. Keep personal details private, use strong passwords, and regularly review the privacy settings on your social media accounts. Before you post, remember that what you share online can be difficult to remove. It's also important to stay informed about the latest digital security practices to protect your data and privacy.

How can I recognize bias in media reporting, and what should I do about it?

Teen: I've heard that media can be biased. How can I spot it, and what should I do when I notice it?

Parent: Bias in media reporting can significantly influence how information is presented and how you perceive it. To recognize bias, look for language that seems loaded or emotionally charged, and check if multiple viewpoints are represented. Consider whether the reporting is one-sided or if it acknowledges different perspectives.

Teen: What should I do if I spot bias in a news article or report?

Parent: If you spot bias, seek out additional sources to get a more balanced view. Compare how different outlets cover the same story and look for inconsistencies or gaps in the coverage. Understanding various perspectives helps you form a more comprehensive and fair opinion. It's also a good idea to question why certain stories are reported in a particular way—what is the potential agenda behind the reporting?

Teen: Should I confront the bias when I see it?

Parent: If you feel comfortable, you can discuss the bias with others, whether in conversations with friends or online forums. The goal isn't necessarily to argue but to raise awareness and encourage critical thinking. You can also support media outlets striving for balanced and fair reporting.

What role does social media play in shaping our opinions, and how can I manage its impact?

Teen: Social media seems to influence how I think about things. How can I make sure it's not shaping my opinions too much?

Parent: Social media can significantly influence your opinions by curating content that aligns with your interests and biases. It often creates echo chambers where you only see viewpoints like yours, limiting your understanding of complex issues.

Teen: How can I manage the impact of social media on my views?

Parent: Diversify your sources of information. Follow accounts and read articles that offer different perspectives, even if they challenge your views. Set limits on your social media use and make time for other activities, like reading books, engaging in face-to-face conversations, or exploring hobbies, to ensure that your views are shaped by a broad range of inputs, not just social media.

Teen: What if I feel like I'm too influenced by what I see on social media?

Parent: Taking regular breaks from social media to regain perspective is important. Reflect on how the content you consume affects your emotions and opinions. If you notice that certain accounts or platforms make you feel anxious, angry, or pressured, consider unfollowing or limiting your exposure. Your mental well-being should always come first.

How can I critically evaluate online reviews and testimonials to determine their reliability?

Teen: I often rely on online reviews before buying something, but I'm unsure how reliable they are. How can I tell?

Parent: Online reviews and testimonials can be helpful but unreliable. Look for reviews from verified users and consider the overall consensus rather than individual opinions. Be cautious of overly positive or negative reviews, as they might be biased or even fake.

Teen: What are some signs that a review or testimonial might not be trustworthy?

Parent: Signs include overly generic language, lack of detail, or patterns of similar phrasing across multiple reviews. Be wary of reviews that seem too extreme—either overly enthusiastic or harsh—without providing specific reasons. Checking reviews across multiple platforms can also help you get a more accurate picture.

Teen: Is there a way to verify if a review is legitimate?

Parent: Yes, you can look for reviews that include detailed descriptions of the product or service and specific experiences. Reviews that mention both pros and cons are often more trustworthy. Some platforms also label reviews from verified purchases, which adds credibility. Additionally, you can cross-reference with professional reviews from reputable sources.

How do echo chambers and filter bubbles impact my understanding of complex issues?

Teen: I've heard about echo chambers and filter bubbles. What impact do they have on how I understand issues?

Parent: Echo chambers and filter bubbles can narrow your understanding by only exposing you to viewpoints that reinforce your existing beliefs. This can limit your awareness of the complexity of issues and hinder critical thinking. When you only see content that aligns with your views, it's easy to overlook or dismiss other perspectives.

Teen: How can I break out of these echo chambers?

Parent: Intentionally seek out diverse sources of information and discuss with people with different perspectives. Reading widely and critically analyzing information from multiple viewpoints will help you gain a more comprehensive understanding of complex issues. It's also helpful to follow social media accounts or join forums that challenge your views, as this encourages you to think critically and consider alternative perspectives.

Teen: What if I'm not sure where to find different viewpoints?

Parent: Start by exploring reputable news outlets worldwide, or look for academic journals and expert analyses on the topics you're interested in. Engaging with communities or groups that hold different views from your own, either online or in person, can also provide valuable insights.

How can I effectively communicate my critical viewpoints in a respectful manner?

Teen: Sometimes, I have strong opinions, but I'm unsure how to express them without causing conflict. How can I communicate my views respectfully?

Parent: Communicating critical viewpoints respectfully involves expressing your ideas clearly and listening to others. Use 'I' statements, like 'I think' or 'I feel,' to share your perspective without accusing or attacking. This way, you focus on your views rather than putting the other person on the defensive.

Teen: What if the conversation gets heated?

Parent: If the conversation becomes tense, try to de-escalate by acknowledging the other person's feelings and steering the discussion back to the issue. It's important to stay calm and avoid personal attacks. If you feel the conversation is becoming unproductive, it might be best to pause and revisit it later when everyone is more composed.

Teen: How can I handle disagreements when communicating my viewpoints?

Parent: Approach disagreements with empathy and a willingness to listen. Focus on finding common ground and understanding the other person's perspective. Even if you don't agree, respecting their viewpoint can lead to a more constructive dialogue. Remember, the goal isn't to win an argument but to exchange ideas and learn from each other.

What are the consequences of spreading misinformation or participating in online debates without proper evidence?

Teen: I see a lot of debates online, and sometimes I want to join in. But what are the consequences if I share something that's not true?

Parent: Spreading misinformation or engaging in debates without evidence can have serious consequences. It can damage your credibility, contribute to the spread of false information, and create unnecessary conflict. It's important to base your arguments on facts and verify information before sharing it.

Teen: What should I do if I realize I've spread misinformation?

Parent: If you realize you've shared something inaccurate, acknowledge the mistake, correct the misinformation, and apologize if necessary. Use the experience as a learning opportunity to improve your media literacy and approach future discussions with a commitment to accuracy and respect. Taking responsibility for your actions online is a key part of being a responsible digital citizen.

Takeaway Points:

1. **Be Critical of Media Messages:** Question who is behind the content and their motives. Distinguish between fact and opinion and recognize persuasive techniques used in advertising.

2. **Verify Information:** Check the credibility of sources and use fact-checking tools. Be cautious of sensational or emotionally charged content.

3. **Develop Critical Thinking Skills:** Practice questioning and analyzing information. Engage in discussions and debates to challenge your assumptions.

4. **Uphold Ethical Standards:** Avoid spreading misinformation and participating in harmful online behaviors. Respect privacy and be a positive online presence.

5. **Promote Responsible Technology Use:** Educate yourself and others about online safety and advocate for ethical digital behaviour.

6. **Recognize and Address Bias:** Identify and critically analyze bias in media reporting. Seek balanced perspectives and verify information from multiple sources.

7. **Manage Social Media Influence:** Diversify your sources of information and be mindful of the impact of social media algorithms on your views.

8. **Evaluate Advertisements Critically:** Analyze the techniques used in advertisements and be cautious of exaggerated claims.

9. **Understand Algorithms and Personalization:** Be aware of how algorithms curate content and actively seek out diverse viewpoints.

10. **Assess Online Reviews Carefully:** Look for reliable reviews, be skeptical of overly positive or negative feedback, and consult multiple sources.

11. **Break Out of Echo Chambers:** Engage with various perspectives and avoid limiting yourself to content that reinforces existing beliefs.

12. **Communicate Respectfully:** Express critical viewpoints clearly and respectfully, focusing on constructive dialogue and mutual understanding.

13. **Avoid Misinformation:** Ensure that your contributions to discussions are evidence-based and correct any mistakes if misinformation is spread.

Parent: By understanding these concepts and practicing media literacy and critical thinking, you'll be better equipped to navigate the complex media landscape and make informed decisions.

Teen: Thanks, I feel like I've got a better handle on approaching media and information now.

Parent: I'm glad to hear that. Remember, it's a continuous learning process. The more you practice these skills, the more confident you'll become in making informed choices and contributing positively to the digital world.

* * *

"It's not your fault. No matter what, you didn't deserve to be hurt."

Chapter 22

Understanding and Preventing Sexual Abuse

Parent: Hey, dear, I wanted to talk about something important today—something that's not always easy to discuss, but it's really crucial. Have you ever considered the issues of sexual abuse and what we can do to prevent it?

Teen: Yeah, I've heard about it in the news and at school, but it's pretty overwhelming. Why do we need to talk about it now?

Parent: It can feel overwhelming, but it's important to talk about these things openly. Sexual abuse is a serious issue that affects many people and understanding it can help us protect ourselves and others. It's about being aware, being prepared, and knowing how to respond if we or someone we know encounters such situations.

What is sexual abuse, and why does it happen?

Teen: So, what exactly is sexual abuse, and why does it happen so often?

Parent: Sexual abuse is any non-consensual sexual activity. This means that it happens without the person's permission and can take many forms, from unwanted touching to more severe forms of assault. Sexual abuse often stems from issues like power imbalances, lack of respect for boundaries, or deeply ingrained societal attitudes. Some people might abuse others because they feel entitled to control or dominate. It's also important to note that such behaviour can happen in various contexts—at home, in schools, or even in seemingly safe environments.

Teen: I get that. But what leads someone to abuse another person?

Parent: Many factors can contribute to abusive behaviour, including a desire for power, control, or dominance. Sometimes, it's about a lack of understanding or respect for boundaries, while other times, it's influenced by societal norms that might condone or ignore such behaviour. It's crucial to understand that no one ever deserves to be abused, and it's never the fault of the victim.

How can I recognize the warning signs of sexual abuse?

Teen: How can I tell if someone I know might be in trouble? What are the warning signs?

Parent: Recognizing sexual abuse can be challenging because victims often feel afraid or ashamed to speak out. However, there are warning signs to watch for. These can include changes in behaviour, such as becoming unusually withdrawn, anxious, or fearful. They might also avoid certain places or people, show sudden changes in their appearance, or lose interest in activities they used to enjoy.

Teen: What should I do if I think someone I know might be in trouble but isn't saying anything?

Parent: It's important to approach the situation with care and sensitivity. Let them know you're there for them and that they can talk to you without judgment. Create a safe and supportive environment where they feel comfortable sharing what's going on. Sometimes, just showing that you care and are willing to listen can make a big difference.

How can I protect myself and others from sexual abuse?

Teen: What can I do to protect myself and others from sexual abuse?

Parent: One of the most empowering things we can do is learn how to protect ourselves and others by understanding and respecting personal boundaries. Everyone has the right to say 'no' and to have their boundaries respected. Trusting your instincts is important—if something feels wrong, it probably is.

Teen: But what if someone tries to cross those boundaries?

Parent: If someone is crossing your boundaries, it's important to stand firm and speak up. You can say something like, 'I'm not comfortable with this,' and remove yourself from the situation if necessary. It's also crucial to seek help from trusted adults, friends, or authorities if you feel threatened. Knowing your rights and having strategies to protect yourself can make a big difference.

How can I support someone who has been a victim of sexual abuse?

Teen: What if I know someone who's been abused? How can I support them?

Parent: Supporting someone who has been abused requires empathy, patience, and understanding. First, listen to them without judgment and offer comfort. Let them know that you believe them and that it's not their fault. Encourage them to seek professional help, like talking to a counselor or therapist, but respect their pace and decisions. It's important to let them know they're not alone.

Teen: What if they don't want to discuss it or seek help?

Parent: It's crucial to respect their boundaries and not push them to talk before they're ready. You can still offer your support by being there for them and checking in regularly. Sometimes just knowing someone is there for them can make a huge difference. If you're really concerned, you might gently suggest that they speak to a trusted adult or professional who can help them navigate their feelings.

How do I report sexual abuse and seek help?

Teen: What should I do if I or someone I know needs help or needs to report abuse?

Parent: If you or someone you know needs help, it's important to contact trusted adults, such as parents, teachers, or school counselors. You can also contact local support organizations, hotlines, or law enforcement. Reporting abuse is a significant step, and it's important to ensure that the victim receives the support and protection they need. Remember, seeking help is a brave and crucial step.

Teen: Is it always necessary to involve authorities?

Parent: Involving authorities can help ensure that the abuse is stopped, and that the abuser is held accountable. It also opens up access to legal protection and resources for the victim. However, the decision to report should be made with the victim's consent whenever possible unless it's a situation where immediate safety is at risk.

How can I contribute to preventing sexual abuse in my community?

Teen: How can I help prevent sexual abuse in my community?

Parent: Preventing sexual abuse starts with promoting respect, consent, and equality in your daily interactions. You can advocate for respectful relationships, educate yourself and others about the importance of consent, and support initiatives that work to prevent abuse. Being an active bystander—standing up and speaking out if you see something wrong—is also a powerful way to contribute.

Teen: What does being an active bystander mean?

Parent: Being an active bystander means recognizing when someone is in a potentially harmful situation and taking steps to intervene safely. This could be by directly addressing the behaviour, supporting the person at risk, or seeking help from others. Even small actions can prevent abuse and make a big difference.

What is consent, and why is it so important?

Teen: I hear a lot about consent. What exactly does it mean, and why is it so important?

Parent: Consent is about giving clear, enthusiastic, and voluntary permission for any sexual activity. It's important because it ensures that both parties agree to what's happening and that their boundaries are respected. Consent must be given freely, without any pressure or coercion, and it can be withdrawn at any time. Ensuring clear communication and mutual respect in any situation is key.

Teen: How can I make sure that consent is clear?

Parent: Always communicate openly with your partner. Ask questions like, 'Are you comfortable with this?' or 'Do you want to keep going?' It's important to check in regularly and ensure that both of you are comfortable and willing. Remember, silence or lack of resistance is not consent, and it's essential to respect the other person's feelings and boundaries.

How does media and culture influence our understanding of sexual abuse?

Teen: How does the media and culture affect how we see and understand sexual abuse?

Parent: Media and cultural messages can sometimes perpetuate harmful stereotypes and normalize abusive behaviour. For example, movies or TV shows might trivialize sexual harassment or portray unhealthy relationships as romantic. It's important to critically evaluate the media you consume and recognize how cultural attitudes might influence perceptions of abuse and consent.

Teen: What should I look out for in media that might be problematic?

Parent: Look for portrayals that trivialize or normalize abusive behaviour, reinforce gender stereotypes, or suggest that consent is not necessary. Question narratives that romanticize controlling or manipulative behaviour and understand how these portrayals can impact real-life attitudes and actions. Challenging these narratives and promoting healthy, respectful relationships in your media is important.

How can trauma from sexual abuse impact a person, and how can I support someone who's experienced it?

Teen: What kind of impact does sexual abuse have on someone, and how can I help them if they're dealing with trauma?

Parent: Experiencing sexual abuse can have profound and long-lasting effects on a person's mental and emotional well-being. Trauma can manifest in various ways, including anxiety, depression, trust issues, and difficulties in relationships. Supporting someone who has experienced trauma involves offering a non-judgmental space where they can share their feelings if they choose to. Encourage them to seek professional support, be patient with their healing process, and respect their boundaries.

Teen: How can I help someone feel safe again?

Parent: Creating a sense of safety involves consistency, reliability, and support. Let them know you're there for them, but don't push them to talk or take steps they're not ready for. Validate their feelings and reassure them that their responses to the trauma are normal. Healing is gradual; your understanding and patience can make a significant difference.

What legal rights and resources are available for victims of sexual abuse?

Teen: What should I know about legal rights and resources if someone I know has been abused?

Parent: It's important to know that there are legal rights and resources available to protect victims of sexual abuse. Different regions have specific laws that provide support and legal aid. Victims have the right to report the abuse to the authorities, seek protective orders, and access counseling and medical services.

Teen: Where can I find this information?

Parent: You can find information through local support organizations, legal aid services, or online resources that guide victims' rights, reporting procedures, and available support. Schools and community centers often have resources as well. It's also important to know that many organizations offer confidential advice and support so victims can seek help without fear of retaliation or exposure.

How can I stay safe online and avoid exploitation?

Teen: The internet seems risky sometimes. How can I stay safe online and avoid being exploited?

Parent: The internet can pose risks, especially when people misuse it to exploit or abuse others. To stay safe online, be cautious about sharing personal information and make sure you understand the privacy settings on your social media accounts. Avoid interacting with strangers, especially if they ask for personal information or try to engage in inappropriate behaviour. If you ever encounter something suspicious or harmful, report it immediately to the appropriate authorities or platforms.

Teen: What should I do if someone makes me uncomfortable online?

Parent: If someone online makes you uncomfortable, trust your instincts and block or report them. You can also talk to a trusted adult about the situation. Never hesitate to remove yourself from a situation that feels wrong, whether it's online or in person.

How can I build healthy relationships based on mutual respect and trust?

Teen: What should I look for in a healthy relationship?

Parent: Healthy relationships are built on mutual respect, trust, and open communication. In a healthy relationship, both partners respect their boundaries, support each other's well-being, and communicate openly about their feelings. There is equality in decision-making, and both individuals feel valued and heard.

Teen: How can I make sure my relationships stay healthy?

Parent: Maintain open and honest communication with your partner. Set and respect boundaries, and make sure both of you are comfortable with the pace and nature of the relationship. It's also important to recognize any signs of unhealthy behaviour, such as jealousy, control, or manipulation, and address them early on. Building a foundation of trust and respect from the start is key to a healthy relationship.

How can I get involved in my community to help prevent sexual abuse?

Teen: How can I contribute to preventing sexual abuse in my community?

Parent: You can get involved by supporting local advocacy groups, educational programs, and campaigns that address sexual abuse prevention. Volunteering, raising awareness, and supporting organizations that combat abuse are valuable ways to contribute. You can also participate in events and workshops that promote consent education and respectful relationships.

Teen: Are there any specific activities I can do?

Parent: You could start by joining or organizing awareness campaigns at your school or community center. You could also volunteer with organizations that support survivors of abuse. No matter how small, every action contributes to creating a safer community.

What myths about sexual abuse should I be aware of?

Teen: Are there any common myths about sexual abuse that I should know about?

Parent: Yes, there are many misconceptions and myths about sexual abuse that can be harmful and misleading. Some people mistakenly believe that only strangers commit sexual abuse, but in reality, it can happen in any context, including with someone the victim knows. Another myth is that victims are to blame for what happens to them, which is never true. Victims are never responsible for the abuse they suffer.

Teen: How can I help challenge these myths?

Parent: You can challenge these myths by educating yourself and others about the realities of sexual abuse. Speak against victim-blaming and support initiatives promoting accurate information and respectful behaviour. By addressing these myths, you help foster a better understanding of the issue and contribute to a more empathetic and informed community.

How can I learn self-defence to protect myself?

Teen: I've heard that self-defence can be helpful. How can I learn it?

Parent: Learning self-defence can empower you to protect yourself in threatening situations. Many community centers, gyms, and organizations offer self-defence classes where you can learn practical skills and strategies to stay safe. These classes often teach techniques for escaping dangerous situations and using your environment to your advantage.

Teen: Is it just about physical defence?

Parent: Self-defence is about physical techniques, awareness, and prevention. Learning to recognize potentially dangerous situations and how to avoid them is a key part of self-defence. It's also about building confidence in asserting your boundaries and reacting quickly.

Takeaway Points:

1. **Understanding and Awareness:** Sexual abuse is a serious issue that can take many forms. Understanding what it is and recognizing the signs is crucial.

2. **Personal Boundaries:** Respecting and communicating personal boundaries is key to protecting oneself and others. Everyone has the right to say 'no' and have their boundaries respected.

3. **Support and Empathy:** Supporting victims involves offering a listening ear, encouraging professional help, and respecting their pace. Empathy and understanding are vital in helping someone heal.

4. **Reporting and Seeking Help:** If you or someone you know is affected by abuse, seeking help from trusted adults or professionals is essential. Reporting to authorities ensures safety and proper support.

5. **Empowering Change:** Advocating for respect and equality and educating others about consent can help prevent abuse and create a safer environment for everyone.

6. **Understanding Consent:** Consent is essential in any sexual activity and must be clear, enthusiastic, and voluntarily given. Always communicate openly and respect boundaries.

7. **Media and Culture Awareness:** Be critical of media portrayals and cultural messages that may normalize or trivialize abusive behaviour.

8. **Impact of Trauma:** Recognize that sexual abuse can have profound psychological effects and offer supportive, non-judgmental care to those affected.

9. **Legal Rights and Resources:** Know your legal rights and available resources for support and reporting abuse. Seek out local organizations and online resources.

10. **Bystander Intervention:** Learn how to intervene and support those affected by abusive behaviour safely. Small actions can contribute to meaningful change.

11. **Online Safety:** Protect yourself from online exploitation by managing privacy settings, being cautious with personal information, and reporting harmful activity.

12. **Healthy Relationships:** Build relationships based on mutual respect, trust, and open communication. Understand the signs of healthy interactions.

13. **Community Involvement:** Engage with community efforts and support organizations working to prevent sexual abuse and promote positive change.

14. **Debunking Myths:** Challenge misconceptions about sexual abuse to foster a more accurate and empathetic understanding of the issue.

15. Self-defence Empowerment: Learn self-defence techniques to build confidence and enhance personal safety.

Parent: I know this is a lot to take in, but having these conversations and being aware is an important step in creating a safer and more respectful world. Remember, you can always come to me with any questions or concerns.

Teen: Thanks for talking about this with me. It's good to know I can rely on you and that there are ways to help and make a difference.

Parent: Absolutely. We're in this together, and by being informed and supportive, we can contribute to positive change. Let's keep this conversation open and ongoing.

* * *

"Injustice anywhere is a threat to justice everywhere."
— Martin Luther King Jr.

Chapter 23

Social Justice and Advocacy

Parent: Let's talk about something really important today—social justice and advocacy. You might often hear these terms, especially when discussing making the world fairer. Social justice ensures everyone has equal rights and opportunities, regardless of background. It's like ensuring everyone gets a fair shot and that no one is held back because of who they are.

Teen: That sounds like something that could make a big difference. But how do we go about making those changes?

Parent: That's a great question. Advocating for social justice means standing up for what's right and working to change unfair systems and practices. It involves understanding the issues, supporting those who are affected, and taking action to create a more equitable world.

What Does Social Justice Mean, and Why Is It Important to Advocate for Change?

Teen: So, what exactly is social justice?

Parent: Social justice means striving for fairness and equality in society. It's about ensuring that everyone has access to the same opportunities and resources, regardless of race, gender, socioeconomic status, or other factors. When we advocate for change, we aim to address the inequalities that have existed and continue to exist, ensuring that everyone can live with dignity and respect.

Teen: Why is it so important to be involved in this?

Parent: Advocating for social justice is crucial because it helps to correct longstanding injustices and inequalities. When we stand up against discrimination and unfair practices, we work towards a society where everyone can succeed and be treated with respect. It's about creating a world with equal rights and opportunities.

How Do I Recognize and Address Systemic Inequalities and Injustices in Society?

Teen: How can I even start to recognize these systemic inequalities?

Parent: Recognizing systemic inequalities involves understanding that these issues are deeply rooted in our institutions and practices. Start by educating yourself about different forms of discrimination—like racial, gender, and economic injustices. Listen to stories from those who experience these inequalities firsthand and be willing to confront your own biases.

Teen: And what can I do once I recognize these issues?

Parent: Once you're aware, you can take action in several ways. Advocate for policy changes, support organizations working towards social justice, and challenge discriminatory behaviors wherever you see them. Use your influence to push for systemic reforms and support marginalized communities in their fight for equality.

What Are Some Ways to Support Marginalized Communities and Promote Inclusivity?

Teen: What practical steps can I take to support marginalized communities?

Parent: There are many ways to make a difference. Start by amplifying the voices of those who are often unheard. Educate yourself about their struggles and advocate for policies that promote inclusivity. Build genuine relationships with people from diverse backgrounds and create safe spaces where everyone feels valued. Supporting minority-owned businesses, volunteering for relevant causes, and participating in local events that promote diversity and inclusion are also impactful ways to contribute.

Teen: What about making sure I'm not contributing to the problem?

Parent: Great point. Self-reflection is key. Regularly examine your own biases and commit to personal growth. Challenge discriminatory attitudes and behaviors in your own life and be proactive about learning and unlearning harmful stereotypes. It's also important to listen to feedback from others, especially those from marginalized groups, and to be willing to change your actions based on what you learn.

How Can I Use My Voice and Privilege to Stand Up for Human Rights and Social Causes?

Teen: How can I effectively use my voice to support human rights?

Parent: Start by educating yourself on the issues that matter to you. Speak out against injustice whenever you see it, whether that's online or in person. Raise awareness by sharing information and supporting causes that align with human rights principles. Your voice can influence others and help drive change, so use it to advocate for policies and practices that promote equality.

Teen: What about challenging my own privilege?

Parent: That's an important aspect. Use your privilege to challenge systems of inequality and advocate for those who may not have the same advantages. Support initiatives that address these disparities and use your influence to push for equity and inclusion. Recognize that privilege comes with the responsibility to stand up for those who are marginalized, and always strive to listen and learn from their experiences.

What Role Does Allyship and Solidarity Play in Creating a More Just and Equitable World?

Teen: What exactly does being an ally involve?

Parent: Being an ally means supporting marginalized communities and actively working to address their struggles. It involves amplifying their voices, advocating for their rights, and challenging systems of oppression. Allyship is about building bridges, confronting biases, and participating in collective action to address and dismantle inequalities.

Teen: How can I be a good ally?

Parent: To be a good ally, listen to and learn from those affected by injustice. Support their efforts and advocate for their rights. Challenge discriminatory practices and policies in your life and promote inclusivity wherever possible. Remember, allyship is an ongoing commitment to learning and taking action. It's not just about words; it's about deeds—standing with others in their fight for justice and being there for them in both big and small ways.

What Are Intersectionality and Its Importance in Social Justice?

Teen: I've heard the term 'intersectionality' a lot lately. What does it mean and why is it important?

Parent: Intersectionality is a concept that describes how different aspects of a person's identity—such as race, gender, class, sexuality, and disability—intersect and create unique experiences of oppression and privilege. Understanding intersectionality helps us to see the complexity of people's experiences and ensures that our advocacy efforts address all aspects of inequality, not just one.

Teen: So, it's about recognizing that people can face multiple forms of discrimination simultaneously?

Parent: Exactly. And by understanding intersectionality, we can ensure that our efforts to fight for social justice are inclusive and consider the full spectrum of people's identities. It's about recognizing that different issues overlap and that addressing them requires a holistic approach.

How Can I Engage in Effective Advocacy Without Overstepping or Speaking for Others?

Teen: How can I advocate effectively without overstepping or speaking for others?

Parent: Effective advocacy involves supporting marginalized communities without overshadowing their voices. To do this, listen actively and amplify the voices of those directly affected by the issues. Use your platform to share their messages and experiences rather than speaking on their behalf. Collaborate with and support organizations led by those communities, and always approach advocacy with humility and respect.

Teen: Is supporting existing movements better than starting my own?

Parent: Often, yes. Supporting existing movements ensures that your efforts align with the needs and goals of those directly affected. It's about standing in solidarity with them rather than taking over. If you do start something new, make sure it's done in consultation with and with the support of the community you're advocating for.

What Are the Challenges of Activism, and How Can I Stay Motivated?

Teen: What are some activism challenges, and how can I stay motivated even when it gets tough?

Parent: Activism can be challenging due to resistance from those opposed to change, burnout from constant engagement, and the slow pace of systemic change. To stay motivated, focus on the positive impact of your efforts, celebrate small victories, and surround yourself with a supportive community. Practicing self-care and setting realistic goals to prevent burnout is also important. Remember, change often takes time, and every action contributes to the larger movement.

Teen: What can I do if I start feeling burned out?

Parent: It's crucial to recognize when you're feeling overwhelmed and take a step back if needed. Engage in self-care, whether taking time off, spending time with loved ones, or doing something that recharges you. It's also helpful to delegate tasks or seek support from others in your community. Remember, activism is a marathon, not a sprint—pacing yourself is key to long-term sustainability.

How Can I Address and Combat Microaggressions in Daily Life?

Teen: What are microaggressions, and how can I address them when I encounter them?

Parent: Microaggressions are subtle, often unintentional, comments or behaviors that perpetuate stereotypes or demean marginalized individuals.

They can be challenging to address because they are sometimes dismissed as minor. To combat microaggressions, educate yourself about what they are and how they affect people. When you witness or experience a microaggression, address it calmly and assertively. Use 'I' statements to express how it impacts you or others, and encourage open dialogue to foster understanding and change.

Teen: What if the person doesn't realize they're being offensive?

Parent: Many times, people don't know they're being hurtful. That's why it's important to approach the conversation empathetically, explaining how their words or actions came across. This can open up a dialogue where they can learn and grow from the experience, leading to positive change.

What Are the Ethical Considerations When Participating in Social Justice Movements?

Teen: What ethical considerations should I consider when participating in social justice movements?

Parent: Yes, there are several ethical considerations. Respect the leadership and decisions of those directly affected by the issues. Avoid performative actions that are more about showing off your involvement than making a real impact. Ensure that your advocacy work is informed and respectful, and avoid co-opting the struggles of marginalized groups for personal gain or visibility. Always strive to be genuine allies and work towards meaningful, collaborative change.

Teen: How can I ensure my actions are genuine and not just performative?

Parent: Focus on the impact of your actions rather than how they appear to others. Engage in advocacy because it's the right thing to do, not because it will make you look good. Be consistent in your efforts, support long-term change, and always center the voices and needs of the communities you advocate for.

How Can I Support Social Justice Efforts in My School or Community?

Teen: How can I support social justice efforts right here in my school or community?

Parent: You can start by educating your peers about social justice issues and organizing or participating in events and discussions that promote awareness. Support or join school clubs or community groups focused on social justice. Advocate for inclusive policies and practices within your school or local organizations. Volunteer with local groups that address social justice issues and collaborate with others to create initiatives that foster equity and inclusion.

Teen: What if I face pushback for my efforts?

Parent: It's not uncommon to encounter resistance when advocating for change. Stay focused on your goals and remember why you're doing this work. Seek support from like-minded individuals and continue to educate yourself and others. Sometimes, persistence and patience are needed to bring about meaningful change.

How Can I Balance Activism with My Other Responsibilities?

Teen: I want to be actively involved in social justice work, but I'm worried about balancing it with my other responsibilities. Do you have any tips?

Parent: Balancing activism with other responsibilities requires time management and prioritization. Set clear goals for your activism work and create a schedule that allows you to manage your time effectively. Break down your tasks into manageable steps and prioritize the most impactful activities. It's also important to communicate your boundaries and ensure you're taking care of your well-being. Remember, you don't have to do everything at once; consistent, small actions can still make a significant difference.

Teen: How do I know what to prioritize?

Parent: Consider what actions will impact you most and align with your skills and passions. Focusing on one or two areas where you can make a meaningful difference rather than spreading yourself too thin is okay. It's also important to be flexible and adjust your priorities as needed.

How Can I Evaluate the Impact of Social Justice Efforts and Ensure They Are Effective?

Teen: How can I assess whether social justice efforts are making a difference?

Parent: To evaluate the impact of social justice efforts, set clear, measurable goals, and assess progress towards them. Seek feedback from the communities you're working to support and be open to their input on improving. Look at both qualitative and quantitative indicators of success, such as policy changes, increased awareness, and tangible improvements in the lives of those affected. Regularly review and adjust your strategies based on what's working and what isn't, and ensure your efforts are aligned with the needs and priorities of the communities you're supporting.

Teen: What if I don't see immediate results?

Parent: Change often takes time, especially when addressing deep-rooted issues. Stay committed to your goals and keep the bigger picture in mind. Even small, incremental progress is valuable. Sometimes, the impact of your efforts may not be immediately visible, but that doesn't mean they're not making a difference.

Takeaway Points:

1. **Understanding Social Justice:** Social justice ensures fairness and equality in society, addresses systemic inequalities, and advocates for equal rights and opportunities.

2. **Recognizing Systemic Inequalities:** Educate yourself about different forms of discrimination and listen to those affected. Take action by supporting reforms and challenging discriminatory practices.

3. **Supporting Marginalized Communities:** Amplify voices, educate yourself, advocate for policy changes, build relationships, create safe spaces, support minority businesses, and engage in self-reflection.

4. **Using Your Voice and Privilege:** Educate yourself on human rights issues, speak out against injustice, raise awareness, support marginalized voices, challenge your own privilege, and participate in advocacy efforts.

5. **Allyship and Solidarity:** Support marginalized communities, amplify their voices, build understanding, challenge oppression, and engage in collective action for justice and equity.

6. **Intersectionality Matters:** Understand how overlapping identities affect experiences of discrimination and privilege, and ensure your advocacy addresses all aspects of inequality.

7. **Effective Advocacy:** Support marginalized voices without overshadowing them and collaborate with those directly affected by the issues.

8. **Challenges of Activism:** Be aware of resistance and burnout, and stay motivated by celebrating progress and practicing self-care.

9. **Combating Microaggressions:** Educate yourself, address microaggressions calmly, and encourage open dialogue.

10. **Ethical Participation:** Respect leadership, avoid performative actions and ensure your advocacy is genuine and collaborative.

11. **Supporting Local Efforts:** Educate peers, engage in community initiatives, and advocate for inclusive practices.

12. **Balancing Responsibilities:** Manage your time effectively, set clear goals, and communicate your boundaries.

13. **Evaluating Impact:** Set measurable goals, seek community feedback, and review strategies regularly to ensure effectiveness.

Parent: I hope this discussion has illuminated the importance of social justice and advocacy. It's about making a real difference and standing up for what's right. Remember, every action counts in the journey towards a more just and equitable world.

Teen: Thanks for this conversation. I feel more equipped to take action and support these important causes.

Parent: I'm proud of your commitment. Let's keep working together to advocate for change and support one another in these efforts.

* * *

"The problem is not the problem. The problem is your attitude about the problem."
— *Captain Jack Sparrow (from Pirates of the Caribbean)*

Chapter 24

Decision-Making and Problem-Solving

Parent: Hey, I've noticed you've been making some big decisions lately, and I thought it might be a good time for us to talk about how you approach decision-making and problem-solving. It can be overwhelming to weigh options and solve problems, and we all face it at different stages in life.

Teen: Yeah, it's been tough. I want to make sure I'm making the right choices, but sometimes I just feel stuck or unsure of what to do.

Parent: I totally get that. Decision-making and problem-solving are skills that can be developed over time. Let's break it down together, and I'll share some strategies and tips to help you feel more confident in your choices.

How Do I Approach Decision-Making Processes and Weigh My Options?

Parent: When you're faced with a decision, it's important to have a systematic approach. Here's a method that can help you make informed choices.

- **Define the Decision:** First, clearly understand what decision needs to be made. What's at stake, and why is it important to you?

- **Gather Information:** Collect all the relevant facts and data. This might include researching options, seeking advice, and understanding potential outcomes.

- **Identify Alternatives:** List all possible options. Don't limit yourself—think creatively about different paths you could take.

- **Evaluate Options:** Assess the pros and cons of each option. Consider how each aligns with your values and goals.

- **Consider Consequences:** Think about the potential long-term effects of each choice. How will it impact your life and the lives of others?

- **Make a Decision:** Choose the option that best fits your criteria and feels right. Trust your judgment and make a decision.

- **Take Action:** Implement your choice with a clear plan. Set goals and timelines to ensure you stay on track.

- **Reflect and Learn:** Afterward, reflect on the decision-making process. What worked well? What could be improved for next time?

Teen: That sounds like a solid approach. It helps to break things down step-by-step rather than feeling overwhelmed.

What Are the Steps Involved in Problem-Solving and Finding Solutions to Challenges?

Parent: Problem-solving can be approached in a structured way. Here's a method to tackle challenges effectively.

- **Define the Problem:** Clearly state the issue you're facing. Understanding the root cause is key to finding a solution.

- **Gather Information:** Collect data and insights related to the problem. Different perspectives can provide valuable context.

- **Generate Options:** Brainstorm possible solutions. Consider both traditional and creative approaches.

- **Evaluate Options:** Assess each solution's feasibility, risks, and benefits to determine which is the most practical and effective.

- **Make a Decision:** Choose the best solution based on your evaluation. Be confident in your choice.

- **Implement the Solution:** Create a plan to execute your chosen solution. Assign tasks and set deadlines.

- **Monitor Progress:** Track how the solution is working. Be prepared to adjust if needed.

- **Evaluate Results:** Assess the effectiveness of the solution. Did it resolve the problem? What can you learn from the experience?

- **Learn and Adapt:** Reflect on what you learned from the process. Use these insights to improve your problem-solving skills for the future.

Teen: I think having a clear process will help me feel more organized when facing problems.

How Can I Overcome Indecision and Develop Confidence in My Choices?

Parent: Indecision can be challenging, but there are ways to build confidence in your decisions.

- **Clarify Your Values:** Identify what's important to you. Your values will guide your decision-making.

- **Set Clear Goals:** Define what you want to achieve. Clear goals can make decision-making easier.

- **Gather Information:** Collect relevant information to support your choices. The more you know, the more confident you'll feel.

- **Trust Your Instincts:** Pay attention to your gut feelings. Sometimes your intuition can offer valuable insights.

- **Practice Decision-Making:** Start with small decisions to build your confidence. Gradually tackle more significant choices.

- **Embrace Imperfection:** Accept that no decision is perfect. Focus on making the best choice with the information you have.

- **Seek Support:** Consult with trusted people when needed. Their perspectives can provide clarity and reassurance.

- **Practice Self-Compassion:** Be kind to yourself. Making mistakes is part of the learning process.

- **Reflect and Learn:** Use past decisions as learning experiences. Reflect on what worked and what didn't.

Teen: I think understanding that it's okay to make mistakes and learn from them will definitely help me be more confident.

What Role Does Intuition and Gut Instinct Play in Decision-Making?

Parent: Intuition and gut instinct can play a significant role in decision-making. Here's how they contribute.

- **Immediate Response:** Intuition often provides a quick, instinctual reaction. It's your subconscious mind's way of guiding you.

- **Pattern Recognition:** Intuition helps you recognize patterns based on past experiences, even if you're unaware of them.

- **Fast Decision-Making:** It allows for quick decisions when time is limited, by trusting your immediate feelings.

- **Integration of Information:** It combines various pieces of information, including your emotions and values, to guide your choices.

- **Risk Assessment:** Gut instinct can alert you to potential risks that aren't immediately obvious.

- **Creativity and Innovation:** Intuition can lead to creative solutions and novel ideas that might not be evident through conventional thinking.

- **Personal Alignment:** It helps you make choices that align with your true self and long-term goals.

Teen: Thinking about how intuition and logic can work together in decision-making is interesting.

How Do I Learn from Past Experiences and Apply Them to Future Decisions?

Parent: Learning from past experiences is a powerful way to improve your decision-making. Here's how you can do it.

- **Reflect on Past Decisions:** Think about past decisions and their outcomes. What went well, and what didn't?

- **Identify Lessons Learned:** Extract key lessons from those experiences. What did you learn about your decision-making process?

- **Adjust Your Approach:** Use these lessons to refine your approach to future decisions. Incorporate successful strategies and avoid past mistakes.

- **Set Goals and Objectives:** Based on your reflections, set goals for future decisions and define success.

- **Seek Feedback:** Ask for feedback from others. Their perspectives can help you see things you might have missed.

- **Stay Flexible:** Be open to new information and adapt your decisions as needed. Each situation is unique.

- **Practice Self-Compassion:** Be kind to yourself. Learn from your experiences without being too hard on yourself.

Teen: I'll try to use what I've learned from past experiences to make better decisions in the future.

How Can I Use a Decision Matrix to Evaluate My Options?

Parent: A decision matrix is a great tool for evaluating multiple options. Here's how you can use it effectively.

- **List Your Options:** List all the options you're considering.

- **Define Criteria:** Identify the criteria that are important for your decision. This could include cost, impact, feasibility, or personal preferences.

- **Rate Each Option:** Rate each option based on your criteria. Use a scale from 1 to 5, where 1 is the least favorable and 5 is the most favorable.

- **Weight the Criteria:** Assign weights to each criterion based on its importance. For example, if cost is more important than convenience, give it a higher weight.

- **Calculate Scores:** Multiply the rating of each option by the weight of each criterion and sum up the scores. This will give you a total score for each option.

- **Compare and Decide:** Compare each option's total score. The option with the highest score should generally be the most suitable choice.

Teen: That sounds like a practical way to compare options objectively. I'll try using a decision matrix for my next big choice.

What Are Some Strategies for Managing Decision-Making Under Pressure?

Parent: Making decisions under pressure can be tough, but there are strategies to help you manage it better.

- **Stay Calm:** Take deep breaths and try to stay calm. Panic can cloud your judgment and make it harder to think clearly.

- **Prioritize:** Identify the most important aspects of the decision. Focus on what really matters and don't get bogged down by less critical details.

- **Limit Your Choices:** If you're overwhelmed by too many options, try to narrow them down to a few key ones. This makes it easier to evaluate and decide.

- **Use a Timeout:** If possible, give yourself a brief break. Sometimes, stepping away from the situation can help you return with a clearer perspective.

- **Consult Others:** If you're unsure, seek advice from trusted friends or family. They can offer valuable perspectives and help you feel more confident.

- **Trust Yourself:** Remember that you've faced tough decisions before and made it through. Trust in your ability to make a good choice.

Teen: I'll definitely remember these strategies, especially the idea of taking a timeout and consulting others.

How Can I Build Resilience in the Face of Decision-Making Setbacks?

Parent: Building resilience is important, especially when things are unplanned. Here's how you can strengthen it.

- **Accept Imperfection:** Understand that not every decision will have a perfect outcome. Accept that setbacks are part of the process.

- **Focus on Growth:** View setbacks as opportunities to learn and grow. Reflect on what went wrong and how you can improve next time.

- **Stay Positive:** Maintain a positive outlook. Remind yourself of past successes and how you've overcome challenges before.

- **Develop Coping Strategies:** Find healthy ways to cope with stress and frustration, such as exercising, talking to friends, or practicing mindfulness.

- **Set Realistic Goals:** Set achievable goals and break them down into smaller, manageable steps. This can make challenges feel less overwhelming.

- **Seek Support:** Don't hesitate to seek support from mentors, counselors, or support groups. They can offer guidance and encouragement.

Teen: I like the idea of viewing setbacks as learning opportunities. It's comforting to know that it's okay not to get everything right.

How Can I Balance Short-Term and Long-Term Goals When Making Decisions?

Parent: Balancing short-term and long-term goals is crucial for making well-rounded decisions. Here's how you can approach it.

1. **Identify Your Goals:** Clearly define your short-term and long-term goals. Understand how each goal aligns with your overall aspirations.

2. **Evaluate Impact:** Consider how each decision impacts both your immediate needs and future objectives. Will it help you achieve your long-term goals while addressing short-term concerns?

3. **Create a Plan:** Develop a plan that includes steps for both short-term and long-term goals. Ensure that your decisions support your broader vision while addressing current needs.

4. **Monitor Progress:** Regularly review your progress toward both short-term and long-term goals. Adjust your plan as needed to stay on track.

5. **Make Trade-Offs:** Sometimes, you may need to trade between short-term and long-term goals. Weigh the benefits and drawbacks of each option carefully.

6. **Stay Flexible:** Be open to adjusting your goals and plans as circumstances change. Flexibility allows you to adapt and stay aligned with your evolving priorities.

Teen: Balancing both types of goals seems challenging but important. I'll try to keep my long-term vision in mind while making decisions for immediate needs.

How Can I Use Decision-Making Frameworks to Improve My Choices?

Parent: Decision-making frameworks can provide structure and clarity. Here are a few frameworks to consider.

1. **SWOT Analysis:** Assess the Strengths, Weaknesses, Opportunities, and Threats related to each option. This helps you understand the broader context of your choices.

2. **Cost-Benefit Analysis:** Compare the costs and benefits of each option. Weighing the pros and cons helps you see the potential value of each choice.

3. **Pareto Principle:** Apply the 80/20 rule by focusing on the 20% of factors that will give you 80% of the results. This helps prioritize what's most impactful.

4. **Decision Tree:** Create a visual representation of different decision paths and their potential outcomes. This helps you see the consequences of each choice more clearly.

5. **Five Whys:** Ask 'Why?' five times to get to the root cause of a problem. This helps clarify the underlying issue and guide you towards effective solutions.

6. **Six Thinking Hats:** Use different perspectives to evaluate a decision: facts (White), emotions (Red), judgment (Black), optimism (Yellow), creativity (Green), and process (Blue). This broadens your approach.

Teen: These frameworks seem like they could help organize my thoughts and make more structured decisions.

Takeaway Points:

1. **Structured Decision-Making:** Use a systematic approach to make informed choices by defining the decision, gathering information, evaluating options, and reflecting on outcomes.

2. **Effective Problem-Solving:** To tackle challenges, follow a step-by-step process from defining the problem to implementing and evaluating solutions.

3. **Overcoming Indecision:** Build confidence by clarifying your values, setting goals, trusting your instincts, and learning from past experiences.

4. **Role of Intuition:** Intuition can provide valuable insights and guide quick decisions, especially when combined with rational analysis.

5. **Learning from Experience:** Reflect on past decisions, identify lessons learned, and use those insights to improve future decision-making.

6. **Decision Matrix:** Use a decision matrix to objectively evaluate and compare options based on defined criteria and weights.

7. **Managing Pressure:** To make effective decisions under pressure, employ strategies like staying calm, prioritizing, and consulting others.

8. **Building Resilience:** Strengthen resilience by accepting imperfection, focusing on growth, and seeking support during setbacks.

9. **Balancing Goals:** Balance short-term and long-term goals by evaluating impacts, creating plans, and staying flexible.

10. **Decision-Making Frameworks:** Utilize frameworks like SWOT Analysis, Cost-Benefit Analysis, and Decision Trees to enhance decision-making clarity and effectiveness.

Parent: I hope these strategies help you feel more confident in your decisions and problem-solving efforts. Remember, it's all about practice and learning from each experience.

Teen: Thanks for the guidance! I feel more equipped to handle decisions and challenges now.

* * *

"You can't pour from an empty cup. Take care of yourself first."

Chapter 25

Self-Care and Well-being

Parent: Hey dear! I've been thinking a lot about how we all juggle so many things in our lives. Between school, work, and everything else, forgetting to care for ourselves is easy. Do you ever feel like you're running on empty and just need a break?

Teen: Absolutely! Sometimes, it feels like there's just no time for me with all the assignments and social stuff. I've heard people talk about self-care, but I'm unsure what it means or how to make it part of my daily routine.

Parent: Self-care is about taking intentional steps to look after yourself, both physically and emotionally. It's crucial because it helps us stay balanced and resilient. Let's explore what self-care is all about and how you can integrate it into your busy life.

What Does Self-Care Mean, and Why Is It Important for Overall Well-Being?

Teen: So, what exactly is self-care? Why should it be a big deal for me?

Parent: Self-care is all about taking time to attend to your own needs and well-being. It's more than just pampering yourself; it's about maintaining a healthy balance in your life. Here's why it's so important:

- **Promotes Physical Health:** Regular self-care practices like exercise, eating well, and getting enough sleep help keep you healthy and prevent illness.

- **Supports Mental Health:** Relaxing and mindfulness can help reduce anxiety and depression and boost your overall mental health.

- **Enhances Emotional Well-being:** Addressing your emotions in healthy ways, like talking to someone you trust or engaging in enjoyable activities, helps improve emotional resilience.

- **Increases Resilience:** By caring for yourself, you build the strength to handle challenges and setbacks more effectively.

- **Improves Relationships:** When you care for yourself, you have more energy and patience to nurture your relationships with others.

- **Boosts Productivity and Creativity:** Taking breaks and engaging in hobbies can enhance your focus and creativity, helping you perform better in various areas of your life.

- **Fosters Self-Compassion:** Self-care helps you develop a kind and compassionate relationship with yourself, which is the foundation for overall well-being.

Teen: That makes a lot of sense! How do I figure out what I need and how to prioritize self-care?

How Do I Identify My Personal Needs and Prioritize Self-Care Practices?

Parent: Identifying your needs and setting up a self-care routine involves a bit of self-reflection and experimentation. Here's how you can do it:

- **Self-Reflection:** Consider your current lifestyle and where you might be feeling depleted or stressed. Consider what areas of your life might need more attention.

- **Journaling:** Keep a journal to track what activities make you feel good and what drains your energy. This can help you identify patterns and areas for improvement.

- **Mindfulness Practices:** Incorporate mindfulness techniques like meditation or deep breathing to help you become more aware of your needs and feelings.

- **Set Boundaries:** Learn to say no to things that don't align with your values or that overextend you. Protect your time and energy.

- **Experimentation:** Try different self-care activities to see what resonates with you. This could include exercise, hobbies, or spending time with loved ones.

- **Listen to Your Body:** Pay attention to physical signs of stress or fatigue. Prioritize activities that help you relax and recharge.

- **Identify Triggers:** Notice what situations or environments cause stress or discomfort, and develop strategies to manage these triggers.

- **Create a Self-Care Plan:** Create a plan that includes regular self-care activities based on your reflections. Make it a priority in your schedule.

- **Practice Self-Compassion:** Be kind to yourself as you navigate this process. Self-care is a journey, and adjusting your approach as needed is okay.

Teen: I think I understand better now. What are some specific self-care activities I could try out?

What Self-Care Activities and Rituals Can I Incorporate into My Daily Routine?

Parent: Great question! Here are some self-care activities you can weave into your daily routine:

- **Morning Routine:** Start your day with something positive, like stretching, journaling, or enjoying a healthy breakfast.

- **Movement and Exercise:** Find an activity you enjoy, such as walking, dancing, or yoga, and make it a regular part of your routine.

- **Mindfulness Practices:** Incorporate mindfulness through deep breathing, meditation, or simply being present in the moment.

- **Healthy Nutrition:** Eat balanced meals with the necessary energy and nutrients. Don't skip meals and try to eat a variety of foods.

- **Hydration:** Drink plenty of water throughout the day to stay hydrated.

- **Rest and Relaxation:** Allocate time to unwind with activities like reading, listening to music, or bathing.

- **Connection:** Spend quality time with friends and family. Meaningful interactions can boost your mood and strengthen relationships.

- **Creativity:** Engage in creative activities such as drawing, writing, or playing a musical instrument to express yourself.

- **Nature Time:** Spend time outdoors to enjoy the natural world. Even a short walk in the park can be rejuvenating.

- **Digital Detox:** Take breaks from screens to reduce stress and engage in offline activities.

Teen: Those sound great! How can I be kinder to myself and cultivate self-compassion?

How Can I Cultivate Self-Compassion and Kindness Towards Myself?

Parent: Cultivating self-compassion is really important. Here's how you can do it:

- **Practice Self-Kindness:** Treat yourself with the same kindness you'd offer a friend. If you make a mistake, be supportive rather than critical.

- **Challenge Negative Self-Talk:** Remember when you're overly critical and replace those thoughts with positive, compassionate ones.

- **Cultivate Mindfulness:** Be present with your emotions and thoughts without judgment. This helps you understand yourself better and be kinder.

- **Practice Self-Care:** Regularly engage in activities that you enjoy and that make you feel good.

- **Set Boundaries:** Establish healthy limits to protect your well-being.

- **Celebrate Your Strengths:** Recognize and celebrate your achievements and positive qualities.

- **Practice Self-Compassion Exercises:** Try exercises like writing a kind letter to yourself or practicing loving-kindness meditation.

- **Seek Support:** Surround yourself with supportive people and seek help when needed.

- **Embrace Imperfection:** Understand that being imperfect is part of being human. Accept and love yourself despite your flaws.

- **Reflect on Common Humanity:** Remember that everyone faces struggles and challenges, and you're not alone in your experiences.

Teen: That's really helpful. Lastly, how can I create a supportive environment that promotes my well-being?

How Do I Create a Supportive Environment That Nurtures My Physical, Emotional, and Mental Health?

Parent: Creating a supportive environment involves several key elements:

- **Prioritize Self-Care:** Make sure self-care is part of your daily routine. This includes physical activities, relaxation, and enjoyable activities.

- **Surround Yourself with Positive Influences:** Build relationships with people who support and uplift you.

- **Create Boundaries:** Set boundaries to protect your energy and well-being. Say no when necessary and focus on what aligns with your values.

- **Practice Mindfulness:** Incorporate mindfulness into your daily life to manage stress and enhance self-awareness.

- **Seek Professional Support:** If you're struggling, don't hesitate to contact mental health professionals for guidance and support.

- **Create a Supportive Physical Environment:** Ensure your space is organized and comfortable and surrounds you with positive influences.

- **Engage in Meaningful Activities:** Pursue activities that give you a sense of purpose and joy.

- **Practice Self-Compassion:** Be kind and understanding with yourself, especially during tough times.

- **Set Realistic Goals:** Set achievable goals and celebrate your progress.

- **Reflect and Adjust:** Regularly evaluate and adjust your environment and habits to support your well-being.

Teen: Thanks for all this information! I better understand self-care and how to make it work for me.

Parent: I'm glad to hear that! Remember, self-care is a journey, and it's important to keep adjusting and finding what works best for you. It's all about nurturing yourself and creating a balanced and fulfilling life.

How Can Self-Care Impact My Daily Life?

Teen: I understand that self-care is important, but how does it affect my daily life?

Parent: Self-care can have a huge impact on your daily life. When you care for yourself, you will likely feel more energized and focused. This means you might find it easier to handle stress, perform better at school, and maintain better relationships with friends and family. Essentially, self-care helps you function at your best.

Teen: So, it's not just about feeling good but also about doing well in other areas of life?

Parent: Exactly! Self-care supports your overall effectiveness and happiness. It's like filling up your gas tank so you can drive smoothly—without it, you might run out of energy and become less effective.

What If I Don't Have Time for Self-Care with My Busy Schedule?

Teen: My schedule includes schoolwork, extracurriculars, and social activities. How can I fit self-care into that?

Parent: It's all about finding small ways to integrate self-care into your routine. It doesn't have to be a big-time commitment. You can start with short, simple practices like taking a 5-minute mindfulness break, doing a quick workout, or even just ensuring you get enough sleep. The key is to prioritize self-care and be creative with how you fit it into your day.

Teen: So, even short bursts of self-care can make a difference?

Parent: Absolutely! Even small acts of self-care can accumulate and greatly impact your overall well-being. The important part is consistency and ensuring that self-care becomes a regular part of your life.

How Can I Balance Self-Care with My Responsibilities and Goals?

Teen: I want to make sure I'm balancing self-care with my responsibilities and goals. How can I manage that?

Parent: Balancing self-care with responsibilities requires good time management and setting priorities. Start by scheduling self-care into your calendar, just like you would with any other important task. Also, be mindful of setting realistic goals for yourself and avoid overcommitting. It's about creating a healthy balance where you care for your needs while still pursuing your responsibilities and goals.

Teen: How can I ensure that self-care doesn't become another source of stress?

Parent: Self-care should be something you look forward to, not something that adds to your stress. To avoid this, make self-care activities enjoyable and stress-free. Choose activities that genuinely make you feel good and relaxed. And remember, it's okay to adjust your self-care practices based on what's working for you.

How Do I Handle Guilt About Taking Time for Myself?

Teen: Sometimes, I feel guilty about taking time for myself when I know there are things I need to do. How can I overcome that guilt?

Parent: It's common to feel guilty, but it's important to recognize that taking time is essential for maintaining your health and productivity. Think of self-care as an investment in your well-being that will ultimately make you more effective and resilient. It's not selfish; it's necessary. You're better equipped to meet your responsibilities and support others by caring for yourself.

Teen: That makes sense. So, is self-care a way to recharge so I can be at my best?

Parent: Exactly! When you recharge, you're more capable of handling your tasks and being there for others. Self-care is a form of self-respect and self-love.

What Role Does Self-Compassion Play in Self-Care?

Teen: How does self-compassion fit into the whole self-care thing?

Parent: Self-compassion is a fundamental aspect of self-care. It means treating yourself with kindness and understanding, especially when things are unplanned. When you practice self-compassion, you're more likely to engage in self-care without judgment or criticism. It helps you acknowledge your imperfections and approach yourself with empathy, which is crucial for long-term well-being.

Teen: So, being kind to myself can help me take better care of myself?

Parent: Yes, exactly! Self-compassion encourages you to be gentle with yourself, which makes it easier to engage in self-care practices and navigate challenges more effectively.

How Can I Create a Self-Care Plan That Works for Me?

Teen: How do I create a self-care plan that fits my life?

Parent: Start by reflecting on what areas of your life need attention and what self-care practices resonate with you. List out activities that support your physical, emotional, and mental health. Create a schedule that incorporates these activities regularly, and be flexible. Adjust your plan based on what's working and what's not. Remember, a personal self-care plan should be tailored to your unique needs and preferences.

Teen: Do I need to always stick to the same self-care activities?

Parent: Not at all! Your self-care plan should evolve with your needs and circumstances. Feel free to experiment with different activities and adjust your plan as needed. The goal is to find what works best for you and helps you feel balanced and fulfilled.

Takeaway Points:

1. **Self-Care is Essential:** It promotes physical health, supports mental well-being, enhances emotional resilience, and improves relationships and productivity.

2. **Identify Needs:** Reflect on your lifestyle, experiment with different activities, and create a personalized self-care plan.

3. **Daily Rituals:** Incorporate exercise, mindfulness, healthy eating, and quality time with loved ones into your routine.

4. **Self-Compassion:** Treat yourself with kindness, challenge negative self-talk and practice self-compassion exercises.

5. **Supportive Environment:** Surround yourself with positive influences, set boundaries, and engage in meaningful activities to create a nurturing space for well-being.

6. **Self-Care Basics:** Self-care involves intentional actions to maintain physical, emotional, and mental health. It is crucial for overall well-being, helping to recharge, reduce stress, and enhance life balance.

7. **Impact on Daily Life:** Self-care improves energy, focus, and effectiveness, supporting better performance in various areas of life, including school, work, and relationships.

8. **Time Management:** Integrate self-care into your routine, even in small ways, to manage a busy schedule effectively. Consistency is key.

9. **Balancing Responsibilities:** Prioritize self-care alongside responsibilities by setting realistic goals and managing time well. Ensure that self-care becomes a regular, enjoyable part of your life.

10. **Overcoming Guilt:** Self-care is not selfish but an essential investment in your health and effectiveness. Address guilt by recognizing the positive impact of self-care on overall well-being.

11. **Role of Self-Compassion:** Self-compassion is integral to self-care. Treat yourself with kindness and understanding, which supports a positive and effective self-care practice.

12. **Creating a Self-Care Plan:** Reflect on your needs, experiment with different activities, and create a flexible self-care plan tailored to your personal preferences and lifestyle.

Parent: By embracing these practices, you can cultivate a lifestyle supporting your overall health and happiness, ensuring you thrive personally and in your interactions with others.

Teen: Thanks for all the tips! I'm ready to start integrating self-care into my life and see how it affects me.

Parent: I'm proud of you for taking this step. Remember, self-care is a lifelong journey, and it's all about finding what works best for you. Let's keep the conversation going and support each other along the way.

* * *

"You are more powerful than you know; you are beautiful just as you are."
— *Melissa Etheridge*

Chapter 26

Growing Up Confident: A Guide for Teenage Girls

Mother: "Hey, Sweetie, I know being a teenager can be exciting and overwhelming. There's so much happening—school, friendships, family, and your future. I thought it would be helpful if we took some time to discuss all these aspects together. We'll cover everything from self-care to planning for your future, and I want us to make sure you feel supported and informed as you navigate this phase of your life. How does that sound?"

Daughter: "That sounds great, Mom. I've been feeling like there's a lot to manage and understand, and talking through it with you will definitely help."

Mother: "Perfect. Let's break this down into key areas of your life and discuss each in detail. We'll talk about your well-being, school, relationships, self-esteem, and future planning, among other things. Ready?"

Daughter: "Absolutely! Let's dive in."

Self-care and Well-Being

Mother: "Self-care is foundational to your overall well-being. It's about taking care of yourself physically, mentally, and emotionally. Let's explore each aspect."

Daughter: "What are some ways I can practice good self-care?"

Mother: "Here's a comprehensive guide:

- **Physical Health:** Regular exercise, balanced nutrition, and sufficient sleep are crucial. Aim for at least 30 minutes of physical activity daily, eat a variety of healthy foods, and get 7-9 hours of sleep each night.

- **Mental Health:** Engage in activities that relax and rejuvenate you, such as reading, listening to music, or practicing mindfulness. Consider keeping a journal to express your thoughts and emotions.

- **Emotional Health:** Surround yourself with supportive friends and family. Practice self-compassion and seek professional help if you're struggling with anxiety, depression, or other emotional challenges."

Daughter: "Sometimes I feel stressed and overwhelmed. What are some effective stress management techniques?"

Mother: "Here are some strategies to manage stress:

- **Time Management:** Create a schedule to manage your tasks and avoid last-minute stress. Use planners or digital tools to keep track of deadlines and commitments.

- **Relaxation Techniques:** Try deep breathing exercises, progressive muscle relaxation, or meditation. Even a few minutes a day can make a big difference.

- **Physical Activity:** Exercise releases endorphins, which help reduce stress. Find a physical activity you enjoy, like dancing, swimming, or jogging.

- **Social Support:** Talk to friends, family, or a mentor when you're feeling overwhelmed. Sometimes, just sharing what you're going through can provide relief."

School and Academic Planning

Mother: "School can be demanding, but you can manage it well with effective planning and strategies. Let's discuss how you can excel academically."

Daughter: "I often feel stressed about schoolwork and exams. How can I stay organized and motivated?"

Mother: "Here are some tips:

- **Organization:** Use a planner or app to keep track of assignments, tests, and deadlines. Break large tasks into smaller, manageable steps.

- **Study Techniques:** Identify what study methods work best for you. This could include making flashcards, summarizing notes, or teaching the material to someone else.

- **Time Management:** Allocate specific times for studying and stick to them. Avoid procrastination by setting clear goals and deadlines for each study session.

- **Seek Help:** Don't hesitate to ask teachers for clarification or extra help if needed. Join study groups for collaborative learning."

Daughter: "I'm also thinking about my future career. How can I start exploring different career options?"

Mother: "Consider these steps:

- **Research:** Look into various careers and their requirements. Websites like O*NET or the Bureau of Labor Statistics can provide detailed information.

- **Internships and Volunteering:** Gain practical experience through internships, part-time jobs, or volunteer work. This will give you a sense of what different jobs are like.

- **Networking:** Talk to professionals in fields that interest you. Ask them about their experiences and the skills required for their roles.

- **Career Counseling:** Utilize school career services or seek advice from a career counselor to explore your interests and options."

Relationships and Social Skills

Mother: "Navigating friendships and social interactions is a significant part of your teenage years. Let's talk about how to build and maintain healthy relationships."

Daughter: "I sometimes struggle with peer pressure and conflicts with friends. What should I do?"

Mother: "Building healthy relationships involves:

- **Effective Communication:** Be open and honest in your conversations. Practice active listening and express your thoughts and feelings clearly.

- **Setting Boundaries:** Establish and respect personal boundaries. It's important to know when to say no and to protect your well-being.

- **Healthy Friendships:** Surround yourself with friends who support and uplift you. Positive friendships can significantly impact your self-esteem and happiness.

- **Conflict Resolution:** Learn to address conflicts calmly and respectfully. Focus on finding solutions rather than placing blame."

Daughter: "What about handling peer pressure? It's hard to stay true to myself sometimes."

Mother: "Peer pressure can be challenging, but you can handle it by:

- **Knowing Your Values:** Be clear about what you stand for and what's important to you. This will help you make decisions that align with your values.

- **Practicing Assertiveness:** It's okay to say no. Practice assertive communication to express your choices firmly but respectfully.

- **Seeking Support:** Find friends who share your values and support your decisions. Having a support system can help you resist negative influences.

Body Image and Self-Esteem

Mother: "Body image and self-esteem are critical aspects of your self-worth. Let's discuss developing a positive body image and strong self-esteem."

Daughter: "I often compare myself to others and feel insecure about my appearance. How can I feel more confident?"

Mother: "Developing a positive body image involves:

- **Self-Acceptance:** Focus on your strengths and what you like about yourself. Practice self-compassion and avoid negative self-talk.

- **Healthy Lifestyle:** Engage in activities that make you feel good and contribute to your well-being. Remember, health is about feeling good in your body, not meeting certain standards.

- **Avoid Comparisons:** Everyone is unique, and comparisons can lead to dissatisfaction. Celebrate your individuality and recognize your value beyond physical appearance.

- **Positive Influences:** Surround yourself with media and people who promote diverse and realistic beauty standards."

Daughter: "How can I build my self-esteem and confidence?"

Mother: "Here are some strategies:

- **Set Achievable Goals:** Set and achieve small goals to build confidence. Celebrate your successes, no matter how small.

- **Self-Care:** Engage in activities that boost your mood and well-being. Taking care of yourself can enhance your self-image.

- **Positive Affirmations:** Practice affirmations to reinforce positive beliefs about yourself. Focus on your strengths and accomplishments.

- **Seek Feedback:** Constructive feedback from trusted sources can help you grow and build confidence."

Future Planning and Life Skills

Mother: "Preparing for the future involves planning and developing life skills. Let's explore how you can get ready for adulthood."

Daughter: "I'm feeling a bit overwhelmed about planning for the future. What are some important areas to focus on?"

Mother: "Consider these key areas:

- **Financial Literacy:** Learn about budgeting, saving, and managing money. Create a budget and practice saving a portion of any money you receive.

- **Career Exploration:** Research career options, set goals, and develop skills relevant to your interests. Consider internships or part-time jobs to gain experience.

- **Life Skills:** Develop essential skills like cooking, laundry, and time management. These skills are crucial for independent living.

- **College and Vocational Training:** Research educational options and application processes. Consider what education or training you need for your desired career path."

Daughter: "What about handling setbacks and adapting to change?"

Mother: "Resilience is key to navigating life's challenges:

- **Adaptability:** Be flexible and open to change. Life rarely goes according to plan, so being adaptable will help you manage unexpected situations.

- **Problem-Solving:** Develop problem-solving skills to address challenges effectively. Break problems into manageable parts and consider possible solutions.

- **Support System:** Seek support from friends, family, or mentors during difficult times. They can provide guidance and encouragement.

- **Reflect and Learn:** Use setbacks as opportunities to learn and grow. Reflect on what happened, what you can improve, and how to move forward."

Personal Development and Growth

Mother: "Personal development is about growing and becoming the best version of yourself. Let's discuss ways to foster personal growth."

Daughter: "What can I do to support my personal development?"

Mother: "Consider these approaches:

- **Goal Setting:** Set short-term and long-term goals for yourself. Goals give you direction and motivation.

- **Self-Reflection:** Take time to reflect on your experiences and personal growth. Consider what you've learned and how you've changed.

- **Learning Opportunities:** Pursue new experiences and challenges. Learning new skills or hobbies can contribute to personal growth.

- **Feedback and Improvement:** Seek feedback from others and use it to improve. Be open to constructive criticism and use it as a tool for growth."

Media Literacy and Critical Thinking

Mother: "In today's digital age, it's important to be media literate and develop critical thinking skills. Let's talk about how to navigate media effectively."

Daughter: "With so much media and information out there, how can I discern what's credible and what's not?"

Mother: "Here are some tips:

- **Source Evaluation:** Check the credibility of sources. Look for reliable and reputable sources rather than those with questionable accuracy.

- **Fact-Checking:** Verify information from multiple sources before accepting it as true. Use fact-checking websites to confirm the accuracy of claims.

- **Critical Thinking:** Analyze and question the information you encounter. Consider the purpose, bias, and evidence behind the content.

- **Digital Citizenship:** Practice responsible technology use. Be mindful of your online presence and respect others in digital spaces."

Family Dynamics and Communication

Mother: "Family dynamics play a significant role in your life. Let's explore how to improve communication and understanding within your family."

Daughter: "Sometimes there are misunderstandings or conflicts at home. How can we improve communication and relationships?"

Mother: "Consider these strategies:

- **Open Communication:** Practice open and honest conversations with family members. Share your thoughts and listen to theirs.

- **Conflict Resolution:** Address conflicts calmly and respectfully. Focus on finding solutions rather than placing blame.

- **Understanding Roles:** Understand and respect each family member's role and contributions. This can help improve family dynamics.

- **Quality Time:** Spend quality time together to strengthen family bonds. Engage in activities that everyone enjoys and that foster connection."

Responsible Behavior and Citizenship

Mother: "Being a responsible citizen involves understanding and fulfilling your responsibilities to yourself and others. Let's discuss what that means."

Daughter: "What does responsible behaviour and citizenship look like?"

Mother: "Here's what to consider:

- **Responsibility:** Take ownership of your actions and their consequences. Be reliable and accountable in your commitments.

- **Community Involvement:** Participate in community activities and volunteer work. Contributing to your community helps you grow as a responsible citizen.

- **Ethics and Integrity:** Uphold ethical standards and act with integrity. Make decisions based on your values and principles.

- **Respect and Inclusivity:** Treat others with respect and promote inclusivity. Embrace diversity and work towards creating a positive and inclusive environment."

Mother: "I'm so proud of how you're navigating these aspects of your life. Remember, seeking help and taking things one step at a time is okay. You have the tools and support you need to thrive."

Daughter: "Thanks, Mom. This has been really helpful. I feel more prepared to handle everything and make informed decisions."

Takeaway Points:

1. **Prioritize Self-Care:** Maintain your physical, mental, and emotional well-being through healthy habits and relaxation techniques.

2. **Manage Stress:** Use time management, stress-relief strategies, and seek social support to cope with stress effectively.

3. **Stay Organized in School:** Use planning tools and effective study methods and seek help to excel academically.

4. **Build Healthy Relationships:** Communicate openly, set boundaries, and confidently handle peer pressure.

5. **Cultivate a Positive Body Image:** Embrace your uniqueness, avoid comparisons, and focus on self-acceptance.

6. **Plan for the Future:** Develop financial literacy, explore career options, and build essential life skills.

7. **Develop Resilience:** Adapt to change, problem-solve effectively, and seek support to overcome challenges.

8. **Foster Personal Growth:** Set goals, reflect on experiences, and seek learning opportunities to develop personally.

9. **Navigate Media Wisely:** Evaluate sources, fact-check information, and practice responsible technology use.

10. **Improve Family Dynamics:** Communicate openly, address conflicts respectfully, and spend quality time with family.

11. **Embrace Responsible Citizenship:** Be accountable for your actions, participate in your community, and act with integrity.

Mother: "This comprehensive guide aims to provide you with the tools and insights you need to navigate every important aspect of your life with confidence, resilience, and a sense of purpose."

Daughter: "Thanks, Mom! I feel more confident and ready to take on whatever comes my way."

Mother: "You've got this, Sweetie! And remember, I'm always here to support you."

* * *

"A father is a man who expects his son to be as good a man as he meant to be."
— *Frank A. Clark*

Chapter 27

A Father and Son's Guide to Growing Up

Father: Hey, my boy! It's great to sit down and have this talk with you. These teenage years are a time of huge changes and challenges, and I want to ensure you feel supported as you navigate through them. We'll cover much ground today—everything from understanding yourself and setting goals to managing relationships and preparing for the future.

Son: I appreciate that, Dad. Sometimes it feels like there's a lot to deal with, and I'm not sure where to start. What's the best way to tackle all of this?

Father: Let's take it step-by-step. We'll start with self-discovery and goal-setting, then move on to managing school, relationships, and more. This way, we'll cover all the important areas and give you practical advice for each one.

Understanding Yourself and Setting Goals

Son: I know having goals is important, but how do I figure out what I really want?

Father: Start by exploring your passions and interests. Think about what activities or subjects make you excited. Also, consider your strengths—what are you naturally good at? Once you sense these, set both short-term and long-term goals. For example, if you enjoy programming, a short-term goal might be to learn a new coding language, while a long-term goal could be pursuing a career in technology.

Son: That makes sense. What if I'm still unsure about my interests?

Father: That's okay. Sometimes it takes time to figure out what you're truly passionate about. Try out different activities, join clubs, or take classes in various subjects. Exposure to different experiences can help you find what resonates with you.

Managing Schoolwork and Academic Challenges

Son: I've been struggling to keep up with my schoolwork. Do you have any tips for staying organized?

Father: Absolutely. One effective method is to create a study schedule. Break your work into manageable tasks and prioritize them. Use a planner or a digital app to keep track of assignments and deadlines. Establishing a dedicated study area that is free from distractions can also be helpful.

Son: What if I'm having trouble with a specific subject?

Father: Don't hesitate to ask for help. Talk to your teacher, seek out tutoring resources, or form a study group with classmates. Sometimes, discussing the material with others can provide new insights and make it easier to understand.

Building Healthy Relationships

Son: How do I handle conflicts with friends or family?

Father: Communication is key. When you disagree, listen to the other person's perspective and express your own feelings calmly. It's important to approach conflicts with a problem-solving mindset rather than being confrontational. Building strong relationships involves mutual respect and understanding.

Son: How can I tell if a relationship is healthy?

Father: A healthy relationship is one where both people feel valued and respected. There should be open communication, trust, and support. It may be worth reassessing if you find that a relationship consistently makes you unhappy or stressed.

Navigating Peer Pressure and Making Choices

Son: I sometimes feel pressured to do things just to fit in. How should I handle that?

Father: It's important to stay true to your values. Practice being assertive and confident in your decisions. Remember, real friends will respect your choices and not pressure you into doing something you're uncomfortable with. Having a few supportive friends who share your values can also be helpful.

Understanding Identity and Self-Esteem

Son: I struggle with self-esteem and comparing myself to others. How can I improve my self-image?

Father: Start by focusing on your strengths and achievements. Celebrate your successes, no matter how small they might seem. Engage in activities that make you feel good about yourself, and practice self-compassion. Everyone has unique qualities, and comparing yourself to others is often unproductive.

Son: What if I still feel insecure?

Father: It's okay to feel insecure at times. Talking about your feelings with someone you trust can be very helpful. Additionally, working on self-acceptance and setting realistic goals can help improve your confidence over time.

Handling Stress and Mental Health

Son: I often feel stressed and overwhelmed. What are some ways to manage stress effectively?

Father: There are several strategies you can use to manage stress. Regular physical activity, such as playing sports or walking, can help relieve tension. Mindfulness practices, like meditation or deep breathing exercises, can also be beneficial. It's important to make time for hobbies and relaxation. And if you're feeling persistently stressed, talking to a mental health professional can provide additional support.

Developing Financial Responsibility

Son: I've started earning some money from a part-time job. How should I manage it wisely?

Father: It's great that you're learning about financial responsibility. Start by creating a simple budget to track your income and expenses. Allocate a portion of your earnings for savings and consider setting aside some money for future goals or emergencies. Learning about basic financial concepts, such as saving and investing, will also help you manage your money more effectively.

Exploring Future Career and Education Paths

Son: I'm thinking about what to do after high school. How do I decide on a career path?

Father: Begin by researching different career options and exploring your interests. Consider what subjects you enjoy and what kind of work environment you thrive in. It's also a good idea to talk to professionals in fields you're interested in and seek internships or volunteer opportunities to gain hands-on experience. This exploration will help you make more informed decisions about your future career and education.

Building Healthy Habits and Personal Responsibility

Son: What habits should I focus on developing now that will benefit me in the future?

Father: Developing good habits early on can set a strong foundation for the future. Focus on maintaining a balanced diet, exercising regularly, and practicing good hygiene. Time management is also crucial—establish routines that help you stay organized and fulfill your commitments. Taking responsibility for your actions and punctuality are important traits that will serve you well in adulthood.

Navigating Technology and Social Media

Son: I spend a lot of time on social media. How can I use technology responsibly?

Father: Set boundaries for screen time and be mindful of how technology affects your daily life. Make sure to engage in offline activities and hobbies. Be cautious about the content you consume and share online and protect your privacy by being selective about the personal information you disclose. Remember that online interactions should be respectful and positive.

Embracing Diversity and Inclusivity

Son: I want to be more aware of diversity and inclusivity. How can I support these values in my community?

Father: Start by educating yourself about different cultures, perspectives, and experiences. Engage in conversations that promote understanding and inclusivity. Support initiatives and organizations that work towards diversity and equality. Being an ally means advocating for those who may be marginalized and standing up against discrimination.

Developing Resilience and Coping Skills

Son: How can I become more resilient when facing challenges?

Father: Resilience is about bouncing back from setbacks and adapting to adversity. Develop a positive mindset and focus on solutions rather than problems. Build a support network of friends, family, and mentors who can offer guidance and encouragement. Learning from your experiences and maintaining a balanced perspective can also help you navigate challenges with greater ease.

Understanding Gender and Sexuality

Son: I'm curious about gender and sexuality. What's important to know?

Father: Gender and sexuality are complex and diverse. It's important to approach these topics with an open mind and respect for others' identities.

Educate yourself about different gender identities and sexual orientations and be supportive of those who may have different experiences from your own. Understanding and respecting diversity in these areas fosters an inclusive environment.

Preparing for Independence and Adulthood

Son: I want to prepare for more independence as I get older. What should I focus on?

Father: Preparing for independence involves developing practical life skills. Learn to manage your finances, cook for yourself, and manage your health. Start practicing self-care and making informed decisions. It's also important to understand the responsibilities of independence and gradually take on more tasks and responsibilities as you grow.

Celebrating Achievements and Learning from Failures

Son: How should I handle my successes and setbacks?

Father: Celebrate your achievements and use them as motivation for future goals. When facing setbacks, view them as opportunities to learn and grow. Reflect on what went wrong, adjust, and move forward with a renewed focus. Both successes and failures are valuable parts of your journey and contribute to your overall growth.

Takeaway Points:

1. **Self-Discovery and Goals:** Explore your interests, set realistic goals, and seek guidance to clarify your path.

2. **Academic Management:** Develop effective time management and organizational skills to stay on top of your studies.

3. **Healthy Relationships:** Communicate openly, maintain respect, and evaluate relationships to ensure they are supportive.

4. **Peer Pressure:** Stay true to your values, practice assertiveness, and choose friends who respect your choices.

5. **Self-Esteem:** Focus on your strengths, practice self-compassion, and engage in activities that boost confidence.

6. **Stress Management:** Use healthy coping strategies, seek support when needed, and prioritize mental well-being.

7. **Financial Responsibility:** Create a budget, save regularly, and learn about financial planning.

8. **Future Planning:** Research career options, seek hands-on experience, and make informed decisions about education.

9. **Healthy Habits:** Establish nutrition, exercise, and personal responsibility routines.

10. **Technology Use:** Set boundaries, be mindful of online interactions, and protect your privacy.

11. **Diversity and Inclusivity:** Educate yourself, support diverse communities, and advocate for equality.

12. **Resilience:** Develop a positive mindset, build support networks, and learn from experiences.

13. **Gender and Sexuality:** Approach these topics with respect and openness, and educate yourself about diverse identities.

14. **Independence:** Learn essential life skills, understand responsibilities, and gradually prepare for adulthood.

15. **Achievements and Failures:** Celebrate successes, learn from setbacks, and use both as opportunities for growth.

Father: I'm really proud of you, son. You're navigating these challenges with maturity, and I'm always here to support you as you grow.

Son: Thanks, Dad. This conversation has helped me feel more prepared and confident in handling what comes my way.

Father: You've got a bright future ahead, and I'm excited to see all the great things you'll achieve.

* * *

"To keep the body in good health is a duty... otherwise we shall not be able to keep our mind strong and clear."
— Buddha

Chapter 28

Understanding Your Body's Needs

Father: Son, I've noticed you're growing up fast, and I can see you're going through a lot of changes. How are you feeling about everything?

Son: Honestly, Dad, it's a bit confusing. My body is changing, and I have so many questions, but I don't know where to start.

Father: I totally get that. Puberty is a big part of growing up, and it's normal to feel a little lost. I'm here to help you understand these changes and answer any questions. Let's talk about everything—no topic is off-limits.

Son: That sounds good. I've heard some things from friends, but I want to get the right information.

Father: That's a smart move. Let's dive into it and go through all the important things together.

Understanding the Male Reproductive System

Son: Can we start with the basics? What are the different parts of the male reproductive system, and what do they do?

Father: Sure. The male reproductive system comprises several key parts, each with an important role. First, there are the testes responsible for producing sperm and the hormone testosterone. Testosterone drives the changes you're seeing now—like your voice getting deeper and the growth of body hair. The scrotum is the sac that holds the testes, keeping them at the right temperature for sperm production.

Then, there's the epididymis, a tube where sperm mature and are stored until ejaculation. The vas deferens is a duct that transports sperm from the epididymis to the urethra. The seminal vesicles and the prostate gland produce the fluid that combines with sperm to form semen. This fluid is crucial because it nourishes the sperm and helps them move. The urethra is the tube that carries semen out of the body during ejaculation, and it's also the pathway for urine. Finally, there's the penis, which becomes erect during sexual arousal and is involved in both urination and sexual intercourse.

Son: That's a lot to take in, but it's starting to make sense now.

Father: It's a lot of information, but understanding how everything works is the first step in caring for your health.

How Puberty Affects Boys

Son: Why does my body go through these changes during puberty?

Father: Puberty is your body's way of preparing you for adulthood, both physically and emotionally. It's driven by hormones, particularly testosterone in your case. This hormone causes your body to develop in several ways: your muscles get bigger, your voice deepens, and you start to grow facial and body hair. Internally, it's also preparing your body for reproduction.

Son: Is everyone's experience with puberty the same?

Father: Not exactly. Everyone goes through puberty at their own pace. Some start earlier, others later, and that's perfectly normal. What's important is that these changes are all part of growing up.

Hormones and Their Role

Son: So, are hormones responsible for all these changes?

Father: Exactly. Hormones like testosterone and growth hormone are the main drivers of puberty. They're responsible for all the physical changes, but they also affect your emotions and mood. That's why you might feel more emotional or have mood swings—it's all part of the process.

Son: That explains a lot. Sometimes I feel like I'm on an emotional rollercoaster.

Father: I've been there, too. It's completely normal, and feeling a wide range of emotions is okay. What's important is learning how to manage them.

The Importance of Self-Care During Puberty

Son: What can I do to take care of myself during all these changes?

Father: Taking care of yourself is crucial during puberty. Regular exercise, a balanced diet, and getting enough sleep are the basics. Staying active helps manage stress and keeps your body healthy as it grows. Eating well gives your body the nutrients it needs to develop properly. And sleep? That's when your body does a lot of its growing and repairing, so don't skip out on it.

Son: What about personal hygiene? I've noticed I sweat a lot more now.

Father: Good observation. During puberty, your sweat glands become more active, which is why you might notice you sweat more, and sometimes it smells stronger. Daily showers, using deodorant, and wearing clean clothes will help you stay fresh. Also, since your skin might get oilier and more prone to acne, washing your face regularly is important.

Sexual Health and Safe Practices

Son: Dad, I've been hearing a lot about sex and protection. What should I know?

Father: That's a big topic, but it's great that you're asking. When it comes to sex, the most important things are consent, respect, and safety. Always ensure you and your partner are on the same page and feel comfortable. Using protection, like condoms, is essential to prevent sexually transmitted infections and unplanned pregnancies. There are also other forms of contraception, but condoms are the only method that protects against STIs.

Son: And what if someone feels pressured into sex?

Father: You should never feel pressured into doing anything you're not ready for. Consent is not just important; it's mandatory. You have every right to say no at any time, and so does your partner.

Emotional Changes and Mental Health

Son: Sometimes I feel really stressed or anxious, and I'm not sure how to handle it. Is that normal?

Father: Absolutely. Puberty can be a stressful time, and it's normal to feel anxious or overwhelmed. The key is to talk about your feelings—whether it's with me, another trusted adult, or even a friend. Sometimes just talking about what's on your mind can help relieve stress. If you ever feel like it's too much, there's no shame in asking for help from a counselor or therapist.

Son: I'll keep that in mind. It's good to know I'm not alone in this.

Father: You're definitely not alone. Everyone goes through this, and it's okay to ask for help whenever you need it.

Navigating Relationships and Social Life

Son: How should I handle relationships and making new friends during this time?

Father: Relationships can be tricky during puberty because everyone is figuring themselves out. My best advice is to be yourself and treat others with respect. Friendships based on honesty and mutual respect will last longer and be more fulfilling. As for romantic relationships, take things slow. It's important to get to know someone and ensure you're both on the same page before moving forward.

Son: That makes sense. Sometimes, it feels like a lot of pressure to have a girlfriend or be popular.

Father: I get it but remember that you don't have to conform to anyone else's expectations. Focus on being the best version of yourself, and the right friendships and relationships will follow.

Dealing with Peer Pressure and Making Wise Choices

Son: Peer pressure is tough. What if I'm in a situation where I feel pressured to do something I'm not comfortable with?

Father: Peer pressure can be challenging, but standing your ground is important. It's okay to say no and to stick to your values. If someone tries to pressure you into doing something you're not comfortable with—whether it's drinking, smoking, or anything else—remember that you don't owe anyone an explanation for your decisions. True friends will respect your choices.

Son: I'll try to remember that. It's just hard sometimes.

Father: It can be, but it gets easier with practice. The more you stand by your values, the stronger you'll become in resisting peer pressure.

Understanding Sexual Orientation and Identity

Son: I've also been thinking a lot about sexual orientation and identity. How do I figure out where I fit?

Father: That's a personal journey and taking your time with it is okay. Your sexual orientation and identity are about who you are, and there's no rush to label yourself. What's most important is that you feel comfortable with who you are. Surround yourself with people who support and accept you, and don't hesitate to talk to me or another trusted adult if you have questions or just need to talk.

Body Image and Confidence

Son: Sometimes I feel self-conscious about how I look. How do I build confidence?

Father: Building confidence starts with appreciating your body for what it can do, not just how it looks. Focus on your strengths—whether it's your abilities, your character, or your achievements. Remember that everyone's body is different, and that's okay. Limiting exposure to unrealistic body images you see in the media is also important. Comparing yourself to those images can be harmful. Instead, focus on being healthy and taking care of your body.

Handling Changes in School and Social Life

Son: School feels different now, too. There's more pressure and more to think about.

Father: That's true. As you grow older, school becomes more challenging, but it's also a time when you can discover your interests and talents. It's important to stay organized and manage your time well. Don't be afraid to ask for help when you need it, whether it's from teachers, friends, or me. And remember, it's okay to take breaks and relax when things get overwhelming.

The Role of Technology and Social Media

Son: What about social media? It's everywhere, and sometimes it feels like too much.

Father: Social media can be a great way to stay connected, but it's also important to use it wisely. Set limits on your time online and be mindful of what you share. Not everything you see on social media is real, and it's easy to fall into the trap of comparing yourself to others. Use social media as a tool, but don't let it control you. And remember, you can always take a break from it if you need to.

Planning for the Future and Setting Goals

Son: I'm starting to think about the future, but it's a bit overwhelming. How do I start planning?

Father: It's great that you're thinking ahead. Start by setting small, achievable goals to help you achieve your larger dreams. Whether it's doing well in school, exploring new hobbies, or thinking about future careers, having goals gives you direction. Take it one step at a time and remember that it's okay to change your goals as you learn more about yourself and the world.

Father: We've covered a lot today, and I'm really proud of you for asking all these important questions. Remember, growing up is a journey, and it's okay to take things one step at a time. Keep asking questions, stay true to yourself, and always make informed decisions.

Son: Thanks, Dad. This talk helped me understand more about what I'm going through.

Father: I'm glad to hear that. You're never alone in this, and I'm always here to talk. Just remember to take care of yourself, respect your own and others' boundaries, and keep an open mind as you grow.

Son: I will. Thanks for being here for me.

Father: Always, son. Let's continue this conversation as you grow and learn more about yourself. You're on a great path.

Takeaway Points:

1. **Understand Your Body:** Learn about the male reproductive system and the changes that occur during puberty.

2. **Manage Hormonal Changes:** Hormones play a crucial role in physical and emotional development; understanding them helps manage hormonal changes.

3. **Prioritize Self-Care:** Exercise, a balanced diet, and good hygiene are essential during puberty.

4. **Practice Safe Sexual Health:** Learn about consent, protection, and the importance of mutual respect in relationships.

5. **Handle Emotional Changes:** It's normal to feel a range of emotions; talking about them can help manage stress and anxiety.

6. **Build Healthy Relationships:** Focus on respect, honesty, and mutual understanding in all relationships.

7. **Resist Peer Pressure:** Stand by your values and make decisions that are right for you.

8. **Explore Your Identity:** Take your time to understand your sexual orientation and identity and seek support if needed.

9. **Develop Body Confidence:** Appreciate your body for its strengths and focus on being healthy.

10. **Navigate School and Social Life:** Stay organized, manage your time well, and ask for help.

11. **Use Technology Wisely:** Limit your social media use and consider its impact on your self-esteem.

12. **Plan for the Future:** Set achievable goals and take one step at a time towards your dreams.

This chapter aims to provide teenage boys with the knowledge and confidence to navigate the physical, emotional, and social changes of growing up, ensuring they feel supported and prepared for the future.

* * *

"The chains of habit are too weak to be felt until they are too strong to be broken."
— *Samuel Johnson*

Chapter 29

Understanding Teenage Addictions

Parent: Hey, my boy and sweetie, can we discuss something important? I want to discuss addiction with you—what it is, how it develops, and what you need to be aware of. It's a serious topic but understanding it can really help.

Teen: Sure, I'm listening. What exactly is addiction?

Parent: Addiction is when someone becomes dependent on a substance, like drugs or alcohol, or a behaviour, like gaming or social media. They start needing more of it to feel the same effects and continue doing it even when it causes problems in their life. It's not just about a lack of willpower—it's actually a chronic condition that changes how the brain works.

Teen: How does someone even get to that point?

Parent: It usually starts with trying something out of curiosity or because of peer pressure. At first, it feels good, and the brain starts associating that substance or activity with pleasure. Over time, the brain needs more of it to feel the same way, leading to tolerance and dependence. Eventually, it can turn into a full-blown addiction where the person can't stop, even if they want to.

Teen: So, does everyone who tries something get addicted?

Parent: Not necessarily. A mix of factors influences addiction. Genetics play a big role—if someone has a family history of addiction, they're at higher risk. But environmental factors like stress, trauma, peer pressure, and even how easily available the substance or behaviour is can also contribute. It's like a puzzle with many pieces.

How to Recognize Signs of Addiction

Teen: That makes sense. But how would I know if someone, like a friend or even me, is struggling with addiction?

Parent: There are several warning signs. Behavior changes are big—like if someone starts being secretive, skipping school, or hanging out with a different crowd. Mood swings, anxiety, and depression can also be signs. You might notice physical changes too, like neglecting hygiene, weight changes, or always looking tired. And if someone is always asking for money or you find drug paraphernalia, those are red flags too.

Teen: That sounds serious. What should someone do if they notice these signs in themselves or someone else?

Parent: The first step is to talk about it openly. Approach the person with care and empathy and let them know you're concerned. It's important to listen and support them, not judge. If it's you, contact someone you trust, like a parent, teacher, or counselor. Professional help is crucial—doctors, therapists, or addiction specialists can provide the right treatment and support. And remember, recovery is possible, but it often requires ongoing support and effort.

The Role of Genetics and the Environment

Teen: I see. Is it true that some people are more likely to get addicted because of their genes?

Parent: Yes, genetics can make someone more susceptible. If addiction runs in the family, the risk is higher. But it's not just about genes—environmental factors also matter. For example, if someone is exposed to a lot of stress or trauma, or if they're in a social environment where substance use is common, it can increase the likelihood of addiction. But just because someone has a genetic predisposition doesn't mean they will become addicted. It's a combination of factors.

Behavioral Addictions: Gaming and Social Media

Teen: What about things like gaming or social media? Can those really be addictive?

Parent: Absolutely. Behavioral addictions, like gaming or social media, can be just as serious as substance addictions. They can take over a person's life, leading to neglect of responsibilities, social isolation, and even mental health issues like anxiety and depression. The brain's reward system gets overstimulated, making it hard to control the behaviour, even when it's causing harm.

Teen: Wow, I didn't realize it could be that bad. How can we protect ourselves from getting addicted?

Parent: Being aware is the first step. Recognize the risks and make informed choices. Set healthy boundaries for things like gaming or social media use, and be mindful of how substances can affect your body and mind. Surround yourself with supportive friends and family, and don't be afraid to seek help if you ever feel like something is becoming too much to handle. Remember, taking care of your mental and physical health is key.

Peer Pressure and Social Influences

Parent: Let's continue our discussion about addiction, especially focusing on how peer pressure and social influences contribute to teenage addictions, and the differences between experimentation and addiction.

Teen: Yeah, I'm curious. How do peer pressure and social influences play a role in this?

Parent: Peer pressure is a major factor during your teenage years. It's natural to want to fit in and be accepted by your friends. This can sometimes lead to experimenting with substances like alcohol or drugs, even if you're not really interested in them. You might feel like you have to try something just to belong.

Teen: So, it's more about wanting to fit in?

Parent: Exactly. The desire for social acceptance is powerful. If your friends are using substances, you might feel pressured to join in so you don't feel left out. Plus, in group settings, risky behaviors like substance use can seem more normal or less dangerous. This kind of indirect pressure can be just as influential as someone directly encouraging you to try something.

Teen: What about social media? Does that make it worse?

Parent: Definitely. Social media often glamorizes substance use. Seeing posts or stories of people drinking, vaping, or using drugs can create the impression that these behaviors are common and acceptable, which might make you more inclined to try them yourself. The fear of missing out, or FOMO, also plays a big role—you might feel like you need to participate to be part of the fun.

Experimentation vs. Addiction

Teen: That makes sense. But how do you tell the difference between just experimenting and being addicted?

Parent: Experimentation is usually about trying something out of curiosity or because of social influence. It's not frequent, and you still have control over whether you do it or not. Addiction, on the other hand, is when you start using a substance regularly, feel like you need it to cope with things, and keep using it even when it's causing problems in your life.

Teen: So, experimentation doesn't always lead to addiction?

Parent: No, not always. But there's a risk, especially if it becomes more frequent. Some people can experiment and then stop, but others might start using more often, develop a tolerance, and eventually become dependent on the substance. That's when it moves from experimentation to addiction.

Teen: What if someone is already experimenting? How can you tell if it's turning into an addiction?

Parent: Look for changes in behaviour. If someone starts using substances more frequently, neglects their responsibilities, or starts losing interest in things they used to enjoy, those are red flags. If they're using substances to cope with stress or emotions, or if they feel like they can't stop, that's a sign that it might be turning into an addiction.

Teen: That sounds serious. How do you prevent it from getting that far?

Parent: It's all about early intervention and making healthy choices. If you ever feel pressured or notice these warning signs in yourself or a friend, it's important to talk to someone you trust, like a parent, teacher, or counselor. The sooner you address it, the better your chances of stopping it before it becomes a bigger problem.

Addiction's Impact on Relationships

Teen: How does addiction affect the relationships I have with my family and friends?

Parent: Addiction can have a big impact on your relationships with those closest to you. When someone is struggling with addiction, they might start breaking promises, like saying they'll stop using but then not following through. This can lead to a loss of trust.

Teen: So, it's like people start to lose faith in them?

Parent: Exactly. When trust is broken, it's really hard to repair. And it's not just about trust—addiction can also create a lot of emotional strain. Arguments become more frequent, and the person struggling with addiction may withdraw emotionally, becoming distant from family and friends.

Teen: I guess that would make everyone feel pretty lonely.

Parent: It does. And in families, addiction can turn things upside down. Sometimes kids have to take on adult responsibilities because their parents are too caught up in their addiction. This role reversal can cause resentment and long-term emotional issues.

Teen: What about with friends?

Parent: Friendships can suffer too. Someone with an addiction might start hanging out only with people who share the same habits, leading to the loss of healthier friendships. Eventually, this can lead to social isolation, where they feel increasingly alone.

Teen: That sounds really tough to come back from.

Parent: It is tough, but it's not impossible. Rebuilding trust and mending those broken relationships takes time, patience, and a lot of effort. It's important for both the person struggling with addiction and their loved ones to seek support, like therapy or support groups, to help navigate these challenges.

Strategies for Preventing Addiction

Teen: What can I do to make sure I don't fall into the trap of addiction?

Parent: One of the best things you can do is educate yourself about the risks and realities of substance use. Understanding the effects that drugs, alcohol, and even prescription medications can have on your body and mind is really important.

Teen: So, it's about knowing the facts?

Parent: Yes, but it's also about making healthy lifestyle choices. Getting involved in activities you enjoy—like sports, music, or art—can give you a positive outlet for stress and keep you busy in a good way.

Teen: And what about at home? How do you and I work together on this?

Parent: We can strengthen our bond by having open, regular conversations about your challenges, like peer pressure. Setting clear rules about substance use is also key, but we must discuss why they exist so you understand and respect them.

Teen: What if I'm feeling stressed or overwhelmed?

Parent: Learning healthy coping strategies is crucial. Techniques like deep breathing, mindfulness, or even talking things out can help manage stress. And remember, you don't have to face everything alone. Building a supportive group of friends who make healthy choices and having mentors or role models to look up to can make a big difference.

Teen: It sounds like it's about balance and support.

Parent: Exactly. It's about creating a balanced life where you feel supported, informed, and empowered to make healthy decisions. By staying engaged in positive activities and maintaining open communication, you can significantly reduce the risk of addiction.

Creating a Supportive Environment for Open Discussion

Teen: How can we have more open conversations about addiction?

Parent: It starts with creating a safe space where you feel comfortable talking about anything, even tough topics like addiction. That means listening without judgment and being open to whatever you need to share.

Teen: It helps when we talk regularly, not just when something goes wrong.

Parent: Absolutely. Making these conversations a normal part of our routine can make them less intimidating. It also helps if I ask open-ended questions, like, 'How do you feel about the pressures you face?' This gives you a chance to express yourself fully.

Teen: What if I don't know all the facts?

Parent: That's okay. We can always learn together. I can provide accurate, age-appropriate information about the risks of substance use and help you understand the realities of addiction. We can also use media, like movies or news stories, to start these conversations.

Teen: What about setting rules?

Parent: Setting clear rules about substance use is important, but discussing them together is just as important. When you're involved in setting these boundaries, you're more likely to respect them. And I'll support and guide you, no matter what.

Teen: I guess it's about trust and understanding on both sides.

Parent: Exactly. By building trust, providing accurate information, setting clear expectations, and being a good role model, I can create a supportive environment where we can talk openly about anything—including addiction.

Healthy Coping Mechanisms

Teen: I sometimes get really stressed or feel down, and I'm unsure how to handle it. What are some good ways to cope?

Parent: It's great that you're thinking about this. It's important to manage stress and emotions in a healthy way. One of the best things you can do is get moving. Physical activity, like running, swimming, or even dancing, can really help lift your mood. Exercise releases endorphins, which are natural mood boosters.

Teen: I've heard about mindfulness, but I'm unsure what it really is. Can that help?

Parent: Definitely. Mindfulness is about staying present in the moment and not letting your mind wander too much into worries about the past or future. You can start small, like focusing on your breathing for a few minutes each day. There are also deep breathing exercises and progressive muscle relaxation, which help calm your body and mind.

Teen: What if I'm not into exercise or meditation?

Parent: That's okay! Everyone has different ways of coping. Creative outlets like drawing, writing, or playing music can be really helpful too. They give you a way to express your feelings and work through them. Even talking to someone you trust, whether it's a friend, family member, or counselor, can make a big difference.

Teen: I guess there are a lot of options, then.

Parent: There are. It's all about finding what works for you. Whether it's through physical activity, mindfulness, creative expression, or social support, the key is to have healthy outlets for your stress and emotions. And remember, it's okay to ask for help when needed.

Understanding Co-occurring Mental Health Disorders

Teen: I've heard that people with mental health issues are more likely to struggle with addiction. Why is that?

Parent: It's true, and there's a close connection between mental health disorders and addiction. Sometimes, people use substances as a way to cope with their mental health symptoms—this is called self-medication. For example, someone with anxiety might turn to alcohol to feel calmer, but over time, this can make their anxiety worse and lead to addiction.

Teen: So, it's like a cycle that's hard to break?

Parent: Exactly. The substance might provide temporary relief, but it often makes the underlying mental health issues worse, which can lead to more substance use. On top of that, both mental health disorders and addiction share common risk factors, like genetics, stress, and trauma. This makes it more likely for someone to develop both issues.

Teen: That sounds really challenging to deal with.

Parent: It is, and that's why treating both the mental health disorder and the addiction at the same time is so important. This is called integrated treatment. Without addressing both, it's hard to achieve long-term recovery.

Teen: So, getting help early is key?

Parent: Absolutely. The sooner someone gets help for both their mental health and substance use, the better their chances of recovery. It's also important for families and friends to understand that addiction is often tied to other mental health challenges, and both need attention and care.

Understanding the Role of Therapy and Counseling in Addiction Treatment

Teen: If someone's dealing with addiction, how can therapy or counseling help?

Parent: Therapy and counseling are really important parts of addiction treatment. They help people understand why they started using substances in the first place, which is often tied to deeper issues like trauma or stress. Therapists can work with you to explore these underlying causes and develop healthier coping methods.

Teen: What kinds of things do people work on in therapy?

Parent: It depends on the person's needs. Cognitive-behavioral therapy (CBT) is common; it helps people identify and change negative thought patterns and behaviors that lead to substance use. Dialectical behaviour therapy (DBT) is also great for managing intense emotions and improving relationships.

Teen: What about family and friends? How do they fit into the picture?

Parent: Family therapy can be really helpful too. Addiction often affects everyone in the family, not just the person struggling with it. In family therapy, everyone can work together to heal, rebuild trust, and set healthy boundaries. There's also couples therapy, which can help partners support each other through recovery.

Teen: So, it's not just about stopping the substance use, but about changing how you deal with things overall?

Parent: Exactly. Therapy helps you develop the tools and strategies to handle life's challenges without turning to substances. It's also about rebuilding relationships, setting goals, and creating a supportive environment for long-term recovery.

The Influence of Media on Teenage Perception of Addiction

Teen: I see a lot of stuff about addiction on TV and social media. How does that affect people, especially Teens?

Parent: How addiction is portrayed in the media can shape how people think about it. Sometimes, the media glamorizes substance use, making it seem exciting or cool. When you see characters on TV or influencers online drinking, smoking, or using drugs without any negative consequences, it can make it seem like it's not a big deal.

Teen: But that's not really how it is in real life, right?

Parent: Right. In real life, substance use often comes with serious risks, like addiction, health problems, or even legal trouble. Unfortunately, the media doesn't always show those consequences. This can lead to many misconceptions, especially among teens who might not have the experience to see through the glamorized portrayals.

Teen: What about the way people with addiction are shown?

Parent: That's another big issue. People with addiction are often shown as weak or morally flawed, which isn't fair or accurate. Addiction is a health issue, not a character flaw. But when the media focuses only on the extremes, like crime or overdoses, it can reinforce negative stereotypes and make it harder for people to get the help they need.

Teen: So, how do we figure out what's real and just media hype?

Parent: It's important to approach media with a critical eye. We can talk about what you see, and I can help you understand the difference between reality and how things are portrayed on screen. By being aware of the media's influence, you can make more informed decisions about substance use and understand the real consequences of addiction.

Risks of Prescription Drug Misuse

Teen: I've heard about people misusing prescription drugs. What are the risks if someone starts doing that?

Parent: Misusing prescription drugs is really dangerous, especially for Teens. One of the biggest risks is overdose. Prescription drugs, especially things like opioids, sedatives, or stimulants, can be very powerful. Taking too much or using them in a way they weren't prescribed can lead to serious health problems, including accidental overdose or poisoning.

Teen: But don't doctors prescribe these drugs? How can they be so dangerous?

Parent: They're safe when used as directed by a doctor, but when misused— like taking someone else's prescription or taking more than prescribed— they can be very harmful. Long-term misuse can damage vital organs, like your liver or heart, and can also lead to addiction. Your brain is still developing, and using these drugs in the wrong way can interfere with that development, leading to long-term cognitive issues.

Teen: That sounds really serious. Are there other risks, too?

Parent: Yes, there are also mental health risks. Misusing these drugs can worsen mental health conditions like anxiety or depression or even cause new psychiatric symptoms. And if someone becomes addicted, they might struggle with withdrawal symptoms, which can be very tough to deal with.

Teen: What about the impact on school or friendships?

Parent: Misusing prescription drugs can definitely affect your schoolwork. It's hard to focus or do well in school if you're dealing with the effects of these drugs. You might also start isolating yourself from friends and family, making you feel even more alone. And don't forget the legal risks—having or using prescription drugs without a prescription is illegal and can lead to serious consequences.

Teen: How can I avoid falling into this trap?

Parent: The best way to avoid these risks is to use medications only as prescribed and never take someone else's prescription. If you're feeling pressured or if you're struggling with stress or other issues, talk to me, a counselor, or another trusted adult. There's always a way to get help without turning to substances.

Addiction to Social Media and Technology

Teen: We talk a lot about substance addiction, but can you get addicted to social media and technology too?

Parent: Absolutely, you can. Social media and technology can be addictive, especially because they're designed to keep you engaged. When someone spends too much time on their phone or computer, it can start to affect their mental health, social life, and even their schoolwork.

Teen: How does it affect mental health?

Parent: For one, social media often leads to comparisons with others, which can make you feel like you're not good enough. This can increase anxiety and depression. Plus, being on your phone late at night can mess with your sleep, which only makes things worse. Lack of sleep can make it harder to focus, manage emotions, and keep up with daily responsibilities.

Teen: I guess it also affects how much time you spend with people in real life.

Parent: It does. Spending too much time online can lead to social isolation because you're not engaging as much with people face-to-face. Online interactions can be shallow, and you might feel lonelier, even if you're constantly connected. It can also lead to conflicts at home, especially if you're always on your phone during family time.

Teen: What about school? Can it really affect your grades?

Parent: Definitely. If you're distracted by social media or online games, focusing on your schoolwork is hard. This can lead to lower grades, missed assignments, and even stress because you're trying to catch up. Social media can also spread misinformation, affecting how you understand certain topics.

Teen: What can we do to keep it from becoming a problem?

Parent: Setting healthy boundaries is key. We can agree on screen time limits, and you can try to engage in more offline activities, like sports, hobbies, or spending time with friends and family in person. It's also important to talk about what you see online and how it affects you, so you can learn to use social media and technology in a healthier way.

Physical Health Effects of Addiction: Sleep and Nutrition

Teen: I've heard that addiction can mess with your sleep and diet. How does that happen?

Parent: Addiction can have a huge impact on your physical health, especially when it comes to sleep and nutrition. When someone is addicted to substances like drugs or alcohol, their sleep patterns can get really disrupted. For example, stimulants like cocaine or meth can make it hard to sleep at all, leading to insomnia. On the flip side, something like alcohol might make you feel sleepy at first, but it messes up the quality of your sleep, especially the REM stage, which is important for feeling rested.

Teen: So, even if it seems like you're sleeping, you're not really getting good sleep?

Parent: Exactly. You might wake up feeling tired, groggy, or just not refreshed. And over time, not getting enough quality sleep can lead to bigger health problems, like weakened immunity, memory issues, and even heart problems.

Teen: What about nutrition? How does addiction affect that?

Parent: Addiction can seriously mess with your eating habits too. Some substances, like stimulants, can suppress your appetite, leading to weight loss and malnutrition because you're just not getting the nutrients your body needs. Others, like marijuana, can increase your appetite but often lead to cravings for unhealthy, high-calorie foods, which can result in weight gain and other related health issues.

Teen: So either way, it's not good for your body.

Parent: Right. Addiction often leads to neglecting proper nutrition because the focus becomes more on getting and using the substance rather than taking care of your body. This can lead to vitamin and mineral deficiencies, a weakened immune system, and other long-term health problems like liver damage from alcohol or digestive issues from various substances.

Teen: That sounds pretty serious. How can someone turn it around?

Parent: Recovery often involves working on restoring healthy sleep and eating habits. This can take time, but it's possible to regain balance with support. Eating nutritious meals, establishing a regular sleep schedule, and getting medical support if needed are all important steps in recovery.

Decision-Making and Risk-Taking Behavior in Addiction

Teen: I've heard that addiction can mess with how you make decisions and take risks. Why does that happen?

Parent: Addiction definitely affects your brain's ability to make good decisions and control impulses. The substances change your brain's reward system, making it hard to think about long-term consequences. Instead, your brain focuses more on the immediate reward of using the substance, even if it's risky or harmful.

Teen: So, it's like your brain starts prioritizing the substance over everything else?

Parent: Exactly. The part of your brain that helps with decision-making called the prefrontal cortex, gets disrupted by addiction. This part is responsible for thinking things through, weighing pros and cons, and controlling impulses. When it's not working properly, you're more likely to take risks without considering the dangers, like using in unsafe places or taking higher doses than you should.

Teen: Does this mean people with addiction can't help themselves when they take these risks?

Parent: It's not that they don't know what they're doing is risky, but the addiction makes it really hard to resist the urge to use, even when they know the risks. Addiction also lowers inhibitions, making it easier to act on impulse rather than thinking things through. It's like the brain is wired to prioritize the immediate reward over anything else, so professional help is so important for recovery.

Teen: What can be done to help with that?

Parent: Treatment often focuses on helping people regain control over their decision-making and reduce impulsive behaviors. Cognitive-behavioral therapy, for example, helps people recognize and change the thought patterns that lead to risky behaviour. It's also important to build new, healthier habits that don't involve substance use.

Alternative Activities to Prevent Addiction

Teen: If someone wants to stay away from addiction, what kinds of activities can they get into instead?

Parent: There are a lot of positive activities that can help keep someone away from addiction. Physical activities like sports are a great option because they help reduce stress and build discipline. Whether it's team sports like soccer or individual activities like running or swimming, staying active can really boost your mood and overall well-being.

Teen: What if I'm not into sports?

Parent: That's okay! There are plenty of other options. Creative activities like drawing, painting, playing an instrument, or even writing can be really fulfilling. These hobbies allow you to express yourself and channel your emotions in a healthy way. Plus, they can give you a sense of accomplishment and pride, which is important for maintaining a positive self-image.

Teen: What about social activities? Can they help too?

Parent: Definitely. Joining clubs, volunteering, or participating in community events can give you a sense of purpose and help you build strong, supportive relationships. Being part of a group that shares your interests can make you feel connected and valued, reducing the temptation to turn to substances.

Teen: It sounds like the key is staying engaged and finding things that make you feel good about yourself.

Parent: Exactly. Engaging in positive activities and hobbies keeps you busy and helps build your self-esteem and resilience. When you feel good about yourself and your abilities, you're less likely to seek out unhealthy ways to cope with stress or boredom.

Recognizing the Need for Professional Help

Teen: If someone is struggling with addiction, how do they know when it's time to get professional help?

Parent: It can be hard to recognize, but there are some signs that it's time to seek help. One big sign is if you feel like you've lost control over your substance use—like you want to stop but can't, or if you're using more than you intended. If you're thinking about using substances all the time, or if it's interfering with your daily life, that's another sign.

Teen: What if it's affecting school or relationships?

Parent: That's definitely a red flag. If your grades are dropping, you're missing school, or you're having conflicts with friends or family because of your substance use, it's a sign that things are getting out of hand. Addiction can also cause physical and mental health problems, like feeling depressed, anxious, or physically unwell. If you're experiencing any of these issues, talking to someone and getting help is important.

Teen: How do you actually ask for help?

Parent: It can be really tough, but reaching out to a trusted adult—like a parent, teacher, or school counselor—is a good first step. You can also talk to your doctor or contact a mental health professional. They can guide you to the right resources and support you need. Remember, asking for help is a sign of strength, not weakness.

Teen: And it's okay to get help even if you're not sure you need it?

Parent: Absolutely. It's better to ask for help early on than wait until things worsen. Even if you're just concerned or have questions, talking to a professional can give you the support and information you need to make healthy choices.

Understanding Self-Esteem and Self-Worth in the Context of Addiction

Teen: How does addiction change the way someone feels about themselves, especially for teens?

Parent: Addiction can really take a toll on a Teen's self-esteem and self-worth. When you're struggling with addiction, it's easy to feel like you're losing control over your life. That loss of control can make you feel powerless and ashamed, which chips away at your self-esteem.

Teen: So, they start to see themselves differently?

Parent: Yes, addiction can lead to a very negative self-image. Teens might feel guilty or ashamed about their behaviour, especially if it hurts their relationships, schoolwork, or health. They might even start to believe that they're a bad person because of their addiction, which can make them feel worthless.

Teen: What about their relationships with other people?

Parent: Addiction often leads to social isolation, which makes things even worse. A Teen might pull away from family and friends who don't use substances, which can make them feel even more alone and misunderstood. Or they might only spend time with others who are also using, which reinforces the addiction and makes it harder to see a way out.

Teen: And that affects how they feel about themselves?

Parent: Definitely. When teens feel isolated or rejected by their peers, it can really damage their self-esteem. They might feel like they don't belong or are not good enough. If they start to face consequences like failing grades or trouble at home, it can reinforce those negative feelings and make them believe they're failures.

Teen: Is there a way to help them feel better about themselves?

Parent: It's important to address both the addiction and the underlying issues that are affecting their self-esteem. Therapy can help them understand why they're feeling the way they are and develop healthier ways to cope. Building a strong support network with family, friends, and possibly a recovery group can also make a big difference. Encouraging them to reconnect with activities they used to enjoy or set new goals can help rebuild their confidence and sense of self-worth.

Teen: So, it's about helping them see that they're more than their addiction?

Parent: Exactly. Addiction doesn't define who they are—it's just one part of their story. Helping them see their strengths, their potential, and the positive things they can achieve is key to rebuilding their self-esteem and self-worth. It's about showing them they can recover and deserve a happy, healthy life.

Impact on Future Goals and Aspirations

Teen: What happens to someone's future goals and dreams if they get caught up in addiction?

Parent: Addiction can have a devastating impact on a Teen's future. When someone is struggling with addiction, it often becomes the central focus of their life, which can derail everything else. For example, academic performance usually suffers because it's hard to concentrate or stay motivated when addiction is in control.

Teen: So their grades start to drop?

Parent: Yes, exactly. Addiction can impair your ability to concentrate, remember things, and solve problems, which leads to poor grades. Over time, this can make it harder to keep up with schoolwork, and some students might even drop out. Dropping out can severely limit your options for the future, making it harder to pursue higher education or even get a good job.

Teen: What about career goals? Does addiction affect that too?

Parent: Absolutely. Addiction can make it difficult to pursue and achieve career aspirations. If someone drops out of school or performs poorly academically, their chances of getting into a good college or training program are reduced. Without the necessary education or skills, finding a job or building a career becomes much harder. Addiction can also lead to behavioral issues or legal troubles, which can damage a person's professional reputation and make it challenging to find or keep a job.

Teen: What happens to their personal growth and relationships?

Parent: Addiction often stunts personal development. It can prevent someone from maturing emotionally and socially, making it hard to form healthy relationships or handle stress. It also tends to isolate people, damaging relationships with family and friends. When addiction takes over, it becomes difficult to focus on self-discovery or personal goals, leaving people feeling lost or unfulfilled.

Teen: Can they recover their goals if they manage to overcome the addiction?

Parent: Recovery is definitely possible, and it's a time when many people reconnect with their dreams and passions. Through therapy and support, they can set new goals and work towards them, even if they've experienced setbacks. Recovery also involves building resilience and life skills to help them pursue a meaningful future.

Teen: So, even if addiction derails things, there's still hope for the future?

Parent: Absolutely. While addiction can cause significant disruptions, recovery offers a chance to rebuild. With the right support and determination, it's possible to overcome addiction and work towards a fulfilling and successful future.

Effects on Teenage Brain Development

Teen: I've heard that addiction can really mess up your brain, especially if you're a Teen. How does it affect brain development?

Parent: The teenage brain is still developing, particularly in areas that control decision-making, impulse control, and emotional regulation. Addiction can interfere with this development in significant ways. For instance, substances can impair the growth of the prefrontal cortex, which is responsible for making decisions and controlling impulses. This can lead to more impulsive behaviour and poor decision-making, which can feed the cycle of addiction.

Teen: So, it makes it harder to make good decisions?

Parent: Yes, exactly. The brain's ability to assess risks and make sound decisions is compromised, which can lead Teens to take more risks without fully understanding the consequences. Additionally, addiction can affect the brain's reward system, making it harder to feel pleasure from everyday activities. This can make it difficult for teens to enjoy things they used to love, which can increase their reliance on substances.

Teen: What about memory and learning?

Parent: Addiction can severely impact memory and learning, especially because it affects the hippocampus, the part of the brain responsible for forming new memories. This can make it difficult for teens to retain information and perform well academically. Over time, these cognitive deficits can persist, even if substance use is reduced or stopped.

Teen: Does it affect emotions too?

Parent: Definitely. Addiction can disrupt the brain's emotional regulation, leading to increased anxiety, depression, and emotional instability. The amygdala, which processes emotions like fear and pleasure, can become overactive or dysfunctional, making it hard to manage stress or emotional responses. This emotional turmoil can make it even more difficult to break free from addiction.

Teen: Is there a chance for the brain to recover if someone stops using substances?

Parent: The good news is that the teenage brain is highly plastic, meaning it has the ability to adapt and heal over time, especially with early intervention and support. Recovery programs focusing on rebuilding cognitive and emotional skills, therapy, and healthy lifestyle changes can help the brain recover and function better.

Teen: So, recovery is possible, but it takes time and effort?

Parent: Exactly. Recovery requires commitment, support, and sometimes professional help, but the brain can heal, and the person can regain many of the cognitive and emotional functions that were affected by addiction.

Addressing Myths and Stereotypes about Addiction

Teen: I hear a lot of things about addiction, but I'm not sure what's true and what's not. What are some common myths or stereotypes about addiction?

Parent: There are quite a few myths that can be really misleading. One of the biggest ones is that addiction is just a moral failing or a lack of willpower. People often think that someone struggling with addiction could just stop if they tried hard enough, but addiction is a complex disease that affects the brain's chemistry and decision-making processes. It's not just about willpower.

Teen: So it's more like a disease that needs treatment?

Parent: Yes, exactly. Addiction changes how the brain works, and those changes make it difficult for someone to quit on their own. It's important to understand that a health issue requires treatment, not just a personal weakness.

Teen: What about the idea that you can't get addicted to prescription drugs if they're from a doctor?

Parent: That's another myth. Prescription drugs, like opioids or stimulants, can be highly addictive, even if a doctor prescribes them. Misusing these medications, like taking them in higher doses or using them in a way not intended by the doctor, can quickly lead to addiction. Just because a drug is legal or prescribed doesn't mean it's safe to misuse.

Teen: Are there certain types of people who are more likely to get addicted?

Parent: That's another stereotype—that addiction only happens to certain types of people. The truth is, that addiction can affect anyone, regardless of their background, education, or social status. It doesn't discriminate. Anyone can be vulnerable to addiction under the right circumstances.

Teen: What about the idea that someone must hit 'rock bottom' before recovering?

Parent: That's a dangerous myth. Waiting for someone to hit rock bottom can lead to serious consequences, including health issues, legal trouble, or even death. Recovery is possible at any stage of addiction, and early intervention can prevent things from getting worse. It's always better to seek help as soon as possible.

Teen: Are there myths about how to recover too?

Parent: Yes, some people think that addiction can be overcome simply by stopping substance use, but recovery is a long-term process. It involves more than just quitting; it's about addressing the underlying issues, learning new coping mechanisms, and often dealing with relapse. Recovery usually requires ongoing support, therapy, and sometimes medication.

Teen: So, addiction is a complex issue that needs understanding and proper treatment.

Parent: Exactly. Understanding these myths and stereotypes is crucial for recognizing addiction as a serious health issue and supporting those who need help.

Cultural Factors in Addiction and Treatment

Teen: Do cultural factors really influence how people view addiction and treatment?

Parent: Yes, cultural factors play a huge role in shaping how addiction is perceived and how people approach treatment. For example, in some cultures, addiction is highly stigmatized and seen as a moral failing or a sign of weakness. This can create shame and make it difficult for people to seek help because they fear being judged.

Teen: So, how does that stigma affect treatment?

Parent: When addiction is stigmatized, people might hide their struggles or avoid treatment altogether. They might fear that admitting to addiction will bring shame to their family or damage their reputation. In some cultures, there's also a strong emphasis on handling problems privately within the family, which can delay or prevent someone from getting professional help.

Teen: What about different religious beliefs?

Parent: Religious beliefs can also shape attitudes toward addiction. In some religious communities, substance use might be strictly prohibited, which can lead to harsh judgment of those who struggle with addiction. On the other hand, some faith-based approaches to treatment can be very supportive, offering a sense of community and spiritual guidance in recovery.

Teen: Do cultural differences affect the types of treatment people choose?

Parent: Definitely. Some cultures might prefer traditional or alternative therapies over conventional medical treatment. For example, they might turn to herbal medicine, spiritual healing, or community rituals as part of the recovery process. Understanding and respecting these preferences is important for providing culturally competent care.

Teen: How do family and community play into this?

Parent: In many cultures, the family and community are central to a person's identity, and their support can be crucial in recovery. However, if the community holds negative views about addiction, it can also lead to isolation and make recovery harder. In cultures where family honour is important, addiction might be seen as bringing shame to the family, which can lead to pressure to conceal the problem.

Teen: So, cultural sensitivity is really important in treating addiction?

Parent: Yes, it's essential. Treatment approaches need to be culturally sensitive and respectful of the individual's background and beliefs. This might mean involving family in the treatment process, integrating cultural practices into the treatment plan, or working with community leaders to reduce stigma and provide support.

Teen: How can schools and communities help?

Parent: Schools and communities can help by offering culturally relevant education and accessible resources to people from different backgrounds. Promoting understanding and reducing stigma can encourage more people to seek help and support those in recovery.

Resources and Support Networks for Teenage Addiction Recovery

Teen: If a Teen is struggling with addiction, what kind of resources and support are out there for them?

Parent: Quite a few resources are available, both in-person and online. For starters, professional treatment programs like inpatient and outpatient rehab centers exist. Inpatient centers offer a structured environment where

Teens can focus on their recovery full-time. At the same time, outpatient programs allow them to continue living at home and attending school while receiving treatment.

Teen: What if they're not ready for something as intense as rehab?

Parent: Counseling and therapy services are also available. Individual therapy, like Cognitive-Behavioral Therapy (CBT), can help Teens understand the root causes of their addiction and develop healthier coping strategies. Family therapy is another option which involves the entire family in the recovery process. Group therapy can also be very helpful because it provides peer support and a sense of community.

Teen: Are there any peer support groups specifically for teens?

Parent: Yes, there are peer support groups through various organizations. Groups like Alcoholics Anonymous India (AA India) and Narcotics Anonymous India (NA India) provide support for those struggling with substance use, including teen-specific meetings. Additionally, organizations such as the Indian Society of Addiction Medicine (ISAM) offer guidance and resources for teens. These groups provide a supportive environment where teens can share their experiences and receive encouragement from others facing similar challenges.

Teen: What about online resources?

Parent: Online resources like the National Institute of Mental Health and Neurosciences (NIMHANS) provide information and support for mental health and addiction. Organizations like YourDOST and iCALL also offer online counseling services for teens seeking help. These platforms are especially useful for teens who might not have access to in-person meetings or prefer the privacy of online support.

Teen: Can schools help too?

Parent: Absolutely. Many schools have Student Assistance Programs (SAPs) that provide counseling, support, and resources for students struggling with substance use. Schools can also offer educational workshops and prevention programs to raise awareness and help students make informed choices.

Teen: What if someone needs help outside of school?

Parent: Community resources like local health departments, community centers, and youth organizations can also provide support. These places often offer counseling, educational programs, and sometimes even treatment services at low or no cost. Faith-based organizations might also offer support tailored to the individual's spiritual needs.

Teen: So, there's a lot of help out there if someone knows where to look?

Parent: Yes, many resources are available, and teens need to know that they don't have to go through this alone. Reaching out for help is the first step toward recovery, and plenty of people and organizations are ready to support them on that journey.

Recognizing When Friends Are Struggling with Addiction

Teen: If I'm worried that one of my friends might be dealing with addiction, how can I tell if they're really struggling?

Parent: You can look out for several signs, but it's important to approach the situation with care and concern. Some of the most noticeable changes might be in their behaviour or personality. For example, if your friend starts having sudden mood swings, becomes more irritable, or withdraws emotionally, these could be signs of substance use.

Teen: What about their physical appearance?

Parent: Physical changes can be a big indicator too. If your friend starts neglecting their hygiene, rapidly loses or gains weight, or has bloodshot eyes or dilated pupils, these could all be signs of something wrong. They might also show physical symptoms like tremors or shakes, which can indicate withdrawal.

Teen: Can addiction affect their school performance?

Parent: Definitely. You might notice that their grades are slipping or that they're missing a lot of school. A friend who used to be engaged in school activities might suddenly lose interest or motivation. These changes can be a red flag that something is interfering with their ability to focus and participate in school.

Teen: What about their social life?

Parent: Changes in social circles can also be telling. If your friend starts hanging out with a new group of people who use substances, or if they suddenly become more isolated and stop spending time with their usual friends, these could be signs of addiction. Risky or uncharacteristic behaviour, like taking more risks or getting into legal trouble, can also be a warning sign.

Teen: How should I approach them if I'm worried?

Parent: Approach them with care and let them know that you're concerned about them because you care. Try to have an open and non-judgmental conversation. Ask them if everything is okay and offer your support. It's important to let them know that you're there for them, no matter what.

Teen: What if they admit they have a problem?

Parent: If they're open about it, encourage them to seek professional help, whether it's talking to a counselor, joining a support group, or seeing a doctor. Offer to help them find resources or even go with them for support. If you think their situation is serious, don't hesitate to involve a trusted adult like a parent or teacher.

Teen: It sounds like it's important to act quickly if you notice these signs.

Parent: Yes, the sooner you can offer support, the better. Addiction can be really tough to deal with, and having a friend who cares enough to reach out can make a huge difference. Even if they're not ready to talk immediately, knowing that you're there for them can be a powerful first step towards getting help.

Teen: How can I rebuild my self-esteem and self-worth after dealing with addiction?

Parent: Rebuilding self-esteem and self-worth after addiction is an important part of the recovery process. Addiction can take a toll on how you see yourself, but with time and effort, you can regain a positive self-image and feel good about who you are again.

Teen: Where do I start?

Parent: Start by acknowledging the progress you've made. Recovery is a huge step, and being on this path shows strength and determination.

Celebrate your successes, no matter how small they might seem. Each day you stay sober is an achievement worth recognizing.

Teen: That's a good point. What else can I do?

Parent: Engage in activities that make you feel good about yourself. This might include pursuing hobbies you enjoy, setting and achieving small goals, or learning something new. These activities help you reconnect with your interests and strengths, reminding you of your capabilities.

Teen: How do I deal with negative thoughts about myself?

Parent: Negative thoughts are common during recovery, but it's important to challenge them. Whenever you think negatively, try reframing those thoughts into something positive. For example, instead of thinking, 'I'm a failure because of my past,' remind yourself, 'I'm strong because I'm working hard to overcome my past.'

Teen: That sounds helpful, but what if I feel like others still see me in a negative light?

Parent: It's natural to worry about how others perceive you, but remember that your recovery is about you, not them. Over time, as you continue to make positive changes, people will notice the new you. Surround yourself with supportive people who see your potential and encourage your growth.

Teen: What if I have trouble forgiving myself for things I did during my addiction?

Parent: Forgiving yourself can be one of the hardest parts of recovery but also one of the most important. Holding on to guilt or shame can weigh you down, making it harder to move forward. Try to view your past actions with compassion—understanding that addiction is a disease and that you're taking steps to heal.

Teen: How can I work on that?

Parent: Therapy can be very helpful for processing guilt and shame and learning self-compassion. A therapist can guide you through exercises that help you let go of the past and focus on your growth. Journaling can also be a good way to express and work through these feelings.

Teen: I guess it's about focusing on the positive changes I'm making now.

Parent: Exactly. Every positive step you take in your recovery builds your self-esteem and self-worth. Remember that you're more than your past—you can change, grow, and achieve great things. Keep focusing on your strengths, your goals, and the person you're becoming.

Teen: Thanks, that makes me feel more hopeful.

Parent: You should feel hopeful. Recovery is a journey; with each step, you're building a stronger, more resilient self. It's not easy, but you're doing it, and that's something to be incredibly proud of.

Teen: How can I balance my recovery with all the responsibilities I have at school?

Parent: Balancing recovery with academic responsibilities can be challenging, but it's definitely possible with some planning and support. The key is prioritizing your health while still keeping up with your schoolwork.

Teen: That sounds tough. Where do I even start?

Parent: Start by creating a structured routine that includes time for both your recovery activities, like therapy or support groups, and your academic work. Having a set schedule can help you manage your time effectively and ensure that you're not neglecting either area.

Teen: What if I feel overwhelmed with everything?

Parent: It's normal to feel overwhelmed, especially in the beginning. If that happens, take things one step at a time. Break down your tasks into smaller, manageable pieces. For example, instead of thinking about completing a whole project, focus on just one section at a time.

Teen: That makes sense. How do I make sure I don't fall behind in school?

Parent: Communication with your teachers is crucial. Tell them about your situation so they can provide support or accommodations if needed. They might be able to give you extensions on assignments, adjust your workload, or offer additional help if you're struggling.

Teen: What if I'm afraid of what they might think?

Parent: It's understandable to feel that way, but most teachers will appreciate your honesty and commitment to recovery and education. They're there to help you succeed, and being open with them can make it easier for them to provide the support you need.

Teen: What about managing stress from school on top of everything else?

Parent: Managing stress is important for your recovery and your academic success. Ensure you're taking care of your physical and mental health—get enough sleep, eat well, exercise, and practice stress-relief techniques like deep breathing or mindfulness. Don't be afraid to ask for help when you need it, whether it's from a teacher, a counselor, or a family member.

Teen: How do I stay motivated when things get tough?

Parent: Staying motivated can be hard but keep your long-term goals in mind. Think about how completing your education can open doors for you in the future. Celebrate your progress, and remind yourself that each step you take, whether it's completing an assignment or attending a support group, is bringing you closer to your goals.

Teen: What if I start to feel like I'm slipping in my recovery because of school stress?

Parent: If you ever feel like school stress affects your recovery, it's important to address it immediately. Reach out to your support network—your therapist, a counselor, or a trusted adult—so you can work together to adjust your routine or find solutions. Remember, your recovery is the foundation for your future success, so it's okay to prioritize it when needed.

Teen: Knowing I don't have to do it alone is good.

Parent: You definitely don't. Balancing recovery and school is a team effort, and there are people who want to help you succeed in both. By staying organized, communicating with your teachers, and taking care of yourself, you can find a balance that works for you and supports your long-term goals.

Teen: How can I rebuild trust with my family after everything that's happened?

Parent: Rebuilding trust after addiction can be challenging, but it's definitely possible. Trust is earned over time through consistent actions, honesty, and communication. It won't happen overnight, but with patience and effort, you can restore those relationships.

Teen: I want to, but I'm unsure where to start.

Parent: The first step is to acknowledge the past and take responsibility for your actions. Being honest about what happened and how it affected your family is important. Apologizing sincerely for any hurt you caused is a crucial part of this process.

Teen: What if they don't believe I've really changed?

Parent: That's understandable, especially if they've been hurt before. Trust is built by showing, not just telling. You can start by being consistent in your actions—follow through on your commitments, keep your promises, and be reliable. Over time, these consistent actions will help rebuild lost trust.

Teen: What if I mess up again? Won't that make things worse?

Parent: Recovery is a process, and setbacks can happen. If you make a mistake, the key is to be honest and take responsibility immediately. Show your family that you're committed to learning from your mistakes and making better choices moving forward. This honesty, even in difficult times, can help strengthen trust over time.

Teen: How can I show them that I'm serious about changing?

Parent: Staying committed to your recovery is one of the best ways to show your family that you're serious. This means attending therapy sessions and support groups and following through with your recovery plan. You can also show your commitment by involving your family in your recovery—sharing your progress with them and being open about your challenges.

Teen: Should I talk to them about how I'm feeling?

Parent: Absolutely. Open communication is key to rebuilding trust. Share your thoughts, feelings, and progress with them. Let them know when you're struggling and ask for their support. This transparency shows that you're willing to be vulnerable and trust them to support you, which can help rebuild your trust.

Teen: What if they're still angry or hurt?

Parent: It's important to give them time to heal. They may need time to process their emotions, and that's okay. Be patient and understanding, and continue to show through your actions that you're committed to change. Over time, their anger and hurt will likely lessen as they see the positive changes in you.

Teen: So, it's about being consistent and patient?

Parent: Exactly. Rebuilding trust takes time, consistency, and patience. It's about showing your family through your actions that you've changed and are committed to staying on a positive path. With time, effort, and honesty, you can rebuild the trust that's been lost and strengthen your relationship with your family.

Teen: How can I create a healthy lifestyle that supports my recovery?

Parent: Creating a healthy lifestyle is an important part of recovery. It's about making choices that support your physical, mental, and emotional well-being. A healthy lifestyle can help you stay focused on your recovery and reduce the risk of relapse.

Teen: Where do I start?

Parent: Start with your diet, exercise, and sleep. Eating a balanced diet, staying physically active, and getting enough sleep are fundamental to maintaining your health and well-being. These habits help your body recover and give you the energy and focus you need to stay on track with your recovery.

Teen: How do I make sure I'm eating right?

Parent: Focus on eating various foods that provide the nutrients your body needs. This means plenty of fruits, vegetables, whole grains, and lean proteins. Try to limit processed foods, sugary snacks, and drinks. Staying hydrated is also important, so drink plenty of water throughout the day.

Teen: What about exercise? How much should I be doing?

Parent: Regular physical activity is great for both your body and mind. It helps reduce stress, improves your mood, and boosts your overall health. Aim for at least 30 minutes of moderate exercise most days of the week.

This could be anything you enjoy, like walking, biking, swimming, or playing a sport. The key is to find something you like so it doesn't feel like a chore.

Teen: I've heard that sleep is really important too. How can I improve my sleep?

Parent: Good sleep is essential for your recovery. Try to go to bed and wake up simultaneously every day to establish a routine. Create a relaxing bedtime routine, like reading or listening to calming music, to help you wind down. Ensure your sleep environment is comfortable—keep the room cool, dark, and quiet, and avoid screens before bed, as the blue light can interfere with your sleep.

Teen: What about mental and emotional health? How do I take care of that?

Parent: Taking care of your mental and emotional health is just as important as your physical health. Practice stress-relief techniques like deep breathing, mindfulness, or meditation. Engage in activities that bring you joy and relaxation, whether it's a hobby, spending time with loved ones, or being in nature. It's also important to stay connected with your support network—friends, family, or a counselor—so you have people to talk to when you need support.

Teen: How do I make all of this a regular part of my life?

Parent: It's about creating a routine that works for you. Start with small changes and build on them over time. For example, you might start by adding a short walk to your daily routine or ensuring you eat a healthy breakfast every morning. As these habits become part of your daily life, you can add healthier behaviors.

Teen: What if I slip up or struggle with my routine?

Parent: It's normal to have ups and downs, so don't be too hard on yourself if you slip up. The important thing is to get back on track as soon as you can. If you find it hard to stick to your routine, consider what might get in the way and adjust as needed. Sometimes, it helps to talk to someone you trust for support or advice.

Teen: So, it's about making healthy choices and being consistent?

Parent: Creating a healthy lifestyle is about making choices that support your recovery and sticking with them. Building new habits takes time, but you'll see the benefits with consistency and patience. A healthy lifestyle will help you stay focused on your recovery, improve your overall well-being, and give you the strength to face challenges along the way.

Teen: How can I manage stress during my recovery?

Parent: Managing stress is really important during recovery because stress can be a trigger for relapse. It's about finding healthy ways to cope with stress, so it doesn't overwhelm you or push you towards old habits.

Teen: What can I do when I start to feel stressed?

Parent: There are many techniques you can use to manage stress. Deep breathing, for example, is a simple but effective way to calm yourself down. Take slow, deep breaths in through your nose, hold for a few seconds, and then slowly exhale through your mouth. This helps activate your body's relaxation response and lower stress levels.

Teen: Are there other techniques I can try?

Parent: Yes, mindfulness and meditation are great tools for managing stress. These practices help you stay focused on the present moment and reduce anxiety about the past or future. Even a few minutes of mindfulness or meditation each day can make a big difference in handling stress.

Teen: What about physical activity? Can that help with stress?

Parent: Absolutely. Physical activity is one of the best ways to reduce stress. Exercise releases endorphins, which are natural mood lifters, and help your body manage stress better. It can be anything from a brisk walk, bike ride, playing a sport, or doing yoga. The important thing is to find something you enjoy so you'll stick with it.

Teen: What if I'm stressed about something specific, like school or relationships?

Parent: It can help to talk about what's stressing you out. Sometimes just sharing your worries with someone you trust, like a friend, family member, or counselor, can relieve some of the pressure. They might offer a different perspective or help you develop solutions you hadn't considered.

Teen: How can I keep stress from building up in the first place?

Parent: Keeping stress from building up involves taking care of yourself regularly. This means getting enough sleep, eating well, staying active, and taking time each day to relax and do something you enjoy. Having a daily routine that includes these elements can help keep stress levels in check.

Teen: What should I do if I feel like I'm getting overwhelmed?

Parent: If you start feeling overwhelmed, taking a step back and giving yourself a break is important. Sometimes, that means taking a few minutes to breathe and calm down, or it could mean taking a day off from your regular activities to rest and recharge. It's okay to ask for help when you need it—whether it's talking to a therapist, reaching out to a support group, or just leaning on a friend or family member.

Teen: So, managing stress is about caring for myself and asking for help when needed?

Parent: Exactly. Managing stress is about recognizing when you're feeling overwhelmed and taking steps to care for yourself. It's also about knowing that it's okay to ask for help. By using healthy coping strategies and staying connected with your support system, you can manage stress effectively and stay on track with your recovery.

Teen: How can I deal with the guilt and shame I feel because of my addiction?

Parent: Guilt and shame are common feelings during recovery, but it's important to address them so they don't hold you back. These emotions can be tough, but with the right approach, you can work through them and focus on moving forward.

Teen: It's hard not to feel guilty about everything I've done.

Parent: It's understandable to feel guilty, but remember that addiction is a disease, not a choice. What's important now is that you're taking steps to get better. Guilt can be a sign that you care deeply about the people you may have hurt and your mistakes, but it's also important to forgive yourself and focus on making positive changes.

Teen: How do I start forgiving myself?

Parent: Forgiving yourself starts with acknowledging your past actions, taking responsibility, and making amends where you can. It's about understanding that everyone makes mistakes, but what matters most is what you do next. Self-forgiveness is a process, and it takes time, but it's essential for your recovery.

Teen: What if I still feel ashamed of what I've done?

Parent: Shame can be a heavy burden, but it's important to separate who you are from the mistakes you've made. Shame tells you that you're a bad person, but that's not true. You're a person who has struggled and is now working hard to change. Focus on your progress and the positive steps you take every day.

Teen: It's hard to let go of the past.

Parent: Letting go of the past doesn't mean forgetting it, but not letting it define you. You can learn from your experiences and use them to become stronger and wiser. It might help to talk to a therapist or counselor who can guide you through this process and help you build a healthier perspective.

Teen: What can I do when those feelings of guilt and shame start to overwhelm me?

Parent: When those feelings overwhelm you, taking a moment to ground yourself is important. Remind yourself of the progress you've made and the reasons you chose recovery. Sometimes, it can help to write down your thoughts or talk to someone you trust who can offer support and reassurance. Practicing self-compassion is key—treat yourself with the kindness you would offer a friend.

Teen: Will these feelings ever go away completely?

Parent: As you continue to heal and grow, these feelings will likely lessen over time. They may not disappear entirely, but they will become more manageable. As you build a new life for yourself, filled with positive experiences and healthy relationships, the weight of guilt and shame will lift. The important thing is to keep moving forward and not let these feelings hold you back.

Teen: So, it's about focusing on my recovery and being kind to myself?

Parent: Yes, focusing on your recovery and practicing self-compassion is key. Guilt and shame can be part of the process, but they don't have to define you. By acknowledging your feelings, seeking support, and focusing on the positive changes you're making, you can overcome these emotions and continue to build a better future for yourself.

Teen: How can I plan for a successful future now that I'm in recovery?

Parent: Planning for a successful future after recovery is about setting goals, building a support system, and staying focused on your goals. It's a great opportunity to create a new chapter in your life that's filled with positive experiences and accomplishments.

Teen: What kind of goals should I be setting?

Parent: Start by setting both short-term and long-term goals. Short-term goals include finishing school, finding a job, or staying sober for a certain period. Long-term goals could involve pursuing higher education, building a career, or achieving personal milestones. Make sure your goals are realistic and achievable, and remember to celebrate your progress along the way.

Teen: How do I stay motivated to reach my goals?

Parent: Staying motivated can be challenging, but it helps to keep your goals in mind and remind yourself why they're important to you. Break your goals down into smaller, manageable steps so they don't feel overwhelming. Surround yourself with supportive people who encourage you and hold you accountable. Regularly review your goals and adjust them as needed to keep moving forward.

Teen: What if I don't know what I want to do with my life yet?

Parent: It's okay not to have everything figured out right now. Recovery is a journey, and it's natural for your goals to evolve over time. Take this time to explore different interests, try new things, and discover what you're passionate about. Volunteering, internships, or taking on different roles can help you figure out what you enjoy and where your strengths lie.

Teen: How can I make sure I stay on track?

Parent: Staying on track involves creating a routine supporting your goals and recovery. This might include setting aside time daily for studying, working, or pursuing hobbies. It's also important to continue with any counseling, therapy, or support groups that are part of your recovery plan. Staying organized and managing your time well will help you keep moving in the right direction.

Teen: What if I face setbacks along the way?

Parent: Setbacks are a part of life, and they don't mean you've failed. What's important is how you respond to them. If you encounter a setback, take some time to reflect on what happened and what you can learn from it. Then, get back on track as soon as you can. Remember, resilience is about bouncing back, not about never making mistakes.

Teen: How can I keep improving myself as I go forward?

Parent: Personal growth is a lifelong process. Keep setting new goals for yourself, continue learning, and seek out opportunities for self-improvement. Whether it's through education, skill-building, or developing healthy relationships, always look for ways to grow and evolve. Staying curious and open to new experiences will help you continue to improve and achieve your full potential.

Teen: So, it's about setting goals, staying motivated, and being open to growth?

Parent: Exactly. By setting clear goals, staying motivated, and embracing personal growth, you can build a successful future for yourself. Remember, your recovery has given you a fresh start, and you have the power to shape your future into something positive and fulfilling. Stay focused on your goals, seek support when needed, and keep moving forward with confidence.

Parent: We've covered a lot today, and I'm really proud of you for being open to this conversation. Remember, addiction is a complex issue, but understanding it and being aware of the risks can help you make informed decisions.

Teen: Thanks, I've learned a lot. Knowing how to handle these situations and where to go for help is good.

* * *

"Obedience to lawful authority is the foundation of manly character."
— *Robert E. Lee*

Chapter 30

Living Lawfully in India

Living lawfully in India goes beyond simply obeying rules; it's about understanding, respecting, and upholding the legal framework that ensures justice, equality, and order. India's rich legal heritage and diverse population are protected by laws designed to safeguard individual rights while promoting the common good. This chapter guides you through the essential aspects of living lawfully in India, including the rights and responsibilities that come with citizenship, the consequences of breaking the law, and the legal protections that uphold the rights of all, particularly the vulnerable and marginalized communities. Understanding these laws is crucial for contributing positively to society and ensuring you are both protected and accountable under the law.

What does it mean to live lawfully in India?

Teen: What does living lawfully in India really mean?

Parent: Living lawfully in India means following the rules and regulations set by the government. It's about respecting the laws in place to ensure peace, order, and fairness in society. Beyond that, it's about understanding your rights as a citizen and fulfilling your duties to contribute positively to the community.

Teen: So, it's like following the rules at school, but on a much larger scale?

Parent: Exactly! Just as school rules maintain discipline, laws help keep our country running smoothly. It's about doing the right thing, respecting others, and being a responsible citizen who understands the importance of laws in protecting everyone's rights.

What are the consequences of breaking the law in India?

Teen: What happens if someone breaks the law?

Parent: Breaking the law in India can lead to serious consequences, ranging from fines to imprisonment, depending on the severity of the offense. Minor offenses might result in warnings or fines, while more serious crimes can lead to long-term imprisonment or even harsher penalties. The idea is not just to punish but also to deter future wrongdoing.

Teen: Does that mean even small mistakes can lead to big trouble?

Parent: Not necessarily. The law takes into account the nature and severity of the offense. However, even small mistakes can have consequences, especially if they involve harm to others or repeated offenses. Understanding the law and acting responsibly is important to avoid getting into trouble.

How does the Indian Penal Code define criminal activities?

Teen: What exactly is the Indian Penal Code?

Parent: The Indian Penal Code (IPC) is a comprehensive document that outlines what actions are considered crimes in India. It covers a wide range of offenses, from theft and assault to more serious crimes like murder and treason. The IPC provides the legal definitions and penalties for each crime, guiding law enforcement and the judiciary in ensuring justice is served.

Teen: So, it's like a rulebook that tells us what's right and wrong?

Parent: The IPC is essentially the country's legal guide defining criminal behaviour and its consequences. By understanding the IPC, you can better understand what is illegal and its potential repercussions.

What are some common offenses outlined in the Indian Penal Code?

Teen: What are some examples of offenses covered by the IPC?

Parent: Common offenses include theft, assault, fraud, and vandalism. The IPC also addresses more serious crimes like kidnapping, rape, and murder. Each offense has specific sections in the IPC that detail the legal repercussions, ensuring that justice is administered fairly based on the nature of the crime.

Teen: I guess it's important to know these laws, so we don't accidentally break them.

Parent: Absolutely. Being aware of the law helps us make informed decisions and stay on the right side of it. It's about being conscious of our actions and their potential impact on others.

What is the role of law enforcement agencies in upholding the law in India?

Teen: What do law enforcement agencies do to maintain law and order?

Parent: Law enforcement agencies, such as the police, are crucial in maintaining law and order. They investigate crimes, apprehend offenders, and ensure that justice is carried out according to the law. They also work to prevent crime through community outreach and by maintaining a visible presence in society.

Teen: So, they're like the guardians of the law?

Parent: In many ways, yes. They protect the public, prevent crime, and ensure that everyone adheres to the rules that keep our society functioning smoothly.

How does the judicial system work to enforce laws and administer justice?

Teen: How does the judicial system fit into all of this?

Parent: The judicial system is responsible for interpreting and applying the law. Courts hear cases, evaluate evidence, and decide based on the law. Judges ensure that justice is done fairly and impartially, whether it's a civil dispute or a criminal case. The judicial system also allows for appeals, so decisions can be reviewed at higher levels if necessary.

Teen: What if someone doesn't agree with a court's decision?

Parent: If someone believes a decision was unfair, they can appeal to a higher court. The judicial system has multiple levels, from lower courts to the Supreme Court, to ensure that justice is thorough and fair. This system helps maintain trust in the law and ensures that everyone has access to justice.

What are the rights and responsibilities of Indian citizens under the law?

Teen: What are our rights and responsibilities as Indian citizens?

Parent: Every citizen in India has certain rights, such as the right to freedom of speech, education, and equality. The Constitution and various laws protect these rights. However, with these rights come responsibilities, such as obeying the law, paying taxes, and respecting the rights of others. It's a two-way street: Our rights are safeguarded, but we must also contribute positively to society.

Teen: So, we get certain freedoms, but we must also play our part in society?

Parent: Exactly. The law protects our rights, but we also have a duty to uphold the law and contribute to the well-being of our community and country. It's about balancing individual freedoms with social responsibilities.

How does Indian law protect the rights of individuals from discrimination and injustice?

Teen: How does the law protect people from being treated unfairly?

Parent: Indian law has several provisions to protect individuals from discrimination based on race, religion, gender, and caste. The Constitution guarantees equality before the law, and there are specific laws like the Scheduled Castes and Scheduled Tribes (Prevention of Atrocities) Act that aim to protect marginalized communities. If someone faces discrimination, they can seek justice through the courts.

Teen: What happens if someone does face discrimination?

Parent: They can file a complaint, and the legal system will investigate and take appropriate action. The law ensures that everyone is treated fairly and that any form of discrimination is addressed and rectified.

What legal rights are related to freedom of speech and expression in India?

Teen: What can you tell me about our rights to freedom of speech and expression?

Parent: Freedom of speech and expression is a fundamental right in India, allowing individuals to freely voice their opinions and ideas. However, this right has certain restrictions to ensure that speech doesn't harm others or incite violence. For example, this right does not protect hate speech, defamation, or speech threatening national security.

Teen: So, we can speak our minds, but we need to be responsible?

Parent: Exactly. It's about balancing freedom with responsibility. Expressing yourself is important, but it should be done in a way that respects others and abides by the law.

How does the Indian Constitution safeguard fundamental rights and liberties?

Teen: What does the Constitution do to protect our rights?

Parent: The Indian Constitution is the supreme law of the land, and it guarantees fundamental rights to all citizens. These rights include equality, freedom, and justice, ensuring that everyone is treated fairly and justly. The Constitution also protects these rights through the judiciary, allowing citizens to challenge any violations of their rights in court.

Teen: So, the Constitution is like a shield for our rights?

Parent: That's a great way to put it! The Constitution protects our rights and ensures that both the government and individuals respect them. It is the foundation of our legal system and the protector of our liberties.

What are the consequences of cybercrime in India, and how are they addressed by law?

Teen: What happens if someone commits a cybercrime in India?

Parent: Cybercrime, such as hacking, identity theft, or online harassment, is taken very seriously in India. The Information Technology Act of 2000 provides strict penalties for those found guilty of these offenses, including fines, imprisonment, or both. The law is designed to protect everyone's privacy and safety online, ensuring that illegal activities on the internet are met with appropriate consequences.

Teen: So, the internet isn't free for all; are there rules here too?

Parent: Absolutely. The internet has rules just like the physical world. The law protects users from harm and ensures that the digital space is safe and secure for everyone.

How does Indian law address issues of violence and harassment against women and children?

Teen: What protections do women and children have against violence and harassment?

Parent: Indian law has strict measures to prevent and punish violence and harassment against women and children. Laws like the Protection of Women from Domestic Violence Act and the Protection of Children from Sexual Offenses Act provide legal remedies and support for victims. These laws are designed to protect the most vulnerable members of society and ensure that perpetrators are held accountable.

Teen: That's really important. It's good to know the law is there to protect those who need it most.

Parent: Yes, and it's equally important for everyone to be aware of these laws so they can stand up against injustice and seek help when needed.

What legal measures are in place to prevent and punish acts of corruption in India?

Teen: What does the law do to stop corruption?

Parent: Corruption is a serious issue in India, and the law has strict measures to combat it. The Prevention of Corruption Act of 1988 and other anti-corruption laws are in place to punish those who misuse power for personal gain. Penalties for corruption can include heavy fines, imprisonment, and dismissal from public office.

Teen: What happens if someone is caught being corrupt?

Parent: They can face severe legal consequences, including imprisonment and fines. Corruption undermines trust in the system, so the law takes it very seriously. It's about ensuring transparency and accountability in all sectors of society.

How does Indian law protect the environment and promote sustainable development?

Teen: What does the law say about protecting the environment?

Parent: Indian law has several provisions to protect the environment and promote sustainable development. Acts like the Environmental Protection Act and the Wildlife Protection Act are designed to conserve natural resources and ensure that development doesn't harm the environment. These laws regulate activities that might impact the environment, such as industrial pollution, deforestation, and wildlife exploitation.

Teen: So, the law helps keep our environment safe?

Parent: Yes, the law plays a crucial role in balancing development with environmental protection. It encourages industries and individuals to act responsibly and sustainably, ensuring that future generations can also enjoy a healthy environment.

What are the penalties for offenses related to drug trafficking and substance abuse in India?

Teen: What are the consequences of drug trafficking and substance abuse?

Parent: Drug trafficking and substance abuse are serious crimes in India, and the law imposes strict penalties, including long-term imprisonment and heavy fines. The Narcotic Drugs and Psychotropic Substances (NDPS)

Act, 1985, is the primary legislation that deals with these offenses, aiming to curb the illegal drug trade and protect society from the dangers of substance abuse.

Teen: Why are the penalties so harsh?

Parent: Because drug trafficking and abuse have devastating effects on individuals and society. The law aims to deter these activities and protect communities from the harmful impacts of drugs. It's about ensuring public safety and health.

How does Indian law address issues of domestic violence and abuse within families?

Teen: What can someone do if they're facing domestic violence?

Parent: Indian law provides strong protection against domestic violence through the Protection of Women from Domestic Violence Act, 2005. This law allows victims to seek legal help, including restraining orders, financial support, and shelter. It's designed to protect individuals from abuse and ensure they have access to justice and safety.

Teen: That sounds like an important law. It's good to know there's help available.

Parent: Yes, the law is there to ensure that no one has to endure violence or abuse. Victims must know their rights and seek help if they or someone they know is in such a situation.

What are the legal rights and protections available to victims of crime in India?

Teen: What rights do victims of crime have in India?

Parent: Victims of crime in India have several rights and protections under the law. They are entitled to a fair trial, the right to be informed about the case's progress, and the right to compensation in certain cases. Victims can also seek legal aid and counseling to help them cope with the trauma and navigate the legal process.

Teen: Does that mean they're not alone in dealing with the aftermath of a crime?

Parent: Exactly. The law ensures that victims receive the support they need, whether it's legal aid, counseling, or protection from further harm. It's about providing justice and helping victims rebuild their lives.

How does Indian law address issues of religious freedom and communal harmony?

Teen: How does the law protect religious freedom in India?

Parent: The Indian Constitution guarantees freedom of religion, allowing everyone to practice, profess, and propagate their faith. Laws also prevent and punish actions threatening communal harmony or inciting violence based on religion. These laws ensure that all religions are treated equally and that everyone can live in peace, regardless of their faith.

Teen: So, the law respects everyone's beliefs?

Parent: Yes, it's about ensuring that all religions are respected and that everyone has the right to practice their faith without fear of discrimination or persecution. The law promotes tolerance and peaceful coexistence among different religious communities.

What are the penalties for offenses related to sexual harassment and assault in India?

Teen: What happens if someone is found guilty of sexual harassment or assault?

Parent: Sexual harassment and assault are serious offenses under Indian law. Penalties include imprisonment, fines, and mandatory counseling or rehabilitation for the offender. The law protects individuals, particularly women, and ensures that perpetrators are held accountable for their actions.

Teen: That's important. It must be hard for victims, so the law must be strict.

Parent: Absolutely. The law protects individuals and ensures that offenders are punished appropriately. It's also important to raise awareness to prevent such offenses.

How does Indian law protect the rights of marginalized communities and minorities?

Teen: How does the law protect marginalized communities in India?

Parent: Indian law has specific provisions to protect the rights of marginalized communities and minorities, including reservations in education and employment and laws that prevent discrimination based on caste, religion, or ethnicity. The Constitution and laws like the Scheduled Castes and Tribes (Prevention of Atrocities) Act are designed to ensure that everyone has equal opportunities and is protected from injustice.

Teen: So, does the law help to level the playing field for everyone?

Parent: The idea is to create a society where everyone has equal rights and opportunities, regardless of background. The law is a tool to promote fairness and social justice for all citizens.

What legal measures are in place to combat terrorism and maintain national security in India?

Teen: What does the law do to combat terrorism?

Parent: Terrorism is a major threat, and Indian law has strict measures to combat it, including laws like the Unlawful Activities (Prevention) Act (UAPA). These laws give authorities the power to take swift action against those involved in terrorist activities, including arresting and detaining suspects and imposing severe penalties such as life imprisonment or even the death penalty for the most serious offenses.

Teen: What happens if someone is suspected of being involved in terrorism?

Parent: They can be arrested, detained, and tried in special courts. The law allows for rigorous investigation and prosecution to ensure that those involved in terrorism are brought to justice. It's about protecting national security and the safety of all citizens.

How does Indian law regulate business practices and ensure fair competition in the market?

Teen: What does the law say about how businesses should operate?

Parent: Indian law, through acts like the Competition Act, ensures that businesses operate fairly and that there's healthy competition in the market. The law prevents monopolies and unfair trade practices and ensures that consumers have access to various goods and services. It also promotes transparency and fairness in business operations.

Teen: So, it's like making sure everyone plays by the rules in the business world?

Parent: Exactly. The law keeps the market fair and competitive, which benefits both businesses and consumers. It's about ensuring that no single business can dominate the market to the detriment of others.

What are the penalties for fraud and financial misconduct offenses in India?

Teen: What happens if someone commits fraud or financial misconduct?

Parent: Fraud and financial misconduct are serious crimes under Indian law, with penalties including imprisonment, fines, and asset confiscation. The law is designed to protect individuals, businesses, and the economy from fraudulent activities. Offenders can face significant legal consequences, including long-term imprisonment and heavy fines.

Teen: Why are these penalties so severe?

Parent: Financial crimes can harm individuals, businesses, and the economy. The law aims to protect people's money and ensure that businesses operate honestly. It's about maintaining trust in the financial system and protecting the market's integrity.

How does Indian law address issues of human trafficking and exploitation?

Teen: What does the law do to stop human trafficking?

Parent: Indian law, through acts like the Immoral Traffic (Prevention) Act, has strict measures to combat human trafficking. Offenders face severe penalties, including long-term imprisonment and fines. The law also provides for the rescue, rehabilitation, and protection of victims of trafficking, ensuring that they receive the support they need to rebuild their lives.

Teen: That's really important. It's terrible that trafficking still happens.

Parent: Yes, it's a serious issue, and the law is working to protect vulnerable people and bring traffickers to justice. It's about ensuring that no one is exploited and those rescued are given the needed help.

What are the legal rights and protections available to migrant workers and labourers in India?

Teen: What protections do migrant workers and labourers have under the law?

Parent: Under Indian law, migrant workers and labourers have specific rights, including fair wages, safe working conditions, and the right to organize. Laws like the Inter-State Migrant Workmen Act provide protections and ensure that their rights are respected, regardless of where they work within the country.

Teen: So, even if someone moves to a different state for work, they're still protected by the law?

Parent: Yes, the law ensures that all workers, regardless of where they're from, are treated fairly and have access to their rights. It's about protecting the dignity and well-being of all workers.

How does Indian law address issues of child labour and exploitation?

Teen: What does the law say about child labour?

Parent: Child labour is strictly prohibited under Indian law, particularly for children under the age of 14. The Child Labour (Prohibition and Regulation) Act lays down rules to prevent exploitation and ensure that children have the opportunity to go to school and enjoy their childhood. There are also penalties for those who employ child labour, including fines and imprisonment.

Teen: That's good. Children should be in school, not working.

Parent: Absolutely. The law is there to protect children and ensure they have a chance to learn, grow, and enjoy their childhood. It's about giving every child the opportunity to build a better future.

What legal measures are in place to promote road safety and prevent accidents in India?

Teen: What does the law do to make sure roads are safe?

Parent: Road safety is a major concern, and Indian law has several measures in place to prevent accidents, such as the Motor Vehicles Act. This law regulates traffic rules, vehicle safety standards, and violation penalties. It also includes driver education and licensing provisions to ensure that only qualified individuals are on the road.

Teen: What happens if someone breaks traffic rules?

Parent: For serious offenses, drivers can face fines, license suspension, or even imprisonment. The law aims to make roads safer for everyone by enforcing strict penalties for violations and encouraging responsible driving behaviour.

How does Indian law regulate the use of firearms and weapons in society?

Teen: What are the rules about owning and using weapons in India?

Parent: Indian law, through the Arms Act, regulates the possession and use of firearms and other weapons. To own a gun, you need a license, and there are strict rules about how weapons can be used and stored. The law aims to ensure that weapons are only in the hands of responsible individuals and are used safely.

Teen: What if someone uses a weapon illegally?

Parent: They can face severe penalties, including imprisonment. The law ensures that weapons don't threaten public safety and that any misuse is dealt with strictly.

What are the penalties for offenses related to cyberbullying and online harassment?

Teen: What happens if someone is caught cyberbullying or harassing someone online?

Parent: Cyberbullying and online harassment are taken very seriously under Indian law. The Information Technology Act and other legal provisions outline penalties that can include fines, imprisonment, or both, depending on the severity of the offense. The law protects individuals from harm in the digital space and ensures that online behaviour is respectful and lawful.

Teen: So, even things said online can have serious consequences?

Parent: Yes, absolutely. Just because something is done online doesn't make it any less real or harmful. The law is there to protect people from abuse, whether it's in person or on the internet.

How does Indian law protect intellectual property rights and innovation?

Teen: How does the law protect things like inventions and creative works?

Parent: Indian law has several provisions to protect intellectual property, such as patents, copyrights, and trademarks. These laws ensure that creators and inventors have exclusive rights to their work, encouraging innovation and creativity. Protecting intellectual property is crucial for fostering innovation and respecting creators' hard work.

Teen: What happens if someone tries to steal someone else's ideas or work?

Parent: If someone infringes on intellectual property rights, they can face legal action, including fines and damages. The law ensures that creators and inventors are rewarded for their work and that others cannot unfairly benefit from their ideas.

What are the legal rights and protections available to prisoners and detainees in India?

Teen: Do people in prison still have rights?

Parent: Yes, even prisoners and detainees have rights under Indian law. These include the right to fair treatment, access to healthcare, and protection from torture or abuse. The law also ensures that prisoners are treated with dignity and that their basic human rights are upheld, even while serving their sentences.

Teen: That's important. Everyone deserves to be treated fairly, no matter what.

Parent: Exactly. The law recognizes that while prisoners are being punished for their crimes, they are still entitled to basic rights and humane treatment.

How does Indian law address issues of pollution and environmental degradation?

Teen: What does the law do about pollution?

Parent: Indian law addresses pollution and environmental degradation through the Air (Prevention and Control of Pollution) Act and the Water (Prevention and Control of Pollution) Act. These laws set air and water quality standards and regulate activities that might harm the environment. Penalties for violating these laws can include fines and imprisonment, depending on the severity of the offense.

Teen: What happens if someone breaks these environmental laws?

Parent: Individuals or companies that violate environmental regulations face penalties, including fines and imprisonment. The law aims to protect the environment and ensure that everyone follows the rules to keep our surroundings clean and safe.

What are the penalties for offenses related to wildlife conservation and animal cruelty?

Teen: What could happen to someone who harms animals or wildlife?

Parent: Wildlife conservation is a major concern, and Indian law has strict penalties for offenses like poaching, illegal trade, and cruelty to animals. The Wildlife Protection Act and Prevention of Cruelty to Animals Act are designed to safeguard animals and their habitats. Offenders can face heavy fines, imprisonment, or both for harming animals or engaging in illegal wildlife activities.

Teen: That's really important. It's terrible that people still harm animals and wildlife.

Parent: Yes, it's a serious issue, and the law protects animals from unnecessary harm and ensures that wildlife is preserved for future generations.

How does Indian law regulate alcohol consumption and public intoxication?

Teen: What are the rules about drinking alcohol in India?

Parent: Indian law regulates alcohol consumption through various state-specific laws. The legal drinking age, sale regulations, and rules about public intoxication vary depending on the state. Public intoxication, especially if it leads to disorderly behaviour, can result in fines or arrest. The law is designed to promote responsible drinking and protect public safety.

Teen: So, it's important to know the local laws wherever you are?

Parent: Exactly. The rules can be different from one state to another, so it's crucial to be aware of the laws in your area to avoid any legal issues.

What are the legal rights and protections available to LGBTQ+ individuals in India?

Teen: What rights do LGBTQ+ people have under Indian law?

Parent: LGBTQ+ individuals have the right to equality and protection from discrimination under Indian law. The decriminalization of Section 377 of the Indian Penal Code was a significant step forward, and there are ongoing efforts to ensure that LGBTQ+ rights are respected and protected. The law is evolving to be more inclusive, but there is still work to ensure full equality and acceptance.

Teen: So, the law is becoming more inclusive?

Parent: Yes, while there's still progress to be made, Indian law is moving towards greater inclusivity and protection for LGBTQ+ individuals, ensuring they can live freely and without fear of discrimination.

How does Indian law address issues of caste discrimination and social inequality?

Teen: How does the law help fight caste discrimination?

Parent: Caste discrimination is illegal under Indian law. The Constitution of India, through articles like Article 15 and Article 17, prohibits discrimination based on caste and has abolished untouchability. Laws like the Scheduled Castes and Tribes (Prevention of Atrocities) Act are also in place to protect marginalized communities from caste-based violence and discrimination.

Teen: So, the law tries to ensure everyone is treated equally, regardless of caste?

Parent: The goal is to create a society with equal rights and opportunities, free from discrimination and social inequality. The law is a powerful tool for promoting all citizens' fairness and justice.

What legal measures are in place to protect consumers from fraudulent and deceptive practices?

Teen: How does the law protect people from getting scammed or tricked when they buy something?

Parent: In India, consumer protection is taken very seriously. The Consumer Protection Act of 2019 is designed to protect consumers from fraudulent and deceptive practices. It gives consumers the right to file complaints against unfair trade practices, defective goods, or deficient services. There are also consumer courts where disputes can be resolved, ensuring that consumers are treated fairly.

Teen: So, if someone buys something that doesn't work as promised, they can take action?

Parent: Exactly. Consumers have the right to get what they pay for, and the law ensures that businesses are held accountable if they don't deliver on their promises.

How does Indian law regulate the use of public spaces and resources?

Teen: Are there laws about how public spaces like parks or streets should be used?

Parent: Yes, public spaces and resources are regulated by various laws to ensure they are used responsibly and for the benefit of everyone. For example, laws like the Municipal Acts govern the use and maintenance of public spaces. There are also specific rules about littering, noise pollution, and unauthorized use of public property, ensuring that these areas are safe and accessible.

Teen: What happens if someone misuses a public space?

Parent: Misusing public spaces can lead to fines, penalties, or other legal actions. The goal is to keep these areas safe, clean, and enjoyable. The law helps maintain the quality and accessibility of public resources for all citizens.

What are the penalties for offenses related to copyright infringement and piracy?

Teen: What happens if someone copies a book, movie, or software without permission?

Parent: Copyright infringement and piracy are serious offenses under Indian law. The Copyright Act of 1957 provides for penalties, including fines and imprisonment. These laws are in place to protect the rights of creators and ensure that they are compensated for their work. It's about respecting intellectual property and encouraging creativity and innovation.

Teen: So, downloading or sharing things illegally can get someone into big trouble?

Parent: Yes, absolutely. It's important to respect intellectual property rights and use content legally, whether it's music, movies, software, or books.

How does Indian law address issues of political corruption and electoral malpractice?

Teen: What does the law say about corruption in politics and cheating in elections?

Parent: Indian law has strict measures to address political corruption and electoral malpractice. The Prevention of Corruption Act of 1988 targets corruption in public offices, and the Representation of the People Act of 1951 governs electoral practices. These laws penalize bribery, vote-buying, and other corrupt practices, ensuring that elections are fair and transparent.

Teen: What happens if a politician is caught being corrupt?

Parent: If found guilty, they can face severe penalties, including imprisonment, fines, and disqualification from holding public office. The law aims to promote clean governance and protect the democratic process, ensuring that public trust in the political system is maintained.

What legal rights and protections are available to individuals with disabilities in India?

Teen: How does the law help people with disabilities in India?

Parent: The Rights of Persons with Disabilities Act, 2016, is a comprehensive law that provides a range of protections and rights for individuals with disabilities. It ensures accessibility, non-discrimination, and equal opportunities in areas like education, employment, and public services. The law is designed to create an inclusive society where people with disabilities can live with dignity and participate fully in all aspects of life.

Teen: That sounds really important. So, does the law help make sure everyone has the same chances, no matter what?

Parent: Exactly. The law ensures that everyone, regardless of their abilities, has the opportunity to succeed and contribute to society. It's about promoting equality and inclusivity for all.

How does Indian law regulate the use of social media and online platforms?

Teen: Are there laws about what people can and can't do on social media?

Parent: Yes, Indian law regulates social media and online platforms through the Information Technology Act of 2000 and the Information Technology (Intermediary Guidelines and Digital Media Ethics Code) Rules, 2021. These laws set guidelines for what is acceptable content, how data should be handled, and how platforms must respond to complaints about illegal or harmful content.

Teen: What happens if someone breaks these rules online?

Parent: Penalties can range from fines to imprisonment, depending on the severity of the offense. Social media platforms are also required to take down harmful content and cooperate with law enforcement to ensure that online activities are safe and lawful.

What are the penalties for offenses related to stalking and harassment?

Teen: What does the law say about stalking and harassment?

Parent: Stalking and harassment are serious offenses under Indian law. The Indian Penal Code includes specific provisions against stalking, with penalties including imprisonment and fines. The law protects individuals from unwanted attention and ensures their safety, whether the harassment occurs in person or online.

Teen: So, if someone is being stalked or harassed, they can get help from the law?

Parent: Absolutely. The law provides strong protection against such behaviour, and victims can seek legal action to stop it and ensure their safety. It's about preventing harm and ensuring that everyone can live without fear.

How does Indian law address issues of workplace discrimination and harassment?

Teen: What protections do people have against discrimination and harassment at work?

Parent: Indian law provides protections against workplace discrimination and harassment through acts like the Sexual Harassment of Women at Workplace (Prevention, Prohibition, and Redressal) Act, 2013, and the Equal Remuneration Act, 1976. These laws ensure that everyone is treated fairly at work, regardless of gender, religion, caste, or other factors, and provide mechanisms for addressing grievances.

Teen: What can someone do if they face discrimination or harassment at work?

Parent: They can file a complaint with their employer, a designated committee, or even approach the courts. The law mandates a safe and respectful workplace, and any violations can lead to serious consequences for the offender, including fines and imprisonment.

What legal measures are in place to promote gender equality and women's empowerment?

Teen: How does the law help promote gender equality and empower women?

Parent: Indian law has several provisions to promote gender equality and empower women, such as the Prohibition of Child Marriage Act of 2006, the Maternity Benefit Act of 1961, and the Domestic Violence Act of 2005. These laws protect women's rights, ensure equal opportunities, and support education, employment, and health.

Teen: So, the law ensures women have the same rights and opportunities as men?

Parent: Exactly. These laws are crucial in breaking down barriers and ensuring that women can participate fully and equally in all aspects of society. It's about promoting gender equality and creating a more just and inclusive society.

How does Indian law protect the rights of indigenous communities and tribal populations?

Teen: How are the rights of indigenous communities and tribal populations protected under the law?

Parent: Indian law provides special protections for indigenous communities and tribal populations through the Constitution and acts like the Scheduled Tribes and Other Traditional Forest Dwellers (Recognition of Forest Rights) Act, 2006. These laws recognize their rights to land, resources, and cultural practices, and aim to preserve their heritage and way of life.

Teen: That's important for protecting their culture and traditions, right?

Parent: Absolutely. The law ensures that their unique identities are respected and that they have the resources they need to thrive while preserving their traditions. It's about balancing development with preserving indigenous cultures and ways of life.

What are the penalties for offenses related to public nuisance and disorderly conduct?

Teen: What happens if someone causes a public nuisance or behaves disorderly in public?

Parent: Public nuisance and disorderly conduct are offenses under the Indian Penal Code, with penalties including fines and imprisonment. These laws are in place to maintain public order and ensure that everyone can enjoy public spaces without being disturbed by the actions of others.

Teen: So, can causing trouble in public places get someone into legal trouble?

Parent: It's important to respect public spaces and the people around us. The law ensures that everyone can live in a peaceful and orderly environment.

How does Indian law address issues of land ownership and property rights?

Teen: What does the law say about owning land and property in India?

Parent: Land ownership and property rights in India are governed by various laws, including the Transfer of Property Act of 1882 and the Land Acquisition Act of 2013. These laws outline how property can be bought, sold, inherited, and transferred and protect the rights of property owners. The law ensures that property transactions are fair and that owners' rights are respected.

Teen: What if there's a dispute over land or property?

Parent: Disputes can be resolved through the legal system, where courts or tribunals will examine the evidence and make a judgment. The law ensures that property transactions are fair and owners' rights are protected.

What legal rights and protections are available to refugees and asylum seekers in India?

Teen: What rights do refugees and asylum seekers have in India?

Parent: While India is not a signatory to the 1951 Refugee Convention, it still protects refugees and asylum seekers under its general legal framework. They are entitled to basic human rights, protection from refoulement (being returned to a country where they face danger), and access to essential services like healthcare and education. The law recognizes their need for protection and provides them with certain rights to ensure their safety and dignity.

Teen: So, even though they're not citizens, they're still protected?

Parent: Yes, Indian law recognizes their need for protection and provides them with certain rights to ensure their safety and dignity while they are in the country.

How does Indian law promote accountability and transparency in governance?

Teen: How does the law ensure the government is transparent and accountable?

Parent: Indian law promotes transparency and accountability in governance through acts like the Right to Information (RTI) Act, 2005. This law allows citizens to request information from public authorities, ensuring that government actions are transparent and officials are held accountable for their decisions. The RTI Act empowers citizens to participate in the democratic process by giving them the tools to seek information and hold the government accountable.

Teen: So, people can ask the government to explain what they're doing?

Parent: Exactly. The RTI Act is a powerful tool for ensuring open and fair governance. It allows citizens to access information and hold officials accountable for their actions.

Takeaway Points:

1. **Understanding the Law:** Living lawfully in India requires a deep understanding of the laws that govern our rights, responsibilities, and conduct as citizens. The Indian Constitution and various statutes ensure justice, equality, and order in society.

2. **Consequences of Breaking the Law:** Violating the law can result in serious consequences, including fines, imprisonment, and other penalties. The severity of the punishment depends on the nature of the offense, highlighting the importance of adhering to legal norms.

3. **Protection of Rights:** Indian law offers robust protection of individual rights, including freedom of speech, protection against discrimination, and safeguards for marginalized communities. These laws are essential for maintaining a fair and just society.

4. **Accountability and Transparency:** Laws like the Right to Information Act promote transparency and accountability in governance, empowering citizens to hold public officials accountable for their actions.

5. **Environmental and Social Responsibility:** Indian law emphasizes the importance of environmental protection, social responsibility, and sustainable development, ensuring that growth and progress do not come at the expense of the environment or vulnerable communities.

6. **Safeguards for Vulnerable Populations:** Indian law provides specific protections for vulnerable populations, including women, children, the LGBTQ+ community, and indigenous peoples, ensuring that their rights are respected and upheld.

7. **Personal Responsibility and Social Order:** Living lawfully means balancing personal freedoms with social responsibilities. It's about making informed decisions, respecting the rights of others, and contributing positively to the community and the nation.

This chapter provides a comprehensive guide to understanding the legal landscape in India. It encourages teenagers to recognize the importance of living lawfully, respecting the rights of others, and contributing to a just and orderly society.

* * *

"Love is an irresistible desire to be irresistibly desired."
— Robert Frost

Chapter 31

Navigating Infatuation and Love: Understanding and Managing Teenage Relationships

Entering the world of teenage relationships is both exciting and challenging. It's a time when emotions run high, and the boundaries between infatuation and love can often blur. As teens navigate these new experiences, they face a host of questions and uncertainties about their feelings and relationships, as well as how to manage both healthily.

This chapter, *Navigating Infatuation and Love: Understanding and Managing Teenage Relationships*, is designed to help Teens understand the nuances of their emotions, recognize the difference between infatuation and love, and build relationships that are based on mutual respect and understanding. Through a thoughtful conversation between a parent and Teen, we will explore the complexities of romantic relationships, the importance of communication, setting healthy boundaries, and maintaining individuality while being part of a couple.

Whether you're experiencing your first crush, wondering how to handle a breakup, or trying to figure out how to balance love with other aspects of life, this chapter offers guidance and insights to help you make informed and confident choices. The goal is to empower you to build relationships that are fulfilling, supportive, and aligned with your values, while also prioritizing your own happiness and well-being.

Parent: So, you're at that age where relationships start becoming a big deal, huh?

Teen: Yeah, it feels like everyone around me is either in a relationship or talking about crushes. It's all kind of confusing.

Parent: I get that. Relationships, especially in your teenage years, can be exciting but overwhelming. Why don't we dive into this together? Let's start with something basic but important—what do you think infatuation is, and how does it differ from love?

What is infatuation, and how does it differ from love?

Teen: I think infatuation is when you're really into someone, but it's more about how they look or the idea of them rather than who they really are.

Parent: That's a great start. Infatuation is often intense and immediate. It's like a crush on steroids, where everything about the person seems perfect. However, infatuation tends to be short-lived and can fade once you get to know the person better or the initial excitement wears off. Love, on the other hand, is deeper. It grows over time as you know and care for someone more meaningfully. Love is about accepting someone's flaws as well as their strengths.

Teen: So, infatuation is more surface-level, while love goes deeper?

Parent: Exactly. Infatuation can feel all-consuming at first, but it doesn't have the staying power of love, which is built on trust, respect, and real emotional connection.

How do you know if you're infatuated with someone?

Teen: I guess you can't stop thinking about them, even if you don't know much about them.

Parent: Yes, that's a common sign. If your feelings are mostly based on how the person looks, or how they make you feel rather than who they are as a person, it's likely infatuation. Another sign is if the relationship moves too quickly—you feel like you're in a whirlwind romance but haven't really gotten to know each other on a deeper level.

Teen: So if I'm more focused on how they look or how they make me feel, it's probably infatuation?

Parent: That's right. And it's totally normal to experience infatuation—everyone does. It's just important to recognize it for what it is.

Can infatuation turn into love over time?

Teen: So if you're infatuated with someone, can it ever become real love?

Parent: It can, but it takes time and effort. If both people get to know each other well and build a strong, respectful connection, what started as infatuation can evolve into love. The key is to slow down and let the relationship develop naturally, rather than rushing into it.

Teen: So, patience is important?

Parent: Absolutely. Letting things grow at their own pace helps ensure that your feelings are real and lasting.

What are the signs of being in love?

Teen: How do you know if you're really in love, then?

Parent: Love feels steady and secure. It's when you genuinely care about the other person's well-being, want to support them, and feel comfortable being yourself around them. It's less about intense highs and more about a deep, ongoing connection. You're not just in it for the good times—you're there for the challenges too.

Teen: So love is more about commitment and caring over the long term?

Parent: Exactly. It's about being there for each other, through thick and thin.

How do you distinguish between genuine feelings and infatuation?

Teen: How can you tell if your feelings are genuine or just infatuation?

Parent: A good question to ask yourself is whether you're interested in the whole person or just certain aspects of them. If your feelings persist and deepen over time, even after seeing the person's imperfections, that's a sign of genuine feelings. Infatuation often fades when you see the person's flaws, while love grows stronger because you accept those flaws.

Teen: So, it's about whether your feelings last and whether you're okay with their imperfections?

Parent: Yes, and whether you're willing to invest in the relationship, not just when it's fun or exciting, but even when it's challenging.

What role does physical attraction play in infatuation and love?

Teen: How does physical attraction fit into all of this?

Parent: Physical attraction is a natural part of both infatuation and love. It's often what initially draws you to someone. Infatuation and physical attraction can sometimes overshadow everything else. But in love, while physical attraction remains important, it's balanced by emotional and intellectual connections. You're attracted to the person, not just how they look.

Teen: So it's normal to be physically attracted to someone, but it shouldn't be the only thing that matters?

Parent: Exactly. Physical attraction is a starting point, but the emotional and intellectual connections make a relationship last.

How can you tell if someone truly loves you?

Teen: How do you know if someone truly loves you?

Parent: Someone who truly loves you will respect, support, and accept you as you are. They'll be interested in your well-being, encourage your growth, and stand by you even when things aren't perfect. They won't pressure you to change or make you feel bad about yourself. Their actions will match their words—they'll show their love through how they treat you daily.

Teen: So it's about consistency and respect?

Parent: Yes, love is shown through consistent actions that demonstrate care, respect, and support.

What are some common misconceptions about love?

Teen: What are some common misconceptions people have about love?

Parent: One big misconception is that love is supposed to be like what you see in movies—full of grand gestures, drama, and perfect moments. Real love is much more about everyday kindness, patience, and working through challenges together. Another misconception is that love means never having conflicts. In reality, even the healthiest relationships have disagreements, but how you handle them matters.

Teen: So, love isn't always about big romantic gestures or avoiding fights?

Parent: Exactly. Real love is about building a life together with all its ups and downs, not just the picture-perfect moments.

How does media influence our perception of love and relationships?

Teen: How does media influence how we see love and relationships?

Parent: Media often portrays love in a very idealized or dramatic way. Movies, TV shows, and even social media can make it seem like love is all about passion, intense emotions, or finding the one who completes you. While these portrayals can be entertaining, they're not always realistic. They can create unrealistic expectations about love, which can lead to disappointment or confusion in real-life relationships.

Teen: So, the media might give us the wrong idea about what to expect in a relationship?

Parent: Yes, it's important to remember that real love is more complex and nuanced than what's often shown in the media. It's about building a deep connection, not just about romance or drama.

What are the dangers of getting too caught up in infatuation?

Teen: What can happen if you get too caught up in infatuation?

Parent: Getting too caught up in infatuation can lead to impulsive decisions, like rushing into a relationship before you know the person. It can also cause you to overlook red flags or ignore your own needs and boundaries.

When you're infatuated, you might idealize the other person and put them on a pedestal, which isn't healthy for either of you. It's important to stay grounded and take time to really understand your feelings.

Teen: So, it's about keeping things in perspective and not getting swept away?

Parent: Exactly. Infatuation can be exciting, but it's important to slow down and make sure your decisions are thoughtful and based on more than just intense emotions.

How do you handle rejection in a relationship?

Teen: What if I really like someone, but they don't feel the same way? How do I deal with that kind of rejection?

Parent: Rejection can be tough, especially when you have strong feelings for someone. The first thing to remember is that rejection doesn't mean there's anything wrong with you—it's just that the other person isn't on the same page, and that's okay. It's important to allow yourself to feel the disappointment and remind yourself that this is just one experience in a lifetime full of possibilities. Focus on what you've learned from the situation and know that this is an opportunity for growth.

Teen: So it's normal to feel hurt, but I shouldn't take it personally?

Parent: Exactly. It's okay to feel hurt but don't let it define your self-worth. Surround yourself with supportive friends and family and keep doing what makes you happy. The pain will fade, and you'll be ready to move forward.

What are healthy boundaries in a romantic relationship?

Teen: What are healthy boundaries, and how do I set them in a relationship?

Parent: Healthy boundaries are the limits you set for yourself in a relationship to protect your well-being. They help ensure that both partners feel respected, valued, and comfortable. For example, a healthy boundary might be deciding how much time you spend together versus apart, or agreeing on how you communicate when you're upset. It's important to have open conversations about your boundaries early on in the relationship and to listen to your partner's boundaries as well.

Teen: How do I know if I'm setting the right boundaries?

Parent: A good boundary is one that makes you feel safe, respected, and true to yourself. If something doesn't feel right to you, speaking up is important. Boundaries are about mutual respect, so both partners should feel comfortable discussing and honoring them.

How do you maintain your individuality in a relationship?

Teen: How do I stay true to myself while being in a relationship?

Parent: Maintaining your individuality means continuing to do the things you love, keeping up with your hobbies, and spending time with your friends and family, even when you're in a relationship. It's easy to get caught up in spending time with your partner, but it's important to remember that a healthy relationship involves two whole people, not two halves making a whole. Your partner should support your interests and encourage you to be the best version of yourself.

Teen: So it's okay to have my own space and interests outside the relationship?

Parent: Absolutely. It's essential. When you maintain your individuality, you bring more to the relationship, and it helps prevent feelings of dependency or losing yourself in the relationship.

What should you do if you feel like you're losing yourself in a relationship?

Teen: What if I start to feel like I'm losing myself in a relationship?

Parent: If you start feeling like you're losing yourself, it's important to take a step back and evaluate what's happening. Are you spending too much time together at the expense of your other relationships and interests? Are you compromising your values or needs to please your partner? If so, it's time to re-establish those boundaries we talked about. Have an open conversation with your partner about your feelings and what you need to do to feel like yourself again.

Teen: And what if my partner doesn't understand or gets upset?

Parent: A supportive partner will understand and respect your need to maintain your identity. If they don't, it might be a sign that the relationship isn't as healthy as it should be. It's important to prioritize your well-being, even if it means making tough decisions.

How do you cope with a breakup?

Teen: Breakups sound really hard. How do you cope if a relationship ends?

Parent: Breakups can be incredibly painful but also a part of life. The most important thing is to give yourself time to grieve and heal. Allow yourself to feel all the emotions of a breakup—sadness, anger, confusion—without rushing the process. It's also important to lean on your support system. Talk to friends, family, or even a counselor about what you're going through. Focus on self-care, whether through exercise, hobbies, or just taking time for yourself. And remember, every breakup is a learning experience that helps you grow and prepares you for future relationships.

Teen: So it's okay to feel bad, but it won't last forever?

Parent: Exactly. Feeling bad after a breakup is normal, but you'll heal and move on with time and support. Every experience helps you learn more about yourself and what you want in a relationship.

Can you be friends with your ex after a breakup?

Teen: Is staying friends with your ex after a breakup possible?

Parent: It's possible, but it depends on the circumstances of the breakup and the feelings involved. If both of you are on the same page and the breakup was mutual, you might be able to transition into a friendship. However, if there are lingering feelings or if the breakup was particularly painful, it might be healthier to take some time apart before considering a friendship. The key is to be honest with yourself about whether you can handle being just friends and to ensure it's not preventing either of you from moving on.

Teen: So, it's not always a good idea to stay friends right away?

Parent: That's right. Sometimes, taking time to heal separately is the best option. It's important to prioritize your emotional well-being.

How do you deal with jealousy in a relationship?

Teen: What about jealousy? How do you handle it if it comes up in a relationship?

Parent: Jealousy is a natural emotion, but it's important to address it in a healthy way. The first step is to recognize why you're feeling jealous. Is it insecurity, fear of losing the person, or something else? Once you understand the root of your jealousy, you can communicate openly with your partner about your feelings. It's important to talk about your concerns without accusing or blaming. Together, you can work on building trust and setting boundaries that help you feel more secure in the relationship.

Teen: So, talking about it openly is the key?

Parent: Yes, communication is crucial. Jealousy can be managed if both partners are willing to understand each other's feelings and work together to address them.

What are the signs of a toxic relationship?

Teen: How can you tell if a relationship is toxic?

Parent: A toxic relationship is one with more negativity than positivity, and it affects your well-being. Some signs include constant criticism, lack of trust, controlling behaviour, frequent arguments, and feeling drained or unhappy most of the time. If you feel like you're walking on eggshells around your partner, or if they're trying to isolate you from friends and family, those are red flags. A healthy relationship should make you feel supported, respected, and happy.

Teen: What should you do if you realize your relationship is toxic?

Parent: If you recognize that you're in a toxic relationship, the best course of action is to have an honest conversation with your partner. If things don't improve or if you feel unsafe, it's important to seek help from trusted friends, family, or a counselor and consider ending the relationship. Your well-being should always come first.

How do you know when it's time to end a relationship?

Teen: How do you know when it's time to end a relationship?

Parent: Ending a relationship is never easy, but sometimes it's the best decision for your well-being. It's time to consider ending a relationship if you're consistently unhappy, if the relationship is draining rather than uplifting, or if there's a lack of respect, trust, or communication. If you've tried to address issues and nothing has changed, it might be time to move on. Trust your instincts—it probably isn't if something doesn't feel right.

Teen: So it might be time to end if it feels more bad than good?

Parent: Yes, relationships should enrich your life, not detract from it. It's important to prioritize your happiness and well-being.

What are the benefits of being single?

Teen: Is there anything good about being single?

Parent: Absolutely! Being single allows you to focus on yourself, explore your interests, and build your confidence. It's a time to grow as an individual without the pressures or responsibilities of a relationship. You can spend time with friends, try new things, and figure out what you really want in life and in a future partner. Being single isn't about being alone—it's about embracing your independence and enjoying the journey of self-discovery.

Teen: So, being single can be a really positive experience?

Parent: Definitely. It's an opportunity to learn more about yourself and to enjoy life on your terms.

How can you build self-esteem and confidence in yourself?

Teen: How can I build my self-esteem and confidence, especially when it feels low?

Parent: Building self-esteem and confidence takes time, but it starts with recognizing your strengths and accomplishments, no matter how small they may seem. Focus on the things you're good at and the qualities you like about yourself. Celebrate your successes, even the little ones, and be kind to yourself when things are unplanned. Surround yourself with positive, supportive people who encourage you. Also, set small, achievable goals that help you grow and challenge yourself, and as you meet them, you'll feel more confident in your abilities.

Teen: What if I keep comparing myself to others? It's hard not to sometimes.

Parent: Comparing yourself to others is a common trap, but it's important to remember that everyone's journey is different. Focus on your path and what makes you unique. Instead of comparing, try to appreciate what others bring to the table while also valuing your contributions. Remember, confidence grows from within, not from comparing yourself to others.

What are some healthy ways to express love and affection?

Teen: How can I show love and affection in a relationship without going too fast?

Parent: Expressing love and affection in healthy ways is about being genuine and respectful of both your feelings and your partner's. Simple gestures like holding hands, giving compliments, spending quality time together, and really listening to each other can go a long way. It's also important to express how you feel verbally—saying things like I care about you or You're important to me helps build a strong emotional connection. Remember, the key is to take things at a comfortable pace for both of you.

Teen: So, it doesn't always have to be big, dramatic gestures?

Parent: Exactly. The small, everyday actions often mean the most and help build a foundation of trust and respect in your relationship.

How do you communicate effectively in a relationship?

Teen: What's the best way to communicate in a relationship, especially when it comes to difficult topics?

Parent: Effective communication in a relationship means being open, honest, and respectful. When discussing difficult topics, try to stay calm and focus on expressing your feelings without blaming or accusing your partner. Use I statements, like I feel… or I need…, to keep the conversation constructive. It's also important to really listen to your partner's perspective and acknowledge their feelings. Good communication is about understanding each other and working together to find solutions.

Teen: What if the conversation gets heated or emotional?

Parent: It's okay for emotions to come up, but if things get too heated, it might be best to take a break and come back to the conversation when you're both calmer. Remember, the goal is to understand each other better, not to win an argument.

What role does trust play in a relationship?

Teen: How important is trust in a relationship?

Parent: Trust is one of the most important foundations of any healthy relationship. It means you can rely on each other, feel safe, and know that your partner has your best interests at heart. Trust allows you to be vulnerable and open without fearing hurt or betrayal. Building trust takes time and consistency—keeping promises, honesty, and showing that you care are all ways to build and maintain trust.

Teen: What if trust is broken? Can it be repaired?

Parent: Trust can be repaired, but both partners need effort and time. It involves honest communication, taking responsibility for mistakes, and demonstrating that the trust can be rebuilt through actions. It's a process, but if both people are committed, it's possible to heal and move forward.

How do you overcome insecurities in a relationship?

Teen: How do I deal with insecurities in my relationship? Sometimes I just feel unsure.

Parent: It's normal to have insecurities, but it's important to address them so they don't create unnecessary tension in the relationship. Start by being honest with yourself about where these insecurities are coming from—are they based on past experiences, fears, or something specific in your current relationship? Then, communicate with your partner about how you're feeling. A supportive partner will listen and help reassure you. Working on your own self-esteem and confidence also helps, as the more secure you feel in yourself, the less those insecurities will affect your relationship.

Teen: So it's okay to talk about my insecurities with my partner?

Parent: Absolutely. Sharing your feelings can bring you closer and help your partner understand what you're going through. A healthy relationship is one where you can be open and supportive of each other.

What are the consequences of rushing into a relationship?

Teen: What happens if you rush into a relationship too quickly?

Parent: Rushing into a relationship can lead to problems because it doesn't give you enough time to really get to know each other and build a strong foundation. It can create unrealistic expectations, and you might overlook important red flags or differences that could cause issues later on. Taking things slowly allows you to develop trust, communication, and a deeper connection, which are all essential for a lasting relationship. Remember, a good relationship isn't a race—it's about building something meaningful over time.

Teen: So taking it slow is actually better in the long run?

Parent: Yes, taking it slow gives you both the chance to build a relationship that's based on mutual respect, understanding, and genuine connection. It's worth the wait.

How can you make sure you're ready for a serious relationship?

Teen: How do I know if I'm ready for a serious relationship?

Parent: Being ready for a serious relationship means you're in a good place with yourself—you feel confident, secure, and happy on your own, and you're not looking for someone else to complete you but rather to complement your life. You should also be ready to commit time, energy, and effort to the relationship, and be willing to communicate openly, set boundaries, and respect your partner's boundaries. If you feel emotionally mature and ready to handle the ups and downs of a relationship, then you're likely ready for something more serious.

Teen: What if I'm not sure yet?

Parent: That's okay too. It's important to listen to your feelings and not rush into anything before you're ready. Take your time to figure out what you want and need in a relationship, and don't feel pressured to dive into something serious before you're fully prepared.

What are some red flags to watch out for in a potential partner?

Teen: Are there any signs that a relationship might not be healthy, even at the start?

Parent: Yes, there are some red flags that can indicate potential problems. If a partner is overly controlling, tries to isolate you from your friends or family, doesn't respect your boundaries, or shows signs of dishonesty, those are all concerns. Other red flags include extreme jealousy, a quick temper, or a lack of empathy for others. Trust your instincts—if something doesn't feel right, it's important to take a step back and evaluate the relationship.

Teen: So if I see these signs, I should really think about whether the relationship is right for me?

Parent: Absolutely. It is better to address concerns early rather than letting them grow into bigger issues. You deserve to be in a relationship where you feel safe, respected, and valued.

How do you know if you're being manipulated in a relationship?

Teen: How can I tell if someone is trying to manipulate me in a relationship?

Parent: Manipulation can be subtle, but there are some signs to watch for. If your partner frequently makes you feel guilty, pressures you to do things you're uncomfortable with, or tries to control your actions or decisions, those are red flags. Manipulators often use emotional tactics, like giving you the silent treatment, making you feel like you owe them something, or twisting your words to make you doubt yourself. If you're constantly questioning your own feelings or decisions because of their influence, that's a sign of manipulation.

Teen: What should I do if I think I'm being manipulated?

Parent: It's important to talk to someone you trust about what's happening, whether it's a friend, family member, or counselor. They can provide perspective and support. You should also consider setting strong boundaries or, if necessary, distancing yourself from the relationship if it's harmful to your well-being.

What are the differences between love, lust, and infatuation?

Teen: How do I know if what I'm feeling is love, lust, or just infatuation?

Parent: Love, lust, and infatuation can feel similar at times, but they're different in important ways. Infatuation is often based on idealized perceptions and can be intense but short-lived. It's more about the excitement of someone new and often focuses on surface-level traits. Lust is primarily physical attraction and desire, and while it can be part of love, on its own, it doesn't build a deep connection. On the other hand, love grows over time and is based on a deep emotional bond, trust, respect, and caring for each other's well-being. Love is less about intense highs and more about steady, enduring feelings that support a healthy relationship.

Teen: So love is more about a lasting connection?

Parent: Exactly. Love develops as you get to know each other deeper and build a relationship based on mutual respect, trust, and shared values.

How can you tell if someone is genuinely interested in you?

Teen: How can I know if someone is really interested in me, or if they're just playing around?

Parent: Genuine interest usually shows through consistent behaviour. If someone is truly interested in you, they'll make an effort to spend time with you, get to know you, and be there for you when you need them. They'll listen to what you have to say, respect your opinions, and make you feel valued. Their actions will match their words—they won't just say they care, they'll show it. If someone is playing around, they might be inconsistent, only showing interest when it's convenient for them, or not taking your feelings seriously.

Teen: So, consistency is key?

Parent: Yes, consistency is a strong indicator of genuine interest. Pay attention to how they treat you over time, not just in the moment. Real interest isn't about grand gestures but about how someone shows up for you every day.

What are some healthy ways to express affection without rushing into a relationship?

Teen: How can I show someone I like them without rushing into things too quickly?

Parent: You can express affection in many healthy ways that don't involve rushing into a relationship. Simple acts like complimenting, spending quality time together, or doing something thoughtful for the person can show that you care. Writing a kind note, sharing a favorite activity, or having meaningful conversations are also great ways to connect without the pressure of labeling the relationship too soon. It's all about enjoying your time together and letting the relationship develop naturally.

Teen: So, it's okay to take my time and just enjoy getting to know them?

Parent: Absolutely. Taking your time allows you both to explore your feelings comfortably, without pressure. It's important to let things unfold naturally and not rush into labels or commitments before you're both ready.

How do you navigate peer pressure in relationships?

Teen: What should I do if my friends pressure me to be in a relationship or do things I'm not ready for?

Parent: Peer pressure can be tough, especially when it comes to relationships, but it's important to stay true to yourself. If you're not ready for a relationship or certain aspects of one, it's okay to say no and set boundaries. You can explain to your friends that you're not rushing into anything and want to ensure it's the right time and person for you. True friends will respect your decisions and support you. Remember, it's your life, and you should choose what's right for you, not just to fit in.

Teen: What if they keep pushing me, though?

Parent: If your friends keep pushing you, it might be time to reassess those friendships. Friends who respect you will understand your boundaries. It's okay to distance yourself from people who pressure you into situations you're not comfortable with. Your well-being and comfort should always come first.

What roles do parents and guardians play in teenage relationships?

Teen: How involved should parents be in their Teen's relationships?

Parent: Parents and guardians play an important role in guiding and supporting their Teens through relationships. It's not about controlling or intruding but about providing advice, support, and a sounding board for your thoughts and feelings. Parents can help you navigate challenges, set healthy boundaries, and understand the difference between healthy and unhealthy relationships. Open communication is key—if you feel comfortable talking to your parents about your relationships, it can help you make more informed and thoughtful decisions.

Teen: But what if I feel like they're too involved?

Parent: It's important to have a balance. If you feel like your parents are too involved, it's okay to have a conversation with them about needing some space while still valuing their guidance. Let them know that you appreciate their support but also want to handle some aspects of your relationship independently, as long as you feel safe and confident doing so.

How do cultural norms and traditions influence teenage relationships?

Teen: How do cultural norms and traditions affect relationships, especially as a Teen?

Parent: Cultural norms and traditions can significantly influence how relationships are viewed and handled. In some cultures, there might be expectations about when it's appropriate to start dating, how relationships should progress, and what role family plays in the relationship. These norms can shape your views and choices, sometimes providing guidance, but they can also create pressure or conflict if they differ from your personal feelings or the norms of your peers.

Teen: What if my cultural background has different expectations than what I feel?

Parent: It's important to navigate this thoughtfully. You might want to discuss openly with your family to understand their perspective while expressing your feelings. Finding a balance between respecting your cultural background and being true to yourself can be challenging, but it's possible with open communication and mutual understanding.

How do you handle disagreements and conflicts in a relationship?

Teen: How should I deal with arguments or conflicts in a relationship?

Parent: Disagreements are normal in any relationship, but how you handle them is key. It's important to approach conflicts with a mindset of wanting to resolve them rather than win the argument. Stay calm, listen to the other person's point of view, and express your feelings clearly and respectfully. Avoid blaming or bringing up past issues irrelevant to the current situation. Sometimes, taking a break to cool off before continuing the discussion can help. The goal is to understand each other better and find a solution that works for both of you.

Teen: What if we can't agree on something?

Parent: It's okay to agree to disagree on some things, as long as the issue isn't fundamental to your values or the health of the relationship. Compromise is often necessary, but it's important that both partners feel heard and respected. If you find yourselves constantly arguing about important issues, it might be a sign that the relationship needs reevaluation.

What are some strategies for building a strong, lasting relationship?

Teen: What can I do to build a strong and lasting relationship?

Parent: Building a strong relationship takes time, effort, and much mutual respect. Start by establishing a foundation of trust and open communication. Be honest with each other and express your feelings and needs clearly. Spend quality time together, but also make sure you maintain your own interests and friendships outside the relationship. Support each other's goals and ambitions, and be there for each other during tough times. It's also important to keep things fun—laugh together, try new things, and keep the romance alive. Remember, a lasting relationship is built on both emotional and practical compatibility.

Teen: So it's about balance and mutual respect?

Parent: Exactly. Balance, respect, and the willingness to work through challenges together are the cornerstones of a strong and lasting relationship.

How do you know if a relationship is worth fighting for?

Teen: How can I tell if a relationship is worth fighting for, especially when things get tough?

Parent: A relationship is worth fighting for if both partners are committed to working through the challenges together and if the relationship adds value to your life. Ask yourself if the relationship makes you happy overall if you both support each other's growth and if there's mutual respect and love. Every relationship has ups and downs, but if the good outweighs the bad and you both want to put in the effort, it's usually worth it. However, if the relationship is consistently causing stress, anxiety, or unhappiness, it might be time to reconsider.

Teen: What if we're just going through a rough patch?

Parent: Rough patches happen in all relationships, and they can often be resolved with communication and effort. The key is to evaluate whether these issues are temporary and can be worked through, or if they're indicative of deeper, unresolved problems. If both of you are willing to put in the work to improve things, it's worth giving it a shot.

What are the benefits of taking things slow in a relationship?

Teen: Why is it important to take things slow in a relationship?

Parent: Taking things slowly allows you to build a strong foundation of trust, understanding, and respect. It gives you time to get to know each other, see how you handle different situations, and ensure that your feelings are genuine and not just a result of infatuation. When you take things slow, you're less likely to overlook red flags or rush into decisions that you might not be ready for. It also helps prevent emotional burnout, ensuring that the relationship remains healthy and fulfilling over time.

Teen: So it's better to let things develop naturally?

Parent: Absolutely. A relationship that develops naturally, without pressure or haste, will likely be stable, fulfilling, and long-lasting.

How do you balance school, extracurricular activities, and a relationship?

Teen: How can I balance school, extracurricular activities, and relationships without feeling overwhelmed?

Parent: Balancing all these aspects of your life requires good time management and setting clear priorities. It's important to make sure that your academic responsibilities come first, as your education is a foundation for your future. Next, consider how much time you need to dedicate to extracurricular activities, which are also important for your personal development. Then, find time for your relationship that doesn't interfere with your other responsibilities. Communication with your partner is key—they should understand and support your need to focus on school and activities, just as you should support theirs. It's about finding a healthy balance where you can enjoy your relationship without sacrificing your goals.

Teen: What if I start feeling too stressed?

Parent: If you start feeling overwhelmed, it's important to reassess your schedule and see where adjustments can be made. Sometimes, this might mean cutting back on activities or having an open conversation with your partner about needing more time for schoolwork. Prioritizing your well-being is crucial, and that includes managing stress effectively.

How do you set boundaries with your partner?

Teen: How can I set boundaries with my partner without hurting their feelings?

Parent: Setting boundaries is essential for a healthy relationship, and it's important to approach this honestly and with care. Start by understanding your boundaries—what makes you comfortable or uncomfortable, and what you need to feel respected and safe. Then, communicate these boundaries to your partner in a calm and respectful way. You can explain that setting boundaries isn't about pushing them away but about ensuring that the relationship remains healthy and comfortable for both of you. For example, you might say I value our time together, but I also need some personal space to focus on my studies. The key is to express your needs clearly while showing that you care about their feelings too.

Teen: What if they don't respect my boundaries?

Parent: If your partner doesn't respect your boundaries, having a serious conversation about why those boundaries are important to you and what they mean for the relationship is important. Boundaries are non-negotiable in a healthy relationship, and if they continue to be ignored, it might be a sign that the relationship isn't right for you. Mutual respect is a fundamental part of any partnership.

What are some warning signs of an abusive relationship?

Teen: What are the warning signs of an abusive relationship?

Parent: There are several warning signs that may indicate an abusive relationship. These include controlling behaviour, such as telling you who you can or cannot spend time with, constant criticism or belittling, isolating you from friends and family, and extreme jealousy. Other signs include physical aggression, threats, manipulation, and any form of intimidation. Emotional abuse can also be subtle, like making you feel guilty for things you haven't done or constantly questioning your worth. If you notice any of these behaviors, it's important to reach out for help and consider ending the relationship. No one deserves to be treated this way.

Teen: What should I do if I think I'm in an abusive relationship?

Parent: If you think you're in an abusive relationship, the first step is to talk to someone you trust—whether it's a parent, teacher, counselor, or friend. It's important not to keep it to yourself. Abusive relationships can be dangerous, and it's crucial to have support as you navigate your next steps. If you feel safe, you can consider confronting your partner about their behaviour, but only if you feel it won't harm you. In many cases, it's best to seek professional help to exit the relationship safely.

How do you support a friend who is in an unhealthy relationship?

Teen: How can I support a friend who's in an unhealthy relationship?

Parent: Supporting a friend in an unhealthy relationship can be challenging, but your concern and care are important. Start by being a good listener— let your friends know you're there for them without judgment. Encourage them to talk about their feelings and what's happening in the relationship. It's important to point out the unhealthy behaviors you've noticed gently, but try to avoid being confrontational. Offer your support and suggest they talk to a trusted adult or counselor. Sometimes, your friend might not be ready to leave the relationship immediately, so be patient and continue offering your support without pushing them too hard. Let them know that they deserve to be treated with respect and that you're there to help them when they're ready.

Teen: What if they don't want to listen?

Parent: It's frustrating when someone doesn't want to see the truth, but staying supportive without pressuring them is important. Keep the lines of communication open and let them know you're always there for them. Sometimes, just knowing they have someone who cares can make a big difference. If the situation becomes dangerous, don't hesitate to involve a trusted adult who can provide the necessary support.

How do you apologize and make amends in a relationship?

Teen: How should I apologize if I've hurt my partner's feelings?

Parent: Apologizing sincerely is an important part of any relationship. Start by acknowledging what you did wrong and how it affected your partner. A good apology isn't just about saying I'm sorry, but about taking responsibility for your actions. For example, you might say, I'm really sorry for not considering your feelings earlier. I understand that it hurt you, and I want to make sure it doesn't happen again. After apologizing, ask how you can make amends and what you can do to avoid repeating the mistake. It's also important to show through your actions that you're committed to changing the behaviour that caused the hurt.

Teen: What if my partner doesn't accept my apology?

Parent: If your partner doesn't accept your apology immediately, give them time and space to process their feelings. It's important to respect their emotions and not pressure them to forgive you on your timeline. Continue to show through your actions that you're committed to making things right. Sometimes, healing takes time, and your partner may need to see that you're genuinely sorry and willing to change before they can fully forgive.

How do you know when it's time to seek professional help for relationship issues?

Teen: How can I tell if my relationship issues are serious enough to need professional help?

Parent: If you're facing challenges in your relationship that you can't resolve on your own—especially if these issues are affecting your mental or emotional well-being—it might be time to seek professional help. This can include recurring arguments, feelings of being stuck or unhappy, or if there are signs of unhealthy or toxic behaviour. A counselor or therapist can provide an outside perspective and help you both work through your issues in a constructive way. It's important to remember that seeking help is a sign of strength, not weakness, showing that you're committed to improving the relationship.

Teen: What if my partner doesn't want to go to counseling?

Parent: If your partner is reluctant to seek counseling, it's important to express why you think it's necessary and how it could help the relationship. You could suggest starting with just one session to see how it goes. If they're still unwilling, you might consider going on your own. Sometimes, individual counseling can help you understand the situation and determine the best course of action for yourself.

What are some ways to practice self-care while in a relationship?

Teen: How can I practice self-care while being in a relationship?

Parent: Practicing self-care in a relationship is all about maintaining a healthy balance between caring for your partner and taking care of yourself. Ensure you're setting aside time for your interests, hobbies, and friendships. It's important to have moments to recharge and focus on your well-being. This might mean spending some time alone, doing things you enjoy, or simply relaxing. Self-care also involves setting boundaries and communicating your needs clearly to your partner. Remember, you can't pour from an empty cup—taking care of yourself helps you be a better partner in the relationship.

Teen: Is it okay to ask for space in a relationship?

Parent: Absolutely. Asking for space isn't a sign that something is wrong in the relationship; it's a sign that you value both the relationship and your own well-being. It's healthy to have some time apart to pursue your own interests and reflect on your feelings. Just be sure to communicate your need for space in a way that reassures your partner that it's about self-care, not distancing from them.

How do you handle long-distance relationships?

Teen: How can I make a long-distance relationship work?

Parent: Long-distance relationships can be challenging, but they can also work if both partners are committed. Communication is key—make an effort to stay in touch regularly through calls, texts, or video chats. It's important to be open and honest about your feelings and any concerns you have. Trust is also crucial in a long-distance relationship, as you won't always be physically present to reassure each other. Planning visits, if possible, can give you something to look forward to and help maintain the connection. Additionally, setting clear expectations and boundaries about what you both want from the relationship can help avoid misunderstandings.

Teen: What if it gets really hard to stay connected?

Parent: It's normal to face challenges in a long-distance relationship; sometimes, you might feel disconnected. When that happens, it's important to talk about it with your partner rather than keeping those feelings to yourself. Finding new ways to connect, like sharing a virtual activity or setting up regular date nights, can help strengthen the bond. If the relationship is important to both of you, you'll find ways to make it work despite the distance.

What are the keys to maintaining a healthy, happy relationship?

Teen: What are the most important things to focus on for a healthy and happy relationship?

Parent: Maintaining a healthy and happy relationship revolves around a few key principles: trust, communication, respect, and mutual support. Trust forms the foundation of any strong relationship, and it's built over time through honesty and reliability. Communication is crucial—both partners should feel comfortable expressing their thoughts, feelings, and needs without fear of judgment. Respect is about valuing each other's opinions, boundaries, and individuality. Finally, mutual support means being there for each other during both good times and bad, encouraging each other's growth and happiness. These elements create a solid framework for a relationship that can thrive and endure when these elements are in place.

Teen: How do you keep the relationship fun and exciting?

Parent: Keeping the relationship fun and exciting involves trying new things together, maintaining a sense of humor, and being open to spontaneity. Whether it's exploring new activities, going on adventures, or simply surprising each other with small gestures, keeping the relationship dynamic helps keep the connection strong. Remember that having fun together is just as important as the serious aspects of a relationship—it helps you bond and creates lasting memories.

How do you know if you're ready to say I love you?

Teen: How do I know when it's the right time to say I love you?

Parent: Saying I love you is a big step in any relationship, and it's important to make sure you really mean it before you say it. You might be ready to say I love you when you feel a deep, genuine connection with your partner and you care about them not just in the moment but in a way that feels enduring and supportive. It's not just about the excitement of being together but about wanting to be there for them through ups and downs and accepting them as they are. When you feel secure in your feelings and confident that they're reciprocated, that's usually a good sign that you're ready to say those three words.

Teen: What if I'm not sure how they'll react?

Parent: It's natural to feel nervous about how your partner will react, but if you're in a healthy relationship, they'll appreciate your honesty and openness. You can express your feelings without pressuring them to say it back immediately. If they're not ready to say it yet, it doesn't necessarily mean they don't care about you—they might just need more time. The most important thing is that you're honest about your feelings and that you give each other the space to grow into that commitment at your own pace.

How do you prioritize your own happiness and well-being in a relationship?

Teen: How can I make sure I'm prioritizing my own happiness while still being in a relationship?

Parent: Prioritizing your happiness and well-being in a relationship starts with self-awareness and self-care. It's important to make sure that you're not neglecting your own needs, goals, and interests for the sake of the relationship. This means maintaining a balance between spending time with your partner and doing things that make you happy on your own—whether that's pursuing hobbies, spending time with friends, or working towards personal goals. Communication is also key—let your partner know what you need to feel fulfilled and supported in the relationship. A healthy relationship should enhance your life, not diminish your sense of self. Remember, you deserve to be happy, and taking care of your own well-being ultimately makes you a better partner too.

Teen: So it's okay to put myself first sometimes?

Parent: Absolutely. Putting yourself first doesn't mean you're being selfish—it means you're taking care of yourself so that you can be your best self in the relationship. When you're happy and fulfilled, it's easier to contribute positively to the relationship and support your partner similarly.

This chapter on Navigating Infatuation and Love aims to equip Teens with the knowledge and tools to understand and manage their romantic relationships healthfully, thoughtfully, and balanced. From recognizing the difference between infatuation and love to understanding the importance of communication, boundaries, and self-care, this conversation between parent and Teen is designed to guide young individuals through the complexities of teenage relationships, helping them build meaningful and respectful connections.

* * *

"A single parent is never really alone in raising a child;
love fills the gaps that circumstances create."
— Anonymous

Chapter 32

Navigating Teenage Challenges with a Single Parent

Navigating life as a teenager can be challenging, and when you're doing it within a single-parent household, those challenges can sometimes feel even more complex. The dynamics of a single-parent family can bring about a unique set of emotions, responsibilities, and questions. This chapter addresses the concerns and experiences of teenagers growing up with a single parent. Through a series of thoughtful and engaging conversations, we explore how to cope with feelings of loss, manage responsibilities, build strong relationships, and find a sense of stability and happiness. Whether it's dealing with the absence of one parent, supporting your single parent, or balancing your own needs, this chapter aims to provide guidance and support as you navigate these important aspects of your life.

Parent: I know that growing up in a single-parent household can bring a lot of questions and emotions. Let's talk about them, one by one, so that you can feel supported and understood.

Teen: Yeah, there's a lot I'm trying to figure out. It feels like everything is more complicated now.

Parent: I'm here to help you navigate these challenges. Let's start with what's on your mind.

Why did my parents divorce or separate, and how do I cope with the changes?

Teen: Why did you and Dad divorce? I still don't fully understand.

Parent: Divorce is complicated, and it often happens because of issues that are difficult for children to see. Sometimes, even if they try, two people can't make their relationship work. But it's important to remember that the separation wasn't your fault. As for coping, feeling sad, angry, or confused is okay. Talking about your feelings, spending time with friends, and finding activities that make you happy can help you cope with these changes.

How do I deal with feelings of abandonment or loss if one of my parents is no longer in my life?

Teen: Sometimes, I feel abandoned since I don't see my other parent much. How do I deal with that?

Parent: Feeling abandoned is a tough emotion to handle. It's important to talk about these feelings rather than keeping them inside. Understand that your other parent's absence doesn't reflect your worth. Sometimes, life circumstances make it hard for them to be present, but it doesn't mean they don't care. Surround yourself with supportive people, and remember, you have a lot of love and support from me and others around you.

What can I do if I feel angry or resentful towards my absent parent?

Teen: I sometimes feel really angry at my other parent for not being around. What should I do with that anger?

Parent: It's normal to feel angry, and it's important to acknowledge those feelings. Try to express your anger in a healthy way—talk to someone you trust, write in a journal, or engage in activities that help you release that frustration. Over time, you might also consider communicating with your absent parent about how you feel if that's something you're comfortable with.

How do I handle questions from peers about my family situation?

Teen: My friends sometimes ask about why I only live with one parent. What should I say?

Parent: You can keep it simple and truthful. You could say, " My parents are divorced/separated, and I live with one of them. It's your choice how much detail you want to share. You don't owe anyone a full explanation unless you feel comfortable giving it. Remember, your family situation doesn't define who you are.

What role does my absent parent play in my identity and sense of self-worth?

Teen: Does the fact that one of my parents isn't around affect who I am?

Parent: Your absent parent is a part of your history, but they don't define your identity or self-worth. Who you are is shaped by your values, your choices, and the love and support you receive. Focusing on what you have rather than what's missing is important. You're a unique individual with your own strengths, and that's something to be proud of.

How do I navigate family gatherings or events without both parents present?

Teen: Family gatherings feel weird without both of you there. How do I handle that?

Parent: It's understandable that family events might feel different now. It's okay to feel that way. Try to focus on the people there and the occasion's joy. You can also talk to me beforehand if you feel anxious about an event. Remember, you can still enjoy these moments even if things aren't how they used to be.

What should I do if I want to reconnect with my absent parent?

Teen: What if I want to reconnect with my other parent? How do I go about it?

Parent: Reconnecting with your absent parent can be a positive step, but it's important to approach it thoughtfully. Start by discussing your feelings with me to discuss what you want and how to go about it. Reconnecting might involve sending a letter, phone call, or email. Keep your expectations realistic and remember that building or rebuilding a relationship takes time.

How do I address feelings of guilt or responsibility for my parents' divorce or separation?

Teen: I sometimes feel like it's my fault that you and Dad split up. How do I deal with that?

Parent: I want you to know that the divorce or separation was not your fault in any way. Adults have their own issues that can lead to these decisions, which are separate from yours. It's natural to feel confused or guilty, but it's important to understand that you didn't cause this. I'm here to listen if you ever need to talk about these feelings.

What are some coping strategies for dealing with the emotional challenges of having a single parent?

Teen: How can I cope with the tough emotions of having just one parent around?

Parent: Acknowledging your feelings and finding healthy ways to express them is important. Talking to someone you trust, whether it's me, a friend, or a counselor, can help. Engaging in activities that you enjoy, like sports, art, or music, can also provide an outlet. Connecting with your friends and participating in social activities can help you feel supported and less isolated.

How do I communicate my needs and feelings to my single parent?

Teen: Sometimes, I'm unsure how to tell you what I need or how I feel. How can I do that better?

Parent: Open communication is key. When you need to talk, try to be honest and specific about what you feel or need. For example, you might say, I'm feeling overwhelmed with school, and I need some help managing my time, or I'm feeling lonely and want to spend more time together. Remember, I'm here to support you and want to understand how you're feeling.

How can I build a strong bond with my single parent?

Teen: How can we strengthen our relationship, especially now that it's just the two of us?

Parent: Building a strong bond takes time and effort from both of us. We can strengthen our relationship by spending quality time together, whether it's through shared activities, open conversations, or just being there for each other. Let's make time for regular check-ins where we talk about our day, our feelings, and anything else on our minds. The more we communicate and support each other, the stronger our bond will become.

What should I do if I feel overwhelmed by my single parent's responsibilities?

Teen: I sometimes feel overwhelmed by all the responsibilities you have. What can I do?

Parent: It's okay to feel that way, and I appreciate your care. One thing we can do is talk about ways you can help out that don't feel overwhelming for you. It's also important for both of us to find a balance—while it's great for you to help, it's equally important for you to focus on your own needs, like school, hobbies, and spending time with friends. We can work together to manage responsibilities in a way that feels fair.

How do I handle conflicts or disagreements with my single parent?

Teen: What should I do when we disagree or have a conflict?

Parent: Disagreements are normal, and the key is handling them respectfully and understanding. When we disagree, let's take a moment to cool off if emotions are running high. Then, we can talk about the issue calmly, listening to each other's perspectives. It's important to communicate openly and to be willing to find a compromise. Remember, we're a team, and working through conflicts together can strengthen our relationship.

What are some ways to support my single parent emotionally and practically?

Teen: How can I support you more, both emotionally and with practical things?

Parent: Your support means a lot to me. Emotionally, just being there and talking to me about your day or how you're feeling can make a big difference. You can help with chores, cooking, or even just keeping your room tidy. It's also helpful when you take initiative—if you see something that needs doing, feel free to step in. But remember, it's important to balance helping out with taking care of your own needs too.

How do I navigate dating and relationships as the child of a single parent?

Teen: How should I approach dating and relationships, especially with you being a single parent?

Parent: Dating is an exciting part of growing up, and I want you to feel supported in your relationships. It's important to be open with me about your feelings and experiences in dating, so I can guide if you need it. Remember, it's okay to set boundaries in your relationships and to take things at your own pace. I'm here to help you navigate this part of your life, and I trust you to make thoughtful decisions.

What role does my single parent play in shaping my future goals and aspirations?

Teen: How do you influence my goals and what I want to do in the future?

Parent: As your parent, my role is to support and guide you as you explore your interests and dreams. I want to help you identify your strengths and passions, and provide the resources or encouragement you need to pursue them. Your goals are your own, but I'm here to help you achieve them by offering advice, helping you plan, and being your biggest cheerleader. Ultimately, I want you to pursue what makes you happy and fulfilled.

How do I address financial concerns or instability in my single-parent household?

Teen: Sometimes I worry about money and how that affects us. What should I do?

Parent: It's natural to be concerned about finances, especially in a single-parent household. If you're worried, let's talk about it. I can explain our situation and what we're doing to manage it. While it's good to be aware, it's important to remember that managing finances is my responsibility, and your main focus should be on your education and well-being. If there are ways you want to help, we can discuss that too, but don't feel pressured to take on more than you're comfortable with.

What should I do if I feel pressure to take on adult responsibilities in my single-parent household?

Teen: I sometimes feel like I have to take on too many adult responsibilities. What can I do?

Parent: It's important that you feel supported rather than overwhelmed. If you're feeling too much pressure, please tell me. We can reassess and make sure you have enough time and space to be a teenager—focusing on school, friends, and your own interests. While it's okay to have some responsibilities, it's also essential that you don't feel burdened by them. We'll work together to find a balance that works for both of us.

How do I deal with feelings of loneliness or isolation as the child of a single parent?

Teen: I sometimes feel lonely or different because it's just you and me. How do I deal with that?

Parent: Feeling lonely or isolated is tough, and it's important to reach out when you're feeling that way. Staying connected with friends and participating in activities you enjoy can help. We can also plan some special times together or find ways to stay close to extended family and friends. Remember, it's okay to feel lonely sometimes, but you're not alone—we're in this together, and there's a lot of love and support around you.

What are some positive aspects of growing up in a single-parent household?

Teen: Are there any positives about growing up with just one parent?

Parent: Absolutely! Growing up in a single-parent household can teach you a lot about resilience, independence, and teamwork. You might become more responsible, self-reliant, and empathetic. We also have a special bond that's unique to our situation. Plus, you get to see firsthand how we navigate challenges together, which can inspire you to face your challenges with confidence. There are plenty of positives, and it's important to recognize and appreciate them.

How do I handle questions or comments from others about my family situation?

Teen: What should I do when people comment or ask questions about our family?

Parent: You can decide how much you want to share. If someone asks about our family, you can keep your response simple, like "It's just me and my parents, and we're doing well." If a comment feels intrusive or hurtful, it's okay to politely let them know you'd rather not discuss it. It's important to remember that your family situation doesn't define you, and you're in control of how you share your story.

How can I support my single parent's well-being while also caring for my needs?

Teen: How can I help you, but still take care of myself?

Parent: The fact that you want to support me means a lot. The best way to help is by taking good care of yourself—doing well in school, pursuing your interests, and being open about your feelings. When you're doing well, it helps me feel supported too. If you want to help with practical things, that's great, but make sure you're not neglecting your own needs. We can always discuss finding a balance that works for both of us.

What role does extended family play in my life as the child of a single parent?

Teen: How should I think about our extended family since it's just you and me most of the time?

Parent: Extended family can be a wonderful source of support and connection. Even though it's just the two of us at home, we're part of a larger family that cares about us. Whether it's grandparents, aunts, uncles, or cousins, staying connected with them can give you a broader support system and a sense of belonging. We can make an effort to spend time with them, and they can be an important part of your life.

How do I cope with the absence of my other parent during important life milestones?

Teen: What should I do when I miss my other parent during big events?

Parent: It's natural to feel that absence, especially during important milestones. It's okay to feel sad or wish they were there. We can find ways to honor their presence in your life, even if they're not physically there—like talking about them, sharing memories, or finding other meaningful ways to include them in your celebrations. Remember, you have people around you who love and support you, and we'll make sure your milestones are special.

What should I do if I feel different or excluded from families with both parents present?

Teen: I sometimes feel different when seeing other families with both parents. How should I handle that?

Parent: Feeling different is understandable, but it's important to remember that every family is unique, and there's no one right way to be a family. What matters most is the love and support within your family, not how it's structured. If you ever feel excluded, we can talk about those feelings, and I can help you find ways to feel more included. Your feelings are valid, and we can work together to make sure you feel valued and loved.

How do I maintain a healthy relationship with my single parent while asserting my independence?

Teen: How can I be close to you but still feel independent as I grow up?

Parent: As you grow, it's natural to want more independence, and I support that. Maintaining a healthy relationship is about finding balance. We can keep our connection strong by communicating openly, spending quality time together, and respecting each other's boundaries. Your independence doesn't mean we'll grow apart—it means our relationship will evolve, with mutual respect and understanding as you take on more responsibility and make more of your own decisions.

What are the ways to celebrate special occasions and holidays in a single-parent household?

Teen: How can we make holidays and special occasions feel complete with just the two of us?

Parent: We can create our own traditions that make these occasions special for us. Whether it's cooking a favorite meal, decorating together, or planning an activity we both enjoy, what matters most is the time we spend together and the memories we create. We can also include extended family or friends if that feels right. It's about making the occasion meaningful in a way that feels good for us, even if it's different from what others do.

How do I address feelings of jealousy or resentment towards friends with two parents?

Teen: I sometimes feel jealous when I see my friends with both of their parents. How do I deal with that?

Parent: Feeling jealous or resentful is completely natural, but it's important to remember that every family has its own challenges, even if they're not visible from the outside. Focus on the strengths and positives of our own situation. It might also help to talk about these feelings, either with me or someone you trust, so they don't build up. By acknowledging and understanding your feelings, you can find peace with your own family situation.

How do I navigate custody arrangements or visitation schedules with my absent parent?

Teen: How do I handle the back and forth with custody or visitation?

Parent: Custody arrangements can be tricky, but the key is to communicate openly with both parents about your needs and feelings. If something isn't working for you, it's important to speak up so we can find a solution that feels fair and manageable. It's also helpful to stay organized, keep track of the schedule, and ensure you have what you need when you go between homes. Remember, expressing your preferences about how time is divided is okay.

What role does communication play in maintaining a strong relationship with my single parent?

Teen: How important is communication in keeping our relationship strong?

Parent: Communication is the foundation of any strong relationship. It helps us understand each other's needs, resolve conflicts, and stay connected. I encourage you to share your thoughts and feelings with me, whether it's something that's bothering you or something you're excited about. By keeping the lines of communication open, we can support each other better and ensure that our relationship remains strong and healthy.

How do I handle feelings of grief or sadness related to the absence of my other parent?

Teen: What should I do when I feel really sad about my other parent not being around?

Parent: Grief and sadness are natural when you miss someone important in your life. It's important to acknowledge those feelings rather than trying to push them away. Talking about your emotions, whether with me, a friend, or a counselor, can help you process them. Finding ways to honor your relationship with your other parent, like keeping a journal, creating something in their memory, or sharing stories, can also be healing. Remember, it's okay to feel sad, and it's okay to seek support.

What are some ways to honor and remember my absent parent?

Teen: How can I honor and remember my other parent even if they're not around?

Parent: There are many meaningful ways to honor and remember your other parent. You might create a scrapbook of photos and memories, write letters to them, or celebrate their birthday or special occasions in a way that feels right to you. These acts of remembrance can help keep their presence in your life, even if they're not physically there. It's about finding what feels meaningful and comforting to you.

How do I find support and understanding from others who have experienced similar family dynamics?

Teen: How can I connect with others who understand what being in a single-parent family is like?

Parent: Finding support from others with similar experiences can be helpful. Consider joining a support group for teens from single-parent families in your community or online. Talking to friends or relatives who've been through similar situations can also provide comfort and understanding. Sharing your experiences with others who get it can help you feel less alone and more supported.

How can I advocate for myself and my family within school or community settings?

Teen: How can I speak up for us in school or other places when people don't understand our situation?

Parent: Advocating for yourself and our family means being clear about your needs and standing up for what's important to you. You might need to communicate with teachers or counselors about your family situation in school, especially if it impacts your schoolwork or participation in activities. In the community, it's about setting boundaries when needed and educating others if they make assumptions about single-parent families. Being confident, assertive, and respectful in these situations is important.

How do I address legal or logistical concerns related to my single-parent household?

Teen: What should I do if I'm worried about legal stuff or how things are managed at home?

Parent: Legal and logistical concerns can be stressful but manageable. If something specific is worrying you, like custody arrangements or financial issues, let's talk about it. I can explain what's happening and how we're handling it. If it's something more complex, we can seek help from a legal expert or counselor who can provide guidance. You must feel secure and understand what's going on in our household.

What role does self-care play in managing the stress and challenges of growing up in a single-parent household?

Teen: How important is self-care when dealing with the stress of our situation?

Parent: Self-care is crucial for managing stress and staying physically and emotionally healthy. It's important to take time for yourself, whether that means engaging in hobbies, exercising, spending time with friends, or just relaxing. Self-care helps you recharge and cope with the challenges that come with our family dynamic. Remember, taking care of yourself isn't selfish—it's necessary and helps you be your best self, both for you and our family.

How do I foster a sense of resilience and perseverance in the face of adversity?

Teen: How can I build resilience to handle our tough times?

Parent: Building resilience is about learning to adapt and grow stronger through challenges. One way to do this is by focusing on your strengths and the positive aspects of your situation. Developing a growth mindset—believing that you can learn and improve from difficult experiences—also helps. Surround yourself with supportive people, and don't be afraid to seek help when needed. Every challenge you overcome makes you stronger and more capable of handling whatever comes next.

How can I develop a positive outlook on my family situation and prospects?

Teen: How can I stay positive about our family and my future?

Parent: Developing a positive outlook starts with focusing on what we're grateful for and recognizing our strengths as a family. It's about setting goals and working towards them, knowing that your circumstances don't define your potential. Stay optimistic by surrounding yourself with positive influences and focusing on what you can control. Remember, your future is bright, and your experiences now are building the resilience and character that will serve you well throughout your life.

How do I balance my responsibilities at home with my social and academic life?

Teen: How can I manage everything—home, school, friends—without feeling overwhelmed?

Parent: Balancing responsibilities is about prioritizing and managing your time effectively. It's important to set realistic goals for school, help out at home, and make time for social activities. We can work together to create a schedule that balances these different areas, ensuring you have time to relax and recharge. Don't hesitate to ask for help if you're feeling overwhelmed—we can adjust your responsibilities to make sure you're not taking on too much at once.

What should I do if I feel overwhelmed by the demands of being the child of a single parent?

Teen: What if I feel like it's all too much to handle?

Parent: If you're feeling overwhelmed, the first step is to talk about it. We can look at what's causing the stress and find ways to lighten your load.

It's important to remember that you don't have to carry everything on your own—we're a team, and we can support each other. Taking breaks, practicing self-care, and finding activities that help you relax can also make a big difference. Your well-being is a top priority, and we can always adjust to ensure you feel supported.

How do I handle questions or curiosity from younger siblings about our family structure?

Teen: How should I talk to my younger siblings if they ask questions about why our family is the way it is?

Parent: It's important to answer their questions in an age-appropriate and reassuring way. You can explain that families come in all shapes and sizes, and what matters most is that we love and support each other. Encourage them to talk about their feelings and let them know it's okay to be curious or confused. We can also work together to create a positive environment where they feel safe and understood.

How can I support my single parent in finding happiness and fulfilment in their own life?

Teen: How can I help you be happy and fulfilled, even with all the challenges we face?

Parent: Your support means a lot to me, and it helps just knowing that you care. You can encourage me to pursue my interests and hobbies, and we can discuss ways to make time for things that bring us joy. Remember, it's not your responsibility to make me happy, but your love and support are always appreciated. We can work together to create a balanced life where we find happiness and fulfilment.

What are some ways to strengthen sibling bonds in a single-parent household?

Teen: How can I ensure we stay close as siblings, especially when it's just us with one parent?

Parent: Strengthening the bond between siblings is about spending time together, supporting each other, and communicating openly. You can plan activities that you both enjoy, help each other with challenges, and try to be there for one another. It's also important to resolve conflicts in a healthy way so you maintain a strong and positive relationship. As siblings, you have a unique bond that can be a source of strength and support throughout your lives.

How do I navigate cultural or societal expectations related to family structure and dynamics?

Teen: What should I do if I feel like society expects something different from our family?

Parent: It's natural to feel pressure from cultural or societal expectations, but it's important to remember that every family is unique and valuable. We can talk about these expectations and how they might affect you, but ultimately, it's about being proud of who we are as a family. Emphasize the strengths and love that define our family, and don't be afraid to challenge stereotypes or misconceptions. Your family structure doesn't determine your worth, and you have the power to shape your own story.

How can I advocate for greater understanding and acceptance of diverse family structures?

Teen: How can I help people understand and accept different families like ours?

Parent: Advocacy starts with being informed and confident in sharing your perspective. You can educate others about the diversity of family structures by speaking up when you hear misconceptions or stereotypes. Encourage open conversations about the value of different types of families, and share your own experiences to help others understand. It's also important to be a role model by showing that your family, like any other, is built on love, respect, and support.

How do I address feelings of insecurity or self-doubt related to my family background?

Teen: What should I do when I feel insecure or doubtful about our family situation?

Parent: It's okay to have moments of insecurity, but it's important to remind yourself of your strengths and the love surrounding you. Focus on the positive aspects of our family and what makes you unique. Surround yourself with supportive people who appreciate you for who you are. If self-doubt becomes overwhelming, we can discuss it, or you might consider speaking with a counselor who can offer additional support. Remember, your family background is just one part of who you are, and it doesn't define your potential or your worth.

How can I find role models or mentors who can provide guidance and support?

Teen: How can I find people to look up to, especially since it's just you and me?

Parent: Finding role models and mentors is a great way to gain guidance and support outside of our immediate family. You can look for mentors in your community, school, or through extracurricular activities—people who inspire you and who you can learn from. Teachers, coaches, family friends, or extended family members can be great mentors. It's important to seek out people who share your values and can provide positive influence as you navigate life's challenges.

How do I handle feelings of guilt or responsibility for my single parent's well-being?

Teen: Sometimes I feel guilty or need to take care of you. What should I do?

Parent: It's natural to care about my well-being, but it's important to remember that it's not your responsibility to take care of me. Your main focus should be on your growth, happiness, and well-being. If you're feeling guilty, let's talk about it. We can work together to make sure you're not taking on too much and that you understand that I'm here to support you, not the other way around. It's okay to care, but it's also okay to prioritize your own needs.

What should I do if I feel pressure to fulfil traditional gender roles or expectations in my single-parent household?

Teen: What if I feel like I'm expected to do certain things just because of my gender?

Parent: Gender roles and expectations can be challenging, especially if they don't align with who you are or what you want. It's important to have an open conversation about these pressures and to challenge stereotypes that don't feel right to you. You should feel free to pursue your interests and responsibilities based on your strengths and passions, not just on traditional gender roles. We can work together to ensure that you're supported in being true to yourself, regardless of societal expectations.

How do I cultivate gratitude and appreciation for the love and support I receive from my single parent?

Teen: How can I make sure I'm grateful and show appreciation for everything you do?

Parent: Cultivating gratitude is about recognizing the love and support you have and expressing appreciation for it. You can do this by simply saying thank you when you feel grateful or by showing your appreciation through actions—helping out around the house, spending quality time together, or writing a note. It's also about reflecting on the positive aspects of our relationship and what we've built together. Gratitude strengthens our bond and helps us focus on the good things in life.

This chapter delves into the challenges and opportunities of growing up in a single-parent household. The conversations cover a wide range of topics, including coping with the emotional impact of a parent's absence, managing responsibilities at home, and dealing with societal expectations. We also discuss how to maintain a strong bond with your single parent, handle conflicts, and support each other's well-being. The chapter emphasizes the importance of open communication, self-care, and resilience, helping you to develop a positive outlook on your family situation and future. Whether you're struggling with feelings of abandonment, guilt, or simply trying to balance your life, this chapter offers practical advice and emotional support to help you thrive.

* * *

"The future belongs to those who believe in the beauty of their dreams."
— *Eleanor Roosevelt*

Chapter 33

Teenagers' Goals, Dreams, Career Aspirations, and Future Hopes

The teenage years are a time of exploration, self-discovery, and big dreams. It's a period when young people begin to think seriously about their futures—about the careers they want to pursue, the goals they want to achieve, and the kind of lives they hope to build. These years are filled with questions, possibilities, and often, uncertainty. How do you figure out what you're truly passionate about? What steps should you take to turn your dreams into reality? And how do you navigate the inevitable challenges and setbacks along the way?

In this chapter, we dive into the complex and exciting journey of setting goals, exploring career options, and planning for the future. Through a conversation between a parent and a teenager, we address the important questions that arise during this pivotal time. From discovering your passions to choosing a college major, from building a resume to managing time effectively, this chapter is designed to guide teenagers through the process of envisioning and achieving their future aspirations.

Teen: Mom, I've been thinking a lot about what I want to do with my life, but it's so overwhelming. How do I even begin to figure out what I'm passionate about?

Parent: It's completely normal to feel that way. Discovering your passions is a journey that takes time and exploration. Start by thinking about what activities excite you—what makes you lose track of time? You could try new things, join clubs, or volunteer. The more you explore, the clearer your passions will become.

Teen: That makes sense. But what if I have several interests? How do I choose a career that aligns with them?

Parent: It's great that you have multiple interests! Sometimes, your skills and interests can intersect in surprising ways. For example, if you love technology and helping people, you might look into careers like healthcare technology, where you can develop tools that improve patient care. The key is to find where your interests overlap and see how they can serve others.

Teen: I've always loved drawing. Can I turn that into a career?

Parent: Absolutely! Many successful careers start as hobbies. If you're passionate about drawing, you could explore fields like graphic design, animation, or even marketing. Your hobby could become a fulfilling career with the right training and persistence.

Teen: That sounds exciting, but I'm unsure where to start. What should be my first step in achieving my long-term goals?

Parent: A good starting point is to set SMART goals—Specific, Measurable, Achievable, Relevant, and Time-bound. Break down your big dreams into smaller, manageable steps. This way, you'll feel a sense of accomplishment as you make progress toward your long-term goals.

Teen: There are so many career options out there. How do I narrow them down without feeling overwhelmed?

Parent: It can be overwhelming, but you don't have to figure it all out simultaneously. Start by researching different fields, talking to professionals, and maybe even shadowing someone in a job you're interested in. This will give you a better idea of what each career involves and help you make a more informed decision.

Teen: I'm torn between a few different college majors. How do I decide which one to choose?

Parent: Think about the subjects you enjoy most and where your strengths lie. Also, consider how different majors align with your long-term career goals. If you're passionate about multiple fields, you could explore interdisciplinary programs that combine your interests.

Teen: Is choosing a college with a good reputation more important, or should I focus on finding one that feels right for me?

Parent: Both factors are important, but ultimately, the environment where you feel supported and inspired is crucial. Look at the programs, campus culture, location, and financial considerations. The right fit is where you'll thrive both academically and personally.

Teen: Everyone talks about going to the best colleges. Does it really matter that much?

Parent: While attending a prestigious college can open doors, it's not the only path to success. What matters most is how you take advantage of the opportunities available, no matter where you go. Your effort, network, and skills will significantly affect your success.

Teen: Do I really need to go to college to be successful?

Parent: College can provide you with specialized knowledge, critical thinking skills, and networking opportunities. It's a place to explore your interests and prepare for various careers. However, success is also about finding the path that works best for you, whether that's college, vocational training, or entrepreneurship.

Teen: College is so expensive. How can we manage the cost?

Parent: There are several ways to manage college expenses, including scholarships, grants, work-study programs, and financial aid. Start researching these options early and consider community colleges or in-state universities, which often have lower tuition rates.

Teen: Where do I even start looking for scholarships?

Parent: There are many scholarships out there, from merit-based to need-based. Start by checking with your school's guidance office, online scholarship databases, and community organizations. Also, fill out the FAFSA to see what federal and state financial aid you qualify for.

Teen: It's hard to find time for everything. How can I balance my studies with extracurriculars?

Parent: Time management is key. Prioritize your activities based on your goals and interests. Use a planner to schedule your time and ensure you're not overcommitting. Remember, quality over quantity—focus on what truly matters to you.

Teen: Do internships really make a difference in the long run?

Parent: Absolutely. Internships and volunteer work give you hands-on experience, help you build a network, and make your resume stand out. They also allow you to explore different fields and see what you enjoy before committing to a career.

Teen: My resume is pretty empty. How do I build it up?

Parent: List your academic achievements, extracurricular activities, volunteer work, and any part-time jobs or internships. As you gain more experience, your resume will grow. Building a professional network can start with your teachers, mentors, and anyone you meet through internships or volunteer work. LinkedIn is also a great tool for networking.

Teen: I'm interested in so many things. How do I narrow it down?

Parent: Research is key. Look into different careers within each field. Technology offers paths in software development, cybersecurity, or data science; healthcare includes medicine, nursing, or public health; business could lead to marketing, finance, or entrepreneurship; and the arts offer careers in design, performance, or media. Consider what excites you and aligns with your skills.

Teen: How do I actually set SMART goals?

Parent: Start by identifying a clear objective. For example, instead of saying, "I want to improve my grades," say, "I want to raise my math grade from a B to an A by the end of the semester." Make sure your goal is measurable, realistic, and has a deadline. This approach helps you stay focused and track your progress.

Teen: I'm considering a gap year, but I'm not sure if it's a good idea.

Parent: A gap year can offer valuable life experiences, time for self-discovery, and a chance to gain work experience or travel. However, planning how you'll spend that time productively is important. Consider your long-term goals and how a gap year could help you achieve them.

Teen: What if I fail or hit a major setback? How do I keep going?

Parent: Setbacks are a natural part of any journey. When they happen, take a step back, assess the situation, and learn from it. Adapt your plan if necessary and keep moving forward. Remember, resilience and persistence are key to achieving your dreams.

Teen: How do mentors really help in the long run?

Parent: Mentors offer guidance, share their experiences, and provide valuable advice as you navigate your career path. They can help you avoid common pitfalls, introduce you to important networks, and offer support when you face challenges. Finding a professional mentor can significantly boost your confidence and career trajectory.

Teen: How do I set up informational interviews or job shadowing?

Parent: Start by contacting professionals in fields you're interested in. You can connect through networking events, LinkedIn, or even family and friends. Ask if they'd be willing to share their experiences or allow you to shadow them for a day. Informational interviews and job shadowing provide a firsthand look at different careers and help you make more informed decisions.

Teen: How do I know if my field will have good job opportunities in the future?

Parent: Research industry trends, job growth projections, and demand for specific skills in your field. Look for reports from professional organizations, government labour statistics, and news articles. Understanding the job market can help you choose a field with strong future prospects.

Teen: Sometimes, it's hard to stay motivated, especially when things get tough. How can I stay focused on my goals?

Parent: Break your goals into smaller, manageable tasks. Celebrate small victories along the way, and remind yourself why you're working towards these goals. Surround yourself with supportive people who encourage you, and keep your long-term vision in mind, even when the road gets rough.

Teen: Is a trade school a good option if I'm unsure about attending a traditional college?

Parent: Vocational and trade schools offer specialized training that can lead to high-demand careers, often with less time and financial investment than a four-year college. If you're interested in hands-on work, such as plumbing, electrical work, or automotive technology, trade school can be a great pathway to a stable and rewarding career.

Teen: What can I do now to build communication, leadership, and problem-solving skills?

Parent: Look for opportunities to practice these skills in your everyday life—join clubs, take on leadership roles in group projects, volunteer, or participate in debates or public speaking events. These experiences help you build the soft skills crucial for success in any career.

Teen: I've always wanted to study abroad. How does it help with my career?

Parent: Studying abroad broadens your perspective, exposes you to different cultures, and helps you develop adaptability and problem-solving skills. It also looks great on a resume, showing employers that you're independent, resourceful, and culturally aware—highly valued in today's global job market.

Teen: Can social media really help with my career?

Parent: Absolutely. Platforms like LinkedIn are great for networking, showcasing your skills, and connecting with industry professionals. You can also use social media to build a personal brand, share your work, and stay informed about industry trends. Just remember to keep your online presence professional and positive.

Teen: Where can I find reliable information to help me plan my career?

Parent: Many resources are available, including career counseling services at school, online career assessments, job search websites, and professional organizations. Books, podcasts, and webinars on career development can also provide valuable insights. Don't hesitate to contact teachers, mentors, or career advisors for guidance.

Teen: What should a career plan include?

Parent: A career plan should outline your long-term goals, the steps needed to achieve them, and a timeline for reaching each milestone. It should include your educational goals, potential job opportunities, skills you need to develop, and networking strategies. Regularly review and adjust your plan as you grow and gain more experience.

Teen: What should I be prepared for when I start working?

Parent: Transitioning from school to the workforce can be challenging. You may face job competition, the need to adapt to a professional environment, or uncertainty about your career path. Being patient, adaptable, and willing to start at an entry-level position to gain experience is important. Building resilience and seeking mentorship can also help you navigate these challenges.

Teen: How can I transition from high school to college or the workforce more smoothly?

Parent: Start by preparing early—develop strong study habits, improve your time management skills, and build a support network. Research what to expect in college or the workforce and consider talking to others who have recently transitioned. Being proactive and open to change will help you adjust more easily.

Teen: Why is self-reflection important for my career?

Parent: Self-reflection helps you understand your strengths, weaknesses, values, and what truly motivates you. It allows you to assess your experiences, learn from them, and make informed decisions about your career path. Regular self-reflection ensures that your goals align with your personal growth and fulfillment.

Teen: What's the difference between growth and fixed mindsets?

Parent: A growth mindset is the belief that one can develop one's abilities and intelligence through effort and learning. With a growth mindset, one is more likely to embrace challenges, persist through setbacks, and see failure as an opportunity to grow. Cultivating this mindset helps one stay adaptable and open to new experiences, which is crucial in a constantly evolving job market.

Teen: I've always been interested in starting my own business. Is it a good idea?

Parent: Entrepreneurship allows you to create something of your own, solve problems, and take control of your career. It can be incredibly rewarding, but it also requires hard work, resilience, and the ability to take risks. Pursuing entrepreneurship could be a fulfilling career path if you're passionate about a business idea. Just make sure you're prepared for the challenges and ready to learn as you go.

Teen: How do I connect with potential mentors?

Parent: Start by identifying people in your field who inspire you—these could be teachers, professionals you've met, or even figures you admire from afar. Contact them through networking events, social media, or mutual connections. Express your admiration for their work and ask if they'd be willing to offer guidance. Building a relationship with a mentor can provide valuable insights and support as you navigate your career.

Teen: How do I know if a career is right for me?

Parent: Reflect on what matters most to you—whether it's creativity, helping others, financial stability, or work-life balance. Choose a career that aligns with your values and brings you personal fulfillment. Pursuing a path that not only meets your professional goals but also enriches your life in a meaningful way is important.

Teen: What should I look for in a job offer?

Parent: Consider factors like salary, benefits, job location, company culture, opportunities for growth, and work-life balance. Think about how the role aligns with your long-term career goals and values. It's also important to assess whether the company's mission and work environment fit you well.

Teen: Why is diversity important in networking?

Parent: A diverse and inclusive network exposes you to different perspectives, ideas, and opportunities. It helps you grow both personally and professionally. Seek connections with people from various backgrounds, industries, and experiences. Engage in professional organizations, attend conferences, and be open to meeting new people.

Teen: How can I keep up with industry trends?

Parent: Stay informed by reading industry publications, following thought leaders on social media, attending webinars or conferences, and joining professional groups. Emerging industries like renewable energy, artificial intelligence, and biotechnology are growing rapidly. Keeping an eye on these trends can help you identify new opportunities and stay competitive in the job market.

Teen: How can I avoid burnout while working hard?

Parent: Prioritize your well-being by setting boundaries between work and personal time. Make time for hobbies, exercise, and relaxation. Learn to say no when necessary and delegate tasks if possible. Remember that maintaining a balance is essential for long-term success and happiness.

Teen: Sometimes I feel like I'm not good enough, even when I succeed. How can I overcome imposter syndrome?

Parent: Imposter syndrome is common, but it's important to recognize your achievements and give yourself credit. Focus on your strengths, seek feedback from trusted mentors, and remind yourself that growth comes from learning and experience. Everyone has moments of self-doubt, but don't let it hold you back from pursuing your goals.

Teen: How can I manage my time better to balance academic, personal, and career-related commitments?

Parent: Use tools like planners or digital calendars to organize your schedule. Prioritize tasks based on urgency and importance, and break larger projects into smaller, manageable steps. Make sure to allocate time for rest and activities that recharge you. Time management is a skill that will help you stay focused and productive throughout your career.

Teen: Can volunteering really help my career?

Parent: Volunteering allows you to gain valuable skills, make connections, and explore different fields. It demonstrates your commitment to making a positive impact, which is attractive to employers. Volunteering can also help you discover new interests and passions that could influence your career path.

Teen: What should I expect when I start working or continue my studies after college?

Parent: The transition can be challenging, but it's also an exciting time. Be prepared to adapt to new environments, whether it's the professional world or graduate school. Build a support system, stay organized, and continue learning. Setting clear goals for this next phase will help you stay focused and motivated.

Teen: Do I really need to go beyond a bachelor's degree?

Parent: It depends on your career goals. Advanced degrees and certifications can provide specialized knowledge, open doors to higher-level positions, and increase your earning potential. However, weighing the benefits against the time and financial investment required is important. In some fields, hands-on experience may be just as valuable as further education.

Teen: How do I turn my weaknesses into strengths?

Parent: Start by being honest with yourself about your strengths and weaknesses. Focus on developing your strengths while finding ways to improve or compensate for your weaknesses. For example, if you struggle with public speaking, consider joining a group like Toastmasters to build your confidence. Understanding and working with both your strengths and weaknesses will help you grow and succeed.

Teen: Why should I care about ethics in my career?

Parent: Ethical considerations are crucial in building a career that aligns with your values and contributes positively to society. Consider how your work impacts others, the environment, and the community. Make decisions that reflect integrity, fairness, and respect for others. Being socially responsible in your career can lead to a more fulfilling and meaningful professional life.

Teen: How can I keep learning after I start working?

Parent: Continuous learning is key to staying competitive in your field. Attend workshops, read industry journals, participate in online courses, and network with professionals. Staying informed about new trends and innovations will help you adapt to changes and keep your skills relevant.

Teen: I have a lot of different interests. How do I find a career that fits them all?

Parent: Look for careers that allow you to combine your interests and skills. For example, if you love technology and the arts, you might explore digital media or graphic design. Consider interdisciplinary fields that draw on multiple areas of expertise. Your unique combination of skills can lead to a rewarding career tailored to your strengths.

Teen: What does success really mean?

Parent: Success is personal and can mean different things to different people. It could be about achieving financial stability, making a difference, or finding joy in your work. Take time to reflect on what fulfilment means to you and set goals that align with your definition of success. Remember, it's about building a career that meets your professional aspirations and enriches your life.

In this chapter, we've covered a wide range of questions that teenagers may have about their goals, dreams, career aspirations, and future hopes. The conversation between a parent and a teenager helps to explore these topics in-depth, providing guidance, advice, and encouragement as young people navigate their way toward a fulfilling and successful future. Whether it's discovering passions, setting SMART goals, or overcoming challenges, this dialogue emphasizes the importance of self-reflection, continuous learning, and resilience in achieving one's dreams.

Takeaway Points:

1. **Exploration of Passions:** Encourage teens to explore various activities and interests to discover what excites them and where their passions lie.

2. **SMART Goals:** Setting Specific, Measurable, Achievable, Relevant, and Time-bound goals helps turn dreams into actionable steps toward success.

3. **Balancing Education and Experience:** Higher education, internships, and volunteering all play crucial roles in career development; balancing these with extracurricular activities is key to a well-rounded experience.

4. **Importance of Mentorship:** Building relationships with mentors can provide valuable guidance, support, and networking opportunities in a chosen field.

5. **Continuous Learning:** Staying informed about industry trends, new technologies, and growth opportunities is essential for long-term career success.

6. **Ethical Considerations:** Aligning career choices with personal values and ethical considerations is important for long-term fulfillment and social responsibility.

7. **Adaptability and Resilience:** Navigating career paths requires resilience and adaptability, especially when faced with challenges and setbacks.

8. **Networking:** Developing a diverse and inclusive professional network can open doors to new opportunities and provide support throughout one's career journey.

9. **Work-Life Balance:** Prioritizing well-being and maintaining a healthy balance between work and personal life is essential for sustained success and happiness.

10. **Self-Reflection:** Regular self-reflection helps align career goals with personal growth, ensuring that the path chosen is fulfilling and meaningful.

* * *

"*Independence is not a gift to be given, but a prize to be earned.*"
— *Mark Twain*

Chapter 34

Navigating Teenage Independence, Decision-Making, Responsibilities, and Freedom

Parent: Independence is an important part of growing up, but it's not always easy to balance your desire for freedom with the responsibilities and decisions that come with it. Let's talk about how you can assert your independence while still making good choices.

Teen: How do I assert my independence without upsetting my parents?

Parent: It's all about finding a balance. Start by having open conversations with us about what you want and why it's important to you. Express your feelings respectfully and be willing to listen to our concerns. We can work together to find a middle ground that gives you more independence while ensuring your safety and well-being.

Teen: What are the benefits of having more freedom and autonomy?

Parent: More freedom allows you to explore your interests, make your own decisions, and learn from your experiences. It helps you develop important life skills like responsibility, time management, and self-discipline. However, with freedom comes the responsibility to make choices that reflect your values and consider the impact on yourself and others.

Teen: How do I balance my desire for independence with my responsibilities at home and school?

Parent: Balancing independence with responsibilities is key. Start by prioritizing your tasks and managing your time effectively. Make sure you fulfill your responsibilities at home and school before taking on additional freedoms. This shows us that you can handle more independence and are ready for new challenges.

Teen: What decisions should I be allowed to make for myself, and which ones require parental guidance?

Parent: As you grow older, you should have more say in decisions about your personal life, such as your hobbies, friendships, and how you spend your free time. However, bigger decisions that impact your future or safety, like career choices, financial decisions, or health-related issues, may still need our guidance and support. The goal is to gradually take on more responsibility for your decisions while still leaning on us when needed.

Teen: How can I gain more trust and autonomy from my parents?

Parent: Trust is earned through consistency, honesty, and responsibility. Show us that you can make good decisions and handle your responsibilities without constant supervision. Communicate openly about your plans, keep your promises, and be accountable for your actions. Over time, this builds trust and gives us confidence in your ability to manage more independence.

Teen: What steps can I take to become more independent and self-reliant?

Parent: Start by setting personal goals and working towards them independently. Learn new skills, take on responsibilities at home, and seek out opportunities to solve problems independently. Whether it's managing your finances, handling your schedule, or making decisions, each step you take towards self-reliance helps build your confidence and independence.

Teen: How do I navigate disagreements with my parents about my desire for independence?

Parent: Disagreements are natural as you assert your independence, but it's important to handle them respectfully. Listen to our perspective and express yours calmly and clearly. Try to understand why we might have concerns and be willing to compromise. We're here to support you, not to hold you back, so finding a solution that works for everyone is key.

Teen: What are the consequences of making decisions without considering their impact on others?

Parent: Every decision you make can have a ripple effect on the people around you. If you make choices without thinking about others, it can strain relationships, create conflicts, or lead to unintended consequences. It's important to consider how your actions affect your family, friends, and community. Responsible decision-making involves empathy, foresight, and an awareness of the bigger picture.

Teen: How can I improve my decision-making skills and become more confident in my choices?

Parent: Improving your decision-making skills starts with gathering information, weighing your options, and considering the potential outcomes. Practice making small decisions on your own and reflect on the results. As you gain experience, you'll become more confident in making bigger decisions. Remember, it's okay to seek advice when you're unsure.

Teen: What role should my parents play in helping me make important life decisions?

Parent: Our role is to guide and support you, not to make decisions for you. We can offer advice, share our experiences, and help you consider your options. But ultimately, the decision should be yours. As you gain more independence, we'll step back and let you take the lead while still supporting you when needed.

Teen: How do I set boundaries with my parents while still respecting their authority?

Parent: Setting boundaries is about mutual respect. It's important to communicate your needs and expectations clearly, while also understanding that we have rules and expectations to keep you safe. We can work together to establish boundaries that allow you to grow and explore your independence while still respecting the structure we provide.

Teen: What freedoms am I entitled to as I age, and how can I earn them?

Parent: As you grow older, you're entitled to more freedoms, such as making your own decisions about your social life, managing your time, and exploring your interests. However, these freedoms come with the responsibility to use them wisely. You earn more freedom by demonstrating maturity, making responsible choices, and being accountable for your actions.

Teen: How do I handle peer pressure to engage in risky behaviors while still asserting my independence?

Parent: Independence means making choices, not just following the crowd. When faced with peer pressure, think about your values, the potential consequences, and what's truly important to you. Assert your independence by standing firm in your decisions, even if it means going against the crowd. True independence comes from being true to yourself.

Teen: What responsibilities come with increased freedom, and how do I manage them effectively?

Parent: Increased freedom comes with the responsibility to make good decisions, manage your time, and fulfill your commitments. To manage these responsibilities effectively, prioritize your tasks, set goals, and stay organized. Remember that freedom isn't just about doing what you want—it's about making choices that reflect your values and responsibilities.

Teen: How do I balance my desire for independence with my obligations to my family and community?

Parent: Balancing independence with your obligations involves understanding that your actions impact those around you. While it's important to pursue your own goals and interests, it's equally important to contribute to your family and community. This balance requires communication, compromise, and a sense of responsibility to both yourself and others.

Teen: What rights do I have as a Teen, and how can I advocate for them responsibly?

Parent: As a Teen, you have rights, such as the right to express your opinions, make decisions about your future, and be treated respectfully.

Advocating for your rights involves communicating your needs clearly and respectfully, understanding the responsibilities of those rights, and working with us to find solutions that honor both your independence and our role as your parents.

Teen: How can I communicate my need for independence to my parents in a respectful and constructive way?

Parent: When communicating your need for independence, being honest and open about your feelings is important. Start by expressing why independence is important to you, and how you plan to manage it responsibly. Listen to our concerns and be willing to discuss potential compromises. A respectful and constructive conversation can help us understand each other better and work together to meet your needs.

Teen: What are the benefits of taking on more responsibilities at home, school, or in my community?

Parent: Taking on more responsibilities helps you develop important life skills like time management, problem-solving, and leadership. It also builds your confidence and prepares you for the challenges of adulthood. By contributing to your home, school, or community, you also strengthen your relationships and gain a sense of purpose and accomplishment.

Teen: How do I handle disagreements with my parents about my desire for more freedom?

Parent: Disagreements are natural, but handling them calmly and respectfully is important. Share your perspective and listen to ours. Understand that our concerns come from a place of love and a desire to keep you safe. By discussing the issue openly and seeking a compromise, we can find a solution that gives you more freedom while addressing our concerns.

Teen: What are the risks and rewards of making my own decisions, even if they differ from my parents' expectations?

Parent: Making your own decisions comes with both risks and rewards. The reward is the growth, confidence, and independence you gain by taking responsibility for your choices. However, there's also the risk of making mistakes or facing challenges. It's important to weigh your options carefully, consider the potential consequences, and be prepared to learn from your experiences—whether they turn out as you hoped or not.

Teen: How can I demonstrate my readiness for independence to my parents?

Parent: You can demonstrate your readiness for independence by consistently making responsible decisions, managing your time effectively, and showing that you can handle challenges independently. Communicate openly with us, take ownership of your actions, and proactively fulfill your responsibilities. The more we see you acting maturely and responsibly, the more confident we'll give you more independence.

Teen: What steps can I take to become more financially independent from my parents?

Parent: Becoming financially independent involves learning how to manage money, setting a budget, and finding ways to earn income. You can start by taking on a part-time job, saving a portion of your earnings, and being mindful of your spending. Financial independence also means making informed decisions about saving, investing, and spending wisely, so you can achieve your financial goals.

Teen: How do I navigate conflicts between my desire for independence and my parents' concerns for my safety and well-being?

Parent: It's important to understand that our primary concern is your safety and well-being. When conflicts arise, try to see things from our perspective and consider the reasons behind our concerns. At the same time, share your thoughts and explain why independence is important to you. We can work together to find a solution that addresses both your desire for freedom and our need to ensure your safety.

Teen: What resources are available to help me learn more about my rights and responsibilities as a Teen?

Parent: Many resources are available to help you understand your rights and responsibilities. You can explore books, websites, and community organizations focusing on youth empowerment, legal rights, and personal development. Schools and libraries often have resources on these topics as well. If you're ever unsure about something, don't hesitate to ask us or another trusted adult for guidance.

Teen: How do I handle situations where my desire for independence conflicts with my parents' rules and expectations?

Parent: When your desire for independence conflicts with our rules, it's important to communicate openly and respectfully. Explain why the rule feels restrictive and offer alternatives that might work for us. We're open to discussing and adjusting rules as you grow older as long as we feel confident that you're ready to handle the added responsibility.

Teen: What are the potential consequences of making impulsive decisions without considering the long-term effects?

Parent: Impulsive decisions can lead to unintended consequences, such as damaging relationships, missing opportunities, or creating challenges that could have been avoided. It's important to take a step back, think through your options, and consider the long-term impact of your choices. This will help you make decisions in your best interest and avoid unnecessary complications.

Teen: How can I advocate for myself and express my opinions and preferences to my parents and other authority figures?

Parent: Advocating for yourself involves expressing your opinions and preferences clearly, confidently, and respectfully. It's important to be assertive, but also to listen to others and consider their perspectives. When you advocate for yourself, you show that you can make thoughtful decisions and value open communication.

Teen: How do I cope with feelings of frustration or resentment when external factors limit my desire for independence?

Parent: It's normal to feel frustrated when your independence is limited, whether by rules, safety concerns, or other factors. When you feel this way, take a moment to acknowledge your feelings and find healthy ways to express them, such as talking to us or journaling. It's also important to recognize that some limitations are temporary and part of the process of gaining more freedom.

Teen: What role does communication play in negotiating boundaries and expectations with my parents?

Parent: Communication is the foundation of negotiating boundaries and expectations. It allows us to understand each other's needs, concerns, and perspectives. Through open and honest dialogue, we can work together to set boundaries that respect your growing independence while ensuring your safety and well-being.

Teen: How do I navigate conflicts between my desire for independence and my obligations to my family?

Parent: Balancing independence with family obligations requires understanding that your choices impact those around you. It's important to communicate with us about your goals and how you plan to fulfil your responsibilities while pursuing your independence. We can work together to find a balance that allows you to grow while contributing to the family.

Teen: What are some practical ways to demonstrate responsibility and maturity to my parents?

Parent: You can demonstrate responsibility and maturity by being reliable, following through on commitments, and taking ownership of your actions. Managing your time well, making thoughtful decisions, and being respectful in your interactions with us and others are all signs of maturity. The more you show that you can handle responsibilities, the more trust and independence you'll earn.

Teen: How can I negotiate compromises with my parents regarding my desire for independence?

Parent: Negotiating compromises involves being open to discussion and willing to find a middle ground. Start by expressing your desires and listening to our concerns. Then, explore options that address both your need for independence and our need to ensure your safety. Compromise is about finding solutions that work for everyone and that help you gradually gain more freedom.

Teen: What strategies can I use to handle conflicts with my parents in a constructive and respectful manner?

Parent: When conflicts arise, staying calm and approaching the situation with a mindset of understanding and resolution is important. Listen to each other's perspectives, avoid blaming or raising your voice, and focus on finding solutions. A constructive approach involves empathy, patience, and a willingness to compromise.

Teen: How do I develop self-discipline and self-control to pursue my goals and desires?

Parent: Developing self-discipline starts with setting clear goals and creating a plan to achieve them. Break your goals into smaller, manageable steps, and hold yourself accountable for completing them. Practice self-control by resisting distractions and staying focused on what's important. Over time, these habits will help you stay on track and achieve your aspirations.

Teen: What steps can I take to earn my parents' trust and respect as I assert my independence?

Parent: You can earn our trust and respect by being honest, responsible, and reliable. Communicate openly about your plans and decisions, follow through on your commitments, and show that you can handle challenges independently. Trust is built through consistent actions demonstrating your maturity and readiness for independence.

Teen: How do I balance my desire for independence with my need for support and guidance from my parents?

Parent: Balancing independence with support involves recognizing that seeking guidance while pursuing your path is okay. Independence doesn't mean you have to do everything alone—it's about making your own decisions with the knowledge and support you need to succeed. We're here to help when you need us, but we also trust you to lead your journey.

Teen: What are the healthy ways to assert my independence without resorting to rebellion or defiance?

Parent: Healthy independence is about making thoughtful, responsible choices rather than acting out of rebellion. Communicate your needs clearly, take on responsibilities willingly, and demonstrate your maturity through your actions. Rebellion often leads to conflict, while the respectful assertion of independence builds trust and strengthens your relationship with us.

Teen: How do I handle situations where my desire for independence conflicts with my parents' values or beliefs?

Parent: When your desire for independence conflicts with our values or beliefs, it's important to have an open and respectful dialogue. Explain why independence is important to you and how it aligns with your values. Listen to our perspective as well, and seek to understand each other's viewpoints. Finding common ground or agreeing to disagree can help you navigate these conflicts while maintaining respect for one another.

Teen: What role do my peers influence my desire for independence, and how can I make informed decisions about my relationships?

Parent: Peers can significantly influence your desire for independence, but it's important to make decisions based on your values and what's right for you. Evaluate your friendships and relationships to ensure they support your goals and well-being. Independence means making choices that are true to yourself, even if they differ from what your peers are doing.

Teen: How do I cope with feelings of guilt or anxiety about asserting my independence from my parents?

Parent: Feeling guilt or anxiety as you assert your independence is natural, especially if you're concerned about how it might affect your relationship. Remember that seeking independence is a normal part of growing up, and it doesn't mean you're distancing yourself from us. Communicate openly about your feelings, and remember that we support your growth and want to see you succeed.

Teen: What are some strategies for building a strong support network of friends, mentors, and trusted adults who can offer guidance and support?

Parent: Building a support network involves seeking out people who share your values, inspire you, and offer guidance. Look for mentors who can provide advice based on their experiences, and surround yourself with friends who uplift and encourage you. Be open to forming connections with teachers, coaches, or community members who can support your journey towards independence.

Teen: How do I develop resilience and adaptability in facing challenges or setbacks related to my desire for independence?

Parent: Resilience and adaptability are essential for navigating the challenges of independence. Develop resilience by viewing setbacks as opportunities to learn and grow. Stay adaptable by being open to change and be willing to adjust your plans when necessary. Practice problem-solving skills and maintain a positive mindset, even when facing difficulties.

Teen: What role does self-awareness play in understanding my motivations and desires for independence?

Parent: Self-awareness helps you understand why independence is important and how it aligns with your values and goals. By reflecting on your motivations, you can make more informed decisions and ensure that your actions are true to who you are. Self-awareness also helps you recognize when you might need support or guidance, making your journey towards independence more balanced and thoughtful.

Teen: How do I navigate conflicts between my desire for independence and my obligations to my family and cultural heritage?

Parent: Balancing your desire for independence with your obligations to family and cultural heritage can be challenging. It's important to honor your roots and the values that have shaped you, while also forging your path. Communicate openly with us about your goals and seek ways to integrate your cultural heritage into your independent life. This balance allows you to respect your background while growing into your unique identity.

Teen: What are the potential risks and benefits of pursuing greater independence at this stage of my life?

Parent: Pursuing greater independence offers many benefits, such as personal growth, self-confidence, and the ability to make decisions. However, it also comes with risks, such as the potential for mistakes or challenges you might not be fully prepared for. It's important to carefully weigh the risks and benefits and seek guidance when needed. Independence is a journey, and taking it step by step helps you build the skills and resilience needed for success.

Teen: How can I cultivate a sense of responsibility and accountability for my actions and decisions?

Parent: Cultivating responsibility and accountability involves taking ownership of your actions and understanding their impact on yourself and others. Set personal goals, follow through on commitments, and be honest with yourself and others about your progress. When you make a mistake, acknowledge it, learn from it, and take steps to make amends. This approach builds trust and helps you grow into a responsible, independent adult.

Teen: How do I handle situations where my desire for independence conflicts with societal norms or expectations?

Parent: When your desire for independence conflicts with societal norms, it is important to think critically about your choices and their potential impact. Reflect on whether these norms align with your values and goals, and consider how you can assert your independence while still respecting the broader community. In some cases, challenging societal norms can be a positive step toward growth and change, but it should be done thoughtfully and responsibly.

Teen: What role does self-advocacy play in asserting my independence and advocating for my needs and preferences?

Parent: Self-advocacy is crucial for asserting your independence. It involves clearly expressing your needs, preferences, and goals, and standing up for yourself respectfully and confidently. Whether you're communicating with us, teachers, or others, self-advocacy helps you take control of your life and ensures that your voice is heard. It's an important skill for navigating the journey to independence.

Teen: How do I develop effective problem-solving skills to address challenges and obstacles related to my desire for independence?

Parent: Effective problem-solving involves identifying the issue, brainstorming potential solutions, and evaluating the pros and cons of each option. Practice approaching challenges methodically, and don't be afraid to seek advice or input from others. By developing these skills, you'll be better equipped to handle obstacles on your path to independence, making your journey smoother and more successful.

Teen: What are some strategies for building healthy, supportive relationships with my parents based on mutual respect, trust, and understanding?

Parent: Building a healthy relationship with us involves open communication, mutual respect, and a willingness to understand each other's perspectives. Try to share your thoughts, listen to ours, and work together to find common ground. Trust is built over time through consistent actions, honesty, and reliability. By fostering this kind of relationship and maintaining a strong, positive connection, we can support your growth and independence.

This conversation is designed to guide Teens as they navigate the complexities of asserting independence while maintaining strong relationships with their parents. By focusing on open communication, mutual respect, and personal responsibility, parents and teens can work together to transition to greater autonomy successfully.

* * *

"There is hope, even when your brain tells you there isn't."
—*John Green*

Chapter 35

Navigating Mental Health: Understanding Depression, Anxiety, and Suicidal Thoughts

Depression, anxiety, and suicidal thoughts are significant mental health challenges that many teens face but often struggle to talk about openly. These topics can evoke feelings of fear, confusion, or even shame, making it difficult to seek help or discuss them with loved ones. This chapter is designed to provide a comprehensive and compassionate exploration of these issues, offering insights, support, and guidance for both teens and parents. We can foster a supportive environment that encourages open dialogue and effective coping strategies by approaching these subjects honestly and empathetically.

The Conversation Begins

Teen: Mom, I've been feeling really down lately, and sometimes I feel so anxious that I can't even focus. I don't really understand what's going on with me. Can we talk about it?

Parent: I'm so glad you're opening up about this. Talking about these feelings is not always easy, but we must do. Let's go through what you've been experiencing and try to make sense of it together.

Teen: Thanks. I guess the first thing I want to know is if my feelings are normal. Is it okay to feel this way?

Parent: It's okay to feel what you're feeling. Many people go through periods of depression and anxiety, especially during their teenage years when there's so much change happening. These feelings can be overwhelming, but you're not alone in this. The important thing is to understand what's happening and know there are ways to manage and overcome these feelings.

Medical Perspective: What the Science Says

Teen: So, does that mean there's something wrong with me? I feel like I'm broken or something.

Parent: Not at all. Depression and anxiety are common mental health conditions that can affect anyone. They're not a sign of weakness or something being wrong with you. From a medical standpoint, these conditions are often caused by a combination of factors, including genetics, brain chemistry, and life events. It's important to remember that these are real health issues, just like any physical illness, and they can be treated effectively with the right support.

Teen: But what about the thoughts I sometimes have? Sometimes, I don't want to be around anymore. Is that normal, too?

Parent: Suicidal thoughts are serious, and we must talk about them openly. Feeling like you don't want to be around anymore signifies that you're in much pain, which we must address together. These thoughts are more common than you might think, but they're also a sign that it's time to reach out for help. Letting someone know what you're going through is crucial so you don't have to face it alone.

Psychological Perspective: Understanding Emotions and Behaviors

Teen: I've been feeling so lost, and sometimes I don't know how to cope. What can I do to feel better?

Parent: It's normal to feel lost when you're dealing with depression and anxiety. These conditions can make it hard to see a way out, but there are ways to manage these feelings. Psychologically, depression often involves feelings of hopelessness, while anxiety can cause overwhelming fear or worry. Understanding that these feelings are part of a mental health condition—not a reflection of who you are—can help you start to find ways to cope. Talking to a therapist or counselor can be incredibly helpful in learning strategies to manage these emotions.

Teen: I feel so guilty all the time, like I'm a burden to everyone. Is that part of it, too?

Parent: Yes, those feelings of guilt and worthlessness are very common in depression. They're often tied to the distorted way the brain processes emotions when someone is depressed. It's important to remember that these feelings are not based on reality—they're a symptom of depression. You're not a burden, and you deserve support and care. Part of improving is learning to challenge these negative thoughts and replace them with more balanced, realistic ones.

Cultural and Social Perspectives: Navigating External Influences

Teen: Sometimes, I feel like I must hide my feelings because everyone expects me to be happy and strong. Is it okay to show that I'm struggling?

Parent: It's okay to show that you're struggling. Our society often pressures people to appear happy and put together, but that's not always realistic for anyone. Mental health challenges are just as valid as physical health challenges, and it's important to be honest about what you're going through. You don't have to hide your feelings to protect others—letting people know what's really going on can help you get the support you need.

Teen: But what if people don't understand? I've heard some of my friends say things like, "Just snap out of it" or "Stop being so dramatic."

Parent: Unfortunately, not everyone understands mental health issues, and sometimes people say hurtful things because they don't know how to respond. It's important to remember that your feelings are valid, even if others don't get it. You can try to educate your friends if you feel comfortable, or you can talk to people who understand and can offer real support. Surrounding yourself with understanding and supportive people can make a big difference.

Parental Perspective: Addressing Concerns and Building Trust

Teen: I'm scared to tell you everything because I don't want you to worry or be disappointed in me.

Parent: I understand that fear, but I want you to know I'm here to support you, not judge you. Feeling worried about how your parents might react is normal, but your well-being is my top priority. I'm not disappointed in you—I'm proud of you for being brave enough to discuss this. Let's work through this together.

Teen: What if I don't want to talk about it right now? Is that okay?

Parent: That's perfectly okay. You don't have to talk about everything all at once. You must feel comfortable and safe when you're ready to share. Just know that I'm here whenever you need to talk, and we can take things at your pace. There's no rush—your feelings and your timing matter.

Exploring Myths and Misconceptions: Dispelling Common Fears

Teen: I've heard people say that if you talk about suicidal thoughts, it just makes them worse. Is that true?

Parent: That's a common myth, but it's not true. Talking about suicidal thoughts doesn't make them worse—it can be the first step toward feeling better. When you keep these thoughts to yourself, they can feel more overwhelming. Sharing them with someone you trust can help you start to process those feelings and find a way to manage them. It's really important to reach out if you have these thoughts to get the support you need.

Teen: I've also heard that people with depression are just lazy or looking for attention. Is that what people really think?

Parent: Unfortunately, there's still much stigma around mental health, and some people might hold those misconceptions. But it's important to understand that depression is a real medical condition, not a character flaw. It's not about being lazy or seeking attention—it's about dealing with a serious health issue that requires care and understanding. The more we talk openly about mental health, the more we can help break down those stigmas and promote a better understanding.

Practical Tips: Navigating Daily Life

Teen: Sometimes, it's hard to even get out of bed or go to school. How can I handle that when I'm feeling so low?

Parent: Those feelings are a very real part of depression, and it's okay to acknowledge that some days are harder than others. One way to manage this is by setting small, achievable goals for yourself. For example, if getting out of bed feels too hard, start with something smaller, like sitting up or getting dressed. Break your day into manageable pieces, and don't be afraid to ask for help when needed. It's also important to communicate with your teachers or school counselor—they can offer support and make accommodations if needed.

Teen: What about when I'm feeling really anxious? Sometimes it feels like I can't breathe, and my heart is racing. What should I do?

Parent: Anxiety can be overwhelming, but there are techniques you can use to help manage those physical symptoms. Deep breathing exercises, grounding techniques, and mindfulness can help calm your body and mind. It can also be helpful to have a plan in place for when anxiety strikes— like taking a few moments to step away, talking to someone you trust, or using an app designed to help manage anxiety. Practicing these techniques regularly can make it easier to handle anxiety when it comes up.

Dealing with Peer Influence and Social Pressure

Teen: I'm worried about how my friends will react if they know what I'm going through. What if they don't want to hang out with me anymore?

Parent: It's natural to worry about how your friends might react, but true friends will want to support you, not distance themselves from you. If they're not sure how to help, you can let them know what you need—whether it's someone to talk to, a distraction, or just someone to be there with you. If someone doesn't react well, that's more about them than it is about you. It might be a sign that they're not equipped to support you right now, and that's okay. Focus on the friends who are there for you and know that you deserve to be surrounded by people who care about you.

Teen: What if I feel burdening them with my problems? I don't want to be that person.

Parent: It's a common fear to feel like you're burdening others, but everyone sometimes needs support. Think about how you would feel if a friend came to you with their struggles—would you want to help them? Your friends likely feel the same way about you. It's okay to lean on others, and it doesn't make you a burden. In fact, opening up can strengthen your friendships because it shows that you trust them.

Fostering a Healthy Dialogue and Building a Support System

Parent: Remember, we don't have to figure everything out right now. What's most important is that you know you're not alone and that there are people who care about you and want to help.

Teen: It helps to hear that. I guess I just need to take it one step at a time.

Parent: Exactly. One step at a time. And remember, we can always talk more about this whenever you're ready. Your feelings are important; I'm here to listen and support you. If we need more help, we can also contact a therapist or counselor specializing in teen mental health.

Conclusion: A Balanced Perspective

In this chapter, we've explored the challenges of dealing with depression, anxiety, and suicidal thoughts from multiple perspectives—medical, psychological, cultural, and social. The goal has been to provide a comprehensive understanding of these issues and to encourage open, honest conversations that can lead to healing and support. Mental health is a critical aspect of overall well-being, and it's important to approach it with compassion, understanding, and the willingness to seek help when needed.

Takeaway Points:

1. **Mental Health is Real:** Depression, anxiety, and suicidal thoughts are real health conditions that can affect anyone. They're not a sign of weakness or failure.

2. **Seek Support:** It's crucial to seek help when dealing with these challenges. Talking to a trusted adult, therapist, or counselor can provide the support and guidance needed to navigate these feelings.

3. **Myths vs. Reality:** Many misconceptions about mental health contribute to stigma. Understanding the facts can help dispel these myths and promote a healthier perspective.

4. **Daily Coping Strategies:** Small, achievable goals and coping techniques like deep breathing and mindfulness can help manage the daily challenges of mental health issues.

5. **Peer Influence:** It's important to surround yourself with supportive friends and not to worry about being a burden. True friends will want to help and support you.

6. **Ongoing Dialogue:** Mental health is an ongoing journey, and it's important to keep the lines of communication open. Regular check-ins and conversations can make a big difference.

7. **Professional Help:** If feelings of depression, anxiety, or suicidal thoughts persist, seeking professional help is essential. Therapists and counselors are trained to provide the support needed to navigate these challenges.

Teen: Thanks for talking about all this with me, Dad. I know it's not easy to bring up these topics, but it really helps to know that I can come to you with my feelings.

Parent: I'm so glad you felt comfortable sharing this with me. It's important to me that you know you're never alone in what you're going through. We're in this together, and I'm here to support you every step of the way.

Teen: I feel better knowing I can talk to you about it. I think having these conversations will make it easier to deal with everything.

Parent: Absolutely. And remember, it's okay to have good days and bad days. What matters is that we keep communicating and working through things together. If we ever need more help, we can contact a therapist or counselor—there's no shame in that.

Teen: That sounds good. It might also help to talk to someone else, like a counselor. But it's nice to know that I have you to lean on.

Parent: I'm glad you feel that way. We'll take it one day at a time and find the right support to help you feel better. Just know that no matter what, I'm always here for you.

Teen: Thanks, Dad. I really appreciate it.

Parent: Anytime. We're a team, and we'll get through this together.

* * *

Conclusion

Recap and Encouragement for the Journey Ahead

As you reach the end of this book, it's important to reflect on the significant journey you've undertaken. The teenage years are a time of immense growth, self-discovery, and learning, and throughout this book, we've explored a wide range of topics designed to guide you through this complex phase of life.

From **understanding your body** and **navigating relationships** to **setting goals for the future** and **embracing your independence**, each chapter has provided insights and practical advice to help you face the challenges of adolescence with confidence and clarity. We also delved into sensitive topics such as **masturbation** and **pornography**, offering a balanced perspective that incorporates medical, psychological, and parental viewpoints. These chapters are designed to encourage open dialogue and informed decision-making like the others.

Remember, this journey is uniquely yours. It's filled with opportunities to learn, grow, and become the person you aspire to be. Challenges and uncertainties are inevitable but also present chances to develop resilience, courage, and wisdom. Embrace the process of becoming, and don't be afraid to seek support when needed. Whether it's from your parents, mentors, or friends, you are not alone on this journey.

As you move forward, carry the lessons you've learned here. Continue to communicate openly with those around you, make decisions that align with your values, and never stop exploring your passions and interests. The road ahead may not always be smooth, but you can navigate it successfully with determination and a positive mindset. This is just the beginning of a lifelong adventure of growth and discovery.

Resources for Further Reading and Support

The topics covered in this book are just the starting point for deeper exploration. As you continue your journey, you may find accessing additional resources for further reading and support helpful. Below is a list of books, websites, and organizations that can provide valuable information and guidance:

Books:

- The 7 Habits of Highly Effective Teens by Sean Covey
- Untangled: Guiding Teenage Girls Through the Seven Transitions into Adulthood by Lisa Damour, Ph.D.
- The Teenage Brain: A Neuroscientist's Survival Guide to Raising Adolescents and Young Adults by Frances E. Jensen, M.D.
- The Book of No: 365 Ways to Say It and Mean It—and Stop People-Pleasing Forever by Susan Newman, Ph.D.
- How to Raise Successful People: Simple Lessons for Radical Results by Esther Wojcicki
- Life Skills for Young Adults: How to Manage Money, Have a Successful Career, and Live Your Best Life by Aruna Sankaranarayanan
- Wings of Fire: An Autobiography by Dr. A.P.J. Abdul Kalam with Arun Tiwari
- The Secret of Leadership: Stories to Awaken, Inspire and Unleash the Leader Within by Prakash Iyer
- The Habit of Winning by Prakash Iyer
- Ignited Minds: Unleashing the Power Within India by Dr. A.P.J. Abdul Kalam

Websites:

- TeensHealth – A comprehensive resource for teen health, emotional well-being, and life skills. https://kidshealth.org/en/teens/

- DoSomething.org – A platform for social change, encouraging teens to get involved in activism and community service. https://dosomething.org/

- The Trevor Project – Support and resources for LGBTQ+ teens, including a 24/7 crisis intervention hotline. https://www.thetrevorproject.org/

- YourDOST – An online emotional wellness platform in India that provides support through expert counseling. https://yourdost.com/

- Young Minds – A UK-based resource for mental health support for young people. https://www.youngminds.org.uk/

Organizations:

- **National Alliance on Mental Illness (NAMI):** Offers mental health resources, support groups, and educational programs for teens and their families. https://www.nami.org/

- **Boys & Girls Clubs of America:** Provides a safe space for teens to engage in educational and recreational activities. https://www.bgca.org/

- **Teen Line:** A confidential helpline for teens offering support on various issues, from peer pressure to mental health. https://www.teenline.org/

- **Snehi – Mental Health Resource Foundation (India):** Provides counseling services, mental health awareness, and support for teens and families in India. https://www.snehi.org.in/

- **SNEHA (Society for Nutrition, Education & Health Action):** An Indian organization that works on adolescent health and provides resources and support for teenagers. https://www.snehamumbai.org/

Here are some Indian government-run organizations and websites that provide valuable resources and support related to health, education, and well-being for teenagers and their families:

Indian Government Organizations and Websites:

1. **National Institute of Mental Health and Neurosciences (NIMHANS)**
   - ➤ **Website:** NIMHANS, https://nimhans.ac.in/
   - ➤ **Description:** NIMHANS offers mental health resources, counseling, and support services for adolescents and their families. It is a premier institution in India for mental health and neuroscience education.

2. **National Health Portal (NHP)**
   - ➤ **Website:** National Health Portal https://www.nhp.gov.in/
   - ➤ **Description:** The NHP provides comprehensive information on health-related topics, including adolescent health, mental health, and sexual health. It is a resource for both teens and parents to learn about various health issues and services.

3. **National Council of Educational Research and Training (NCERT)**
   - ➤ **Website:** NCERT, https://ncert.nic.in/
   - ➤ **Description:** NCERT offers educational resources, including counseling services and life skills education for teenagers. The website also provides access to textbooks and learning materials focused on adolescent education.

4. **Ministry of Health and Family Welfare (MoHFW)**
   - ➤ **Website:** Ministry of Health and Family Welfare https://www.mohfw.gov.in/
   - ➤ **Description:** The MoHFW provides information on various health initiatives, including adolescent health programs like Rashtriya Kishor Swasthya Karyakram (RKSK), which focuses on the health and well-being of teenagers in India.

5. **Digital Infrastructure for Knowledge Sharing (DIKSHA)**
   - ➤ **Website:** DIKSHA https://diksha.gov.in/
   - ➤ **Description:** DIKSHA is an initiative of the Ministry of Education that provides educational content for school students. It includes resources on career planning, life skills, and health education.

6. **National Commission for Protection of Child Rights (NCPCR)**
   - ▷ **Website:** NCPCR https://ncpcr.gov.in/
   - ▷ **Description:** NCPCR is a statutory body under the Government of India that protects child rights, including the rights of adolescents. It provides resources and support for education, health, and child protection issues.

7. **National Institute of Open Schooling (NIOS)**
   - ▷ **Website:** NIOS, https://www.nios.ac.in/
   - ▷ **Description:** NIOS offers flexible schooling options and educational resources for teenagers. It includes programs on life skills, career guidance, and health education.

Here are some Indian government initiatives and resources that provide support for teens struggling with addictions and suicidal thoughts:

1. **National Mental Health Programme (NMHP)**
   - ▷ **Service:** Launched by the Ministry of Health and Family Welfare, NMHP aims to address mental health issues, including substance abuse and suicide prevention, through various initiatives at the national and state levels.
   - ▷ **Website:** Ministry of Health and Family Welfare https://www.mohfw.gov.in/

2. **Kiran Mental Health Rehabilitation Helpline**
   - ▷ **Service:** A 24/7 helpline launched by the Ministry of Social Justice and Empowerment to provide support for mental health issues, including addiction and suicidal thoughts.
   - ▷ **Helpline Number:** 1800-599-0019

3. **Integrated Rehabilitation Centre for Addicts (IRCA)**
   - ▷ **Service:** These centers, supported by the Ministry of Social Justice and Empowerment, provide treatment, counseling, and rehabilitation services for individuals with substance abuse issues.
   - ▷ **Website:** National Institute of Social Defence http://www.nisd.gov.in/

4. **Lifeline Foundation**
   - ▷ **Service:** An initiative supported by the Indian government that provides counseling and support for individuals facing mental health challenges, including suicidal thoughts.
   - ▷ **Helpline Number:** 91-9152987821

5. **Ministry of Health and Family Welfare's Tele-MANAS Initiative**
   - ▷ **Service:** Tele-MANAS provides tele-counseling services for mental health, offering support for issues like addiction and suicidal ideation through trained professionals.
   - ▷ **Website:** Tele-MANAS https://www.telemanas.in/

6. **Childline India Foundation**
   - ▷ **Service:** A 24/7 helpline (1098) for children in distress, including those dealing with addiction and suicidal thoughts. Childline offers counseling and connects individuals to relevant support services.
   - ▷ **Website:** Childline India https://www.childlineindia.org/

These resources can provide valuable support and information as you navigate the challenges and opportunities of adolescence. Whether you're seeking further education on specific topics, seeking mental health support, or getting involved in social change, these books, websites, and organizations offer tools and guidance to help you along the way.

Your journey doesn't end with this book—it continues with the choices you make, the challenges you overcome, and the dreams you pursue. Keep learning, keep growing, and remember that every step forward is a step toward becoming the best version of yourself.

Timeless Wisdom: Reflections on Life, Growth, and Resilience

As we conclude this journey through the complexities and challenges of teenage life, it's fitting to end with words of wisdom from those who have walked the path of life before us. These quotes encapsulate the essence of the themes explored in this book—personal growth, resilience, understanding, and the enduring bond between parents and teens. May these reflections inspire you, offer guidance, and remind you that you are never alone in your journey.

"The greatest glory in living lies not in never falling, but in rising every time we fall."
— Nelson Mandela

"You must be the change you wish to see in the world."
— Mahatma Gandhi

"It is not the strongest of the species that survive, nor the most intelligent, but the one most responsive to change."
— Charles Darwin

"In the end, it's not the years in your life that count. It's the life in your years."
— Abraham Lincoln

"Happiness is not something ready-made. It comes from your own actions."

— Dalai Lama

"Courage doesn't always roar. Sometimes courage is the quiet voice at the end of the day saying, 'I will try again tomorrow.'"
— Mary Anne Radmacher

"You don't have to see the whole staircase, just take the first step."
— Martin Luther King Jr.

"Do not let what you cannot do interfere with what you can do."
— John Wooden

"Arise, awake, and stop not until the goal is reached."
— Swami Vivekananda

"Our greatest glory is not in never failing, but in rising every time we fall."
— Confucius

"To succeed in life and achieve results, you must understand and master three mighty forces—desire, belief, and expectation."
— A.P.J. Abdul Kalam

"The best way to predict the future is to create it."
— Peter Drucker

"Life is 10% what happens to us and 90% how we react to it."
— Charles R. Swindoll

"The only limit to our realization of tomorrow is our doubts of today."
— Franklin D. Roosevelt

References

Chapter 1: Understanding the Body

References:

- Marieb, E. N., & Hoehn, K. (2018). *Human Anatomy & Physiology.* Pearson.

- Sherwood, L. (2015). *Human Physiology: From Cells to Systems.* Cengage Learning.

Chapter 2: Relationships and Communication

References:

- Gottman, J. M., & Silver, N. (2015). *The Seven Principles for Making Marriage Work.* Harmony Books.

- Collins, W. A., & Laursen, B. (2004). Changing relationships, changing youth: Interpersonal contexts of adolescent development. *Journal of Early Adolescence,* 24(1), 55-62.

Chapter 3: Sexual Health and Education

References:

- Kirby, D. (2007). *Emerging Answers 2007: Research Findings on Programs to Reduce Teen Pregnancy and Sexually Transmitted Diseases.* The National Campaign to Prevent Teen and Unplanned Pregnancy.

- Santelli, J. S., Lindberg, L. D., Finer, L. B., & Singh, S. (2007). Explaining recent declines in adolescent pregnancy in the United States: The contribution of abstinence and improved contraceptive use. *American Journal of Public Health,* 97(1), 150-156.

Chapter 4: Navigating Personal Boundaries: A Guide to Self-Understanding for Teens and Parents

References:

➤ Levine, S. B. (2002). *Sexuality in Mid-Life*. Springer.

➤ Laumann, E. O., Gagnon, J. H., Michael, R. T., & Michaels, S. (1994). *The Social Organization of Sexuality: Sexual Practices in the United States*. University of Chicago Press.

Chapter 5: Understanding Pornography: Consequences and Conversations

References:

➤ Owens, E. W., Behun, R. J., Manning, J. C., & Reid, R. C. (2012). The impact of internet pornography on adolescents: A review of the research. *Sexual Addiction & Compulsivity*, 19(1-2), 99-122.

➤ Flood, M. (2009). The harms of pornography exposure among children and young people. *Child Abuse Review*, 18(6), 384-400.

Chapter 6: Premarital Sex and Marriage

References:

➤ Finer, L. B. (2007). Trends in premarital sex in the United States, 1954-2003. *Public Health Reports*, 122(1), 73-78.

➤ Stanley, S. M., & Markman, H. J. (1992). Assessing commitment in personal relationships. *Journal of Marriage and the Family, 54*(3), 595–608.

Chapter 7: Navigating Life as a Teenager of Divorced Parents

References:

➤ Hetherington, E. M., & Kelly, J. (2002). *For Better or For Worse: Divorce Reconsidered*. W. W. Norton & Company.

➤ Amato, P. R. (2001). Children of divorce in the 1990s: An update of the Amato and Keith (1991) meta-analysis. *Journal of Family Psychology*, 15(3), 355-370.

Chapter 8: Mental Health and Well-being

References:

➤ Kessler, R. C., et al. (2005). Lifetime prevalence and age-of-onset distributions of DSM-IV disorders in the National Comorbidity Survey Replication. *Archives of General Psychiatry*, 62(6), 593-602.

➤ Burns, D. D. (1999). *The Feeling Good Handbook*. Penguin Books.

Chapter 9: Peer Pressure and Decision-Making

References:

➤ Steinberg, L. (2014). *Age of Opportunity: Lessons from the New Science of Adolescence*. Houghton Mifflin Harcourt.

➤ Gardner, M., & Steinberg, L. (2005). Peer influence on risk taking, risk preference, and risky decision making in adolescence and adulthood: An experimental study. *Developmental Psychology*, 41(4), 625.

Chapter 10: Online Safety and Cyberbullying

References:

➤ Hinduja, S., & Patchin, J. W. (2014). *Bullying Beyond the Schoolyard: Preventing and Responding to Cyberbullying*. Corwin Press.

➤ Willard, N. E. (2007). *Cyber-Safe Kids, Cyber-Savvy Teens: Helping Young People Learn to Use the Internet Safely and Responsibly*. John Wiley & Sons.

Chapter 11: Gender and Sexuality

References:

➤ Diamond, L. M. (2008). *Sexual Fluidity: Understanding Women's Love and Desire*. Harvard University Press.

➤ Butler, J. (2006). *Gender Trouble: Feminism and the Subversion of Identity*. Routledge.

Chapter 12: Body Image and Self-Esteem

References:

➤ Cash, T. F. (2008). *The Body Image Workbook: An Eight-Step Program for Learning to Like Your Looks*. New Harbinger Publications.

➤ Grogan, S. (2016). *Body Image: Understanding Body Dissatisfaction in Men, Women, and Children*. Routledge.

Chapter 13: Responsible Behavior and Citizenship

References:

➤ Westheimer, J., & Kahne, J. (2004). What kind of citizen? The politics of educating for democracy. *American Educational Research Journal*, 41(2), 237-269.

➤ Dalton, R. J. (2008). *The Good Citizen: How a Younger Generation is Reshaping American Politics*. CQ Press.

Chapter 14: Life Skills and Future Planning

References:

➤ Covey, S. R. (1989). *The 7 Habits of Highly Effective People: Powerful Lessons in Personal Change*. Simon & Schuster.

➤ Goleman, D. (1995). *Emotional Intelligence: Why It Can Matter More Than IQ*. Bantam Books.

Chapter 15: Family Dynamics and Communication

References:

➤ Gottman, J. M., & Silver, N. (2015). *The Seven Principles for Making Marriage Work*. Harmony Books.

➤ Minuchin, S. (1974). *Families and Family Therapy*. Harvard University Press.

Chapter 16: Academic and Career Planning

References:

- Niles, S. G., & Harris-Bowlsbey, J. (2016). *Career Development Interventions*. Pearson.

- Super, D. E. (1990). A life-span, life-space approach to career development. *Journal of Vocational Behavior*, 16(3), 282-298.

Chapter 17: Financial Literacy and Responsibility

References:

- Lusardi, A., & Mitchell, O. S. (2014). The economic importance of financial literacy: Theory and evidence. *Journal of Economic Literature*, 52(1), 5-44.

- Dave Ramsey (2011). *Smart Money Smart Kids: Raising the Next Generation to Win with Money*. Ramsey Press.

Chapter 18: Health and Wellness

References:

- Sizer, F. S., & Whitney, E. N. (2017). *Nutrition: Concepts and Controversies*. Cengage Learning.

- Ogden, J. (2011). *Health Psychology: A Textbook*. McGraw-Hill Education.

Chapter 19: Peer Relationships and Social Skills

References:

- Rubin, K. H., Bukowski, W. M., & Laursen, B. (2011). *Handbook of Peer Interactions, Relationships, and Groups*. The Guilford Press.

- Sullivan, H. S. (1953). *The Interpersonal Theory of Psychiatry*. W. W. Norton & Company.

Chapter 20: Personal Development and Growth

References:

- ➤ Dweck, C. S. (2006). *Mindset: The New Psychology of Success.* Random House.

- ➤ Csikszentmihalyi, M. (1990). *Flow: The Psychology of Optimal Experience.* Harper & Row.

Chapter 21: Media Literacy and Critical Thinking

References:

- ➤ Hobbs, R. (2010). *Digital and Media Literacy: Connecting Culture and Classroom.* Corwin Press.

- ➤ Thoman, E., & Jolls, T. (2005). *Media Literacy Education: Lessons from the Center for Media Literacy.* Sage Publications.

Chapter 22: Understanding and Preventing Sexual Abuse

References:

- ➤ Finkelhor, D. (2009). The prevention of childhood sexual abuse. *Future of Children*, 19(2), 169-194.

- ➤ Bass, E., & Davis, L. (2008). *The Courage to Heal: A Guide for Women Survivors of Child Sexual Abuse.* Harper & Row.

Chapter 23: Social Justice and Advocacy

References:

- ➤ Freire, P. (2000). *Pedagogy of the Oppressed.* Continuum.

- ➤ Adams, M., Bell, L. A., & Griffin, P. (2007). *Teaching for Diversity and Social Justice.* Routledge.

Chapter 24: Decision-Making and Problem-Solving

References:

- Kahneman, D. (2011). *Thinking, Fast and Slow*. Farrar, Straus, and Giroux.

- Johnson, S. (1998). *Who Moved My Cheese? An Amazing Way to Deal with Change in Your Work and in Your Life*. G. P. Putnam's Sons.

Chapter 25: Self-Care and Well-being

References:

- Neff, K. (2011). *Self-Compassion: The Proven Power of Being Kind to Yourself*. William Morrow.

- Schaffner, A. K. (2016). *Exhaustion: A History*. Columbia University Press.

Chapter 26: Growing Up Confident: A Guide for Teenage Girls

References:

- Wiseman, R. (2002). *Queen Bees and Wannabes: Helping Your Daughter Survive Cliques, Gossip, Boyfriends, and the New Realities of Girl World*. Crown Publishing.

- Damour, L. (2016). *Untangled: Guiding Teenage Girls Through the Seven Transitions into Adulthood*. Ballantine Books.

Chapter 27: A Father and Son's Guide to Growing Up

References:

- Gurian, M. (2006). *The Wonder of Boys: What Parents, Mentors, and Educators Can Do to Shape Boys into Exceptional Men*. TarcherPerigee.

- Pollack, W. (1998). *Real Boys: Rescuing Our Sons from the Myths of Boyhood*. Henry Holt and Co.

Chapter 28: Understanding Your Body's Needs

References:

- Whitney, E., & Rolfes, S. R. (2019). *Understanding Nutrition*. Cengage Learning.

- McArdle, W. D., Katch, F. I., & Katch, V. L. (2015). *Exercise Physiology: Nutrition, Energy, and Human Performance*. Wolters Kluwer.

Chapter 29: Understanding Teenage Addictions

References:

- Volkow, N. D., & Li, T. K. (2005). The neuroscience of addiction. *Nature Neuroscience*, 8(11), 1429-1430.

- Goldstein, R. Z., & Volkow, N. D. (2002). Drug addiction and its underlying neurobiological basis: Neuroimaging evidence for the involvement of the frontal cortex. *American Journal of Psychiatry*, 159(10), 1642-1652.

Chapter 30: Living Lawfully in India

References:

- The Constitution of India, Government of India.

- Indian Penal Code, Government of India.

- Ministry of Law and Justice, Government of India. (2018). *Legal Information and Legal Literacy*. Available at: https://lawmin.gov.in/

Chapter 31: Navigating Infatuation and Love

References:

- Hatfield, E., & Rapson, R. L. (1993). *Love, Sex, and Intimacy: Their Psychology, Biology, and History*. HarperCollins.

- Fisher, H. E. (2004). *Why We Love: The Nature and Chemistry of Romantic Love*. Henry Holt and Co.

Chapter 32: Navigating Teenage Challenges with a Single Parent

References:

- Amato, P. R., & Gilbreth, J. G. (1999). Nonresident fathers and children's well-being: A meta-analysis. *Journal of Marriage and Family*, 61(3), 557-573.

- Ahrons, C. R. (2004). *We're Still Family: What Grown Children Have to Say about Their Parents' Divorce*. HarperCollins.

Chapter 33: Teenagers' Goals, Dreams, Career Aspirations, and Future Hopes

References:

- Savickas, M. L. (2005). The theory and practice of career construction. In S. D. Brown & R. W. Lent (Eds.), *Career Development and Counseling: Putting Theory and Research to Work*. John Wiley & Sons.

- Blustein, D. L. (2013). *The Psychology of Working: A New Perspective for Career Development, Counseling, and Public Policy*. Routledge.

Chapter 34: Navigating Teenage Independence, Decision-Making, Responsibilities, and Freedom

References:

- Steinberg, L. (2014). *Age of Opportunity: Lessons from the New Science of Adolescence*. Houghton Mifflin Harcourt.

- Arnett, J. J. (2000). Emerging adulthood: A theory of development from the late teens through the twenties. *American Psychologist*, 55(5), 469.

Chapter 35: Navigating Mental Health: Understanding Depression, Anxiety, and Suicidal Thoughts

References:

- "The Anxiety and Phobia Workbook" by Edmund J. Bourne, **ISBN** 978-1684034833

- "Feeling Good: The New Mood Therapy" by David D. Burns, **ISBN** 978-0380810338

➤ "The Depression Cure: The 6-Step Program to Beat Depression without Drugs" by Stephen S. Ilardi, **ISBN** 978-0738213880

➤ "Lost Connections: Uncovering the Real Causes of Depression – and the Unexpected Solutions" by Johann Hari, **ISBN** 978-1408878682

➤ "The Suicidal Mind" by Edwin S. Shneidman, **ISBN** 978-0195118018

➤ "Mind Over Mood: Change How You Feel by Changing the Way You Think" by Dennis Greenberger and Christine A. Padesky, **ISBN** 978-1462520428

Organizations:

➤ **American Psychological Association (APA)** - "Understanding Depression and Anxiety in Adolescents." https://www.apa.org.

➤ **National Institute of Mental Health (NIMH)** - "Depression in Children and Adolescents." https://www.nimh.nih.gov.

➤ **Mayo Clinic** - "Teen Depression: Symptoms and Causes." https://www.mayoclinic.org.

➤ **World Health Organization (WHO)** - "Adolescent Mental Health." https://www.who.int.

➤ **Mind** - "Understanding Anxiety and Panic Attacks." https://www.mind.org.uk

➤ **Centers for Disease Control and Prevention (CDC)** - "Suicide Prevention for Teens." https://www.cdc.gov

➤ **DoSomething.org**. (n.d.). *Home*. https://www.dosomething.org/

➤ **National Institute of Mental Health.** (n.d.). *Teen Depression*. https://www.nimh.nih.gov/health/topics/teen-depression/index.shtml

➤ **Trevor Project.** (n.d.). *Crisis Services for LGBTQ Youth*. https://www.thetrevorproject.org/

➤ **Office of Adolescent Health, U.S. Department of Health and Human Services.** (n.d.). *Talking With Teens*. https://www.hhs.gov/ash/oah/resources-and-publications/learning/talking-with-teens/index.html

Appendix

Additional Resources and Tools

The appendix of this book provides a curated list of additional resources and tools that can help you continue your journey of personal growth and self-discovery. Whether you're looking for further reading on a particular topic, practical tools to help you manage your time and set goals, or contact information for support services, this section has you covered.

1. **Further Reading and Online Resources**
   - **Personal Development:**
     - *Atomic Habits* by James Clear – A guide to building good and breaking bad habits. https://jamesclear.com/habits
     - MindTools – Online resources for personal effectiveness, including articles on goal setting, time management, and more.
   - **Mental Health and Well-being:**
     - *Dare to Lead* by Brené Brown – Insights into leadership and the power of vulnerability. **ISBN □: □** 1984854038
     - National Institute of Mental Health and Neurosciences (NIMHANS) – Information on mental health conditions, treatments, and support options. https://nimhans.ac.in/
   - **Career Planning:**
     - *What Color Is Your Parachute? for Teens* by Carol Christen and Richard N. Bolles – A guide to teen career planning. ISBN-13: 978-1607745778

- ○ O*NET OnLine – A tool for exploring various career options and understanding the skills required.

2. **Practical Tools and Applications**
   - ➤ **Goal Setting Apps:**
     - ○ **GoalsOnTrack:** A web-based tool designed to help you set and track goals with specific, measurable outcomes.
     - ○ **Strides:** A goal and habit tracker that helps you focus on your objectives by breaking them down into manageable steps.
   - ➤ **Time Management Tools:**
     - ○ **Trello:** A visual project management tool that helps you organize tasks, set deadlines, and track progress.
     - ○ **RescueTime:** A time management app that tracks your digital activity to help you identify time-wasting habits and improve productivity.
   - ➤ **Mindfulness and Relaxation:**
     - ○ **Headspace:** A mindfulness and meditation app that offers guided sessions to help you manage stress and improve focus.
     - ○ **Calm:** An app designed to help you relax, meditate, and sleep better with guided sessions and soothing sounds.

Worksheets for Goal Setting, Time Management, and More

To help you apply the concepts from this book, we've included a series of worksheets designed to help you with goal setting, time management, and self-reflection. These worksheets can be printed and filled out at your own pace, allowing you to tailor them to your needs and goals.

1. **Goal Setting Worksheet**
   - ➤ **Step 1:** Define Your Long-Term Goals
   - ➤ **Step 2:** Break Down Goals into Short-Term Objectives
   - ➤ **Step 3:** Identify Action Steps for Each Objective
   - ➤ **Step 4:** Set Deadlines and Milestones
   - ➤ **Step 5:** Track Progress and Adjust as Needed

2. **Time Management Planner**
   - ➢ **Step 1:** List Daily and Weekly Tasks
   - ➢ **Step 2:** Prioritize Tasks by Importance and Urgency
   - ➢ **Step 3:** Allocate Time Slots for Each Task
   - ➢ **Step 4:** Review and Adjust Your Schedule Daily
   - ➢ **Step 5:** Reflect on Productivity and Make Improvements

3. **Self-Reflection Journal**
   - ➢ **Prompt 1:** What Are My Strengths and How Can I Build on Them?
   - ➢ **Prompt 2:** What Challenges Am I Facing and How Can I Overcome Them?
   - ➢ **Prompt 3:** What Are My Personal Values and How Do They Guide My Decisions?
   - ➢ **Prompt 4:** What Goals Have I Achieved Recently and What Did I Learn from the Process?
   - ➢ **Prompt 5:** What Areas of My Life Would I Like to Improve, and How Will I Start?

Contact Information for Support Services

Knowing where to turn for help is crucial in times of need. Below is a list of contact information for support services that offer assistance in various areas, from mental health to academic counseling.

1. **Mental Health Support:**

International:

- **Crisis Text Line:** Text HOME to 741741 for free, 24/7 support in the U.S.

- **National Suicide Prevention Lifeline:** Call 1-800-273-TALK (8255) for confidential support in the U.S.

- **The Trevor Project:** Call 1-866-488-7386 for crisis intervention and suicide prevention services for LGBTQ+ youth in the U.S.

India:

- **Kiran Mental Health Rehabilitation Helpline:** Call 1800-599-0019 for 24/7 mental health support provided by the Ministry of Social Justice and Empowerment.

- **NIMHANS Helpline:** Call 080-4611-0007 for mental health support from the National Institute of Mental Health and Neurosciences (NIMHANS).

- **Snehi:** Provides crisis intervention services for suicide prevention. Visit Snehi or call 91-9152987821.

- **Tele-MANAS:** Provides tele-counseling services for mental health, including support for addiction and suicidal ideation. Visit Tele-MANAS.

2. **Academic Support:**

International:

- **Khan Academy:** Free online courses and resources for students of all ages. Visit Khan Academy.

- **College Board:** Resources for college planning, including SAT prep and scholarship information. Visit College Board.

India:

- **National Career Service (NCS):** Offers career counseling, job search assistance, and vocational training. Visit National Career Service.

- **CBSE Counseling:** The Central Board of Secondary Education (CBSE) offers counseling services for students during exam seasons. Visit CBSE for more information.

- **ePathshala:** A platform by NCERT offering free educational resources for students, teachers, and parents. Visit ePathshala.

- **Diksha Platform:** An initiative by the Ministry of Education, India, providing digital educational resources. Visit Diksha.

3.   **Career Counseling:**

- **CareerOneStop:** A U.S. Department of Labor resource for career exploration and job search assistance. Visit www.careeronestop.org.

- **National Career Service:** Indian Government website. https://www.ncs.gov.in/ Ministry of labour & Employment.

- **National Career Development Association (NCDA):** Provides career counseling resources and a directory of certified counselors. Visit www.ncda.org.

- **National Government Services Portal:** https://services.india.gov.in/

4.   **National Career Service (NCS)**

- **Website:** National Career Service (NCS)

- **Description:** The National Career Service is an initiative by the Ministry of Labour & Employment, Government of India. It offers career counseling, job search assistance, and information on training programs. The portal connects job seekers, employers, and career counselors.

5.   **National Institute for Career Service (NICS)**

- **Website:** National Institute for Career Service (NICS)

- **Description:** The National Institute for Career Service, under the Ministry of Labour & Employment, provides career counseling services, training programs, and employment services. It is a central hub for career-related resources and support.

6.   **Counseling and Placement Cell - University Grants Commission (UGC)**

- **Website:** University Grants Commission (UGC)

- **Description:** The UGC provides guidelines for universities and colleges to establish Counseling and Placement Cells. These cells offer career counseling, placement assistance, and skill development programs to students in higher education institutions across India.

7. Disha - Career Counselling and Guidance Portal by CBSE

- **Website**: CBSE Disha

- **Description**: The Central Board of Secondary Education (CBSE) provides career counseling through its Disha portal. It offers guidance on career options, skill development, and higher education opportunities for students in CBSE-affiliated schools.

8. State Employment Exchanges

- **Website**: Varies by state (e.g., Maharashtra State Employment Exchange)

- **Description**: State Employment Exchanges, managed by the respective state governments, provide career counseling, vocational guidance, and job placement services to job seekers. They also offer training programs and career workshops.

Legal and Financial Advice:

1. National Legal Services Authority (NALSA)
  - ▷ **Website**: National Legal Services Authority (NALSA)

  - ▷ **Description**: NALSA provides free legal services to eligible persons and organizes Lok Adalats for amicable settlement of disputes. It ensures that justice is accessible to all, especially marginalized communities.

2. Ministry of Law and Justice
  - ▷ **Website**: Ministry of Law and Justice

  - ▷ **Description**: The Ministry of Law and Justice is responsible for administrating legal affairs, legislative activities, and framing laws in India. It provides information on legal rights, access to legal resources, and updates on new laws and amendments.

3. **eCourts Services**
   - ➤ **Website**: eCourts Services
   - ➤ **Description**: Managed by the Department of Justice, this portal provides access to case status, cause lists, and judgments of the courts across India. It also offers information on legal services and resources.

4. **Department of Justice - Legal Aid Services**
   - ➤ **Website**: Department of Justice
   - ➤ **Description**: The Department of Justice provides legal aid services to the underprivileged sections of society. It oversees various legal aid programs and collaborates with state legal services authorities.

Indian Government Financial Services:

1. **National Securities Depository Limited (NSDL) - Financial Literacy Programs**
   - ➤ **Website**: NSDL Financial Literacy
   - ➤ **Description**: NSDL conducts financial literacy programs under the guidance of the Ministry of Finance. These programs educate citizens about financial planning, investments, savings, and the importance of financial security.

2. **Pradhan Mantri Jan Dhan Yojana (PMJDY)**
   - ➤ **Website**: Pradhan Mantri Jan Dhan Yojana (PMJDY)
   - ➤ **Description**: PMJDY is a financial inclusion initiative by the Government of India to provide affordable access to financial services, including banking, savings accounts, remittance, credit, insurance, and pensions.

3. **Investor Education and Protection Fund Authority (IEPFA)**
   - ➤ **Website**: IEPFA

   - ➤ **Description**: Under the Ministry of Corporate Affairs, IEPFA promotes investor awareness and protection. It offers resources on safe investment practices, financial literacy, and redressal of investor grievances.

4. **Ministry of Finance - Financial Services**
   - ➤ **Website**: Ministry of Finance

   - ➤ **Description**: The Ministry of Finance oversees the financial sector, including banking, insurance, and financial market regulations. It provides information on government financial schemes, banking policies, and financial inclusion initiatives.

5. **Reserve Bank of India (RBI) - Financial Education**
   - ➤ **Website**: RBI Financial Education

   - ➤ **Description**: The Reserve Bank of India offers financial education resources to promote financial literacy nationwide. It guides managing personal finances, understanding banking services, and making informed financial decisions.

This appendix is designed to be a living resource that you can return to as you continue your journey. Use these tools, worksheets, and contact information to support your ongoing growth, learning, and development.

Goal Setting Worksheet

Step 1: Define Your Long-Term Goals

What do you want to achieve in the next few years? Think about your career, education, personal life, and health.

Goal 1: ____

Goal 2: ____

Goal 3: ____

Step 2: Break Down Goals into Short-Term Objectives

For each long-term goal, identify smaller objectives that will help you reach your main goal.

Objective 1.1: ____

Objective 1.2: ____

Objective 2.1: ____

Objective 2.2: ____

Objective 3.1: ____

Objective 3.2: ____

Step 3: Identify Action Steps for Each Objective

What specific actions will you take to achieve each objective?

Objective 1.1: ____

Action Step 1: ____

Action Step 2: ____

Objective 2.1: ____

Action Step 1: ____

Action Step 2: ____

Objective 3.1: ____

Action Step 1: ____

Action Step 2: ____

Step 4: Set Deadlines and Milestones

Determine when you want to achieve each goal and objective and identify milestones to track your progress.

Goal 1 Deadline: ____

Objective 1.1 Deadline: ____

Objective 1.2 Deadline: ____

Goal 2 Deadline: ____

Objective 2.1 Deadline: ____

Objective 2.2 Deadline: ____

Goal 3 Deadline: ____

Objective 3.1 Deadline:_______________________________________

Objective 3.2 Deadline:_______________________________________

Step 5: Track Progress and Adjust as Needed

Regularly review your progress. If necessary, adjust your goals, objectives, or action steps.

Goal 1 Progress:____

Milestone 1: ____

Milestone 2: ____

Goal 2 Progress:____

Milestone 1: ____

Milestone 2: ____

Goal 3 Progress:____

Milestone 1: ____

Milestone 2: ____

This worksheet provides a structured way to set and track goals, helping to break them down into manageable steps and ensuring you stay on track to achieve them. You can use this template to create your own worksheet or as a guide for setting up a similar worksheet in a digital format like Excel or Google Sheets.

Time Management Planner Worksheet

Step 1: List Daily and Weekly Tasks

Identify the tasks you need to complete each day and week. Include work, study, personal, and leisure activities.

Daily Tasks:

Task 1: ____

Task 2: ____

Task 3: ____

Task 4: ____

Weekly Tasks:

Task 1: ____

Task 2: ____

Task 3: ____

Task 4: ____

Step 2: Prioritize Tasks by Importance and Urgency

Rank your tasks based on how important and urgent they are. Use a scale from 1 to 4 (1 = High Importance/Urgency, 4 = Low Importance/Urgency).

Daily Tasks:

Task 1: _____ (Importance/Urgency Level)

Task 2: _____ (Importance/Urgency Level)

Task 3: _____ (Importance/Urgency Level)

Task 4: _____ (Importance/Urgency Level)

Weekly Tasks:

Task 1: _____ (Importance/Urgency Level)

Task 2: _____ (Importance/Urgency Level)

Task 3: _____ (Importance/Urgency Level)

Task 4: _____ (Importance/Urgency Level)

Step 3: Allocate Time Slots for Each Task

Assign specific times in your day or week to complete each task. Make sure to account for breaks and realistic timeframes.

Daily Schedule:

Task 1: _____ AM/PM – _____ AM/PM

Task 2: _____ AM/PM – _____ AM/PM

Task 3: _____ AM/PM – _____ AM/PM

Task 4: _____ AM/PM – _____ AM/PM

Weekly Schedule:

Task 1: ____ (Day and Time)

Task 2: ____ (Day and Time)

Task 3: ____ (Day and Time)

Task 4: ____ (Day and Time)

Step 4: Review and Adjust Your Schedule Daily

At the end of each day, review your schedule. Did you complete all your tasks? If not, adjust your schedule for the following day.

Daily Reflection:

What tasks were completed? ____

What tasks were not completed? ____

Adjustments for tomorrow: ____

Step 5: Reflect on Productivity and Make Improvements

At the end of each week, reflect on your productivity. Identify areas for improvement and adjust your time management strategies accordingly.

Weekly Reflection:

What worked well this week? ____

What didn't work well? ____

How can I improve next week? ____

Adjustments for next week: ____

This **Time Management Planner Worksheet** is designed to help you organize your tasks, prioritize effectively, and reflect on your productivity to make continuous improvements. You can print out this worksheet and fill it in daily and weekly to keep track of your tasks and manage your time efficiently.

Self-Reflection Journal Worksheet

Prompt 1: What Are My Strengths and How Can I Build on Them?

Reflect on your personal strengths. How can you leverage these strengths in different areas of your life?

My Strengths:

Strength 1: ____

Strength 2: ____

Strength 3: ____

How I Can Build on These Strengths:

Action 1: ____

Action 2: ____

Action 3: ____

Prompt 2: What Challenges Am I Currently Facing and How Can I Overcome Them?

Identify any challenges or obstacles you're dealing with. Consider strategies or resources that can help you overcome these challenges.

Current Challenges:

Challenge 1: ____

Challenge 2: ____

Challenge 3: ____

Strategies to Overcome These Challenges:

Strategy 1: ____

Strategy 2: ____

Strategy 3: ____

Prompt 3: What Are My Personal Values, and How Do They Guide My Decisions?

Think about the core values that are most important to you. How do these values influence the decisions you make?

My Personal Values:

Value 1: ____

Value 2: ____

Value 3: ____

How These Values Guide My Decisions:

Example 1: ____

Example 2: ____

Example 3: ____

Prompt 4: What Goals Have I Achieved Recently and What Did I Learn from the Process?

Reflect on recent achievements. What did you learn from the process of achieving these goals?

Goals I Have Achieved:

Goal 1: ____

Goal 2: ____

Goal 3: ____

Lessons Learned:

Lesson 1: ____

Lesson 2: ____

Lesson 3: ____

Prompt 5: What Areas of My Life Would I Like to Improve and How Will I Start?

Consider areas of your life where you'd like to see growth or improvement. What steps will you take to begin this journey?

Areas for Improvement:

Area 1: ____

Area 2: ____

Area 3: ____

First Steps to Start Improving:

Step 1: ____

Step 2: ____

Step 3: ____

This **Self-Reflection Journal Worksheet** is designed to encourage deep personal reflection and to help you create actionable plans for growth and improvement. Each section can be revisited regularly to track progress and adjust your strategies as needed.

Real-Life Case Studies: Applying Insights to Real Situations

Introduction to Case Studies As a counseling psychologist, I have worked with numerous individuals and families navigating the complex challenges of adolescence. Through these experiences, I have gathered a wealth of knowledge that can immensely benefit both teens and parents. In this section, I present a series of real-life case studies that illustrate the concepts discussed throughout this book. These case studies offer practical examples of applying the strategies and advice in the chapters, making the content more relatable and actionable.

Each case study has been carefully selected to highlight a particular issue or challenge that teenagers and their families commonly face. While the identities of the individuals have been anonymized to protect their privacy, the situations depicted are based on real-life experiences. I hope these case studies will enhance your understanding of the topics and empower you to apply these lessons to your own life.

Case Study 1: Navigating Peer Pressure and Decision-Making

- **Overview: Ravi,** a 16-year-old high school student, was struggling with peer pressure from his friends to experiment with alcohol and smoking. Despite knowing the potential consequences, Ravi found it challenging to say no, fearing that his peers might ostracize him.

- **Challenges Faced:** Ravi's internal conflict was significant. On the one hand, he wanted to fit in with his friends, but on the other, he was concerned about the health risks and their impact on his academic performance. His parents were unaware of the extent of the pressure he was facing, and Ravi felt isolated in his dilemma.

- **Steps Taken:** During counseling sessions, Ravi was guided through self-reflection, helping him identify his personal values and priorities. He was encouraged to communicate openly with his parents about the pressures he was facing. Through role-playing exercises, Ravi practiced assertiveness skills, learning how to set boundaries without damaging his friendships.

- **Outcome:** Ravi was able to have an open and honest conversation with his parents, who offered their support and understanding. With their guidance and his newfound assertiveness, Ravi successfully navigated the situation, maintaining his friendships while staying true to his values.

Key Takeaways:

- Understanding personal values is crucial in decision-making.
- Open communication with trusted adults can provide the necessary support.
- Assertiveness is a key skill in resisting peer pressure.

Case Study 2: Coping with Academic Pressure and Anxiety

- **Overview: Priya**, a 17-year-old student preparing for her board exams, was experiencing severe anxiety. The pressure to perform well academically was overwhelming, leading to sleepless nights, panic attacks, and a constant feeling of inadequacy.

- **Challenges Faced:** Priya's anxiety was compounded by her fear of disappointing her parents, who had high expectations for her academic success. Despite her hard work, Priya felt she could never do enough, and her self-esteem plummeted.

- **Steps Taken:** Through counseling, Priya was introduced to stress management techniques, including mindfulness and time management strategies. She learned to set realistic goals and break down her study sessions into manageable chunks. Priya's parents were also involved in the process, learning how to offer emotional support without adding to the pressure.

- **Outcome:** Priya's anxiety gradually decreased as she implemented the techniques learned in counseling. She developed a healthier approach to studying and began seeing her self-worth separate from her academic achievements. Her relationship with her parents improved as they learned to support her emotionally rather than just focusing on her grades.

Key Takeaways:

- Effective stress management techniques can significantly reduce anxiety.
- Parental support is crucial, but it must be balanced and empathetic.
- Self-worth should not be solely tied to academic performance.

Case Study 3: Addressing Depression and Suicidal Thoughts

- **Overview: Arjun**, an 18-year-old, was battling severe depression, which led to suicidal thoughts. He felt isolated and misunderstood and struggled to find a reason to continue living. His parents were unaware of the severity of his condition, attributing his behaviour to typical teenage moodiness.

- **Challenges Faced:** Arjun's depression was deep-rooted, exacerbated by academic pressure and a recent breakup. His parents, although loving, lacked the awareness and knowledge to recognize the signs of depression and did not know how to help.

- **Steps Taken:** Arjun was encouraged to seek professional help and worked through his despair. Cognitive-behavioral therapy (CBT) was introduced to help him challenge negative thought patterns and develop healthier coping mechanisms. His parents were also educated about depression, learning to recognize warning signs and provide the support Arjun needed.

- **Outcome:** Through therapy and with his parents' support, Arjun's mental health began to improve. He found new ways to cope with his emotions and started to rebuild his life, focusing on activities that brought him joy and fulfilment. His parents became more attuned to his needs, fostering a supportive and understanding environment at home.

Key Takeaways:

- Professional help is essential in addressing severe mental health issues.

- Parental awareness and support can significantly impact a teen's recovery.

- Developing healthy coping mechanisms is crucial for managing depression.

Conclusion: Learning from Real-Life Experiences

These case studies demonstrate the importance of understanding, communication, and support in navigating the challenges of adolescence. Each story is a testament to teenagers' resilience and parents' vital role in their journey. By reflecting on these examples, you can gain insights into approaching similar situations in your own life or those you care about.

The key to overcoming challenges lies in open communication, seeking support when needed, and being willing to learn and grow from each experience. Whether you are a teenager or a parent, these case studies offer valuable lessons on navigating life's complexities with empathy, understanding, and courage.

Acknowledgments

This book is the culmination of countless hours of work, thoughtful discussions, and invaluable support from many individuals who have played an essential role in its creation. I am deeply grateful to all who have contributed to this project.

First and foremost, I would like to express my heartfelt thanks to the teenagers and parents who have shared their stories, experiences, and insights. Your honesty and willingness to engage in meaningful conversations have laid the foundation for this book. Without your contributions, this work would not have been possible.

To my colleagues and friends, Ph.D. students (Sowjanya, Jeena, Hajeesh, Megha, and Smriti), and fellow educators, thank you for your encouragement and feedback and for challenging me to think critically about the issues teenagers face today. Your expertise and dedication to empowering young people have inspired many of the ideas presented in these pages.

I am profoundly grateful to my family for their unwavering support and patience throughout the writing process. To my spouse, who has been my steadfast partner, thank you for your love and understanding and for always believing in the importance of this work. To my children, thank you for your curiosity and questions and for constantly reminding me of the importance of open and honest communication.

A special thank you to my mentors and advisors, who have guided me throughout my career as both a scientist and a counseling psychologist.

Your wisdom and experience have shaped my approach to understanding and supporting the needs of teenagers and their families.

I would also like to acknowledge the professionals and organizations (and Microsoft Designer and Adobe Firefly softwares) who have provided invaluable resources, including AI-generated images and research, that have informed the content of this book. Your support is vital to the ongoing effort to support and empower young people.

I extend my gratitude to those who provided invaluable support, feedback, and insights during the creation of this book. Special thanks go to the countless sources of knowledge and inspiration that helped refine my ideas and brought clarity to complex topics, making this project possible.

Finally, I extend my deepest gratitude to the readers of this book. Whether you are a teenager, a parent, or someone supporting a young person, I hope this book serves as a helpful guide and a source of inspiration. Thank you for exploring these important topics and for your commitment to fostering understanding, growth, and communication.

With sincere appreciation,

Prof. Dr. Kiran Mangalampalli

27-August-2024

Chennai